Fri. Nov. 11

A MAN DAMNE

"Yet to those who know him best, Coleridge
is neither the inadvertent clown nor the
Pagliacci-figure whose outward demeanor
conceals by simulated gaiety the drowning and
redrowning of his soul in liquid fire. If he
does not wear his heart upon his sleeve, its
steady bleeding is all too apparent both in
his poetry and in his personal letters, to
say nothing of his private journals. For
Coleridge is the type of Man Damned,
too introspective not to know it, too
retrospective to sustain for long the
determination to face futurity with any
reasonable expectation of being able to overcome
the causes of his damnation."

From the Introduction

CARLOS BAKER is Woodrow Wilson Professor of
English Literature at Princeton University. He is the
author of *Major English Romantic Poets, Masters of
English Literature* and *Shelley's Poetry and Prose.*
He also edited *Keats: Poems and Selected Letters* for
the Bantam Classic series.

COLERIDGE:
POETRY AND PROS

EDITED AND
WITH AN INTRODUCTION BY
CARLOS BAKER
Princeton University

BANTAM BOOKS

NEW YORK / TORONTO / LONDON

COLERIDGE: POETRY AND PROSE
A Bantam Classic / published September 1965

ACKNOWLEDGMENTS

*Clarendon Press: Selections from the Coleridge Griggs edition;
the E. H. Coleridge edition of* The Poems of Coleridge; *the
Shawcross edition of* Biographia Literaria; *and* Wordsworthian
and Other Studies *by Ernest De Selincourt. Reprinted by
permission of Clarendon Press, Oxford.*
*Thomas M. Raysor: From Coleridge's Miscellaneous Criticism by
Thomas M. Raysor. Reprinted by permission of the author.*

Library of Congress Catalog Card Number: 65-22483

*Bantam Books are published by Bantam Books, Inc., a subsidiary
of Grosset & Dunlap, Inc. Its trade-mark, consisting of the words
"Bantam Books" and the portrayal of a bantam, is registered in the
United States Patent Office and in other countries. Marca Registrada.
Bantam Books, Inc., 271 Madison Avenue, New York, N. Y. 10016.*

PRINTED IN THE UNITED STATES OF AMERICA

PREFATORY NOTE

This book is designed as a readers' Coleridge. Its purpose is to offer the student and the general reader an introduction to four major facets of the many-sided genius whose complete works fill nearly a dozen closely printed volumes. The Coleridge here represented is the poet, the critic, the letter-writer, and the conversationalist. The book opens with a substantial selection from his verse, beginning with the justly famous "mystery poems," continuing with the series of reflective lyrics which are usually called the "conversation poems," and concluding with the odes, hymns, songs, and lesser pieces which best illustrate the varieties of his verse. The second subdivision contains selections from his prose, including key chapters from the *Biographia Literaria* as well as significant examples of his most original work in both theoretical and practical criticism. Since Coleridge the man, in his glory and his misery, is nowhere better revealed than in his communications to his friends, fifty-one of his best letters are here reprinted. And since his prowess as conversationalist is one of his most noteworthy, endearing, awesome, and irritating characteristics, a selection from his *Table Talk* rounds out the volume. At the end of each poem, and other selections where relevant, the composition date appears on the left and the publication date on the right.

Much of Coleridge's most rigorous thinking is preserved in the most arid prose imaginable, while much that he wrote within the disciplines of moral and metaphysical philosophy, theology and ecclesiastical polity, or political economy is now of interest only to the specialist for whom the present volume is not primarily intended. But the vividly imaginative, myriad-minded, and almost unendurably harassed man who wrote the poetry, criticism, and letters, or delivered his critical opinions by word of mouth to anyone who would listen, is the Coleridge on whom the book which follows is designed to concentrate.

In preparing the text, the editor has had the valuable assistance of Mr. J. C. Douglas Marshall, whose careful labors he gratefully acknowledges.

C. B.

CONTENTS

COLERIDGE: POETRY AND PROSE

INTRODUCTION

If what a man was may be summed up in what other men said of him, Coleridge is the leading figure of the English Romantic Movement. Soon after his death in the summer of 1834, the social philosopher John Stuart Mill classed Coleridge with Jeremy Bentham as originator and promulgator of most of the major ideas on which early nineteenth-century England subsisted, and also as one who had effected nothing less than a revolution among the thinkers and investigators of the age. George Saintsbury, again, spoke of Coleridge as "one of the greatest critics of the world," and did not balk at grouping him with Aristotle and Longinus. In our time, Professor René Wellek has called him, without visible hesitation, "the intellectual center of the English romantic movement." Had Coleridge never existed, says Wellek, we should be likely to feel "that [English] Romanticism, glorious as its poetry and prose is in its artistic achievements, remained dumb in matters of intellect." For we are able to discover "a point of view, a certain attitude" in the writings of Keats and Shelley. "We find the expression of a creed in Wordsworth." But it is only in the work of Coleridge that we "leave thought which is an integral part of poetry for thought which can be expressed in logical form, and can claim comparison with the systems of the great German philosophers" like Immanuel Kant.

One may wish to quarrel with certain of the foregoing judgments. Yet their cumulative effect is beyond question to raise Coleridge to a very high level indeed. To call him one of the world's greatest critics is remarkable enough. To praise him as one of two leading revolutionary thinkers in an age of revolutions, and as the only major English romantic poet who knew how to use his head, makes him something like a paragon of paragons. Even if the case has been slightly overstated, too many respectable voices have been raised in laudatory chorus to be ignored. The most cautious possible summary of the situation would be to say that in spite of certain ups and downs Coleridge's reputation as poet and critic has been relatively secure since his death.

Yet to many of his contemporaries, himself included, this

strange and harassed man seemed to be a failure. He left Cambridge University without having taken a degree; he projected a Utopian community in America only to abandon the plan. He married in haste but shortly discovered that his temperament was almost completely incompatible with that of his wife; he sired more children than he knew how to support. Two journals which he undertook to edit came quickly to nothing. A combination of illness, self-doubt, laziness, and indecision constantly inhibited and often destroyed his plans for writing and lecturing. He moved restlessly across the English landscape, pursued by demons which he could not escape because they were inside him. He tried to forget his woes in Germany, Malta, Sicily, and Italy—without success. And through a large part of his adult life he fought vainly against the opium habit, more or less innocently contracted as a means of relief from pain, yet soon so boldly tyrannous that he might have died raving long before his earthly work was finished, and would doubtless have done so if it had not been for the frequent intercession of his friends.

Without success. Had he succumbed at forty, these two words could almost have served as his epitaph. He was already thinking of death, and of the example of his own misspent life, when he summarized his sense of failure in a letter to his friend Josiah Wade in the summer of 1814. "Conceive," he cried, "a poor miserable wretch, who for many years has been attempting to beat off pain, by a constant recurrence to the vice that reproduces it. Conceive a spirit in hell, employed in tracing out for others the road to that heaven, from which his crimes exclude him! In short, conceive whatever is most wretched, helpless, and hopeless, and you will form as tolerable a notion of my state, as it is possible for a good man to have. . . . In the one crime of OPIUM, what crime have I not made myself guilty of!—Ingratitude to my Maker! and to my benefactors—injustice! *and unnatural cruelty to my poor children!*—self-contempt for my repeated promise—breach, nay, too often, actual falsehood! After my death, I earnestly entreat, that a full and unqualified narration of my wretchedness, and of its guilty cause, may be made public, that at least some little good may be effected by the direful example!"

This is but one passage drawn from the long train of self-recriminations in which Coleridge repeatedly sought to state, and thus perhaps to alleviate, the horror that assailed him whenever his conscience rose up to point an accusing finger.

Restless, wretched, seemingly helpless, and often literally hopeless, he could have composed a "history" very nearly as
"tragicall" as that of Marlowe's *Faustus*.

Faustus: Where are you damned?

Mephistopheles: In hell.

Faustus: How comes it then that thou art out of hell?

Mephistopheles: Why this is hell, nor am I out of it.

If not among us, at least among his contemporaries, the
temptation was strong to condemn this man for his short-
comings. So it was with William Hazlitt, despite his own
foibles and failures, in a retrospective account of Coleridge
preaching in the north of England. "His forehead was broad
and high, light as if built of ivory, with large projecting eye-
brows, and his eyes rolling beneath them, like a sea with
darkened lustre. His mouth gross, voluptuous, open, eloquent
... but his nose, the rudder of the face, index of the will, was
small, feeble, nothing—like what he has done." For Carlyle, too,
the contrast between Coleridge's promise and his actual achievement carried the overtones of tragedy. "A ray of heavenly inspiration," says Carlyle, "struggled in Coleridge, in a tragically
ineffectual degree, with the weakness of flesh and blood . . . To
the man himself, Nature had given in high measure the seeds
of a noble endowment . . . a subtle, lynx-eyed intellect; tremulous, pious sensibility to all good and all beautiful . . . but
imbedded in such weak laxity of character . . . as made
strange work with it." Once more, says Carlyle, in the Scottish
moralist's typical summing-up, "once more, the tragic story of
a high endowment with an insufficient will."

It is all too easy to laugh over Coleridge—the cavalryman,
for example, who ran off and enlisted in the Light Dragoons
only to discover that he was allergic to horses. Or the young
Cantabrigian dandy disporting himself in a swanskin waistcoat.
Or the inexperienced, adenoidal lover who dreams of establishing a blissful American abode with one of the nubile daughters
of a bankrupt tinware manufacturer from the city of Bristol,
only to propose with idealistic haste and henceforth to find
himself hooked for the long duration of his life. Or the end-
lessly inventive projector whose ever-springing hopes are invariably quashed by his own bumbling ineptitudes and
procrastinations. Or the talker whose fascination with the
musical murmur of his own polysyllabic discourse denies to

others the opportunity to intrude with so much as a monosyllable of their own.

Yet to those who know him best, Coleridge is neither the
inadvertent clown nor the Pagliacci-figure whose outward
demeanor conceals by simulated gaiety the drowning and
redrowning of his soul in liquid fire. If he does not wear
his heart upon his sleeve, its steady bleeding is all too apparent
both in his poetry and in his personal letters, to say nothing of
his private journals. For Coleridge is the type of Man Damned,
too introspective not to know it, too retrospective to sustain
for long the determination to face futurity with any reasonable
expectation of being able to overcome the causes of his damnation.

These causes, naturally, originate within himself. In certain
quarters it has long been held that all the male world is split
between two camps: father's boys and mother's boys. If the
hypothesis has any psychological validity, Coleridge must
clearly qualify as his father's son. For he seems to have revered
his philoprogenitive but otherworldly sire, whom he lost when
he was only nine, and to have entertained emotions of mild
scorn towards his mother. Her determination that the children
in her charge should amount to something in the everyday
society of her time must on occasion have driven Mrs. Coleridge
towards a kind of practical dynamism to which her son, like his
father before him, was temperamentally indisposed. Coleridge
remembered his father, softened and gilded in the gathering
mist of time, as the "perfect Parson Adams"—simple, learned,
generously improvident, and (unlike Adams) "conscientiously
indifferent to the good and evil of this world." In Coleridge's
own paternal improvidence, in his voluminous and thronging
fantasies, in his perpetual abhorrence of business arrangements
and other forms of practical management, he is his father's ally
and his mother's enemy.

Yet, such are the vagaries of subtle and precariously balanced
minds, he could not evade feelings of remorse and guilt whenever his own failure to fulfill his mother's (and later his wife's)
desires for normal worldly respectability and success was borne
in upon him. The love he was unable to develop towards his
mother he tendered, rather sentimentally, to other women
during adolescence and young manhood. His sense of bereave-
ment upon the early death of his father led him to seek in male
friendships a whole series of father-substitutes, among whom
Wordsworth for some magical years reigned uppermost, though

he failed Coleridge in the end by outstripping him as poet if
not as sage, and as paterfamilias if not as philosopher.

Among his masculine benefactors, none did him more good
than Dr. Gillman, the surgeon of Highgate, into whose pleasant
household he entered, like a kind of downtrodden Übermensch,
just as the leaves were beginning to bud in the spring of 1816.
He was nearly forty-four, too old to accept the doctor and his
wife as spiritual foster-parents, yet so far gone in decrepitude
and despair that his need for them was infinitely greater than
theirs for him. They literally raised the roof to accommodate
Coleridge. His cheerful attic room was reached by a flight of
nine steep stairs. All of one side of his chamber was lined with
bookshelves from floor to ceiling. Centered in the opposite wall
was a fireplace before which stood his writing table. A yard
away was the large spool bed where, except for occasional out-
ings at the seaside and one trip to the Rhineland with Wordsworth during his middle fifties, Coleridge spent nearly all the
nights of his final eighteen years.

Beside the west window stood a dresser, ornamented by Mrs.
Gillman with potted geraniums and dark green myrtle, his
favorite house plants. On good days the view was fine, with
the Nightingale Valley stretching away in the evening sunlight,
and the tree-covered vistas of Hampstead dotted with half-
visible villas from whose chimneys, morning and evening, rose
companionable evidence of human habitation. Here, said
Carlyle, sat the sage, on the very brow of Highgate Hill, three
hundred feet above the uttermost northern fringe of the vast
city, "looking down on London and its smoke-tumult" as if he
had escaped from "the inanity of life's battle" . . . a "heavy-
laden, high-aspiring, and surely much-suffering man." And
here, in his sixty-second year, his sufferings ended.

— 2 —

Behind the public Coleridge—Mill's epoch-making philosopher, Saintsbury's critical Colossus, De Quincey's eloquent
discourser, Lamb's metaphysician and logician, Shelley's "sub-
tle-souled psychologist"—stood another and far less confident
creature: Coleridge the dreamer, or as one of his biographers
called him, "the sublime somnambulist." This was the man of
private dread, that curiously fragile victim of parlous circumstance whose trembling and pious sensibility discovered itself

to the young Carlyle whenever he sat at the feet of the master
in the tall old house at Highgate.

The forms of private dread are among the keys to Coleridge's
innermost personality. With many another sedentary scholar he
showed some degree of physical cowardice. Yet the impulse to
fear took its origin far less from outward stimuli than from
causes inside his psyche itself. Sporadically throughout his
life, though chiefly in his youth and young manhood, he seems
to have been

Like one, that on a lonesome road
Doth walk in fear and dread,
And having once turned round walks on,
And turns no more his head;
Because he knows, a frightful fiend
Doth close behind him tread.

Although he protested that he did not believe in ghosts, having met too many of them personally, there were frequent occasions when his disbelief was unwillingly suspended while
fiends of awful aspect stalked his errant footsteps. He well
knew what he calls in *Limbo* "the mere horror of blank Naught-
at-all." Far worse was the horror of what he might have
denominated "Something-indeed." For thick recurrent crowds
of "shapes and thoughts" rose round him as he lay writhing
on the borderlands of the subconscious. *The Pains of Sleep*
records his shocked realization of his own innate capacity for
sin; he recoiled at the discovery that he could desire hugely
what he hugely loathed. Shame, terror, guilt, remorse, and woe
roared like the gusts of a rising tempest down the walls of that
vast gulf which he once called "the unfathomable hell within."

It is a curious fact that many of Coleridge's deepest fears
partake somehow in the emotion of desolation—what D. G.
James speaks of as "the desert island feeling." At bottom this is
a dread, not so much of being alone as of being so profoundly
alone that one is out of touch, perhaps irrevocably, with the
whole range of the living universe. In *The Dungeon*, an extract
from his tragedy *Osorio* which he printed in the second edition
of *Lyrical Ballads*, Coleridge mentions with evident dismay the
idea of *"friendless solitude."* The adjective here makes all the
difference. For in a *friendless* as opposed to a *friendly* solitude,
one is conscious of being encircled by stagnation and corruption, by all that rots and reeks, until the soul itself "unmoulds
its essence" and becomes as "hopelessly deformed" as that of the

dungeoned prisoner in Coleridge's play. The bearing of all this on his figure of the Ancient Mariner is obvious.

Even the dejection of which the poet complains in the memorable and moving ode of April 1802 owes its origin to his conviction of an essential disunity between his own (as it were) orphaned sensibility and those multiple and potentially friendly sensibilities which make up the natural and familial world around him. As with Satan after the wars in paradise, Coleridge feels himself damned while yet capable of "beholding good." In this condition, like his ancient mariner becalmed on the surface of an empty sea, he can evoke no harmonies, bring nothing into formal being. For the duration of the ode, at least, he inhabits "that inanimate cold world"—that spectral wasteland where the "poor loveless ever-anxious crowd" blindly gropes in perpetual unawareness, having, as Coleridge said in another context, "eyes that see not, ears that hear not, and hearts that neither feel nor understand."

The antidote to all this is the dream of an earthly paradise. We are not sure how it may have looked to him while his head was submerged under the glittering surfaces of his most golden visions. As it comes out in the reflective poems, however, it is nothing so grand as Kubla's pleasure-dome inside the walled domain of Xanadu. Humbly enough in these verses he asks no more than a place of peace where in times of spiritual agoraphobia he can take refuge and find solace. Such was the lime-tree bower just over the wall from his cottage in Nether Stowey where he somnolently waited out a long June evening in 1797, gazing about at the sun-dappled foliage of the nearby walnuts and elms, hearing no other sounds than the twittering of swallows and the placid drone of a bumblebee. This was a friendly, not a friendless, solitude, made companionable both by the proximity of his own dwelling and by his thoughts of Charles Lamb and William and Dorothy Wordsworth as they set their course over the low hills and meadows between Nether Stowey and the sea. Such, too, was the interior of the same cottage one frosty midnight in the next winter when Coleridge sat dreaming of his own rural childhood and planning a happier and better one for his infant son, Hartley. On an April afternoon two months later he found "a green and silent spot" among the same hills his friends had explored—a "quiet spirit-healing nook" where he reclined on the golden coverlet of the "never-bloomless furze" to watch the descending sun and listen to the song of the ascending skylark. Here, as always, he permitted himself to dream of another world, one in which pure meditative joy in the flowering lap of nature might be prolonged rather than periodically interrupted and destroyed.

Interruption and destruction are in fact among his worst nightmares. Though his nature-worship is a good deal less intense than that of his friend Wordsworth, he has known enough of meditative joy in the lap of nature to wish for its perpetual continuance. At the same time, the best of experiential evidence —his own—convinces him that such joy can never last long. It is the possibility of interruption and destruction that sets him trembling even as he lolls half-asleep "on fern or withered heath" in seeming content. He fittingly calls his poem *Fears in Solitude*. Its subtitle provides the date and the cause of his fear: "Written in April, 1798, during the alarm of an invasion." Even in his vernal haven he cannot erase the indelible threat of what he knows so well—things changing for the worse. "My God!" he cries, "it is a melancholy thing" when a man who wishes only to "preserve his soul in calmness" must think of imminent war and its human consequences. Who is able to say that martial-minded France has not already set her men ashore? Even now strife may be stirring just beyond these silent hills—"invasion, and the thunder and the shout, and all the crash of onset."

It goes without saying that the war he feared did not reach English soil. Neither then nor later did Coleridge's "divine and beauteous island" fall victim to a foreign conqueror. What arrests our attention in this reflective poem is rather the architectural image through which the poet summarizes his sense of what England has meant to him. It is, he says, a "most magnificent temple" where he has been able to "walk with awe" and sing his stately songs. If the image is of no great consequence when taken alone, it assumes a striking pertinence when we think of it in connection with the pleasure-dome of Kubla Khan, another earthly temple whose owner dwelt in peace, though warned by ancestral voices that war and invasion might one day occur. It is this sense of possible destruction which gives dramatic force to Coleridge's autobiographical *Fears in Solitude*. It is also of use in the interpretation of that enigmatic parable which the author could have called *The Fall of the House of Kubla*.

In this brief fragment the pleasure-dome does not fall as did Poe's House of Usher, nor is Xanadu invaded and laid waste by barbarian hordes. Yet the poem hints clearly enough that both are distinct possibilities. The presiding concept in these fifty-four lines may indeed be summed up in the word *precariousness,* which is exactly the emotion Coleridge felt as he lay in apparently blissful ease in the dell above Nether Stowey.

The most important feature of the poem's internal structure is the series of contrasts there developed. Coleridge, with whom the device of thesis-antithesis was a fetish, thought habitually in terms of polar oppositions. Part One of the poem shows four of these: the light and the darkness, civilization and savagery, heat and cold, peace and war. The descriptive imagery of the opening lines at once establishes a bright and sun-filled landscape, green, fertile, and orderly. Yet the poem is not five lines old before we are reminded of the sunless waste of water far below. Another contrast is made with similar economy: the well-tended gardens of the Khan as over against the deep, wild, cedar-shaded gorge where the River Alph bursts out of the earth like a Niagara in reverse. This region of Xanadu, which Coleridge calls "romantic" in the eighteenth-century sense of "wildly but pleasurably awesome," is as different from Kubla Khan's domesticated grounds as is an Alpine chasm from the clipped formality of an English manor-house garden. "A savage place" is another of Coleridge's epithets. In Xanadu the rude and the civilized stand side by side.

The third contrast is not fully apparent until we have visualized the topographical features inside the protective wall. The pleasure-dome stands about halfway between the roaring fountain where the river springs up and the echoing caverns through which it dives in final tumult. Between appearance and disappearance, the Alph meanders some five miles. As the Tartarean crow flies, the distance between the dome and either end of the river is not great, since Kubla Khan within his castle can hear the "mingled measure" of the water's rise and fall. Lines 31–36 describe the miraculous situation of the pleasure-dome, which rests on a foundation of ice-caves either beside or astride the River Alph.

> The shadow of the dome of pleasure
> Floated midway on the waves; . . .
> It was a miracle of rare device,
> A sunny pleasure-dome with caves of ice.

Rare and miraculous indeed! The co-presence of heat and cold, of fire and ice, is enough to suggest the possibility that the dome's situation is precarious. Should the ice-caves melt, or should the Alph wear them away, the whole structure would dissolve and vanish, never to reappear except as flotsam on the dark subterranean ocean.

One then asks whether the possible destruction of the pleasure-dome is elsewhere implied. The answer brings out the final contrast in Part One: the opposition of peace and war. The dome is dedicated to peace, plenty, domesticated beauty, and the gentle arts of contemplation. The roar of the water as it dives below ground would not be oppressive if the Khan did not hear through the tumult the sinister sound of "ancestral voices prophesying war."

In all four contrasts we are made aware of the precariousness of the Khan's situation. During the second part of the poem, when the narrator-observer comes to speak for himself, it is to ally his interests with the forces of order and creativity. Like Kubla Khan he wishes to be the builder of an earthly paradise. Unhappily his inspiration—which is here represented by the strains of music from the visionary maiden's dulcimer—has departed. Even if he could "build that dome in air," he would still be in Kubla Khan's predicament; he would have to take into account the always imminent forces of destruction. For the magical creation of castles in the air is involved with a long history of popular distrust and superstition. People are all too ready to suppose that such unearthly pageants are the work of enchanters, possibly of demons. Does not this one show the flashing eyes of a man possessed? Clearly the wisest course among law-abiding citizens of the orthodox persuasion is to begin a ceremony of exorcism, weaving a circle three times round, closing their eyes in holy dread of his hypnotic stare. He has fed on honey-dew, the celestial ichor, and drunk the milk of paradise, a celestial liquor. So had Satan, before he fell.

In the face of such opposition, the builder might well expect to see his cloud-capped towers dissolve into thin air before he could get them suitably mapped and blueprinted. By Coleridge's account this was what happened to his own vision of Xanadu when his reverie was interrupted and his privacy invaded by the arrival of a rank outsider—on *business,* too. Although he afterwards retained "a vague and dim recollection of the general purport of the vision," all his "phantom world" had otherwise vanished.

Luckily, and despite the brevity of the fragment, its general purport is quite clear. It follows the normal lyrical mode of statement, application, and resolution. The statement hints four times that the earthly paradise is in imminent danger of dissolution. If it does not come from within—by crumbling foundations like those of the House of Usher—it may come from outside—by assault. The application and resolution combine to show that the visionary poet faces similar dangers. He has already lost his power to revive within him the music of inspiration. At the hands of a suspicious and antagonistic public he may likewise have to reckon with a "war" from outside.

— 3 —

We have already noticed Coleridge's refusal to believe in ghosts on the grounds that he had seen too many of them. Enough of these experiences are on record in his writings to indicate that his mind was always playing him tricks. His generic term for this process was "somnial magic" by which he meant a spectrum broad enough to cover not only those times when he was actually asleep but also those varying degrees of wakefulness running from the simple daydream (when one is in full and relaxed command of his mind) all the way down to a kind of reverie where the "comparative powers" are suspended and images of mental origin seem as real as images of actual visible objects.

The *Biographia Literaria* asserts that psychology had long been one of Coleridge's hobbyhorses. If he had ever undertaken his proposed work on dreams, visions, ghosts, and witchcraft, he would have treated all such phenomena systematically and offered "scientific" explanations for them. Luther's encounter with the devil could, for example, be subjectively explained. It was nothing more supernatural than the result of a "deranged digestion" in a man of sedentary habits who had been intensively worrying about the problem of evil. Having himself passed through many similar adventures along the frontiers of sleep, Coleridge understood perfectly how Luther was able to see both his actual room, with all its furniture and appurtenances, and also a superimposed "brain-image of the devil, vivid enough to have acquired apparent outness." It is clear that Coleridge would have had no difficulty whatever in analyzing the case of Ebenezer Scrooge and the three ghosts of Christmastide.

Illness and bodily pain stimulated the image-making powers. He believed that "the optics and acoustics of the inner sense" helped to explain the "mode in which our thought, in states of morbid slumber, is delirium." When his friend Charles

Lloyd, an epileptic, fell seriously ill in November, 1796, Coleridge carefully observed and recorded Lloyd's state of mind. Most remarkable was the way in which actual events and sounds were assimilated and transformed into the substance of his imaginings. "All the Realities round him," said Coleridge, "mingle with, and form part of the strange dream. All his voluntary powers are suspended; but he perceives every thing and hears every thing, and whatever he perceives and hears he perverts into the substance of his delirious vision."

At the other extreme from Lloyd's delirium was the daydream or semicontrolled reverie like that recorded in *Frost at Midnight*. Here the poet was perfectly aware of time and place, yet free to range at will over the past, into the future, and far outside the confines of the cottage where he ruminated at midnight beside a dying fire. His reveries were not always so pleasant. In the ode, *Dejection*, he recalls himself from a state of choking regret over the decay of his imaginative powers, the same decay presaged in *Kubla Khan* some years earlier, with an image suggestive of the Laocoön:

Hence, viper thoughts, that coil around my mind,
Reality's dark dream!
I turn from you and listen to the wind,
Which long has raved unnoticed.

He has sunk so deep into the buried life that he has forgotten to listen for the rising storm, a phenomenon earlier wished for in the hope that it might startle him out of his lethargic temper.

Two poems called *Day-dream* show, when they are compared, what a range of consciousness Coleridge meant his term to embrace. One says simply: "My eyes make pictures, when they are shut." The other states that "no deeper trance e'er wrapt a yearning spirit" than that from which the child Frederic awakened him. Whenever he dozed in his chair, regrets and nostalgias, hopes and fears rose up in his mind as pictures. The various states and levels of reverie show what he once called "that *complexus* of visual images, cycles or customs of sensations, and fellow-traveling circumstances (as the ship to the mariner) which make up our empirical self."

Such phenomena sometimes occurred even when Coleridge was fully awake and actively engaged in writing. One of his letters to Southey mentions their old room in College Street. Then he interrupts his letter to explain that even as he wrote the sentence about their former association in a particular house beside a familiar street, he was struck by an "ocular spectrum" of the room itself. He goes on to say that this ocular picture illustrates his own theory of association. When association occurs, it is often less a linkage between trains of ideas than of "resembling states of feeling." The notebooks are full of his comments on cycles of sensations and fellow-traveling circumstances. "Renew the state of affection or bodily Feeling," says one entry, "same or similar—sometimes dimly similar, and instantly the trains of forgotten thought rise from their living catacombs."

Opium was not for Coleridge the "onlie begetter" of daydreams, but no one who has read his letters can doubt that it served him both as a narcotic and a stimulant. "Laudanum gave me repose, not sleep," he wrote in March, 1798, and the distinction helps to explain the state in which after 1796 he often voluntarily placed himself. The repose (not sleep) which the dosage induced he once called "a spot of enchantment, a green spot of fountain and flowers and trees in the very heart of waste sands." The language here is plainly figurative, like Shelley's "green isle" in the "sea of misery." What it meant to Coleridge is what aspirin means to lesser mortals: a joyous relief from the gnawing edge of pain, a sense of euphoria in which the mind is set free from bodily misery (or even spiritual remorse), though always and only for the time being.

But opium was also a stimulant. If he did not enter the dopetaker's nirvana of popular belief, he nevertheless found this "pernicious drug" oddly beneficial to him as a mode of liberation. Sometimes it released "thoughts, hidden in him before," yet happily capable of producing the deepest emotional responses among "his best, greatest, and sanest contemporaries." For a "delusive time" this poison seemed to make the body a "fitter instrument for the all-powerful soul." Not only could it deaden the pain of affliction; it also opened inner doors to nobler traffic. In such a situation, he said, writing itself becomes a kind of "mental somnambulism, the somnial magic superinduced on, without suspending, the active powers of the mind." What ensues is a series of vivid and dramatic metaphors, closely accompanied by the very words that will best express them. One need not wonder at his gradual addiction to such a drug as this. The catch, and well he knew it, lay in the paralysis of the will power which accompanied this magical liberation and made him incapable of setting down more than the merest fraction of the wonders he had seen.

Great minds, said Coleridge in one of his aphoristic moments, are never wrong except as a consequence of being in the right, but imperfectly. In this, as in so much else he wisely summarized, he was drawing on personal experience. Of his own imperfections he was the best expositor and the severest judge. Modern psychology and psychiatry, though they have surpassed the levels of achievement he could only dream of, yet confirm many of his affirmations about the phenomena of the human mind under various forms of stress and stimulation. He was often wrong. But he was also often in the right, however imperfectly.

— 4 —

What a man was may be summed up not only in what other men said of him but also in what he said of other men. For he is likely to select for admiration and emulation those qualities in his predecessors and contemporaries to which he himself aspires. It is clear that one of Coleridge's leading aspirations was to excel in a whole variety of modes of expression. He was, it has been said, a man of many facets with all the facets turned on to the full. If he was, in the end, neither the greatest of poets nor the most systematic of philosophers, neither the wisest of moralists nor the best of psychologists, neither (certainly) the wittiest of playwrights nor the cleverest of wits, he did manage to excel, though sporadically, in each of his chosen fields. And if the term *universal genius* must finally be denied him, he came close enough to that lofty station so that some examination of his views on the subject of genius may fittingly conclude these introductory remarks.

He disagreed with Dr. Samuel Johnson's view that genius was little more than a generalized talent developed in a particular direction by the force of circumstance. He wished, in fact, to distinguish sharply between the poetic power of genius and, on the other hand, "a general talent determined to poetic composition by accidental motives, by an act of will rather than by the inspiration of a genial and productive nature." Johnson's formula suggested that true geniuses appear more frequently than they actually do. "Poetic genius," said Coleridge, "is not only a very delicate but a very rare plant."

When genius occurred, he believed, one could always recognize it by the degree of its dominance over the materials it worked with. Shakespeare, whom Coleridge never tired of exploring because each fresh investigation disclosed new powers in the master, was assuredly no "mere child of nature; no automaton of genius; no passive vehicle of inspiration possessed by the spirit, not possessing it." On the contrary, he "studied patiently, meditated deeply, understood minutely, till knowledge, become habitual and intuitive, wedded itself to his habitual feelings." The inspiration, when it came, had to be a positive act of the whole man. The whole man must possess wholly the knowledge he projected. He must be autonomous rather than automatic. Whatever he did must be based on an empirical observation—examined, ruminated upon, and at last comprehended with the lordly grasp of the master. Like that of any true genius, the kind of poetry Shakespeare wrote required an activity of the will, but in a quite different connection from what one was likely to find in the work of a merely talented man. For in genius, said Coleridge, one discovers not so much a partnership as a *union* of powers: "interpenetration of passion and will, of spontaneous impulse and of voluntary purpose." Few commentators have put the matter better.

"Idly talk they," cried Coleridge, "who speak of poets as indulgers of fancy, imagination, superstition, etc. They are the bridlers by delight, the purifiers; they that combine all these with reason and order—the true protoplasts—Gods of love who tame the chaos." Out of deference to reason and order, Coleridge defined one side of genius as "originality in intellectual construction." But the definition did not wholly satisfy him. For it omitted one great activating principle of genius which consisted, as he often said, in the ability to carry on into the powers of manhood the freshness and feelings of childhood. The genius can so re-present familiar objects as to "awaken the minds of others to a like freshness of sensation concerning them."

The skeptic or idle talker may seek to depreciate the genius as a blind man offering to lead the blind, or at best as one "talking the language of sight to those who do not possess the sense of seeing"—a statement, incidentally, which exactly describes William Blake. Coleridge's response to such depreciation is to say that we are not all blind, though all of us from time to time may be subject to "distempers of the mental sight." We are all in error, though not all in the same error, or at the same time. It is the conceivable office of some great men to help heal others, to open their eyes to truths hitherto concealed. Such men are the true geniuses of any age.

The genius, therefore, is the bugler blowing reveille in the dormitory of the soul. He is the awakener, the freshener, the reactivator, and the discoverer or rediscoverer. "The character and privilege of genius," said Coleridge, is to "find no contradiction in the union of the old and new, to contemplate the Ancient of Days with feelings as fresh as if they then sprang forth at his own fiat." Like the poet in Keats's second *Hyperion*, such men will "feel the riddle of the world, and may help to unravel it." But Coleridge insistently returns to the idea of an educated innocence as the *sine qua non* of true genius. So equipped, a man may somehow manage to "carry on the feelings of childhood into the powers of manhood" and to look with "the child's sense of wonder and novelty" upon those appearances which "every day for perhaps forty years have rendered familiar."

In this sense, Wordsworth was for Coleridge the living illustration of genius. When they began collaborating on *Lyrical Ballads*, Wordsworth's task was to "awaken the mind's attention from the lethargy of custom" directing it rather to "the loveliness and the wonders of the world before us." His performance, in Coleridge's judgment, proved the wisdom of the assignment. For Wordsworth had that kind of genius which "neither distorts nor false-colours its objects." Instead he brought out "many a vein and many a tint which escapes the eye of common observation, thus raising to the rank of gems what had been often kicked away by the hurrying foot of the traveller on the dusty high road of custom."

How exactly Coleridge conforms to his own conception of greatness is a question for continuing debate. Whatever we may think of him as poet or philosopher, psychologist or moralist or metaphysician, he is literally a man to reckon with—if not (like Immanuel Kant) to tell time by. Compared to that industrious utilitarian Jeremy Bentham, the garrulous and often querulous Coleridge seems the very image of the *until*-itarian: a perpetual procrastinator, a John-a-dreams unpregnant of the means by which his best aspirations may be realized. Yet we may remind ourselves that it was no less a person than John Stuart Mill who classed both men as the supreme "seminal thinkers" of the early nineteenth century. In the minds of all the thinking part of mankind, these two had managed to sow those ideological seeds which would sooner or later spring up and flourish. For both men, Mill's metaphor is just.

Chief Dates in the Life of Coleridge

1772   October 21: Samuel Taylor Coleridge born, Ottery St. Mary, Devonshire, youngest child of Rev. John Coleridge and Anne Bowdon, his second wife.

1781   Death of father.

1782   Entered the famous old charity school of Christ's Hospital, London. Formed lifelong friendship with Charles Lamb, his schoolmate.

1791   Entered as sizar at Jesus College, Cambridge.

1793   Returned to London. Enlisted in 15th Light Dragoons under pseudonym of Silas Tomkyn Comberbach.

1794   His brothers bought him free of military service. Returned to Cambridge. Met Robert Southey at Oxford and hatched scheme of "Pantisocratic" settlement in America. Engaged to marry Sara Fricker of Bristol. Collaborated with Southey on revolutionary tragedy, *The Fall of Robespierre*. Formed friendship with Thomas Poole. Abortive love affair with Mary Evans. Left Cambridge without degree.

1795   Abandoned Pantisocracy. Married Sara Fricker, October 4. First meeting with William Wordsworth and with publisher Joseph Cottle.

1796   His periodical, *The Watchman,* failed in May in its tenth number. Published *Poems on Various Subjects.* Began use of laudanum for medicinal purposes. Birth of son Hartley.

1797   In residence at Nether Stowey. In June paid visit to William and Dorothy Wordsworth at Racedown. In July they moved to Alfoxden, and friendship ripened. Coleridge wrote play, *Osorio;* published *Poems,* second edition; and under stimulus of Wordsworth produced *The Rime of the Ancient Mariner, Kubla Khan,* and the first part of *Christabel.*

1798   Climaxed two years of preaching with offer of pastorate
       at Unitarian Chapel, Shrewsbury, where he first met
       William Hazlitt, later his literary enemy. Declined offer
       on strength of annuity from Josiah and Thomas Wedg-
       wood. Birth of son Berkeley. Collaborated with Words-
       worth on first edition of *Lyrical Ballads*. Left for Ger-
       many with William and Dorothy Wordsworth.

1799   Returned from Germany. Began another hopeless love
       affair, this time with Sara, sister of Mary Hutchinson,
       Wordsworth's wife-to-be. Translated Schiller's *Wallen-
       stein* and wrote journalism and poetry for the London
       Morning Post. Death of son Berkeley.

1800   Second edition of *Lyrical Ballads* with a long preface by
       Wordsworth. Coleridge settled family at Greta Hall,
       Keswick, Lake District. Marked domestic unhappiness,
       illness, and increasing addiction to opium. Wrote second
       part of *Christabel*.

1802   Birth of daughter Sara.

1804   April: Sailed for 17-month stay in Malta. Employed as
       private secretary in the Governor's Palace.

1805   September: Left Malta for Syracuse, Naples, Rome,
       Florence, Pisa, and Leghorn.

1806   August: Returned to England. October: Rejoined wife
       and children at Keswick. Marriage now in severe diffi-
       culties.

1807   First meeting with Thomas De Quincey at Bridgwater.

1808   First subscription lecture series, London. Frequent visits
       to the Wordsworths at Grasmere in this and next two
       years.

1809–1810   Periodical publication of *The Friend* (essays).

1810   Breach with Wordsworth. Virtually final separation from
       wife.

1810–1813   Offered further lecture series.

1813   His play *Osorio,* retitled *Remorse,* successfully produced.

1815   Composed *Biographia Literaria.* Began composition of *Zapolya.*

1816   April: For release from opium habit placed self in household of Dr. James Gillman at Highgate "in the leafy environs of London" for duration of life. *The Statesman's Manual* and the *Christabel* volume published.

1817   July: Publication of *Biographia Literaria, Sibylline Leaves* (poems). Publication of *Lay Sermons* and *Zapolya: A Christmas Tale* (play).

1818–1819   Further lecture series.

1825   Publication of *Aids to Reflection.* Coleridge of Highgate now at height of fame as a conversationalist.

1830   Publication of the *Constitution of Church and State.*

1834   July 25: Death of Coleridge, aged 61.

~Poetry~

MYSTERY POEMS

Except for the second part of *Christabel,* done in 1800, the mystery poems belong to the productive years of 1797–1798 when Coleridge's powers as poet reached the highest point of their development under the immediate stimulus of his new friendship with Wordsworth. It is a curious commentary on his habitual indolence that, even in these years of intellectual and emotional excitation, he should have left incomplete two of the three poems by which his future fame as poet was chiefly to be spread.

Many reasons exist for calling them the mystery poems. How much of Coleridge's personal feeling of guilt, for example, went into the literally marvelous fable of crime and punishment which he put into the mouth of the Ancient Mariner? What personal dream of a perilous Eden underlies the evocative fragment which he called *Kubla Khan?* Why did he finally abandon the tale of sexual enchantment, with its marked pre-Freudian overtones, just when the story of *Christabel* had begun to approach its climactic moments?

Yet the chief mystery is perhaps the matter of interpretation. What are we to make of these three quite different accounts of actual or incipient incursions of evil into human life, the release and play of chthonic forces among innocents like Christabel; unwitting criminals like the young sailor who shoots the albatross; or benign rulers like Kubla Khan, whose domains may be laid waste, as his "ancestral voices" seem to prophesy? Why was Coleridge's subconscious mind so laden with images of imminent destruction in the very years when his creative powers stood at their highest peak? Why, above all, does none of his other poetry bear resemblances to this famous trio of narratives? After all the speculation, an essential mystery remains.

THE RIME OF THE ANCIENT MARINER

IN SEVEN PARTS

Facile credo, plures esse Naturas invisibiles quam visibiles in rerum universitate. Sed horum omnium familiam quis nobis enarrabit? et gradus et cognationes et discrimina et singulorum munera? Quid agunt? quae loca habitant? Harum rerum notitiam semper ambivit ingenium humanum, nunquam attigit. Juvat, interea, non diffiteor, quandoque in animo, tanquam in tabulâ, majoris et melioris mundi imaginem contemplari: ne mens assuefacta hodiernae vitae minutiis se contrahat nimis, et tota subsidat in pusillas cogitationes. Sed veritati interea invigilandum est, modusque servandus, ut certa ab incertis, diem a nocte, distinguamus.—
T. Burnet, *Archaeol. Phil.* p. 68.

ARGUMENT

How a Ship having passed the Line was driven by storms to the cold Country towards the South Pole; and how from thence she made her course to the tropical Latitude of the Great Pacific Ocean; and of the strange things that befell; and in what manner the Ancyent Marinere came back to his own Country.

PART I

An ancient Mariner meeteth three Gallants bidden to a wedding-feast, and detaineth one.

It is an ancient Mariner,
And he stoppeth one of three.
"By thy long grey beard and glittering eye,
Now wherefore stopp'st thou me?

The Bridegroom's doors are opened wide,
And I am next of kin;
The guests are met, the feast is set:
May'st hear the merry din."

He holds him with his skinny hand,
"There was a ship," quoth he.

5

10

24

"Hold off! unhand me, grey-beard loon!"
Eftsoons his hand dropt he.

The Wedding-Guest is spell-bound by the eye of the old seafaring man, and constrained to hear his tale.

He holds him with his glittering eye—
The Wedding-Guest stood still,
And listens like a three years' child: 15
The Mariner hath his will.

The Wedding-Guest sat on a stone:
He cannot choose but hear;
And thus spake on that ancient man,
The bright-eyed Mariner.   20

"The ship was cheered, the harbour
      cleared,
Merrily did we drop
Below the kirk, below the hill,
Below the lighthouse top.

The Mariner tells how the ship sailed southward with a good wind and fair weather, till it reached the Line.

The Sun came up upon the left,   25
Out of the sea came he!
And he shone bright, and on the right
Went down into the sea.

Higher and higher every day,
Till over the mast at noon—"   30
The Wedding-Guest here beat his breast,
For he heard the loud bassoon.

The Wedding-Guest heareth the bridal music; but the Mariner continueth his tale.

The bride hath paced into the hall,
Red as a rose is she;
Nodding their heads before her goes   35
The merry minstrelsy.

The Wedding-Guest he beat his breast,
Yet he cannot choose but hear;
And thus spake on that ancient man,
The bright-eyed Mariner.   40

The ship driven by a storm toward the south pole.

"And now the STORM-BLAST came, and he
Was tyrannous and strong;
He struck with his o'ertaking wings,
And chased us south along.

With sloping masts and dipping
      prow,   45

As who pursued with yell and blow
Still treads the shadow of his foe,
And forward bends his head,
The ship drove fast, loud roared the blast,
And southward aye we fled.   50

And now there came both mist and snow,
And it grew wondrous cold:
And ice, mast-high, came floating by,
As green as emerald.

The land of ice,
and of fearful
sounds where no
living thing was
to be seen.

And through the drifts the snowy
            clifts   55
Did send a dismal sheen:
Nor shapes of men nor beasts we ken—
The ice was all between.

The ice was here, the ice was there,
The ice was all around: 60
It cracked and growled, and roared and
        howled,
Like noises in a swound!

Till a great sea-
bird, called the
Albatross, came
through the
snow-fog, and
was received
with great joy
and hospitality.

At length did cross an Albatross,
Thorough the fog it came;
As if it had been a Christian soul,   65
We hailed it in God's name.

It ate the food it ne'er had eat,
And round and round it flew.
The ice did split with a thunder-fit;
The helmsman steered us through!   70

And lo! the Al-
batross proveth
a bird of good
omen, and fol-
loweth the ship
as it returned
northward
through fog and
floating ice.

And a good south wind sprung up be-
            hind;
The Albatross did follow,
And every day, for food or play,
Came to the mariners' hollo!

In mist or cloud, on mast or shroud,   75
It perched for vespers nine;
Whiles all the night, through fog-smoke
            white,
Glimmered the white Moon-shine."

*The ancient
Mariner inhospi-
tably killeth the
pious bird of
good omen.*

"God save thee, ancient Mariner!
From the fiends, that plague thee
   thus!—   80
Why look'st thou so?"—"With my cross-
   bow
I shot the ALBATROSS.

PART II

The Sun now rose upon the right:
Out of the sea came he,
Still hid in mist, and on the left   85
Went down into the sea.

And the good south wind still blew be-
   hind,
But no sweet bird did follow,
Nor any day for food or play
Came to the mariners' hollo!   90

*His shipmates
cry out against
the ancient Mar-
iner, for killing
the bird of good
luck.*

And I had done a hellish thing,
And it would work 'em woe:
For all averred, I had killed the bird
That made the breeze to blow.
Ah wretch! said they, the bird to slay,   95
That made the breeze to blow!

*But when the
fog cleared off,
they justify the
same, and thus
make themselves
accomplices in
the crime.*

Nor dim nor red, like God's own head,
The glorious Sun uprist:
Then all averred, I had killed the bird
That brought the fog and mist.   100
'Twas right, said they, such birds to slay,
That bring the fog and mist.

*The fair breeze
continues; the
ship enters the
Pacific Ocean,
and sails north-
ward, even till it
reaches the Line.*

The fair breeze blew, the white foam
   flew,
The furrow followed free;
We were the first that ever burst   105
Into that silent sea.

*The ship hath
been suddenly
becalmed.*

Down dropt the breeze, the sails dropt
   down,
'Twas sad as sad could be;
And we did speak only to break
The silence of the sea!   110

All in a hot and copper sky,
The bloody Sun, at noon,
Right up above the mast did stand,
No bigger than the Moon.

Day after day, day after day,   115
We stuck, nor breath nor motion;
As idle as a painted ship
Upon a painted ocean.

And the Alba-
tross begins to
be avenged.

Water, water, every where,
And all the boards did shrink;   120
Water, water, every where,
Nor any drop to drink.

The very deep did rot: O Christ!
That ever this should be!
Yea, slimy things did crawl with legs   125
Upon the slimy sea.

About, about, in reel and rout
The death-fires danced at night;
The water, like a witch's oils,
Burnt green, and blue and white.   130

And some in dreams assuréd were
A Spirit had
followed them;
one of the invis-
ible inhabitants
of this planet,
Of the Spirit that plagued us so;
Nine fathom deep he had followed us
From the land of mist and snow.

neither departed souls nor angels; concerning whom the learned Jew, Josephus, and
the Platonic Constantinopolitan, Michael Psellus, may be consulted. They are very
numerous, and there is no climate or element without one or more.

And every tongue, through utter
   drought,   135
Was withered at the root;
We could not speak, no more than if
We had been choked with soot.

The shipmates,
in their sore dis-
tress, would fain
throw the whole
guilt on the an-
cient Mariner: in
Ah! well a-day! what evil looks
Had I from old and young!
Instead of the cross, the Albatross   140
About my neck was hung.

sign whereof they hang the dead sea-bird round his neck.

PART III

There passed a weary time. Each throat
Was parched, and glazed each eye.
A weary time! a weary time!   145
How glazed each weary eye,
When looking westward, I beheld
A something in the sky.

*The ancient Mar-
iner beholdeth a
sign in the ele-
ment afar off.*

At first it seemed a little speck,
And then it seemed a mist;   150
It moved and moved, and took at last
A certain shape, I wist.

A speck, a mist, a shape, I wist!
And still it neared and neared:
As if it dodged a water-sprite,   155
It plunged and tacked and veered.

*At its nearer ap-
proach, it seem-
eth him to be a
ship; and at a
dear ransom he
freeth his speech
from the bonds
of thirst.*

With throats unslaked, with black lips
    baked,
We could nor laugh nor wail;
Through utter drought all dumb we
    stood!
I bit my arm, I sucked the blood,   160
And cried, A sail! a sail!

With throats unslaked, with black lips
    baked,
Agape they heard me call:
A flash of joy;
Gramercy! they for joy did grin,
And all at once their breath drew in,   165
As they were drinking all.

*And horror fol-
lows. For can it
be a ship that
comes onward
without wind or
tide?*

See! see! (I cried) she tacks no more!
Hither to work us weal;
Without a breeze, without a tide,
She steadies with upright keel!   170

The western wave was all a-flame.
The day was well nigh done!
Almost upon the western wave
Rested the broad bright Sun;
When that strange shape drove sud-
    denly   175
Betwixt us and the Sun.

It seemeth him but the skeleton of a ship.

And straight the Sun was flecked with
  bars,
(Heaven's Mother send us grace!)
As if through a dungeon-grate he peered
With broad and burning face.   180

And its ribs are seen as bars on the face of the setting Sun.

Alas! (thought I, and my heart beat loud)
How fast she nears and nears!
Are those *her* sails that glance in the Sun,
Like restless gossameres?

The Spectre-Woman and her Deathmate, and no other on board the skeleton ship. Like vessel, like crew!

Are those *her* ribs through which the
  Sun   185
Did peer, as through a grate?
And is that Woman all her crew?
Is that a DEATH? and are there two?
Is DEATH that woman's mate?

Death and Life-in-Death have diced for the ship's crew, and she (the latter) winneth the ancient Mariner.

Her lips were red, *her* looks were
  free,   190
Her locks were yellow as gold:
Her skin was as white as leprosy,
The Night-mare LIFE-IN-DEATH was she,
Who thicks man's blood with cold.

The naked hulk alongside came,   195
And the twain were casting dice;
'The game is done! I've won! I've won!'
Quoth she, and whistles thrice.

No twilight within the courts of the Sun.

The Sun's rim dips; the stars rush out:
At one stride comes the dark;   200
With far-heard whisper, o'er the sea,
Off shot the spectre-bark.

At the rising of the Moon,

We listened and looked sideways up!
Fear at my heart, as at a cup,
My life-blood seemed to sip!   205
The stars were dim, and thick the night,
The steersman's face by his lamp gleamed
  white;
From the sails the dew did drip—
Till clomb above the eastern bar
The hornéd Moon, with one bright
  star   210
Within the nether tip.

*One after an-
other,*

One after one, by the star-dogged Moon,
Too quick for groan or sigh,
Each turned his face with ghastly pang,
And cursed me with his eye.   215

*His shipmates
drop down dead.*

Four times fifty living men,
 (And I heard nor sigh nor groan)
With heavy thump, a lifeless lump,
They dropped down one by one.

*But Life-in-
Death begins her
work on the an-
cient Mariner.*

The souls did from their bodies
     fly,—   220
They fled to bliss or woe!
And every soul, it passed me by,
Like the whizz of my cross-bow!"

PART IV

*The Wedding-
Guest feareth
that a Spirit is
talking to him;*

"I fear thee, ancient Mariner!
I fear thy skinny hand!   225
And thou art long, and lank, and brown,
As is the ribbed sea-sand.[1]

I fear thee and thy glittering eye,
And thy skinny hand, so brown."—

*But the ancient
Mariner assureth
him of his bodily
life, and pro-
ceedeth to relate
his horrible pen-
ance.*

"Fear not, fear not, thou Wedding-
     Guest!   230
This body dropt not down.

Alone, alone, all, all alone,
Alone on a wide wide sea!
And never a saint took pity on
My soul in agony.   235

*He despiseth the
creatures of the
calm,*

The many men, so beautiful!
And they all dead did lie:
And a thousand thousand slimy things
Lived on; and so did I.

*And envieth that
they should live,
and so many lie
dead.*

I looked upon the rotting sea,   240
And drew my eyes away;
I looked upon the rotting deck,
And there the dead men lay.

[1] For the last two lines of this stanza, I am indebted to Mr. Wordsworth. It was
on a delightful walk from Nether Stowey to Dulverton, with him and his sister,
in the Autumn of 1797, that this Poem was planned, and in part composed.—
S. T. C. [Coleridge's Note]

I looked to heaven, and tried to pray;
But or ever a prayer had gusht,   245
A wicked whisper came, and made
My heart as dry as dust.

I closed my lids, and kept them close,
And the balls like pulses beat;
For the sky and the sea, and the sea and
      the sky   250
Lay like a load on my weary eye,
And the dead were at my feet.

But the curse
liveth for him in
the eye of the
dead men.

The cold sweat melted from their limbs,
Nor rot nor reek did they:
The look with which they looked on
      me   255
Had never passed away.

An orphan's curse would drag to hell
A spirit from on high;
But oh! more horrible than that
Is the curse in a dead man's eye!   260
Seven days, seven nights, I saw that curse,
And yet I could not die.

In his loneliness
and fixedness he
yearneth towards
the journeying
Moon, and the
stars that still
sojourn, yet still
move onward;
and everywhere
the blue sky be-
longs to them,
and is their ap-
pointed rest, and
their native

The moving Moon went up the sky,
And no where did abide:
Softly she was going up,   265
And a star or two beside—

Her beams bemocked the sultry main,
Like April hoar-frost spread;
But where the ship's huge shadow lay,
The charméd water burnt alway   270
A still and awful red.

country and their own natural homes, which they enter unannounced, as lords that
are certainly expected and yet there is a silent joy at their arrival.

By the light of
the Moon he be-
holdeth God's
creatures of the
great calm.

Beyond the shadow of the ship,
I watched the water-snakes:
They moved in tracks of shining white,
And when they reared, the elfish
      light   275
Fell off in hoary flakes.

Within the shadow of the ship
I watched their rich attire:
Blue, glossy green, and velvet black,
They coiled and swam; and every
    track   280
Was a flash of golden fire.

*Their beauty
and their happi-
ness.*

O happy living things! no tongue
Their beauty might declare:
A spring of love gushed from my heart,

*He blesseth them
in his heart.*

And I blessed them unaware: 285
Sure my kind saint took pity on me,
And I blessed them unaware.

*The spell begins
to break.*

The self-same moment I could pray;
And from my neck so free
The Albatross fell off, and sank   290
Like lead into the sea.

PART V

Oh sleep! it is a gentle thing,
Beloved from pole to pole!
To Mary Queen the praise be given!
She sent the gentle sleep from
    Heaven,   295
That slid into my soul.

*By grace of the
holy Mother, the
ancient Mariner
is refreshed with
rain.*

The silly buckets on the deck,
That had so long remained,
I dreamt that they were filled with dew;
And when I awoke, it rained.   300

My lips were wet, my throat was cold,
My garments all were dank;
Sure I had drunken in my dreams,
And still my body drank.

I moved, and could not feel my
    limbs: 305
I was so light—almost
I thought that I had died in sleep,
And was a blessèd ghost.

And soon I heard a roaring wind:
It did not come anear;   310
But with its sound it shook the sails,
That were so thin and sere.

The upper air burst into life!
And a hundred fire-flags sheen,
To and fro they were hurried about!   315
And to and fro, and in and out,
The wan stars danced between.

And the coming wind did roar more loud,
And the sails did sigh like sedge;
And the rain poured down from one black
      cloud;   320
The Moon was at its edge.

The thick black cloud was cleft, and still
The Moon was at its side:
Like waters shot from some high crag,
The lightning fell with never a jag,   325
A river steep and wide.

The loud wind never reached the ship,
Yet now the ship moved on!
Beneath the lightning and the Moon
The dead men gave a groan.   330

They groaned, they stirred, they all up-
      rose,
Nor spake, nor moved their eyes;
It had been strange, even in a dream,
To have seen those dead men rise.

The helmsman steered, the ship moved
      on;   335
Yet never a breeze up-blew;
The mariners all 'gan work the ropes,
Where they were wont to do;
They raised their limbs like lifeless tools—
We were a ghastly crew.   340

The body of my brother's son
Stood by me, knee to knee:
The body and I pulled at one rope,
But he said nought to me."

"I fear thee, ancient Mariner!"   345
"Be calm, thou Wedding-Guest!
'Twas not those souls that fled in pain,
Which to their corses came again,
But a troop of spirits blest:

But not by the souls of the men, nor by dæmons of earth or middle air, but by a blessed troop of angelic spirits, sent down by the invocation of the guardian saint.

For when it dawned—they dropped their
      arms,   350
And clustered round the mast;
Sweet sounds rose slowly through their
      mouths,
And from their bodies passed.

Around, around, flew each sweet sound,
Then darted to the Sun;   355
Slowly the sounds came back again,
Now mixed, now one by one.

Sometimes a-dropping from the sky
I heard the sky-lark sing;
Sometimes all little birds that are,   360
How they seemed to fill the sea and air
With their sweet jargoning!

And now 'twas like all instruments,
Now like a lonely flute;
And now it is an angel's song,   365
That makes the heavens be mute.

It ceased; yet still the sails made on
A pleasant noise till noon,
A noise like of a hidden brook
In the leafy month of June,   370
That to the sleeping woods all night
Singeth a quiet tune.

Till noon we quietly sailed on,
Yet never a breeze did breathe:
Slowly and smoothly went the ship,   375
Moved onward from beneath.

The lonesome Spirit from the south-pole carries on the ship as far as the Line, in obedi-

Under the keel nine fathom deep,
From the land of mist and snow,
The spirit slid: and it was he
That made the ship to go.   380

*ence to the an-
gelic troop, but
still requireth
vengeance.*

The sails at noon left off their tune,
And the ship stood still also.

The Sun, right up above the mast,
Had fixed her to the ocean:
But in a minute she 'gan stir,   385
With a short uneasy motion—
Backwards and forwards half her length
With a short uneasy motion.

Then like a pawing horse let go,
She made a sudden bound: 390
It flung the blood into my head,
And I fell down in a swound.

*The Polar
Spirit's fellow-
dæmons, the in-
visible inhabit-
ants of the ele-
ment, take part
in his wrong;
and two of them
relate, one to the
other, that pen-
ance long and
heavy for the
ancient Mariner
hath been ac-
corded to the
Polar Spirit, who
returneth south-
ward.*

How long in that same fit I lay,
I have not to declare;
But ere my living life returned,   395
I heard and in my soul discerned
Two voices in the air.

'Is it he?' quoth one, 'Is this the man?
By him who died on cross,
With his cruel bow he laid full low   400
The harmless Albatross.

The spirit who bideth by himself
In the land of mist and snow,
He loved the bird that loved the man
Who shot him with his bow.'   405

The other was a softer voice,
As soft as honey-dew:
Quoth he, 'The man hath penance done,
And penance more will do.'

PART VI

FIRST VOICE

'But tell me, tell me! speak again,   410
Thy soft response renewing—
What makes that ship drive on so fast?
What is the ocean doing?'

SECOND VOICE

'Still as a slave before his lord,
The ocean hath no blast;   415
His great bright eye most silently
Up to the Moon is cast—

If he may know which way to go;
For she guides him smooth or grim.
See, brother, see! how graciously   420
She looketh down on him.'

FIRST VOICE

The Mariner
hath been cast
into a trance; for
the angelic
power causeth
the vessel to
drive northward
faster than hu-
man life could
endure.

'But why drives on that ship so fast,
Without or wave or wind?'

SECOND VOICE

'The air is cut away before,
And closes from behind.   425

Fly, brother, fly! more high, more high!
Or we shall be belated:
For slow and slow that ship will go,
When the Mariner's trance is abated.'

The supernatural
motion is re-
tarded; the
Mariner awakes,
and his penance
begins anew.

I woke, and we were sailing on   430
As in a gentle weather:
'Twas night, calm night, the moon was
    high;
The dead men stood together.

All stood together on the deck,
For a charnel-dungeon fitter: 435
All fixed on me their stony eyes,
That in the Moon did glitter.

The pang, the curse, with which they
    died,
Had never passed away:
I could not draw my eyes from
    theirs,   440
Nor turn them up to pray.

*The curse is
finally expiated.*

And now this spell was snapt: once more
I viewed the ocean green,
And looked far forth, yet little saw
Of what had else been seen—   445

Like one, that on a lonesome road
Doth walk in fear and dread,
And having once turned round walks on,
And turns no more his head;
Because he knows, a frightful fiend   450
Doth close behind him tread.

But soon there breathed a wind on me,
Nor sound nor motion made:
Its path was not upon the sea,
In ripple or in shade.   455

It raised my hair, it fanned my cheek
Like a meadow-gale of spring—
It mingled strangely with my fears,
Yet it felt like a welcoming.

Swiftly, swiftly flew the ship,   460
Yet she sailed softly too:
Sweetly, sweetly blew the breeze—
On me alone it blew.

*And the ancient
Mariner behold-
eth his native
country.*

Oh! dream of joy! is this indeed
The light-house top I see?   465
Is this the hill? is this the kirk?
Is this mine own countree?

We drifted o'er the harbour-bar,
And I with sobs did pray—
O let me be awake, my God!   470
Or let me sleep alway.

The harbour-bay was clear as glass,
So smoothly it was strewn!
And on the bay the moonlight lay,
And the shadow of the Moon.   475

The rock shone bright, the kirk no less,
That stands above the rock:
The moonlight steeped in silentness
The steady weathercock.

And the bay was white with silent
    light,   480
Till rising from the same,

*The angelic
spirits leave the
dead bodies,*

Full many shapes, that shadows were,
In crimson colours came.

*And appear in
their own forms
of light.*

A little distance from the prow
Those crimson shadows were: 485
I turned my eyes upon the deck—
Oh, Christ! what saw I there!

Each corse lay flat, lifeless and flat,
And, by the holy rood!
A man all light, a seraph-man,   490
On every corse there stood.

This seraph-band, each waved his hand:
It was a heavenly sight!
They stood as signals to the land,
Each one a lovely light;   495

This seraph-band, each waved his hand,
No voice did they impart—
No voice; but oh! the silence sank
Like music on my heart.

But soon I heard the dash of oars,   500
I heard the Pilot's cheer;
My head was turned perforce away
And I saw a boat appear.

The Pilot and the Pilot's boy,
I heard them coming fast: 505
Dear Lord in Heaven! it was a joy
The dead men could not blast.

I saw a third—I heard his voice:
It is the Hermit good!
He singeth loud his godly hymns   510
That he makes in the wood.
He'll shrieve my soul, he'll wash away
The Albatross's blood.

PART VII

This Hermit good lives in that wood
Which slopes down to the sea.   515
How loudly his sweet voice he rears!
He loves to talk with marineres
That come from a far countree.

He kneels at morn, and noon, and eve—
He hath a cushion plump: 520
It is the moss that wholly hides
The rotted old oak-stump.

The skiff-boat neared: I heard them talk,
'Why, this is strange, I trow!
Where are those lights so many and
         fair,   525
That signal made but now?'

'Strange, by my faith!' the Hermit said—
'And they answered not our cheer!
The planks looked warped! and see those
         sails,
How thin they are and sere!   530
I never saw aught like to them,
Unless perchance it were

Brown skeletons of leaves that lag
My forest-brook along;
When the ivy-tod is heavy with
         snow,   535
And the owlet whoops to the wolf below,
That eats the she-wolf's young.'

'Dear Lord! it hath a fiendish look—
(The Pilot made reply)
I am a-feared'—'Push on, push on!'   540
Said the Hermit cheerily.

The boat came closer to the ship,
But I nor spake nor stirred;
The boat came close beneath the ship,
And straight a sound was heard.   545

Under the water it rumbled on,
Still louder and more dread:

It reached the ship, it split the bay;
The ship went down like lead.

*The ancient
Mariner is saved
in the Pilot's
boat.*

Stunned by that loud and dreadful
        sound,   550
Which sky and ocean smote,
Like one that hath been seven days
        drowned
My body lay afloat;
But swift as dreams, myself I found
Within the Pilot's boat: 555

Upon the whirl, where sank the ship,
The boat spun round and round;
And all was still, save that the hill
Was telling of the sound.

I moved my lips—the Pilot shrieked   560
And fell down in a fit;
The holy Hermit raised his eyes,
And prayed where he did sit.

I took the oars: the Pilot's boy,
Who now doth crazy go,   565
Laughed loud and long, and all the while
His eyes went to and fro.
'Ha! ha!' quoth he, 'full plain I see
The Devil knows how to row.'

And now, all in my own countree,   570
I stood on the firm land!
The Hermit stepped forth from the boat,
And scarcely he could stand.

*The ancient
Mariner ear-
nestly entreateth
the Hermit to
shrieve him; and
the penance of
life falls on him.*

'O shrieve me, shrieve me, holy man!'
The Hermit crossed his brow.   575
'Say quick,' quoth he, 'I bid thee say—
What manner of man art thou?'

Forthwith this frame of mine was
        wrenched
With a woful agony,
Which forced me to begin my tale;   580
And then it left me free.

*And ever and
anon throughout
his future life an
agony constrain-
eth him to travel
from land to
land;*

Since then, at an uncertain hour,
That agony returns:
And till my ghastly tale is told,
This heart within me burns.   585

I pass, like night, from land to land;
I have strange power of speech;
That moment that his face I see,
I know the man that must hear me:
To him my tale I teach.   590

What loud uproar bursts from that door!
The wedding-guests are there:
But in the garden-bower the bride
And bride-maids singing are:
And hark the little vesper bell,   595
Which biddeth me to prayer!

O Wedding-Guest! this soul hath been
Alone on a wide wide sea:
So lonely 'twas, that God himself
Scarce seeméd there to be.   600

O sweeter than the marriage-feast,
'Tis sweeter far to me,
To walk together to the kirk
With a goodly company!—

To walk together to the kirk,   505
And all together pray,
While each to his great Father bends,
Old men, and babes, and loving friends
And youths and maidens gay!

*And to teach, by
his own exam-
ple, love and
reverence to all
things that God
made and lov-
eth.*

Farewell, farewell! but this I tell   610
To thee, thou Wedding-Guest!
He prayeth well, who loveth well
Both man and bird and beast.

He prayeth best, who loveth best
All things both great and small;   615
For the dear God who loveth us,
He made and loveth all."

The Mariner, whose eye is bright,
Whose beard with age is hoar,

Is gone: and now the Wedding-
    Guest   620
Turned from the bridegroom's door.

He went like one that hath been stunned,
And is of sense forlorn:
A sadder and a wiser man,
He rose the morrow morn.   625

1797–1798   *1798*

CHRISTABEL

PREFACE

*The first part of the following poem was written in the year
1797, at Stowey, in the county of Somerset. The second part,
after my return from Germany, in the year 1800, at Keswick,
Cumberland. It is probable that if the poem had been finished at either of the former periods, or if even the first and
second part had been published in the year 1800, the impression of its originality would have been much greater than
I dare at present expect. But for this I have only my own
indolence to blame. The dates are mentioned for the exclusive purpose of precluding charges of plagiarism or servile
imitation from myself. For there is amongst us a set of critics,
who seem to hold, that every possible thought and image is
traditional; who have no notion that there are such things as
fountains in the world, small as well as great; and who would
therefore charitably derive every rill they behold flowing,
from a perforation made in some other man's tank. I am confident, however, that as far as the present poem is concerned,
the celebrated poets whose writings I might be suspected of
having imitated, either in particular passages, or in the tone
and the spirit of the whole, would be among the first to
vindicate me from the charge, and, on any striking coincidence, would permit me to address them in this doggerel
version of two monkish Latin hexameters.*

> *'Tis mine and it is likewise yours;*
> *But an if this will not do;*
> *Let it be mine, good friend! for I*
> *Am the poorer of the two.*

*I have only to add that the metre of Christabel is not,
properly speaking, irregular, though it may seem so from its
being founded on a new principle: namely, that of counting
in each line the accents, not the syllables. Though the latter
may vary from seven to twelve, yet in each line the accents
will be found to be only four. Nevertheless, this occasional
variation in number of syllables is not introduced wantonly,
or for the mere ends of convenience, but in correspondence
with some transition in the nature of the imagery or passion.*

PART

'Tis the middle of night by the castle clock,
And the owls have awakened the crowing cock;
Tu—whit!——Tu—whoo!
And hark, again! the crowing cock,
How drowsily it crew.   5
Sir Leoline, the Baron rich,
Hath a toothless mastiff bitch;
From her kennel beneath the rock
She maketh answer to the clock,
Four for the quarters, and twelve for the hour;   10
Ever and aye, by shine and shower,
Sixteen short howls, not over loud;
Some say, she sees my lady's shroud.

Is the night chilly and dark?
The night is chilly, but not dark.   15
The thin gray cloud is spread on high,
It covers but not hides the sky.
The moon is behind, and at the full;
And yet she looks both small and dull.
The night is chill, the cloud is gray: 20
'Tis a month before the month of May,
And the Spring comes slowly up this way.

The lovely lady, Christabel,
Whom her father loves so well,
What makes her in the wood so late,   25
A furlong from the castle gate?
She had dreams all yesternight
Of her own betrothéd knight;
And she in the midnight wood will pray
For the weal of her lover that's far away.   30

She stole along, she nothing spoke,
The sighs she heaved were soft and low,
And naught was green upon the oak
But moss and rarest misletoe:
She kneels beneath the huge oak tree,   35
And in silence prayeth she.

The lady sprang up suddenly,
The lovely lady, Christabel!
It moaned as near, as near can be,
But what it is she cannot tell.—
On the other side it seems to be,   40
Of the huge, broad-breasted, old oak tree.

The night is chill; the forest bare;
Is it the wind that moaneth bleak?
There is not wind enough in the air   45
To move away the ringlet curl
From the lovely lady's cheek—
There is not wind enough to twirl
The one red leaf, the last of its clan,
That dances as often as dance it can,   50
Hanging so light, and hanging so high,
On the topmost twig that looks up at the sky.

Hush, beating heart of Christabel!
Jesu, Maria, shield her well!
She folded her arms beneath her cloak,
And stole to the other side of the oak.   55
    What sees she there?

There she sees a damsel bright,
Drest in a silken robe of white,
That shadowy in the moonlight shone: 60
The neck that made that white robe wan,
Her stately neck, and arms were bare;
Her blue-veined feet unsandal'd were,
And wildly glittered here and there
The gems entangled in her hair.   65
I guess, 'twas frightful there to see
A lady so richly clad as she—
Beautiful exceedingly!

Mary mother, save me now!
(Said Christabel,) And who art thou?   70

The lady strange made answer meet,
And her voice was faint and sweet:—
Have pity on my sore distress,
I scarce can speak for weariness:

Stretch forth thy hand, and have no fear!   75
Said Christabel, How camest thou here?
And the lady, whose voice was faint and sweet,
Did thus pursue her answer meet:—

My sire is of a noble line,
And my name is Geraldine: 80
Five warriors seized me yestermorn,
Me, even me, a maid forlorn:
They choked my cries with force and fright,
And tied me on a palfrey white.
The palfrey was as fleet as wind,   85
And they rode furiously behind.
They spurred amain, their steeds were white:
And once we crossed the shade of night.
As sure as Heaven shall rescue me,
I have no thought what men they be;   90
Nor do I know how long it is
(For I have lain entranced I wis)
Since one, the tallest of the five,
Took me from the palfrey's back,
A weary woman, scarce alive.   95
Some muttered words his comrades spoke:
He placed me underneath this oak;
He swore they would return with haste;
Whither they went I cannot tell—
I thought I heard, some minutes past,   100
Sounds as of a castle bell.
Stretch forth thy hand (thus ended she),
And help a wretched maid to flee.

Then Christabel stretched forth her hand,
And comforted fair Geraldine: 105
O well, bright dame! may you command
The service of Sir Leoline;
And gladly our stout chivalry
Will he send forth and friends withal
To guide and guard you safe and free   110
Home to your noble father's hall.

She rose: and forth with steps they passed
That strove to be, and were not, fast.
Her gracious stars the lady blest,

And thus spake on sweet Christabel: 115
All our household are at rest,
The hall as silent as the cell;
Sir Leoline is weak in health,
And may not well awakened be,
But we will move as if in stealth,   120
And I beseech your courtesy,
This night, to share your couch with me.

They crossed the moat, and Christabel
Took the key that fitted well;
A little door she opened straight,   125
All in the middle of the gate;
The gate that was ironed within and without,
Where an army in battle array had marched out.
The lady sank, belike through pain,
And Christabel with might and main   130
Lifted her up, a weary weight,
Over the threshold of the gate:
Then the lady rose again,
And moved, as she were not in pain.

So free from danger, free from fear,   135
They crossed the court: right glad they were.
And Christabel devoutly cried
To the lady by her side,
Praise we the Virgin all divine
Who hath rescued thee from thy distress!   140
Alas, alas! said Geraldine,
I cannot speak for weariness.
So free from danger, free from fear,
They crossed the court: right glad they were.

Outside her kennel, the mastiff old   145
Lay fast asleep, in moonshine cold.
The mastiff old did not awake,
Yet she an angry moan did make!
And what can ail the mastiff bitch?
Never till now she uttered yell   150
Beneath the eye of Christabel.
Perhaps it is the owlet's scritch:
For what can ail the mastiff bitch?

They passed the hall, that echoes still,
Pass as lightly as you will!   155
The brands were flat, the brands were dying,
Amid their own white ashes lying;
But when the lady passed, there came
A tongue of light, a fit of flame;
And Christabel saw the lady's eye,   160
And nothing else saw she thereby,
Save the boss of the shield of Sir Leoline tall,
Which hung in a murky old niche in the wall.
O softly tread, said Christabel,
My father seldom sleepeth well.   165

Sweet Christabel her feet doth bare,
And jealous of the listening air
They steal their way from stair to stair,
Now in glimmer, and now in gloom,
And now they pass the Baron's room,   170
As still as death, with stifled breath!
And now have reached her chamber door;
And now doth Geraldine press down
The rushes of the chamber floor.

The moon shines dim in the open air,   175
And not a moonbeam enters here.
But they without its light can see
The chamber carved so curiously,
Carved with figures strange and sweet,
All made out of the carver's brain,   180
For a lady's chamber meet:
The lamp with twofold silver chain
Is fastened to an angel's feet.

The silver lamp burns dead and dim;
But Christabel the lamp will trim.   185
She trimmed the lamp, and made it bright,
And left it swinging to and fro,
While Geraldine, in wretched plight,
Sank down upon the floor below.

O weary lady, Geraldine,   190
I pray you, drink this cordial wine!
It is a wine of virtuous powers;
My mother made it of wild flowers.

And will your mother pity me,
Who am a maiden most forlorn?
Christabel answered—Woe is me!   195
She died the hour that I was born.
I have heard the grey-haired friar tell
How on her death-bed she did say,
That she should hear the castle-bell   200
Strike twelve upon my wedding-day.
O mother dear! that thou wert here!
I would, said Geraldine, she were!

But soon with altered voice, said she—
"Off, wandering mother! Peak and pine!   205
I have power to bid thee flee."
Alas! what ails poor Geraldine?
Why stares she with unsettled eye?
Can she the bodiless dead espy?
And why with hollow voice cries she,   210
"Off, woman, off! this hour is mine—
Though thou her guardian spirit be,
Off, woman, off! 'tis given to me."

Then Christabel knelt by the lady's side,
And raised to heaven her eyes so blue—   215
Alas! said she, this ghastly ride—
Dear lady! it hath wildered you!
The lady wiped her moist cold brow,
And faintly said, " 'tis over now!"

Again the wild-flower wine she drank: 220
Her fair large eyes 'gan glitter bright,
And from the floor whereon she sank,
The lofty lady stood upright:
She was most beautiful to see,
Like a lady of a far countrée.   225

And thus the lofty lady spake—
"All they who live in the upper sky,
Do love you, holy Christabel!
And you love them, and for their sake
And for the good which me befel,   230
Even I in my degree will try,
Fair maiden, to requite you well.

But now unrobe yourself; for I
Must pray, ere yet in bed I lie."

Quoth Christabel, So let it be!   235
And as the lady bade, did she.
Her gentle limbs did she undress,
And lay down in her loveliness.

But through her brain of weal and woe
So many thoughts moved to and fro,   240
That vain it were her lids to close;
So half-way from the bed she rose,
And on her elbow did recline
To look at the lady Geraldine.

Beneath the lamp the lady bowed,   245
And slowly rolled her eyes around;
Then drawing in her breath aloud,
Like one that shuddered, she unbound
The cincture from beneath her breast:
Her silken robe, and inner vest,   250
Dropt to her feet, and full in view,
Behold! her bosom and half her side——
A sight to dream of, not to tell!
O shield her! shield sweet Christabel!

Yet Geraldine nor speaks nor stirs;   255
Ah! what a stricken look was hers!
Deep from within she seems half-way
To lift some weight with sick assay,
And eyes the maid and seeks delay;
Then suddenly, as one defied,   260
Collects herself in scorn and pride,
And lay down by the Maiden's side!—
And in her arms the maid she took,
                    Ah wel-a-day!
And with low voice and doleful look   265
These words did say:
"In the touch of this bosom there worketh a spell,
Which is lord of thy utterance, Christabel!
Thou knowest to-night, and wilt know to-morrow,
This mark of my shame, this seal of my sorrow;   270
        But vainly thou warrest,

        For this is alone in
    Thy power to declare,
        That in the dim forest
        Thou heard'st a low moaning,   275
And found'st a bright lady, surpassingly fair;
And didst bring her home with thee in love and in
            charity,
To shield her and shelter her from the damp air."

THE CONCLUSION TO PART I

It was a lovely sight to see
The lady Christabel, when she   280
Was praying at the old oak tree.
        Amid the jaggéd shadows
        Of mossy leafless boughs,
        Kneeling in the moonlight,
        To make her gentle vows;   285
Her slender palms together prest,
Heaving sometimes on her breast;
Her face resigned to bliss or bale—
Her face, oh call it fair not pale,
And both blue eyes more bright than clear,   290
Each about to have a tear.

With open eyes (ah woe is me!)
Asleep, and dreaming fearfully,
Fearfully dreaming, yet, I wis,
Dreaming that alone, which is—   295
O sorrow and shame! Can this oe she,
The lady, who knelt at the old oak tree?
And lo! the worker of these harms,
That holds the maiden in her arms,
Seems to slumber still and mild,   300
As a mother with her child.

A star hath set, a star hath risen,
O Geraldine! since arms of thine
Have been the lovely lady's prison.
O Geraldine! one hour was thine—   305
Thou'st had thy will! By tairn and rill,
The night-birds all that hour were still.
But now they are jubilant anew,

From cliff and tower, tu—whoo! tu—whoo!
Tu—whoo! tu—whoo! from wood and fell!   310

And see! the lady Christabel
Gathers herself from out her trance;
Her limbs relax, her countenance
Grows sad and soft; the smooth thin lids
Close o'er her eyes; and tears she sheds—   315
Large tears that leave the lashes bright!
And oft the while she seems to smile
As infants at a sudden light!

Yea, she doth smile, and she doth weep,
Like a youthful hermitess,   320
Beauteous in a wilderness,
Who, praying always, prays in sleep.
And, if she move unquietly,
Perchance, 'tis but the blood so free
Comes back and tingles in her feet.   325
No doubt, she hath a vision sweet.
What if her guardian spirit 'twere,
What if she knew her mother near?
But this she knows, in joys and woes,
That saints will aid if men will call: 330
For the blue sky bends over all!

1797

PART II

Each matin bell, the Baron saith,
Knells us back to a world of death.
These words Sir Leoline first said,
When he rose and found his lady dead: 335
These words Sir Leoline will say
Many a morn to his dying day!

And hence the custom and law began
That still at dawn the sacristan,
Who duly pulls the heavy bell,   340
Five and forty beads must tell

Between each stroke—a warning knell,
Which not a soul can choose but hear
From Bratha Head to Wyndermere.

Saith Bracy the bard, So let it knell!   345
And let the drowsy sacristan
Still count as slowly as he can!
There is no lack of such, I ween,
As well fill up the space between.
In Langdale Pike and Witch's Lair,   350
And Dungeon-ghyll so foully rent,
With ropes of rock and bells of air
Three sinful sextons' ghosts are pent,
Who all give back, one after t'other,
The death-note to their living brother;   355
And oft too, by the knell offended,
Just as their one! two! three! is ended,
The devil mocks the doleful tale
With a merry peal from Borodale.

The air is still! through mist and cloud   360
That merry peal comes ringing loud;
And Geraldine shakes off her dread,
And rises lightly from the bed;
Puts on her silken vestments white,
And tricks her hair in lovely plight,   365
And nothing doubting of her spell
Awakens the lady Christabel.
"Sleep you, sweet lady Christabel?
I trust that you have rested well."

And Christabel awoke and spied   370
The same who lay down by her side—
O rather say, the same whom she
Raised up beneath the old oak tree!
Nay, fairer yet! and yet more fair!
For she belike hath drunken deep   375
Of all the blessedness of sleep!
And while she spake, her looks, her air
Such gentle thankfulness declare,
That (so it seemed) her girded vests
Grew tight beneath her heaving breasts.   380
"Sure I have sinn'd!" said Christabel,

"Now heaven be praised if all be well!"
And in low faltering tones, yet sweet,
Did she the lofty lady greet
With such perplexity of mind   385
As dreams too lively leave behind.

So quickly she rose, and quickly arrayed
Her maiden limbs, and having prayed
That He, who on the cross did groan,
Might wash away her sins unknown,   390
She forthwith led fair Geraldine
To meet her sire, Sir Leoline.

The lovely maid and the lady tall
Are pacing both into the hall,
And pacing on through page and groom,   395
Enter the Baron's presence-room.

The Baron rose, and while he prest
His gentle daughter to his breast,
With cheerful wonder in his eyes
The lady Geraldine espies,   400
And gave such welcome to the same,
As might beseem so bright a dame!

But when he heard the lady's tale,
And when she told her father's name,
Why waxed Sir Leoline so pale,   405
Murmuring o'er the name again,
Lord Roland de Vaux of Tryermaine?

Alas! they had been friends in youth;
But whispering tongues can poison truth;
And constancy lives in realms above;   410
And life is thorny; and youth is vain;
And to be wroth with one we love
Doth work like madness in the brain.
And thus it chanced, as I divine,
With Roland and Sir Leoline.   415
Each spake words of high disdain
And insult to his heart's best brother:
They parted—ne'er to meet again!
But never either found another

To free the hollow heart from paining—   420
They stood aloof, the scars remaining,
Like cliffs which had been rent asunder;
A dreary sea now flows between;—
But neither heat, nor frost, nor thunder,
Shall wholly do away, I ween,   425
The marks of that which once hath been.

Sir Leoline, a moment's space,
Stood gazing on the damsel's face:
And the youthful Lord of Tryermaine
Came back upon his heart again.   430

O then the Baron forgot his age,
His noble heart swelled high with rage;
He swore by the wounds in Jesu's side
He would proclaim it far and wide,
With trump and solemn heraldry,   435
That they, who thus had wronged the dame,
Were base as spotted infamy!
"And if they dare deny the same,
My herald shall appoint a week,
And let the recreant traitors seek   440
My tourney court—that there and then
I may dislodge their reptile souls
From the bodies and forms of men!"
He spake: his eye in lightning rolls!
For the lady was ruthlessly seized; and he kenned   445
In the beautiful lady the child of his friend!

And now the tears were on his face,
And fondly in his arms he took
Fair Geraldine, who met the embrace,
Prolonging it with joyous look.   450
Which when she viewed, a vision fell
Upon the soul of Christabel,
The vision of fear, the touch and pain!
She shrunk and shuddered, and saw again—
(Ah, woe is me! Was it for thee,   455
Thou gentle maid! such sights to see?)

Again she saw that bosom old,
Again she felt that bosom cold,

And drew in her breath with a hissing sound:
Whereat the Knight turned wildly round,   460
And nothing saw, but his own sweet maid
With eyes upraised, as one that prayed.

The touch, the sight, had passed away,
And in its stead that vision blest,
Which comforted her after-rest   465
While in the lady's arms she lay,
Had put a rapture in her breast,
And on her lips and o'er her eyes
Spread smiles like light!
                         With new surprise,
"What ails then my belovèd child?"   470
The Baron said—His daughter mild
Made answer, "All will yet be well!"
I ween, she had no power to tell
Aught else: so mighty was the spell.

Yet he, who saw this Geraldine,   475
Had deemed her sure a thing divine:
Such sorrow with such grace she blended,
As if she feared she had offended
Sweet Christabel, that gentle maid!
And with such lowly tones she prayed   480
She might be sent without delay
Home to her father's mansion.
                                 "Nay!
Nay, by my soul!" said Leoline.
"Ho! Bracy the bard, the charge be thine!
Go thou, with music sweet and loud,   485
And take two steeds with trappings proud,
And take the youth whom thou lov'st best
To bear thy harp, and learn thy song,
And clothe you both in solemn vest,
And over the mountains haste along,   490
Lest wandering folk, that are abroad,
Detain you on the valley road.

"And when he has crossed the Irthing flood,
My merry bard! he hastes, he hastes
Up Knorren Moor, through Halegarth Wood,   495

And reaches soon that castle good
Which stands and threatens Scotland's wastes.

"Bard Bracy! bard Bracy! your horses are fleet,
Ye must ride up the hall, your music so sweet,
More loud than your horses' echoing feet!
And loud and loud to Lord Roland call,   500
Thy daughter is safe in Langdale hall!
Thy beautiful daughter is safe and free—
Sir Leoline greets thee thus through me!
He bids thee come without delay   505
With all thy numerous array
And take thy lovely daughter home:
And he will meet thee on the way
With all his numerous array
White with their panting palfreys' foam: 510
And, by mine honour! I will say,
That I repent me of the day
When I spake words of fierce disdain
To Roland de Vaux of Tryermaine!—
—For since that evil hour hath flown,   515
Many a summer's sun hath shone;
Yet ne'er found I a friend again
Like Roland de Vaux of Tryermaine."

The lady fell, and clasped his knees,
Her face upraised, her eyes o'erflowing;   520
And Bracy replied, with faltering voice,
His gracious Hail on all bestowing!—
"Thy words, thou sire of Christabel,
Are sweeter than my harp can tell;
Yet might I gain a boon of thee,   525
This day my journey should not be,
So strange a dream hath come to me,
That I had vowed with music loud .
To clear yon wood from thing unblest,
Warned by a vision in my rest!   530
For in my sleep I saw that dove,
That gentle bird, whom thou dost love,
And call'st by thy own daughter's name—
Sir Leoline! I saw the same
Fluttering, and uttering fearful moan,   535
Among the green herbs in the forest alone.

Which when I saw and when I heard,
I wonder'd what might ail the bird;
For nothing near it could I see,
Save the grass and green herbs underneath the old tree.   540

"And in my dream methought I went
To search out what might there be found;
And what the sweet bird's trouble meant,
That thus lay fluttering on the ground.
I went and peered, and could descry   545
No cause for her distressful cry;
But yet for her dear lady's sake
I stooped, methought, the dove to take,
When lo! I saw a bright green snake
Coiled around its wings and neck.   550
Green as the herbs on which it couched,
Close by the dove's its head it crouched;
And with the dove it heaves and stirs,
Swelling its neck as she swelled hers!
I woke; it was the midnight hour,   555
The clock was echoing in the tower;
But though my slumber was gone by,
This dream it would not pass away—
It seems to live upon my eye!
And thence I vowed this self-same day   560
With music strong and saintly song
To wander through the forest bare,
Lest aught unholy loiter there."

Thus Bracy said: the Baron, the while,
Half-listening heard him with a smile;   565
Then turned to Lady Geraldine,
His eyes made up of wonder and love;
And said in courtly accents fine,
"Sweet maid, Lord Roland's beauteous dove,
With arms more strong than harp or song,   570
Thy sire and I will crush the snake!"
He kissed her forehead as he spake,
And Geraldine in maiden wise
Casting down her large bright eyes,
With blushing cheek and courtesy fine   575
She turned her from Sir Leoline;
Softly gathering up her train,

That o'er her right arm fell again;
And folded her arms across her chest,
And couched her head upon her breast,   580
And looked askance at Christabel—
Jesu, Maria, shield her well!

A snake's small eye blinks dull and shy;
And the lady's eyes they shrunk in her head,
Each shrunk up to a serpent's eye,   585
And with somewhat of malice, and more of dread,
At Christabel she looked askance!—
One moment—and the sight was fled!
But Christabel in dizzy trance
Stumbling on the unsteady ground   590
Shuddered aloud, with a hissing sound;
And Geraldine again turned round,
And like a thing, that sought relief,
Full of wonder and full of grief,
She rolled her large bright eyes divine   595
Wildly on Sir Leoline.

The maid, alas! her thoughts are gone.
She nothing sees—no sight but one!
The maid, devoid of guile and sin,
I know not how, in fearful wise,   600
So deeply had she drunken in
That look, those shrunken serpent eyes,
That all her features were resigned
To this sole image in her mind:
And passively did imitate   605
That look of dull and treacherous hate!
And thus she stood, in dizzy trance,
Still picturing that look askance
With forced unconscious sympathy
Full before her father's view—   610
As far as such a look could be
In eyes so innocent and blue!

And when the trance was o'er, the maid
Paused awhile, and inly prayed:
Then falling at the Baron's feet,   615
"By my mother's soul do I entreat
That thou this woman send away!"

She said: and more she could not say:
For what she knew she could not tell,
O'er-mastered by the mighty spell.   620

Why is thy cheek so wan and wild,
Sir Leoline? Thy only child
Lies at thy feet, thy joy, thy pride,
So fair, so innocent, so mild;
The same, for whom thy lady died!   625
O by the pangs of her dear mother
Think thou no evil of thy child!
For her, and thee, and for no other,
She prayed the moment ere she died:
Prayed that the babe for whom she died,   630
Might prove her dear lord's joy and pride!
    That prayer her deadly pangs beguiled,
            Sir Leoline!
    And wouldst thou wrong thy only child,
            Her child and thine?   635

Within the Baron's heart and brain
If thoughts, like these, had any share,
They only swelled his rage and pain,
And did but work confusion there.
His heart was cleft with pain and rage,   640
His cheeks they quivered, his eyes were wild,
Dishonoured thus in his old age;
Dishonoured by his only child,
And all his hospitality
To the wronged daughter of his friend   645
By more than woman's jealousy
Brought thus to a disgraceful end—
He rolled his eye with stern regard
Upon the gentle minstrel bard,
And said in tones abrupt, austere—   650
"Why, Bracy! dost thou loiter here?
I bade thee hence!" The bard obeyed;
And turning from his own sweet maid,
The agéd knight, Sir Leoline,
Led forth the lady Geraldine!   655
                                                           1800

THE CONCLUSION TO PART I

A little child, a limber elf,
Singing, dancing to itself,
A fairy thing with red round cheeks,
That always finds, and never seeks,
Makes such a vision to the sight   660
As fills a father's eyes with light;
And pleasures flow in so thick and fast
Upon his heart, that he at last
Must needs express his love's excess
With words of unmeant bitterness.   665
Perhaps 'tis pretty to force together
Thoughts so all unlike each other;
To mutter and mock a broken charm,
To dally with wrong that does no harm.
Perhaps 'tis tender too and pretty   670
At each wild word to feel within
A sweet recoil of love and pity.
And what, if in a world of sin
  (O sorrow and shame should this be true!)
Such giddiness of heart and brain   675
Comes seldom save from rage and pain,
So talks as it's most used to do.

1797–1800   *1816*

KUBLA KHAN

OR, A VISION IN A DREAM

A FRAGMENT

The following fragment is here published at the request of a poet of great and deserved celebrity [Lord Byron], and, as far as the Author's own opinions are concerned, rather as a psychological curiosity, than on the ground of any supposed poetic merits.

In the summer of the year 1797, the Author, then in ill health, had retired to a lonely farm-house between Porlock and Linton, on the Exmoor confines of Somerset and Devonshire. In consequence of a slight indisposition, an anodyne had been prescribed, from the effects of which he fell asleep in his chair at the moment that he was reading the following sentence, or words of the same substance, in "Purchas's Pilgrimage": "Here the Khan Kubla commanded a palace to be built, and a stately garden thereunto. And thus ten miles of fertile ground were inclosed with a wall." The Author continued for about three hours in a profound sleep, at least of the external senses, during which time he has the most vivid confidence, that he could not have composed less than from two to three hundred lines; if that indeed can be called composition in which all the images rose up before him as things, with a parallel production of the correspondent expressions, without any sensation or consciousness of effort. On awaking he appeared to himself to have a distinct recollection of the whole, and taking his pen, ink, and paper, instantly and eagerly wrote down the lines that are here preserved. At this moment he was unfortunately called out by a person on business from Porlock, and detained by him above an hour, and on his return to his room, found, to his no small surprise and mortification, that though he still retained some vague and dim recollection of the general purport of the vision, yet, with the exception of some eight or ten scattered lines and images, all the rest had passed away like the images on the surface of a stream into which a stone has been cast, but, alas! without the after restoration of the latter!

In Xanadu did Kubla Khan
A stately pleasure-dome decree:
Where Alph, the sacred river, ran
Through caverns measureless to man

   Down to a sunless sea.
So twice five miles of fertile ground   5
With walls and towers were girdled round:
And there were gardens bright with sinuous rills,
Where blossomed many an incense-bearing tree;
And here were forests ancient as the hills,   10
Enfolding sunny spots of greenery.

But oh! that deep romantic chasm which slanted
Down the green hill athwart a cedarn cover!
A savage place! as holy and enchanted
As e'er beneath a waning moon was haunted   15
By woman wailing for her demon-lover!
And from this chasm, with ceaseless turmoil seething,
As if this earth in fast thick pants were breathing,
A mighty fountain momently was forced:
Amid whose swift half-intermitted burst   20
Huge fragments vaulted like rebounding hail,
Or chaffy grain beneath the thresher's flail:
And 'mid these dancing rocks at once and ever
It flung up momently the sacred river.
Five miles meandering with a mazy motion   25
Through wood and dale the sacred river ran,
Then reached the caverns measureless to man,
And sank in tumult to a lifeless ocean:
And 'mid this tumult Kubla heard from far
Ancestral voices prophesying war!   30
    The shadow of the dome of pleasure
    Floated midway on the waves;
    Where was heard the mingled measure
    From the fountain and the caves.
It was a miracle of rare device,   35
A sunny pleasure-dome with caves of ice!

   A damsel with a dulcimer
   In a vision once I saw:
   It was an Abyssinian maid,
   And on her dulcimer she played,
   Singing of Mount Abora.   40
   Could I revive within me
   Her symphony and song,
   To such a deep delight 'twould win me,
That with music loud and long,
                              45

I would build that dome in air,
That sunny dome! those caves of ice!
And all who heard should see them there,
And all should cry, Beware! Beware!
His flashing eyes, his floating hair!
Weave a circle round him thrice,
And close your eyes with holy dread,
For he on honey-dew hath fed,
And drunk the milk of Paradise.

1797?   *1816*

CONVERSATION POEMS

Coleridge's subtitle for *The Nightingale* is "A Conversation Poem." He might have used the same subtitle for that whole series of reflective lyrics which begins with *The Eolian Harp* and more or less terminates with the laudatory poem *To William Wordsworth*. Indeed it is Wordsworth's biographer, George McLean Harper, who well summarizes the quality of mind, the literary intention, which sets these poems somewhat apart from the rest of Coleridge's work in verse. "Even when they are soliloquies," wrote Harper, "the sociable man who wrote them could not even think without supposing a listener."

In form, they resemble the Elizabethan, and more especially the Shakespearean, dramatic soliloquy—a device through which the actor-persona is able to convey what is passing in his inmost mind, communicating with an unknown audience with which, however, he feels himself to be in intimate contact. For a considered moment he is thus able to put aside his public mask, to display that "which passeth show" within, before he resumes his life of action within the play. Yet Coleridge, in his proper person, has this advantage over a Hamlet or a Brutus—that he can take psychological comfort in the thought of someone near him, whether it is his good friends coursing through the Quantocks while he must remain chair-ridden under the leafy lime trees; or his infant son Hartley encradled and asleep, or gazing wide-eyed at the moon from the protection of his father's arms; or the circle of "beloved faces" of those who have listened to the oral presentation of Wordsworth's *Prelude* through a succession of winter evenings.

It is a critical commonplace to call these poems Wordsworthian. One notices a marked difference between those which were composed before the friendship with Wordsworth had ripened and those which belong to the period 1798–1807 when Coleridge, in spite of some divagations, was closer to his friend than he would ever be again. Yet the point of dependence can be overemphasized, especially if one means to imply a slavish copying. In fact, M. H. Abrams has credited Coleridge with the development of a particular reflective genre on which his personal imprimatur is perfectly visible, and of which the following poems are excellent examples.

THE EOLIAN HARP

Composed at Clevedon, Somersetshire

My pensive Sara! thy soft cheek reclined
Thus on mine arm, most soothing sweet it is
To sit beside our Cot, our Cot o'ergrown
With white-flower'd Jasmin, and the broad-leav'd Myrtle,
  (Meet emblems they of Innocence and Love!)   5
And watch the clouds, that late were rich with light,
Slow saddening round, and mark the star of eve
Serenely brilliant (such should Wisdom be)
Shine opposite! How exquisite the scents
Snatch'd from yon bean-field! and the world *so* hush'd!   10
The stilly murmur of the distant Sea
Tells us of silence.

            And that simplest Lute,
Placed length-ways in the clasping casement, hark!
How by the desultory breeze caress'd,
Like some coy maid half yielding to her lover,   15
It pours such sweet upbraiding, as must needs
Tempt to repeat the wrong! And now, its strings
Boldlier swept, the long sequacious notes
Over delicious surges sink and rise,
Such a soft floating witchery of sound   20
As twilight Elfins make, when they at eve
Voyage on gentle gales from Fairy-Land,
Where Melodies round honey-dropping flowers,
Footless and wild, like birds of Paradise,
Nor pause, nor perch, hovering on untam'd wing!   25
O! the one Life within us and abroad,
Which meets all motion and becomes its soul,
A light in sound, a sound-like power in light,
Rhythm in all thought, and joyance every where—
Methinks, it should have been impossible   30
Not to love all things in a world so fill'd;
Where the breeze warbles, and the mute still air
Is Music slumbering on her instrument.

And thus, my Love! as on the midway slope
Of yonder hill I stretch my limbs at noon,   35
Whilst through my half-clos'd eye-lids I behold

The sunbeams dance, like diamonds, on the main,
And tranquil muse upon tranquillity;
Full many a thought uncall'd and undetain'd,
And many idle flitting phantasies,   40
Traverse my indolent and passive brain,
As wild and various as the random gales
That swell and flutter on this subject Lute!
    And what if all of animated nature
Be but organic Harps diversely fram'd,   45
That tremble into thought, as o'er them sweep
Plastic and vast, one intellectual breeze,
At once the Soul of each, and God of all?
    But thy more serious eye a mild reproof
Darts, O belovéd Woman! nor such thoughts   50
Dim and unhallow'd dost thou not reject,
And biddest me walk humbly with my God.
Meek Daughter in the family of Christ!
Well hast thou said and holily disprais'd
These shapings of the unregenerate mind;   55
Bubbles that glitter as they rise and break
On vain Philosophy's aye-babbling spring.
For never guiltless may I speak of him,
The Incomprehensible! save when with awe
I praise him, and with Faith that inly *feels;*   60
Who with his saving mercies healéd me,
A sinful and most miserable man,
Wilder'd and dark, and gave me to possess
Peace, and this Cot, and thee, heart-honour'd Maid!

1795   *1796*

REFLECTIONS ON HAVING LEFT A PLACE
OF RETIREMENT

Sermoni propriora.—HORACE

Low was our pretty Cot: our tallest Rose
Peep'd at the chamber-window. We could hear
At silent noon, and eve, and early morn,
The Sea's faint murmur. In the open air
Our Myrtles blossom'd; and across the porch   5
Thick Jasmins twined: the little landscape round
Was green and woody, and refresh'd the eye.
It was a spot which you might aptly call
The Valley of Seclusion! Once I saw
(Hallowing his Sabbath-day by quietness)   10
A wealthy son of Commerce saunter by,
Bristowa's citizen: methought, it calm'd
His thirst of idle gold, and made him muse
With wiser feelings: for he paus'd, and look'd
With a pleas'd sadness, and gaz'd all around,   15
Then eyed our Cottage, and gaz'd round again,
And sigh'd, and said, it was a Blesséd Place.
And we *were* bless'd. Oft with patient ear
Long-listening to the viewless sky-lark's note
(Viewless, or haply for a moment seen   20
Gleaming on sunny wings) in whisper'd tones
I've said to my Belovéd, "Such, sweet Girl!
The inobtrusive song of Happiness,
Unearthly minstrelsy! then only heard
When the Soul seeks to hear; when all is hush'd,   25
And the Heart listens!"

                    But the time, when first
From that low Dell, steep up the stony Mount
I climb'd with perilous toil and reach'd the top,
Oh! what a goodly scene! *Here* the bleak mount,
The bare bleak mountain speckled thin with sheep;   30
Grey clouds, that shadowing spot the sunny fields;
And river, now with bushy rocks o'er-brow'd,
Now winding bright and full, with naked banks;
And seats, and lawns, the Abbey and the wood,
And cots, and hamlets, and faint city-spire;   35

The Channel *there*, the Islands and white sails,
Dim coasts, and cloud-like hills, and shoreless Ocean—
It seem'd like Omnipresence! God, methought,
Had built him there a Temple: the whole World
Seem'd *imag'd* in its vast circumference: 40
No *wish* profan'd my overwhelméd heart.
Blest hour! It was a luxury,—to be!

   Ah! quiet Dell! dear Cot, and Mount sublime!
I was constrain'd to quit you. Was it right,
While my unnumber'd brethren toil'd and bled,   45
That I should dream away the entrusted hours
On rose-leaf beds, pampering the coward heart
With feelings all too delicate for use?
Sweet is the tear that from some Howard's eye
Drops on the cheek of one he lifts from earth: 50
And he that works me good with unmov'd face,
Does it but half: he chills me while he aids,
My benefactor, not my brother man!
Yet even this, this cold beneficence
Praise, praise it, O my Soul! oft as thou scann'st   55
The sluggard Pity's vision-weaving tribe!
Who sigh for Wretchedness, yet shun the Wretched,
Nursing in some delicious solitude
Their slothful loves and dainty sympathies!
I therefore go, and join head, heart, and hand   60
Active and firm, to fight the bloodless fight
Of Science, Freedom, and the Truth in Christ.

Yet oft when after honourable toil
Rests the tir'd mind, and waking loves to dream,
My spirit shall revisit thee, dear Cot!   65
Thy Jasmin and thy window-peeping Rose,
And Myrtles fearless of the mild sea-air.
And I shall sigh fond wishes—sweet Abode!
Ah!—had none greater! And that all had such!
It might be so—but the time is not yet.   70
Speed it, O Father! Let thy Kingdom come!

1795   *1796*

THIS LIME-TREE BOWER MY PRISON

[ADDRESSED TO CHARLES LAMB, OF THE INDIA HOUSE, LONDON]

In the June of 1797 some long-expected friends paid a visit to the author's cottage; and on the morning of their arrival, he met with an accident, which disabled him from walking during the whole time of their stay. One evening, when they had left him for a few hours, he composed the following lines in the garden-bower.

Well, they are gone, and here must I remain,
This lime-tree bower my prison! I have lost
Beauties and feelings such as would have been
Most sweet to my remembrance even when age
Had dimm'd mine eyes to blindness! They, meanwhile,   5
Friends, whom I never more may meet again,
On springy heath, along the hill-top edge,
Wander in gladness, and wind down, perchance,
To that still roaring dell, of which I told;
The roaring dell, o'erwooded, narrow, deep,   10
And only speckled by the mid-day sun;
Where its slim trunk the ash from rock to rock
Flings arching like a bridge;—that branchless ash,
Unsunn'd and damp, whose few poor yellow leaves
Ne'er tremble in the gale, yet tremble still,   15
Fann'd by the water-fall! and there my friends
Behold the dark green file of long lank weeds,
That all at once (a most fantastic sight!)
Still nod and drip beneath the dripping edge
Of the blue clay-stone.   20

     Now, my friends emerge
Beneath the wide wide Heaven—and view again
The many-steepled tract magnificent
Of hilly fields and meadows, and the sea,
With some fair bark, perhaps, whose sails light up
The slip of smooth clear blue betwixt two Isles   25
Of purple shadow! Yes! they wander on
In gladness all; but thou, methinks, most glad,
My gentle-hearted Charles! for thou hast pined
And hunger'd after Nature, many a year,
In the great City pent, winning thy way   30

With sad yet patient soul, through evil and pain
And strange calamity! Ah! slowly sink
Behind the western ridge, thou glorious Sun!
Shine in the slant beams of the sinking orb,
Ye purple heath-flowers! richlier burn, ye clouds!   35
Live in the yellow light, ye distant groves!
And kindle, thou blue Ocean! So my friend
Struck with deep joy may stand, as I have stood,
Silent with swimming sense; yea, gazing round
On the wide landscape, gaze till all doth seem   40
Less gross than bodily, and of such hues
As veil the Almighty Spirit, when yet he makes
Spirits perceive his presence.

                    A delight
Comes sudden on my heart, and I am glad
As I myself were there! Nor in this bower,   45
This little lime-tree bower, have I not mark'd
Much that has sooth'd me. Pale beneath the blaze
Hung the transparent foliage; and I watch'd
Some broad and sunny leaf, and lov'd to see
The shadow of the leaf and stem above   50
Dappling its sunshine! And that walnut-tree
Was richly ting'd, and a deep radiance lay
Full on the ancient ivy, which usurps
Those fronting elms, and now, with blackest mass
Makes their dark branches gleam a lighter hue   55
Through the late twilight: and though now the bat
Wheels silent by, and not a swallow twitters,
Yet still the solitary humble-bee
Sings in the bean-flower! Henceforth I shall know
That Nature ne'er deserts the wise and pure;   60
No plot so narrow, be but Nature there,
No waste so vacant, but may well employ
Each faculty of sense, and keep the heart
Awake to Love and Beauty! and sometimes
'Tis well to be bereft of promis'd good,   65
That we may lift the soul, and contemplate
With lively joy the joys we cannot share.
My gentle-hearted Charles! when the last rook
Beat its straight path along the dusky air
Homewards, I blest it! deeming its black wing   70
(Now a dim speck, now vanishing in light)

Had cross'd the mighty Orb's dilated glory,
While thou stood'st gazing; or, when all was still,
Flew creeking o'er thy head, and had a charm   75
For thee, my gentle-hearted Charles, to whom
No sound is dissonant which tells of Life.

1797   1800

FROST AT MIDNIGHT

The Frost performs its secret ministry,
Unhelped by any wind. The owlet's cry
Came loud—and hark, again! loud as before.
The inmates of my cottage, all at rest,
Have left me to that solitude, which suits   5
Abstruser musings: save that at my side
My cradled infant slumbers peacefully.
'Tis calm indeed! so calm, that it disturbs
And vexes meditation with its strange
And extreme silentness. Sea, hill, and wood,   10
This populous village! Sea, and hill, and wood,
With all the numberless goings-on of life,
Inaudible as dreams! the thin blue flame
Lies on my low-burnt fire, and quivers not;
Only that film, which fluttered on the grate,   15
Still flutters there, the sole unquiet thing.
Methinks, its motion in this hush of nature
Gives it dim sympathies with me who live,
Making it a companionable form,
Whose puny flaps and freaks the idling Spirit   20
By its own moods interprets, every where
Echo or mirror seeking of itself,
And makes a toy of Thought.

                        But O! how oft,
How oft, at school, with most believing mind,
Presageful, have I gazed upon the bars,   25
To watch that fluttering *stranger*! and as oft
With unclosed lids, already had I dreamt
Of my sweet birth-place, and the old church-tower,
Whose bells, the poor man's only music, rang,
From morn to evening, all the hot Fair-day,   30
So sweetly, that they stirred and haunted me
With a wild pleasure, falling on mine ear
Most like articulate sounds of things to come!
So gazed I, till the soothing things, I dreamt,
Lulled me to sleep, and sleep prolonged my dreams! 35
And so I brooded all the following morn,
Awed by the stern preceptor's face, mine eye
Fixed with mock study on my swimming book:

Save if the door half opened, and I snatched
A hasty glance, and still my heart leaped up,   40
For still I hoped to see the *stranger's* face,
Townsman, or aunt, or sister more beloved,
My play-mate when we both were clothed alike!

    Dear Babe, that sleepest cradled by my side,
Whose gentle breathings, heard in this deep calm,   45
Fill up the interspersèd vacancies
And momentary pauses of the thought!
My babe so beautiful! it thrills my heart
With tender gladness, thus to look at thee,
And think that thou shalt learn far other lore,   50
And in far other scenes! For I was reared
In the great city, pent 'mid cloisters dim,
And saw nought lovely but the sky and stars.
But *thou,* my babe! shalt wander like a breeze
By lakes and sandy shores, beneath the crags   55
Of ancient mountain, and beneath the clouds,
Which image in their bulk both lakes and shores
And mountain crags: so shalt thou see and hear
The lovely shapes and sounds intelligible
Of that eternal language, which thy God   60
Utters, who from eternity doth teach
Himself in all, and all things in himself.
Great universal Teacher! he shall mould
Thy spirit, and by giving make it ask.

    Therefore all seasons shall be sweet to thee,   65
Whether the summer clothe the general earth
With greenness, or the redbreast sit and sing
Betwixt the tufts of snow on the bare branch
Of mossy apple-tree, while the nigh thatch
Smokes in the sun-thaw; whether the eave-drops fall   70
Heard only in the trances of the blast,
Or if the secret ministry of frost
Shall hang them up in silent icicles,
Quietly shining to the quiet Moon.

1798   *1798*

FEARS IN SOLITUDE

WRITTEN IN APRIL 1798, DURING THE
ALARM OF AN INVASION

A green and silent spot, amid the hills,
A small and silent dell! O'er stiller place
No singing sky-lark ever poised himself.
The hills are heathy, save that swelling slope,
Which hath a gay and gorgeous covering on,   5
All golden with the never-bloomless furze,
Which now blooms most profusely: but the dell,
Bathed by the mist, is fresh and delicate
As vernal corn-field, or the unripe flax,
When, through its half-transparent stalks, at eve,   10
The level sunshine glimmers with green light.
Oh! 'tis a quiet spirit-healing nook!
Which all, methinks, would love; but chiefly he,
The humble man, who, in his youthful years,
Knew just so much of folly, as had made   15
His early manhood more securely wise!
Here he might lie on fern or withered heath,
While from the singing lark (that sings unseen
The minstrelsy that solitude loves best),
And from the sun, and from the breezy air,   20
Sweet influences trembled o'er his frame;
And he, with many feelings, many thoughts,
Made up a meditative joy, and found
Religious meanings in the forms of Nature!
And so, his senses gradually wrapt   25
In a half sleep, he dreams of better worlds,
And dreaming hears thee still, O singing lark,
That singest like an angel in the clouds!

    My God! it is a melancholy thing
For such a man, who would full fain preserve   30
His soul in calmness, yet perforce must feel
For all his human brethren—O my God!
It weighs upon the heart, that he must think
What uproar and what strife may now be stirring
This way or that way o'er these silent hills—   35
Invasion, and the thunder and the shout,

And all the crash of onset; fear and rage,
And undetermined conflict—even now,
Even now, perchance, and in his native isle:
Carnage and groans beneath this blessed sun!   40
We have offended, Oh! my countrymen!
We have offended very grievously,
And been most tyrannous. From east to west
A groan of accusation pierces Heaven!
The wretched plead against us; multitudes   45
Countless and vehement, the sons of God,
Our brethren! Like a cloud that travels on,
Steamed up from Cairo's swamps of pestilence,
Even so, my countrymen! have we gone forth
And borne to distant tribes slavery and pangs,   50
And, deadlier far, our vices, whose deep taint
With slow perdition murders the whole man,
His body and his soul! Meanwhile, at home,
All individual dignity and power
Engulfed in Courts, Committees, Institutions,   55
Associations and Societies,
A vain, speech-mouthing, speech-reporting Guild
One Benefit-Club for mutual flattery,
We have drunk up, demure as at a grace,
Pollutions from the brimming cup of wealth;   60
Contemptuous of all honourable rule,
Yet bartering freedom and the poor man's life
For gold, as at a market! The sweet words
Of Christian promise, words that even yet
Might stem destruction, were they wisely preached,   65
Are muttered o'er by men, whose tones proclaim
How flat and wearisome they feel their trade:
Rank scoffers some, but most too indolent
To deem them falsehoods or to know their truth
Oh! blasphemous! the Book of Life is made   70
A superstitious instrument, on which
We gabble o'er the oaths we mean to break;
For all must swear—all and in every place,
College and wharf, council and justice-court;
All, all must swear, the briber and the bribed,   75
Merchant and lawyer, senator and priest,
The rich, the poor, the old man and the young;
All, all make up one scheme of perjury,
That faith doth reel; the very name of God

Sounds like a juggler's charm; and, bold with joy,   80
Forth from his dark and lonely hiding-place,
   (Portentous sight!) the owlet Atheism,
Sailing on obscene wings athwart the noon,
Drops his blue-fringéd lids, and holds them close,
And hooting at the glorious sun in Heaven,   85
Cries out, "Where is it?"

                                    Thankless too for peace,
   (Peace long preserved by fleets and perilous seas)
Secure from actual warfare, we have loved
To swell the war-whoop, passionate for war!
Alas! for ages ignorant of all   90
Its ghastlier workings, (famine or blue plague,
Battle, or siege, or flight through wintry snows,)
We, this whole people, have been clamorous
For war and bloodshed; animating sports,
The which we pay for as a thing to talk of,   95
Spectators and not combatants! No guess
Anticipative of a wrong unfelt,
No speculation on contingency,
However dim and vague, too vague and dim
To yield a justifying cause; and forth,   100
   (Stuffed out with big preamble, holy names,
And adjurations of the God in Heaven,)
We send our mandates for the certain death
Of thousands and ten thousands! Boys and girls,
And women, that would groan to see a child   105
Pull off an insect's leg, all read of war,
The best amusement for our morning meal!
The poor wretch, who has learnt his only prayers
From curses, who knows scarcely words enough
To ask a blessing from his Heavenly Father,   110
Becomes a fluent phraseman, absolute
And technical in victories and defeats,
And all our dainty terms for fratricide;
Terms which we trundle smoothly o'er our tongues
Like mere abstractions, empty sounds to which   115
We join no feeling and attach no form!
As if the soldier died without a wound;
As if the fibres of this godlike frame
Were gored without a pang; as if the wretch,
Who fell in battle, doing bloody deeds,   120

Passed off to Heaven, translated and not killed;
As though he had no wife to pine for him,
No God to judge him! Therefore, evil days
Are coming on us, O my countrymen!
And what if all-avenging Providence,   125
Strong and retributive, should make us know
The meaning of our words, force us to feel
The desolation and the agony
Of our fierce doings?

             Spare us yet awhile,
Father and God! O! spare us yet awhile!   130
Oh! let not English women drag their flight
Fainting beneath the burthen of their babes,
Of the sweet infants, that but yesterday
Laughed at the breast! Sons, brothers, husbands, all
Who ever gazed with fondness on the forms   135
Which grew up with you round the same fire-side,
And all who ever heard the sabbath-bells
Without the infidel's scorn, make yourselves pure!
Stand forth! be men! repel an impious foe,
Impious and false, a light yet cruel race,   140
Who laugh away all virtue, mingling mirth
With deeds of murder; and still promising
Freedom, themselves too sensual to be free,
Poison life's amities, and cheat the heart
Of faith and quiet hope, and all that soothes,   145
And all that lifts the spirit! Stand we forth;
Render them back upon the insulted ocean,
And let them toss as idly on its waves
As the vile sea-weed, which some mountain-blast
Swept from our shores! And oh! may we return   150
Not with a drunken triumph, but with fear,
Repenting of the wrongs with which we stung
So fierce a foe to frenzy!

             I have told,
O Britons! O my brethren! I have told
Most bitter truth, but without bitterness.   155
Nor deem my zeal or factious or mistimed;
For never can true courage dwell with them,
Who, playing tricks with conscience, dare not look
At their own vices We have been too long

Dupes of a deep delusion! Some, belike,   160
Groaning with restless enmity, expect
All change from change of constituted power;
As if a Government had been a robe,
On which our vice and wretchedness were tagged
Like fancy-points and fringes, with the robe   165
Pulled off at pleasure. Fondly these attach
A radical causation to a few
Poor drudges of chastising Providence,
Who borrow all their hues and qualities
From our own folly and rank wickedness,   170
Which gave them birth and nursed them. Others, mean-
       while,
Dote with a mad idolatry; and all
Who will not fall before their images,
And yield them worship, they are enemies
Even of their country!

                     Such have I been deemed.—   175
But, O dear Britain! O my Mother Isle!
Needs must thou prove a name most dear and holy
To me, a son, a brother, and a friend,
A husband, and a father! who revere
All bonds of natural love, and find them all   180
Within the limits of thy rocky shores.
O native Britain! O my Mother Isle!
How shouldst thou prove aught else but dear and holy
To me, who from thy lakes and mountain-hills,
Thy clouds, thy quiet dales, thy rocks and seas,   185
Have drunk in all my intellectual life,
All sweet sensations, all ennobling thoughts,
All adoration of the God in nature,
All lovely and all honourable things,
Whatever makes this mortal spirit feel   190
The joy and greatness of its future being?
There lives nor form nor feeling in my soul
Unborrowed from my country! O divine
And beauteous island! thou hast been my sole
And most magnificent temple, in the which   195
I walk with awe, and sing my stately songs,
Loving the God that made me!—

                                        May my fears,
My filial fears, be vain! and may the vaunts
And menace of the vengeful enemy
Pass like the gust, that roared and died away   200
In the distant tree: which heard, and only heard
In this low dell, bowed not the delicate grass.

   But now the gentle dew-fall sends abroad
The fruit-like perfume of the golden furze:
The light has left the summit of the hill,   205
Though still a sunny gleam lies beautiful,
Aslant the ivied beacon. Now farewell,
Farewell, awhile, O soft and silent spot!
On the green sheep-track, up the heathy hill,
Homeward I wind my way; and lo! recalled   210
From bodings that have well-nigh wearied me,
I find myself upon the brow, and pause
Startled! And after lonely sojourning
In such a quiet and surrounded nook,
This burst of prospect, here the shadowy main,   215
Dim-tinted, there the mighty majesty
Of that huge amphitheatre of rich
And elmy fields, seems like society—
Conversing with the mind, and giving it
A livelier impulse and a dance of thought!   220
And now, belovéd Stowey! I behold
Thy church-tower, and, methinks, the four huge elms
Clustering, which mark the mansion of my friend;
And close behind them, hidden from my view,
Is my own lowly cottage, where my babe   225
And my babe's mother dwell in peace! With light
And quickened footsteps thitherward I tend,
Remembering thee, O green and silent dell!
And grateful, that by nature's quietness
And solitary musings, all my heart   230
Is softened, and made worthy to indulge
Love, and the thoughts that yearn for human kind.

1798   *1798*

THE NIGHTINGALE

A CONVERSATION POEM, APRIL 1798

No cloud, no relique of the sunken day
Distinguishes the West, no long thin slip
Of sullen light, no obscure trembling hues.
Come, we will rest on this old mossy bridge!
You see the glimmer of the stream beneath,   5
But hear no murmuring: it flows silently,
O'er its soft bed of verdure. All is still,
A balmy night! and though the stars be dim,
Yet let us think upon the vernal showers
That gladden the green earth, and we shall find   10
A pleasure in the dimness of the stars.
And hark! the Nightingale begins its song,
"Most musical, most melancholy" bird!
A melancholy bird? Oh! idle thought!
In Nature there is nothing melancholy.   15
But some night-wandering man whose heart was pierced
With the remembrance of a grievous wrong,
Or slow distemper, or neglected love,
 (And so, poor wretch! filled all things with himself,
And made all gentle sounds tell back the tale   20
Of his own sorrow) he, and such as he,
First named these notes a melancholy strain.
And many a poet echoes the conceit;
Poet who hath been building up the rhyme
When he had better far have stretched his limbs   25
Beside a brook in mossy forest-dell,
By sun or moon-light, to the influxes
Of shapes and sounds and shifting elements
Surrendering his whole spirit, of his song
And of his fame forgetful! so his fame   30
Should share in Nature's immortality,
A venerable thing! and so his song
Should make all Nature lovelier, and itself
Be loved like Nature! But 'twill not be so;
And youths and maidens most poetical,   35
Who lose the deepening twilights of the spring
In ball-rooms and hot theatres, they still
Full of meek sympathy must heave their sighs

O'er Philomela's pity-pleading strains

My Friend, and thou, our Sister! we have learnt   40
A different lore: we may not thus profane
Nature's sweet voices, always full of love
And joyance! 'Tis the merry Nightingale
That crowds, and hurries, and precipitates
With fast thick warble his delicious notes,   45
As he were fearful that an April night
Would be too short for him to utter forth
His love-chant, and disburthen his full soul
Of all its music!
           And I know a grove
Of large extent, hard by a castle huge,   50
Which the great lord inhabits not; and so
This grove is wild with tangling underwood,
And the trim walks are broken up, and grass,
Thin grass and king-cups grow within the paths.
But never elsewhere in one place I knew   55
So many nightingales; and far and near,
In wood and thicket, over the wide grove,
They answer and provoke each other's song,
With skirmish and capricious passagings,
And murmurs musical and swift jug jug,   60
And one low piping sound more sweet than all—
Stirring the air with such a harmony,
That should you close your eyes, you might almost
Forget it was not day! On moonlight bushes,
Whose dewy leaflets are but half-disclosed,   65
You may perchance behold them on the twigs,
Their bright, bright eyes, their eyes both bright and full,
Glistening, while many a glow-worm in the shade
Lights up her love-torch.
           A most gentle Maid
Who dwelleth in her hospitable home   70
Hard by the castle, and at latest eve
(Even like a Lady vowed and dedicate
To something more than Nature in the grove)
Glides through the pathways; she knows all their notes,
That gentle Maid! and oft, a moment's space,   75
What time the moon was lost behind a cloud,
Hath heard a pause of silence; till the moon
Emerging, hath awakened earth and sky

With one sensation, and those wakeful birds
Have all burst forth in choral minstrelsy,   80
As if some sudden gale had swept at once
A hundred airy harps! And she hath watched
Many a nightingale perch giddily
On blossomy twig still swinging from the breeze
And to that motion tune his wanton song   85
Like tipsy Joy that reels with tossing head.

Farewell, O Warbler! till to-morrow eve,
And you, my friends! farewell, a short farewell!
We have been loitering long and pleasantly,
And now for our dear homes.—That strain again!   90
Full fain it would delay me! My dear babe,
Who, capable of no articulate sound,
Mars all things with his imitative lisp,
How he would place his hand beside his ear,
His little hand, the small forefinger up,   95
And bid us listen! And I deem it wise
To make him Nature's play-mate. He knows well
The evening-star; and once, when he awoke
In most distressful mood (some inward pain
Had made up that strange thing, an infant's dream—)   100
I hurried with him to our orchard-plot,
And he beheld the moon, and, hushed at once,
Suspends his sobs, and laughs most silently,
While his fair eyes, that swam with undropped tears,
Did glitter in the yellow moon-beam! Well!—   105
It is a father's tale: But if that Heaven
Should give me life, his childhood shall grow up
Familiar with these songs, that with the night
He may associate joy.—Once more, farewell,
Sweet Nightingale! once more, my friends! farewell.   110

1798   *1798*

TO WILLIAM WORDSWORTH

COMPOSED ON THE NIGHT AFTEP HIS RECITATION OF A POEM
ON THE GROWTH OF AN INDIVIDUAL MIND

Friend of the wise! and Teacher of the Good!
Into my heart have I received that Lay
More than historic, that prophetic Lay
Wherein (high theme by thee first sung aright)
Of the foundations and the building up   5
Of a Human Spirit thou hast dared to tell
What may be told, to the understanding mind
Revealable; and what within the mind
By vital breathings secret as the soul
Of vernal growth, oft quickens in the hear   10
Thoughts all too deep for words!—

                         Theme hard as high!
Of smiles spontaneous, and mysterious fears
(The first-born they of Reason and twin-birth),
Of tides obedient to external force,
And currents self-determined, as might seem,   15
Or by some inner Power; of moments awful,
Now in thy inner life, and now abroad,
When power streamed from thee, and thy soul received
The light reflected, as a light bestowed—
Of fancies fair, and milder hours of youth,   20
Hyblean murmurs of poetic thought
Industrious in its joy, in vales and glens
Native or outland, lakes and famous hills!
Or on the lonely high-road, when the stars
Were rising; or by secret mountain-streams,   25
The guides and the companions of thy way!

Of more than Fancy, of the Social Sense
Distending wide, and man beloved as man,
Where France in all her towns lay vibrating
Like some becalmèd bark beneath the burst   30
Of Heaven's immediate thunder, when no cloud
Is visible, or shadow on the main.

For thou wert there, thine own brows garlanded,
Amid the tremor of a realm aglow,
Amid a mighty nation jubilant,   35
When from the general heart of human kind
Hope sprang forth like a full-born Deity!
——Of that dear Hope afflicted and struck down,
So summoned homeward, thenceforth calm and sure
From the dread watch-tower of man's absolute self,   40
With light unwaning on her eyes, to look
Far on—herself a glory to behold,
The Angel of the vision! Then (last strain)
Of Duty, chosen Laws controlling choice,
Action and joy!—An Orphic song indeed,   45
A song divine of high and passionate thoughts
To their own music chaunted!

           O great Bard!
Ere yet that last strain dying awed the air,
With stedfast eye I viewed thee in the choir
Of ever-enduring men. The truly great   50
Have all one age, and from one visible space
Shed influence! They, both in power and act,
Are permanent, and Time is not with them,
Save as it worketh for them, they in it.
Nor less a sacred Roll, than those of old,   55
And to be placed, as they, with gradual fame
Among the archives of mankind, thy work
Makes audible a linkéd lay of Truth,
Of Truth profound a sweet continuous lay,
Not learnt, but native, her own natural notes!   60
Ah! as I listened with a heart forlorn,
The pulses of my being beat anew:
And even as Life returns upon the drowned,
Life's joy rekindling roused a throng of pains—
Keen pangs of Love, awakening as a babe   65
Turbulent, with an outcry in the heart;
And fears self-willed, that shunned the eye of Hope;
And Hope that scarce would know itself from Fear;
Sense of past Youth, and Manhood come in vain,
And Genius given, and Knowledge won in vain;   70
And all which I had culled in wood-walks wild,
And all which patient toil had reared, and all,

Commune with thee had opened out—but flowers
Strewed on my corse, and borne upon my bier
In the same coffin, for the self-same grave!   75

That way no more! and ill beseems it me,
Who came a welcomer in herald's guise,
Singing of Glory, and Futurity,
To wander back on such unhealthful road,
Plucking the poisons of self-harm! And ill   80
Such intertwine beseems triumphal wreaths
Strew'd before thy advancing!

                                    Nor do thou,
Sage Bard! impair the memory of that hour
Of thy communion with my nobler mind
By pity or grief, already felt too long!   85
Nor let my words import more blame than needs.
The tumult rose and ceased: for Peace is nigh
Where Wisdom's voice has found a listening heart.
Amid the howl of more than wintry storms,
The Halcyon hears the voice of vernal hours   90
Already on the wing.

                            Eve following eve,
Dear tranquil time, when the sweet sense of Home
Is sweetest! moments for their own sake hailed
And more desired, more precious, for thy song,
In silence listening, like a devout child,   95
My soul lay passive, by thy various strain
Driven as in surges now beneath the stars,
With momentary stars of my own birth,
Fair constellated foam, still darting off
Into the darkness; now a tranquil sea,   100
Outspread and bright, yet swelling to the moon.

And when—O Friend! my comforter and guide!
Strong in thyself, and powerful to give strength!—
Thy long sustainéd Song finally closed,
And thy deep voice had ceased—yet thou thyself   105
Wert still before my eyes, and round us both
That happy vision of belovéd faces—
Scarce conscious, and yet conscious of its close
I sate, my being blended in one thought

(Thought was it? or aspiration? or resolve?)   110
Absorbed, yet hanging still upon the sound—
And when I rose, I found myself in prayer.

1807   *1817*

POEMS BEFORE WORDSWORTH, 1790–1794

Coleridge was a poet before he met Wordsworth, and continued to be at least a poet of sorts for a long time after his path had widely diverged from that of his friend. Like many of his romantic coevals, Coleridge began versifying with a manner and a style scarcely to be distinguished from that of scores of poetasters at the end of the eighteenth century. When Byron attacked him (along with many another British bard and Scottish critic), he spoke slightingly of the "turgid odes" and "tumid stanzas" which Coleridge held dear. Whether or not the young lord had particular examples in mind other than *To a Young Ass*, it is clear enough that the turgid and the tumid are not foreign to the early work of Coleridge. The sonnet to the autumnal moon, composed in the very year of Byron's birth, is neither tumid nor turgid but simply the typical out-of-school exercise of an eighteenth-century adolescent. The monody on Chatterton and the imitation of the Ossianic poems are equally of this time, while the two sonnets on Pantisocracy reflect the political idealism which pervaded the emotions of certain young liberal-minded Englishmen whenever they thought of the new republic being reared in the west-running wilderness across the vast Atlantic.

SONNET

TO THE AUTUMNAL MOON

Mild Splendour of the various-vested Night!
  Mother of wildly-working visions! hail!
I watch thy gliding, while with watery light
  Thy weak eye glimmers through a fleecy veil;
And when thou lovest thy pale orb to shroud   5
  Behind the gather'd blackness lost on high;
And when thou dartest from the wind-rent cloud
  Thy placid lightning o'er the awaken'd sky.

Ah such is Hope! as changeful and as fair!
  Now dimly peering on the wistful sight;   10
Now hid behind the dragon-wing'd Despair:
  But soon emerging in her radiant might
She o'er the sorrow-clouded breast of Care
  Sails, like a meteor kindling in its flight.

1788   *1796*

MONODY ON THE DEATH OF CHATTERTON

[FIRST VERSION, IN CHRIST'S HOSPITAL BOOK—1790]

> Cold penury repress'd his noble rage,
> And froze the genial current of his soul

Now prompts the Muse poetic lays,
And high my bosom beats with love of Praise!
But, Chatterton! methinks I hear thy name,
For cold my Fancy grows, and dead each Hope of Fame.

When Want and cold Neglect had chill'd thy soul,   5
Athirst for Death I see thee drench the bowl!
    Thy corpse of many a livid hue
    On the bare ground I view,
Whilst various passions all my mind engage;
    Now is my breast distended with a sigh,   10
    And now a flash of Rage
Darts through the tear, that glistens in my eye.

    Is this the land of liberal Hearts!
    Is this the land, where Genius ne'er in vain
Pour'd forth her soul-enchanting strain?   15
    Ah me! yet Butler 'gainst the bigot foe
    Well-skill'd to aim keen Humour's dart,
    Yet Butler felt Want's poignant sting;
    And Otway, Master of the Tragic art,
    Whom Pity's self had taught to sing,   20
    Sank beneath a load of Woe;
This ever can the generous Briton hear,
And starts not in his eye th' indignant Tear?

    Elate of Heart and confident of Fame,
From vales where Avon sports, the Minstrel came,   25
    Gay as the Poet hastes along
    He meditates the future song,
How Ælla battled with his country's foes,
    And whilst Fancy in the air
    Paints him many a vision fair   30
His eyes dance rapture and his bosom glows.
With generous joy he views th' ideal gold:
    He listens to many a Widow's prayers,

And many an Orphan's thanks he hears;
 He soothes to peace the care-worn breast,   35
 He bids the Debtor's eyes know rest,
 And Liberty and Bliss behold:
And now he punishes the heart of steel,
And her own iron rod he makes Oppression feel.

Fated to heave sad Disappointment's sigh,   40
To feel the Hope now rais'd, and now deprest,
To feel the burnings of an injur'd breast,
 From all thy Fate's deep sorrow keen
 In vain, O Youth, I turn th' affrighted eye;
 For powerful Fancy evernigh   45
The hateful picture forces on my sight.
 There, Death of every dear delight,
 Frowns Poverty of Giant mien!
In vain I seek the charms of youthful grace,
Thy sunken eye, thy haggard cheeks it shews,   50
The quick emotions struggling in the Face
 Faint index of thy mental Throes,
When each strong Passion spurn'd controll,
And not a Friend was nigh to calm thy stormy soul.

Such was the sad and gloomy hour   55
When anguish'd Care of sullen brow
Prepared the Poison's death-cold power.
Already to thy lips was rais'd the bowl,
When filial Pity stood thee by,
Thy fixéd eyes she bade thee roll   60
On scenes that well might melt thy soul—
Thy native cot she held to view,
Thy native cot, where Peace ere long
Had listen'd to thy evening song;
Thy sister's shrieks she bade thee hear,   65
And mark thy mother's thrilling tear,
She made thee feel her deep-drawn sigh,
And all her silent agony of Woe.

And from *thy* Fate shall such distress ensue?
Ah! dash the poison'd chalice from thy hand!   70
And thou had'st dash'd it at her soft command;
But that Despair and Indignation rose,
And told again the story of thy Woes,

Told the keen insult of th' unfeeling Heart,
The dread dependence on the low-born mind, 75
Told every Woe, for which thy breast might smart,
Neglect and grinning scorn and Want combin'd—
    Recoiling back, thou sent'st the friend of Pain
To roll a tide of Death thro' every freezing vein.
      O Spirit blest! 80
   Whether th' eternal Throne around,
   Amidst the blaze of Cherubim,
   Thou pourest forth the grateful hymn,
   Or, soaring through the blest Domain,
   Enraptur'st Angels with thy strain,— 85
   Grant me, like thee, the lyre to sound,
   Like thee, with fire divine to glow—
   But ah! when rage the Waves of Woe,
   Grant me with firmer breast t'oppose their hate,
And soar beyond the storms with upright eye elate! 90

1790   *1893*

MUSIC

Hence, soul-dissolving Harmony
  That lead'st th' oblivious soul astray—
Though thou sphere-descended be—
  Hence away!—
Thou mightier Goddess, thou demand'st my lay,   5
  Born when earth was seiz'd with cholic;
Or as more sapient sages say,
  What time the Legion diabolic
    Compell'd their beings to enshrine
    In bodies vile of herded swine,   10
    Precipitate adown the steep
    With hideous rout were plunging in the deep,
And hog and devil mingling grunt and yell
  Seiz'd on the ear with horrible obtrusion:—
Then if aright old legendaries tell,   15
  Wert thou begot by Discord on Confusion!

What though no name's sonorous power
Was given thee at thy natal hour!—
Yet oft I feel thy sacred might,
While concords wing their distant flight.   20
  Such Power inspires thy holy son
    Sable·clerk of Tiverton!
And oft where Otter sports his stream,
I hear thy banded offspring scream.
Thou Goddess! thou inspir'st each throat;   25
'Tis thou who pour'st the scritch-owl note!
Transported hear'st thy children all
Scrape and blow and squeak and squall;
And while old Otter's steeple rings,
Clappest hoarse thy raven wings!   30

1791   *1834*

IMITATED FROM OSSIAN

The stream with languid murmur creeps,
   In Lumin's *flowery* vale:
Beneath the dew the Lily weeps
   Slow-waving to the gale.

'Cease, restless gale!' it seems to say,   5
   'Nor wake me with thy sighing!
The honours of my vernal day
   On rapid wing are flying.

'To-morrow shall the Traveller come
   Who late beheld me blooming: 10
His searching eye shall vainly roam
   The *dreary* vale of Lumin.'

With eager gaze and wetted cheek
   My wonted haunts along,
Thus, faithful Maiden! *thou* shalt seek   15
   The Youth of simplest song.

But I along the breeze shall roll
   The voice of feeble power;
And dwell, the Moon-beam of thy soul,
   In Slumber's nightly hour.   20

1793   *1796*

TO A YOUNG ASS

ITS MOTHER BEING TETHERED NEAR IT

Poor little Foal of an oppresséd race!
I love the languid patience of thy face:
And oft with gentle hand I give thee bread,
And clap thy ragged coat, and pat thy head.
But what thy dulled spirits hath dismay'd,   5
That never thou dost sport along the glade?
And (most unlike the nature of things young)
That earthward still thy moveless head is hung?
Do thy prophetic fears anticipate,
Meek Child of Misery! thy future fate?   10
The starving meal, and all the thousand aches
"Which patient Merit of the Unworthy takes"?
Or is thy sad heart thrill'd with filial pain
To see thy wretched mother's shorten'd chain?
And truly, very piteous is *her* lot—   15
Chain'd to a log within a narrow spot,
Where the close-eaten grass is scarcely seen,
While sweet around her waves the tempting green!

Poor Ass! thy master should have learnt to show
Pity—best taught by fellowship of Woe!   20
For much I fear me that *He* lives like thee,
Half famish'd in a land of Luxury!
How *askingly* its footsteps hither bend?
It seems to say, "And have I then *one* friend?"
Innocent foal! thou poor despis'd forlorn!   25
I hail thee *Brother*—spite of the fool's scorn!
And fain would take thee with me, in the Dell
Where high-soul'd Pantisocracy shall dwell!
Where Mirth shall tickle Plenty's ribless side,
And smiles from Beauty's Lip on sunbeams glide,   30
Where Toil shall wed young Health that charming Lass!
And use his sleek cows for a looking-glass—
Where Rats shall mess with Terriers hand-in-glove
And Mice with Pussy's Whiskers sport in Love.
How thou wouldst toss thy heels in gamesome play,   35
And frisk about, as lamb or kitten gay!
Yea! and more musically sweet to me

Thy dissonant harsh bray of joy would be,
Than warbled melodies that soothe to rest
The aching of pale Fashion's vacant breast!

1794   *1794*

SONNET

TO THE RIVER OTTER

Dear native Brook! wild Streamlet of the West!
  How many various-fated years have past,
  What happy and what mournful hours, since last
I skimm'd the smooth thin stone along thy breast,
Numbering its light leaps! yet so deep imprest   5
Sink the sweet scenes of childhood, that mine eyes
  I never shut amid the sunny ray,
But straight with all their tints thy waters rise,
  Thy crossing plank, thy marge with willows grey,
And bedded sand that vein'd with various dyes   10
Gleam'd through thy bright transparence! On my way,
  Visions of Childhood! oft have ye beguil'd
Lone manhood's cares, yet waking fondest sighs:
  Ah! that once more I were a careless Child!

1793   *1796*

PANTISOCRACY

No more my visionary soul shall dwell
On joys that were; no more endure to weigh
The shame and anguish of the evil day,
Wisely forgetful! O'er the ocean swell
Sublime of Hope, I seek the cottag'd dell   5
Where Virtue calm with careless step may stray,
And dancing to the moonlight roundelay,
The wizard Passions weave an holy spell.
Eyes that have ach'd with Sorrow! Ye shall weep
Tears of doubt-mingled joy, like theirs who start   10
From Precipices of distemper'd sleep,

On which the fierce-eyed Fiends their revels keep,
And see the rising Sun, and feel it dart
New rays of pleasance trembling to the heart.

1794   *1849*

ON THE PROSPECT OF ESTABLISHING
A PANTISOCRACY IN AMERICA

Whilst pale Anxiety, corrosive Care,
The tear of Woe, the gloom of sad Despair,
   And deepen'd Anguish generous bosoms rend;—
Whilst patriot souls their country's fate lament;
Whilst mad with rage demoniac, foul intent,   5
   Embattled legions Despots vainly send
To arrest the immortal mind's expanding ray
   Of everlasting Truth;—I other climes
Where dawns, with hope serene, a brighter day
   Than e'er saw Albion in her happiest times,   10
With mental eye exulting now explore,
   And soon with kindred minds shall haste to enjoy
(Free from the ills which here our peace destroy)
Content and Bliss on Transatlantic shore.

1794   *1826*

ODES, HYMNS, AND SONGS

"I write melancholy, always melancholy," said Coleridge in a notebook entry of 1803. "You will suspect that it is a fault of my natural temper. Alas! no.—This is the great Occasion that my Nature is made for Joy—impelling me to Joyance—& I never —never can yield to it.—I am a genuine Tantalus." Now the hapless figure of Tantalus in Greek mythology was one set in Hades beside a pool of water in the midst of an orchard, and afflicted with perpetual thirst and hunger. Yet such was his punishment that the water in the pool always ebbed when he bent to drink, while the fruit-laden branches of the trees always swayed out of his reach as he stretched to pluck them clean. So, thinks Coleridge, it has been with him and joy.

His prevalent sense of the Tantalus-situation helps to explain why the power of darkness seems to preponderate in the poems. If joy, though always visible, is perpetually unattainable, Coleridge is in what has been called "the true hell-situation—heaven glimpsed but unrealized." Like Wordsworth on occasion, he seems to recall a time when things were better than they are now. Unlike Wordsworth, he is never quite willing to settle for anything less than what he has lost. Not for him are the lesser consolations; nor, at least in his poetry, does he find "strength in what remains behind." Even the "philosophic mind" which the years had brought him by 1802 struck him as a poor substitute, a compensatory habit of "abstruse research" in place of the "shaping spirit of imagination" which for a few years suffused his life with an aureate glow.

In the end, however, he managed to work his way through the vein of melancholia which darkens the texture of these odes and hymns, and to emerge into benign middle age. If it was never wholly serene, it was at least a situation in which Tantalus was content to sit beneath the trees and talk, leaning forward from time to time to ruffle with a finger the placid surface of the pool, yet able to repress the impulse to bend and drink.

FRANCE: AN ODE

ARGUMENT

"First Stanza. *An invocation to those objects in Nature the contemplation of which had inspired the Poet with a devotional love of Liberty.* Second Stanza. *The exultation of the Poet at the commencement of the French Revolution, and his unqualified abhorrence of the Alliance against the Republic.* Third Stanza. *The blasphemies and horrors during the domination of the Terrorists regarded by the Poet as a transient storm, and as the natural consequence of the former despotism and of the foul superstition of Popery. Reason, indeed, began to suggest many apprehensions; yet still the Poet struggled to retain the hope that France would make conquests by no other means than by presenting to the observation of Europe a people more happy and better instructed than under other forms of Government.* Fourth Stanza. *Switzerland, and the Poet's recantation.* Fifth Stanza. *An address to Liberty, in which the Poet expresses his conviction that those feelings and that grand ideal of Freedom which the mind attains by its contemplation of its individual nature, and of the sublime surrounding objects (see Stanza the First) do not belong to men, as a society, nor can possibly be either gratified or realised, under any form of human government; but belong to the individual man, so far as he is pure, and inflamed with the love and adoration of God in Nature."*

Ye Clouds! that far above me float and pause,
   Whose pathless march no mortal may controul!
   Ye Ocean-Waves! that, wheresoe'er ye roll,
Yield homage only to eternal laws!
Ye Woods! that listen to the night-birds singing,   5
   Midway the smooth and perilous slope reclined,
Save when your own imperious branches swinging,
   Have made a solemn music of the wind!
Where, like a man beloved of God,
Through glooms, which never woodman trod,   10
     How oft, pursuing fancies holy,
My moonlight way o'er flowering weeds I wound,

Inspired, beyond the guess of folly,
By each rude shape and wild unconquerable sound!
O ye loud Waves! and O ye Forests high!   15
    And O ye Clouds that far above me soared!
Thou rising Sun! thou blue rejoicing Sky!
    Yea, every thing that is and will be free!
    Bear witness for me, wheresoe'er ye be,
    With what deep worship I have still adored   20
        The spirit of divinest Liberty.

When France in wrath her giant-limbs upreared,
    And with that oath, which smote air, earth, and sea,
    Stamped her strong foot and said she would be free,
Bear witness for me, how I hoped and feared!   25
With what a joy my lofty gratulation
    Unawed I sang, amid a slavish band:
And when to whelm the disenchanted nation,
    Like fiends embattled by a wizard's wand,
        The Monarchs marched in evil day,   30
        And Britain joined the dire array;
    Though dear her shores and circling ocean,
Though many friendships, many youthful loves
    Had swoln the patriot emotion
And flung a magic light o'er all her hills and groves;   35
Yet still my voice, unaltered, sang defeat
    To all that braved the tyrant-quelling lance,
And shame too long delayed and vain retreat!
For ne'er, O Liberty! with partial aim
I dimmed thy light or damped thy holy flame;   40
    But blessed the paeans of delivered France,
And hung my head and wept at Britain's name.

III

"And what," I said, "though Blasphemy's loud scream
    With that sweet music of deliverance strove!
    Though all the fierce and drunken passions wove   45
A dance more wild than e'er was maniac's dream!
    Ye storms, that round the dawning East assembled,

The Sun was rising, though ye hid his light!"
　　And when, to soothe my soul, that hoped and
　　　　trembled,
The dissonance ceased, and all seemed calm and
　　　　bright;   50
　　When France her front deep-scarr'd and gory
　　Concealed with clustering wreaths of glory;
　　　　When, insupportably advancing,
　　Her arm made mockery of the warrior's ramp;
　　　　While timid looks of fury glancing,   55
　　Domestic treason, crushed beneath her fatal stamp,
Writhed like a wounded dragon in his gore;
　　Then I reproached my fears that would not flee;
"And soon," I said, "shall Wisdom teach her lore
In the low huts of them that toil and groan!   60
And, conquering by her happiness alone,
　　Shall France compel the nations to be free,
Till Love and Joy look round, and call the Earth their
　　　　own."

                                   IV

Forgive me, Freedom! O forgive those dreams!
　　I hear thy voice, I hear thy loud lament,   65
　　From bleak Helvetia's icy caverns sent—
I hear thy groans upon her blood-stained streams!
　　Heroes, that for your peaceful country perished,
And ye that, fleeing, spot your mountain-snows
　　With bleeding wounds; forgive me, that I cher-
　　　　ished   70
One thought that ever blessed your cruel foes!
　　To scatter rage, and traitorous guilt,
　　Where Peace her jealous home had built;
　　　　A patriot-race to disinherit
Of all that made their stormy wilds so dear;   75
　　　　And with inexpiable spirit
To taint the bloodless freedom of the mountaineer—
O France, that mockest Heaven, adulterous, blind,
　　And patriot only in pernicious toils!
Are these thy boasts, Champion of human kind?   80
　　To mix with Kings in the low lust of sway,
Yell in the hunt, and share the murderous prey;

To insult the shrine of Liberty with spoils
   From freemen torn; to tempt and to betray?

V

  The Sensual and the Dark rebel in vain,   85
Slaves by their own compulsion! In mad game
   They burst their manacles and wear the name
     Of Freedom, graven on a heavier chain!
  O Liberty! with profitless endeavour
Have I pursued thee, many a weary hour;   90
   But thou nor swell'st the victor's strain, nor ever
Didst breathe thy soul in forms of human power.
   Alike from all, howe'er they praise thee,
    (Nor prayer, nor boastful name delays thee)
    Alike from Priestcraft's harpy minions,   95
   And factious Blasphemy's obscener slaves,
    Thou speedest on thy subtle pinions,
The guide of homeless winds, and playmate of the
      waves!
And there I felt thee!—on that sea-cliff's verge,
   Whose pines, scarce travelled by the breeze
     above,   100
Had made one murmur with the distant surge!
Yes; while I stood and gazed, my temples bare,
And shot my being through earth, sea, and air,
   Possessing all things with intensest love,
    O Liberty! my spirit felt thee there.   105

1798   *1798*

LEWTI

OR THE CIRCASSIAN LOVE-CHAUNT

At midnight by the stream I roved,
To forget the form I loved.
Image of Lewti! from my mind
Depart; for Lewti is not kind.
The Moon was high, the moonlight gleam   5
  And the shadow of a star
Heaved upon Tamaha's stream;
  But the rock shone brighter far,
The rock half sheltered from my view
By pendent boughs of tressy yew.—   10
So shines my Lewti's forehead fair,
Gleaming through her sable hair.
Image of Lewti! from my mind
Depart; for Lewti is not kind.

I saw a cloud of palest hue,   15
  Onward to the moon it passed;
Still brighter and more bright it grew,
With floating colours not a few,
Till it reached the moon at last:
Then the cloud was wholly bright,   20
With a rich and amber light!
And so with many a hope I seek,
  And with such joy I find my Lewti;
And even so my pale wan cheek
  Drinks in as deep a flush of beauty!   25
Nay, treacherous image! leave my mind,
If Lewti never will be kind.

The little cloud—it floats away,
  Away it goes; away so soon!
Alas! it has no power to stay:
Its hues are dim, its hues are grey—   30
  Away it passes from the moon!
How mournfully it seems to fly,

Ever fading more and more,
To joyless regions of the sky—   35
   And now 'tis whiter than before!
As white as my poor cheek will be,
   When, Lewti! on my couch I lie,
A dying man for love of thee.
Nay, treacherous image! leave my mind—   40
And yet, thou didst not look unkind.

I saw a vapour in the sky,
Thin, and white, and very high;
I ne'er beheld so thin a cloud:
   Perhaps the breezes that can fly   45
   Now below and now above,
Have snatched aloft the lawny shroud
   Of Lady fair—that died for love.
For maids, as well as youths, have perished
From fruitless love too fondly cherished.   50
Nay, treacherous image! leave my mind—
For Lewti never will be kind.

Hush! my heedless feet from under
   Slip the crumbling banks for ever:
Like echoes to a distant thunder,   55
   They plunge into the gentle river.
The river-swans have heard my tread,
And startle from their reedy bed.
O beauteous birds! methinks ye measure
   Your movements to some heavenly tune!   60
O beauteous birds! 'tis such a pleasure
   To see you move beneath the moon,
I would it were your true delight
To sleep by day and wake all night.

I know the place where Lewti lies,   65
When silent night has closed her eyes:
   It is a breezy jasmine-bower,
The nightingale sings o'er her head:
   Voice of the Night! had I the power

That leafy labyrinth to thread,   70
And creep, like thee, with soundless tread,
I then might view her bosom white
Heaving lovely to my sight,
As these two swans together heave
On the gently-swelling wave.   75

Oh! that she saw me in a dream,
   And dreamt that I had died for care;
All pale and wasted I would seem,
   Yet fair withal, as spirits are!
I'd die indeed, if I might see   80
Her bosom heave, and heave for me!
Soothe, gentle image! soothe my mind!
To-morrow Lewti may be kind.

1798   *1798*

DEJECTION: AN ODE
(Original version)

A LETTER TO SARA HUTCHINSON

Intimations of Immortality

April 4, 1802.   Sunday Evening.

Well! if the Bard was weatherwise, who made
The grand old Ballad of Sir Patrick Spence,
This Night, so tranquil now, will not go hence
Unrous'd by winds, that ply a busier trade
Than that, which moulds yon clouds in lazy flakes,   5
Or the dull sobbing Draft, that drones and rakes
Upon the Strings of this Eolian Lute,
Which better far were mute.
For, lo! the New Moon, winter-bright!
And overspread with phantom Light   10
(With swimming phantom Light o'erspread
But rimm'd and circled with a silver Thread)
I see the Old Moon in her Lap, foretelling
The coming-on of Rain and squally Blast—
O! Sara! that the Gust ev'n now were swelling,   15
And the slant Night-shower driving loud and fast!

A Grief without a pang, void, dark and drear,
A stifling, drowsy, unimpassion'd Grief
That finds no natural outlet, no Relief
In word, or sigh, or tear—   20
This, Sara! well thou know'st,
Is that sore Evil, which I dread the most,
And oft'nest suffer! In this heartless Mood,
To other thoughts by yonder Throstle woo'd,
That pipes within the Larch tree, not unseen,   25
(The Larch, which pushes out in tassels green
It's bundled Leafits) woo'd to mild Delights
By all the tender Sounds and gentle Sights
Of this sweet Primrose-month—and *vainly* woo'd
O dearest Sara! in this heartless Mood   30
All this long Eve, so balmy and serene,
Have I been gazing on the western Sky
And its peculiar Tint of Yellow Green—

And still I gaze—and with how blank an eye!
And those thin Clouds above, in flakes and bars,   35
That give away their Motion to the Stars;
Those Stars, that glide behind them, or between,
Now sparkling, now bedimm'd, but always seen;
Yon crescent Moon, as fix'd as if it grew
In it's own cloudless, starless Lake of Blue—   40
A boat becalm'd! dear William's Sky Canoe!
—I see them all, so excellently fair!
I see, not feel, how beautiful they are.

My genial Spirits fail—
And what can these avail   45
To lift the smoth'ring Weight from off my Breast?
It were a vain Endeavor,
Tho' I should gaze for ever
On that Green Light which lingers in the West!
I may not hope from outward Forms to win   50
The Passion and the Life, whose Fountains are within!

These lifeless Shapes, around, below, Above,
    O what can they impart?
When even the gentle Thought, that thou, my Love!
Art gazing, now, like me,
And see'st the Heaven, I see—   55
Sweet Thought it is—yet feebly stirs my Heart!

Feebly! O feebly!—Yet
  (I well remember it)
In my first Dawn of Youth that Fancy stole
With many secret Yearnings on my Soul   60
At eve, sky-gazing in 'ecstatic fit'
(Alas! for cloister'd in a city School
The Sky was all, I knew, of Beautiful)
At the barr'd window often did I sit,   65
And oft upon the leaded School-roof lay,
And to myself would say—
There does not live the Man so stripp'd of good affections
As not to love to see a Maiden's quiet Eyes
Uprais'd, and linking on sweet Dreams by dim
        Connections   70
To Moon, or Evening Star, or glorious western Skies—

While yet a Boy, this Thought would so pursue me,
That often it became a kind of Vision to me!

Sweet Thought! and dear of old
To Hearts of finer Mould!
Ten thousand times by Friends and Lovers blest!   75
I spake with rash Despair,
And ere I was aware,
The Weight was somewhat lifted from my Breast!
O Sara! in the weather-fended Wood,   80
Thy lov'd haunt! where the Stock-doves coo at Noon
I guess, that thou hast stood
And watch'd yon Crescent, and it's ghost-like Moon.
And yet, far rather in my present Mood
I would, that thou'dst been sitting all this while   85
Upon the sod-built Seat of Camomile—
And tho' thy Robin may have ceas'd to sing,
Yet needs for *my* sake must thou love to hear
The Bee-hive murmuring near,
That ever-busy and most quiet Thing   90
Which I have heard at Midnight murmuring.

I feel my spirit moved.
And wheresoe'er thou be,
O Sister! O Beloved!
Those dear mild Eyes, that see   95
Even now the Heaven, *I* see—
There is a Prayer in them! It is for *me*—
And I, dear Sara, *I* am blessing *thee*!

It was as calm as this, that happy night
When Mary, thou, and I together were,   100
The low decaying Fire our only Light,
And listen'd to the Stillness of the Air!
O that affectionate and blameless Maid,
Dear Mary! on her Lap my head she lay'd—
Her Hand was on my Brow,   105
Even as my own is now;
And on my Cheek I felt the eye-lash play.
Such joy I had, that I may truly say,
My Spirit was awe-stricken with the Excess
And trance-like Depth of it's brief Happiness.   110

Ah fair Remembrances, that so revive
The Heart, and fill it with a living Power,
Where were they, Sara?—or did I not strive
To win them to me?—on the fretting Hour
Then when I wrote thee that complaining Scroll,   115
Which even to bodily Sickness bruis'd thy Soul!
And yet thou blam'st thyself alone! And yet
Forbidd'st me all Regret!

And must I not regret, that I distress'd
Thee, best belov'd, who lovest me the best?   120
My better mind had fled, I know not whither,
For O! was this an absent Friend's Employ
To send from far both Pain and Sorrow thither
Where still his Blessings should have call'd down Joy!
I read thy guileless Letter o'er again—   125
I hear thee of thy blameless Self complain—
And only this I learn—and this, alas! I know—
That thou art weak and pale with Sickness,
      Grief, and Pain—
And I,—I made thee so!

O for my own sake I regret perforce   130
Whatever turns thee, Sara! from the course
Of calm Well-being and a Heart at rest!
When thou, and with thee those, whom thou lov'st best,
Shall dwell together in one happy Home,
One House, the dear *abiding* Home of All,   135
I too will crown me with a Coronal—
Nor shall this Heart in idle Wishes roam
      Morbidly soft!

No! let me trust, that I shall wear away
In no inglorious Toils the manly Day,   140
And only now and then, and not too oft,
Some dear and memorable Eve will bless
Dreaming of all your Loves and Quietness.
Be happy, and I need thee not in sight.
Peace in thy Heart, and Quiet in thy Dwelling,   145
Health in thy Limbs, and in thine eyes the Light
Of Love and Hope and honourable Feeling—
Where e'er I am, I shall be well content!
Not near thee, haply shall be more content!

To all things I prefer the Permanent.   150
And better seems it, for a Heart, like mine,
Always to *know*, than sometimes to behold,
    Their Happiness and thine—
For Change doth trouble me with pangs untold!
To see thee, hear thee, feel thee—then to part   155
    Oh! it weighs down the heart!
To *visit* those, I love, as I love thee,
Mary, and William, and dear Dorothy,
It is but a temptation to repine—
The transientness is Poison in the Wine,   160
Eats out the pith of Joy, makes all Joy hollow,
All Pleasure a dim Dream of Pain to follow!
My own peculiar Lot, my house-hold Life
It is, and will remain, Indifference or Strife.
While *Ye* are *well* and *happy*, 'twould but wrong you   165
If I should fondly yearn to be among you—
Wherefore, O wherefore! should I wish to be
A wither'd branch upon a blossoming Tree?

But (let me say it! for I vainly strive
To beat away the Thought), but if thou pin'd   17(
Whate'er the Cause, in body or in mind,
I were the miserablest Man alive
To know it and be absent! Thy Delights
Far off, or near, alike I may partake—
But O! to mourn for thee, and to forsake   175
All power, all hope, of giving comfort to thee—
To know that thou art weak and worn with pain,
And not to hear thee, Sara! not to view thee—
    Not sit beside thy Bed,
    Not press thy aching Head,   180
    Not bring thee Health again—
    At least to hope, to try—
By this Voice, which thou lov'st, and by this earnest Eye—
Nay, wherefore did I let it haunt my Mind
The dark distressful Dream!   185
I turn from it, and listen to the Wind
Which long has rav'd unnotic'd! What a Scream
Of agony, by Torture lengthen'd out
That Lute sent forth! O thou wild Storm without!
Jagg'd Rock, or mountain Pond, or blasted Tree,   190
Or Pine-Grove, whither Woodman never clomb,

Or lonely House, long held the Witches' Home,
Methinks were fitter Instruments for Thee,
Mad Lutanist! that in this month of Showers,
Of dark brown Gardens and of peeping Flowers,   195
Mak'st Devil's Yule with worse than wintry Song
The Blossoms, Buds, and timorous Leaves among!
Thou Actor, perfect in all tragic Sounds!
Thou mighty Poet, even to frenzy bold!
What tell'st thou now about?   200
'Tis of the Rushing of an Host in Rout
And many groans for men with smarting Wounds—
At once they groan with smart, and shudder
     with the cold!
'Tis hush'd! there is a Trance of deepest Silence,
Again! but all that Sound, as of a rushing Crowd,   205
And Groans and tremulous Shudderings, all are over.
And it has other Sounds, and all less deep, less loud!
A Tale of less Affright,
And temper'd with Delight,
As William's self had made the tender Lay—   21c
'Tis of a little Child
Upon a heathy Wild,
Not far from home, but it has lost its way—
And now moans low in utter grief and fear—
And now screams loud, and hopes to make its   215
     Mother hear!

'Tis Midnight! and small Thoughts have I of Sleep.
Full seldom may my Friend such Vigils keep—
O breathe She softly in her gentle Sleep!
Cover her, gentle Sleep! with wings of Healing.
And be this Tempest but a Mountain Birth!   220
May all the Stars hang bright above her Dwelling,
Silent, as though they *watch'd* the sleeping Earth!
Healthful and light, my Darling! may'st thou rise
With clear and chearful Eyes—
And of the same good Tidings to me send!   225
For oh! beloved Friend!
I am not the buoyant Thing I was of yore
When like an own Child, I to Joy belong'd:
For others mourning oft, myself oft sorely wrong'd,
Yet bearing all things then, as if I nothing bore!   23c

Yes, dearest Sara, yes!
There *was* a time when tho' my path was rough,
The Joy within me dallied with Distress;
And all Misfortunes were but as the Stuff
Whence Fancy made me Dreams of Happiness; 235
For Hope grew round me, like the climbing Vine,
And Leaves and Fruitage, not my own, seem'd mine!
But now Ill Tidings bow me down to earth,
Nor care I that they rob me of my Mirth—
But oh! each Visitation 240
Suspends what Nature gave me at my Birth,
My shaping Spirit of Imagination!

I speak not now of those habitual Ills
That wear out Life, when two unequal Minds
Meet in one House and two discordant Wills— 245
    This leaves me, where it finds,
Past Cure, and past Complaint,—a fate austere
Too fix'd and hopeless to partake of Fear!

But thou, dear Sara! (dear indeed thou art,
My Comforter! a Heart within my Heart!) 250
Thou, and the Few, we love, tho' few ye be,
Make up a World of Hopes and Fears for me.
And if Affliction, or distemp'ring Pain,
Or wayward Chance befall you, I complain
Not that I mourn—O Friends, most dear! most true! 255
    Methinks to weep with you
Were better far than to rejoice alone—
But that my coarse domestic Life has known
No Habits of heart-nursing Sympathy,
No Griefs but such as dull and deaden me, 260
No mutual mild Enjoyments of it's own,
No Hopes of its own Vintage, None O! none—
Whence when I mourn'd for you, my Heart might borrow
Fair forms and living Motions for it's Sorrow.
For not to think of what I needs must feel, 265
But to be still and patient all I can;
And haply by abstruse Research to steal
From my own Nature, all the Natural man—
This was my sole Resource, my wisest plan!
And that, which suits a part, infects the whole, 270
And now is almost grown the Temper of my Soul.

My little Children are a Joy, a Love,
　　A good Gift from above!
But what is Bliss, that still calls up a Woe,
　　And makes it doubly keen   275
Compelling me to *feel*, as well as *know*,
What a most blessed Lot mine might have been.
Those little Angel Children (woe is me!)
There have been hours when feeling how they bind
And pluck out the Wing-feathers of my Mind,   280
Turning my Error to Necessity,
I have half-wish'd they never had been born!
That seldom! but sad Thoughts they always bring,
And like the Poet's Philomel, I sing
My Love-song, with my breast against a Thorn.   285
With no unthankful Spirit I confess,
This clinging Grief, too, in it's turn, awakes
That Love, and Father's Joy; but O! it makes
The Love the greater, and the Joy far less.
These Mountains too, these Vales, these Woods,   290
　　these Lakes,
Scenes full of Beauty and of Loftiness
Where all my Life I fondly hop'd to live—
I were sunk low indeed, did they *no* solace give;
But oft I seem to feel, and evermore I fear,
They are not to me now the Things, which once   295
　　they were.

O Sara! we receive but what we give,
And in *our* life alone does Nature live
Our's is her Wedding Garment, our's her Shroud—
And would we aught behold of higher Worth
Than that inanimate cold World allow'd   300
To the poor loveless ever anxious Crowd,
Ah! from the Soul itself must issue forth
A Light, a Glory, and a luminous Cloud
Enveloping the Earth!
And from the Soul itself must there be sent   305
A sweet and potent Voice, of it's own Birth,
Of all sweet Sounds, the Life and Element.
O pure of Heart! thou need'st not ask of me
What this strong music in the Soul may be,
What and wherein it doth exist,
This Light, this Glory, this fair luminous Mist,   310

This beautiful and beauty-making Power!
Joy, innocent Sara! Joy, that ne'er was given
Save to the Pure, and in their purest Hour,
Joy, Sara! is the Spirit and the Power,
That wedding Nature to us gives in Dower   315
   A new Earth and new Heaven,
Undreamt of by the Sensual and the Proud!
Joy is that strong Voice, Joy that luminous Cloud—
   We, we ourselves rejoice!
And thence flows all that charms or ear or sight,   320
All melodies, the Echoes of that Voice,
All Colours a Suffusion of that Light.
Sister and Friend of my devoutest Choice
Thou being innocent and full of love,
And nested with the Darlings of thy Love,   325
And feeling in thy Soul, Heart, Lips, and Arms
Even what the conjugal and mother Dove,
That borrows genial Warmth from those, she warms,
Feels in the thrill'd wings, blessedly outspread—
Thou free'd awhile from Cares and human Dread   330
By the Immenseness of the Good and Fair
   Which thou seest everywhere—
Thus, thus, should'st thou rejoice!
To thee would all things live from Pole to Pole;
Their Life the Eddying of thy living Soul—   335
O dear! O Innocent! O full of Love!
A very Friend! A Sister of my Choice—
O dear, as Light and Impulse from above,
Thus may'st thou ever, evermore rejoice!
                                                                        340

1802   *1937*

DEJECTION: AN ODE

(Final version)

> Late, late yestreen I saw the new Moon,
> With the old Moon in her arms;
> And I fear, I fear, my Master dear!
> We shall have a deadly storm.
> *Ballad of Sir Patrick Spence.*

I

Well! If the Bard was weather-wise, who made
  The grand old ballad of Sir Patrick Spence,
  This night, so tranquil now, will not go hence
Unroused by winds, that ply a busier trade
Than those which mould yon cloud in lazy flakes,   5
Or the dull sobbing draft, that moans and rakes
Upon the strings of this Æolian lute,
    Which better far were mute.
  For lo! the New-moon winter-bright!
  And overspread with phantom light,   10
  (With swimming phantom light o'erspread
  But rimmed and circled by a silver thread)
I see the old Moon in her lap, foretelling
  The coming-on of rain and squally blast.
And oh! that even now the gust were swelling,   15
  And the slant night-shower driving loud and fast!
Those sounds which oft have raised me, whilst they awed,
    And sent my soul abroad,
Might now perhaps their wonted impulse give,
Might startle this dull pain, and make it move and live!   20

II

A grief without a pang, void, dark, and drear,
  A stifled, drowsy, unimpassioned grief,
  Which finds no natural outlet, no relief
    In word, or sigh, or tear—
O Lady! in this wan and heartless mood,   25
To other thoughts by yonder throstle woo'd,
  All this long eve, so balmy and serene,
Have I been gazing on the western sky,
  And its peculiar tint of yellow green:

And still I gaze—and with how blank an eye!   30
And those thin clouds above, in flakes and bars,
That give away their motion to the stars;
Those stars, that glide behind them or between,
Now sparkling, now bedimmed, but always seen:
Yon crescent Moon, as fixed as if it grew   35
In its own cloudless, starless lake of blue;
I see them all so excellently fair,
I see, not feel, how beautiful they are!

III

　　My genial spirits fail;
　　And what can these avail   40
To lift the smothering weight from off my breast?
　　It were a vain endeavour,
　　Though I should gaze for ever
On that green light that lingers in the west:
I may not hope from outward forms to win   45
The passion and the life, whose fountains are within.

Locke

IV

O Lady! we receive but what we give,
And in our life alone does Nature live:
Ours is her wedding garment, ours her shroud!
　　And would we aught behold, of higher worth,   50
Than that inanimate cold world allowed
To the poor loveless ever-anxious crowd,
　　Ah! from the soul itself must issue forth
A light, a glory, a fair luminous cloud
　　　　Enveloping the Earth—   55
And from the soul itself must there be sent
　　A sweet and potent voice, of its own birth,
Of all sweet sounds the life and element!

*camera
obscura*

V

O pure of heart! thou need'st not ask of me
What this strong music in the soul may be!   60
What, and wherein it doth exist,
This light, this glory, this fair luminous mist,
This beautiful and beauty-making power.
　　Joy, virtuous Lady! Joy that ne'er was given,
Save to the pure, and in their purest hour,   65
Life, and Life's effluence, cloud at once and shower,

Joy, Lady! is the spirit and the power,
Which wedding Nature to us gives in dower
　　A new Earth and new Heaven,
Undreamt of by the sensual and the proud—　　　　　70
Joy is the sweet voice, Joy the luminous cloud—
　　　　We in ourselves rejoice!
And thence flows all that charms or ear or sight,
　　All melodies the echoes of that voice,
All colours a suffusion from that light.　　　　　75

VI

There was a time when, though my path was rough,
　　This joy within me dallied with distress,
And all misfortunes were but as the stuff
　　Whence Fancy made me dreams of happiness:
For hope grew round me, like the twining vine,　　　80
And fruits, and foliage, not my own, seemed mine.
But now afflictions bow me down to earth:
Nor care I that they rob me of my mirth;
　　But oh! each visitation
Suspends what nature gave me at my birth,　　　　85
　　My shaping spirit of Imagination.
For not to think of what I needs must feel,
　　But to be still and patient, all I can;
And haply by abstruse research to steal
　　From my own nature all the natural man—　　　90
　　This was my sole resource, my only plan:
Till that which suits a part infects the whole,
And now is almost grown the habit of my soul.

VII

Hence, viper thoughts, that coil around my mind,
　　　　Reality's dark dream!　　　　　　　　　95
I turn from you, and listen to the wind,
　　Which long has raved unnoticed. What a scream
Of agony by torture lengthened out
That lute sent forth! Thou Wind, that rav'st without,
　　Bare crag, or mountain-tairn, or blasted tree,　　100
Or pine-grove whither woodman never clomb,
Or lonely house, long held the witches' home,
　　Methinks were fitter instruments for thee,
Mad Lutanist! who in this month of showers,
Of dark-brown gardens, and of peeping flowers,　　105

Mak'st Devils' yule, with worse than wintry song,
The blossoms, buds, and timorous leaves among.
   Thou Actor, perfect in all tragic sounds!
Thou mighty Poet, e'en to frenzy bold!
     What tell'st thou now about?   110
      'Tis of the rushing of an host in rout,
   With groans, of trampled men, with smarting wounds—
At once they groan with pain, and shudder with the cold!
But hush! there is a pause of deepest silence!
   And all that noise, as of a rushing crowd,   115
With groans, and tremulous shudderings—all is over—
   It tells another tale, with sounds less deep and loud!
     A tale of less affright,
     And tempered with delight,
As Otway's self had framed the tender lay,—   120
      'Tis of a little child
      Upon a lonesome wild,
Not far from home, but she hath lost her way:
And now moans low in bitter grief and fear,
And now screams loud, and hopes to make her mother
        hear.   125

VIII

'Tis midnight, but small thoughts have I of sleep:
Full seldom may my friend such vigils keep!
Visit her, gentle Sleep! with wings of healing,
   And may this storm be but a mountain-birth,
May all the stars hang bright above her dwelling,   130
   Silent as though they watched the sleeping Earth!
     With light heart may she rise,
     Gay fancy, cheerful eyes,
   Joy lift her spirit, joy attune her voice;
To her may all things live, from pole to pole,   135
Their life the eddying of her living soul!
   O simple spirit, guided from above,
Dear Lady! friend devoutest of my choice,
Thus mayest thou ever, evermore rejoice.

1802   *1802*

THE PICTURE

OR THE LOVER'S RESOLUTION

Through weeds and thorns, and matted underwood
I force my way; now climb, and now descend
O'er rocks, or bare or mossy, with wild foot
Crushing the purple whorts; while oft unseen,
Hurrying along the drifted forest-leaves,   5
The scared snake rustles. Onward still I toil,
I know not, ask not whither! A new joy,
Lovely as light, sudden as summer gust,
And gladsome as the first-born of the spring,
Beckons me on, or follows from behind,   10
Playmate, or guide! The master-passion quelled,
I feel that I am free. With dun-red bark
The fir-trees, and the unfrequent slender oak,
Forth from this tangle wild of bush and brake
Soar up, and form a melancholy vault   15
High o'er me, murmuring like a distant sea.

Here Wisdom might resort, and here Remorse;
Here too the love-lorn man, who, sick in soul,
And of this busy human heart aweary,
Worships the spirit of unconscious life   20
In tree or wild-flower.—Gentle lunatic!
If so he might not wholly cease to be,
He would far rather not be that he is;
But would be something that he knows not of,
In winds or waters, or among the rocks!   25

    But hence, fond wretch! breathe not contagion here!
No myrtle-walks are these: these are no groves
Where Love dare loiter! If in sullen mood
He should stray hither, the low stumps shall gore
His dainty feet, the briar and the thorn   30
Make his plumes haggard. Like a wounded bird
Easily caught, ensnare him, O ye Nymphs,
Ye Oreads chaste, ye dusky Dryades;
And you, ye Earth-winds! you that make at morn
The dew-drops quiver on the spiders' webs!   35
You, O ye wingless Airs! that creep between

The rigid stems of heath and bitten furze,
Within whose scanty shade, at summer-noon,
The mother-sheep hath worn a hollow bed—
Ye, that now cool her fleece with dropless damp,   40
Now pant and murmur with her feeding lamb.
Chase, chase him, all ye Fays, and elfin Gnomes!
With prickles sharper than his darts bemock
His little Godship, making him perforce
Creep through a thorn-bush on yon hedgehog's back.   45

    This is my hour of triumph! I can now
With my own fancies play the merry fool,
And laugh away worse folly, being free.
Here will I seat myself, beside this old,
Hollow, and weedy oak, which ivy-twine   50
Clothes as with net-work: here will I couch my limbs,
Close by this river, in this silent shade,
As safe and sacred from the step of man
As an invisible world—unheard, unseen,
And listening only to the pebbly brook   55
That murmurs with a dead, yet tinkling sound;
Or to the bees, that in the neighbouring trunk
Make honey-hoards. The breeze, that visits me,
Was never Love's accomplice, never raised
The tendril ringlets from the maiden's brow,   60
And the blue, delicate veins above her cheek;
Ne'er played the wanton—never half disclosed
The maiden's snowy bosom, scattering thence
Eye-poisons for some love-distempered youth,
Who ne'er henceforth may see an aspen-grove   65
Shiver in sunshine, but his feeble heart
Shall flow away like a dissolving thing.

Sweet breeze! thou only, if I guess aright,
Liftest the feathers of the robin's breast,
That swells its little breast, so full of song,   70
Singing above me, on the mountain-ash.
And thou too, desert stream! no pool of thine,
Though clear as lake in latest summer-eve,
Did e'er reflect the stately virgin's robe,
The face, the form divine, the downcast look   75
Contemplative! Behold! her open palm
Presses her cheek and brow! her elbow rests

On the bare branch of half-uprooted tree,
That leans towards its mirror! Who erewhile
Had from her countenance turned, or looked by stealth,   80
(For Fear is true-love's cruel nurse), he now
With steadfast gaze and unoffending eye,
Worships the watery idol, dreaming hopes
Delicious to the soul, but fleeting, vain,
E'en as that phantom-world on which he gazed,   85
But not unheeded gazed: for see, ah! see,
The sportive tyrant with her left hand plucks
The heads of tall flowers that behind her grow,
Lychnis, and willow-herb, and fox-glove bells:
And suddenly, as one that toys with time,   90
Scatters them on the pool! Then all the charm
Is broken—all that phantom world so fair
Vanishes, and a thousand circlets spread,
And each mis-shape the other. Stay awhile,
Poor youth, who scarcely dar'st lift up thine eyes!   95
The stream will soon renew its smoothness, soon
The visions will return! And lo! he stays:
And soon the fragments dim of lovely forms
Come trembling back, unite, and now once more
The pool becomes a mirror; and behold   100
Each wildflower on the marge inverted there,
And there the half-uprooted tree—but where,
O where the virgin's snowy arm, that leaned
On its bare branch? He turns, and she is gone!
Homeward she steals through many a woodland maze   105
Which he shall seek in vain. Ill-fated youth!
Go, day by day, and waste thy manly prime
In mad love-yearning by the vacant brook,
Till sickly thoughts bewitch thine eyes, and thou
Behold'st her shadow still abiding there,   110
The Naiad of the mirror!
                                    Not to thee,
O wild and desert stream! belongs this tale:
Gloomy and dark art thou—the crowded firs
Spire from thy shores, and stretch across thy bed,
Making thee doleful as a cavern-well: 115
Save when the shy king-fishers build their nest
On thy steep banks, no loves hast thou, wild stream!

     This be my chosen haunt—emancipate

From Passion's dreams, a freeman, and alone,
I rise and trace its devious course. O lead,   120
Lead me to deeper shades and lonelier glooms.
Lo! stealing through the canopy of firs,
How fair the sunshine spots that mossy rock,
Isle of the river, whose disparted waves
Dart off asunder with an angry sound,   125
How soon to re-unite! And see! they meet,
Each in the other lost and found: and see
Placeless, as spirits, one soft water-sun
Throbbing within them, heart at once and eye!
With its soft neighbourhood of filmy clouds,   130
The stains and shadings of forgotten tears,
Dimness o'erswum with lustre! Such the hour
Of deep enjoyment, following love's brief feuds;
And hark, the noise of a near waterfall!
I pass forth into light—I find myself   135
Beneath a weeping birch (most beautiful
Of forest trees, the Lady of the Woods),
Hard by the brink of a tall weedy rock
That overbrows the cataract. How bursts
The landscape on my sight! Two crescent hills   140
Fold in behind each other, and so make
A circular vale, and land-locked, as might seem,
With brook and bridge, and grey stone cottages,
Half hid by rocks and fruit-trees. At my feet,
The whortle-berries are bedewed with spray,   145
Dashed upwards by the furious waterfall.
How solemnly the pendent ivy-mass
Swings in its winnow: All the air is calm.
The smoke from cottage-chimneys, tinged with light,
Rises in columns; from this house alone,   150
Close by the water-fall, the column slants,
And feels its ceaseless breeze. But what is this?
That cottage, with its slanting chimney-smoke,
And close beside its porch a sleeping child,
His dear head pillowed on a sleeping dog—   155
One arm between its fore-legs, and the hand
Holds loosely its small handful of wild-flowers
Unfilletted, and of unequal lengths.
A curious picture, with a master's haste
Sketched on a strip of pinky-silver skin,   160
Peeled from the birchen bark! Divinest maid!

Yon bark her canvas, and those purple berries
Her pencil! See, the juice is scarcely dried
On the fine skin! She has been newly here;
And lo! yon patch of heath has been her couch—   165
The pressure still remains! O blesséd couch!
For this may'st thou flower early, and the sun,
Slanting at eve, rest bright, and linger long
Upon thy purple bells! O Isabel!
Daughter of genius! stateliest of our maids!   170
More beautiful than whom Alcaeus wooed,
The Lesbian woman of immortal song!
O child of genius! stately, beautiful,
And full of love to all, save only me,
And not ungentle e'en to me! My heart,   175
Why beats it thus? Through yonder coppice-wood
Needs must the pathway turn, that leads straightway
On to her father's house. She is alone!
The night draws on—such ways are hard to hit—
And fit it is I should restore this sketch,   180
Dropt unawares, no doubt. Why should I yearn
To keep the relique? 'twill but idly feed
The passion that consumes me. Let me haste!
The picture in my hand which she has left;
She cannot blame me that I followed her: 185
And I may be her guide the long wood through.

1802   *1802*

HYMN BEFORE SUN-RISE IN THE VALE OF CHAMOUNI

Besides the Rivers, Arve and Arveiron, which have their sources in the foot of Mont Blanc, five conspicuous torrents rush down its sides; and within a few paces of the Glaciers, the Gentiana Major grows in immense numbers, with its 'flowers of loveliest blue.'

Hast thou a charm to stay the morning-star
In his steep course? So long he seems to pause
On thy bald awful head, O sovran BLANC,
The Arve and Arveiron at thy base
Rave ceaselessly; but thou, most awful Form!   5
Risest from forth thy silent sea of pines,
How silently! Around thee and above
Deep is the air and dark, substantial, black,
An ebon mass: methinks thou piercest it,
As with a wedge! But when I look again,   10
It is thine own calm home, thy crystal shrine,
Thy habitation from eternity!
O dread and silent Mount! I gazed upon thee,
Till thou, still present to the bodily sense,
Didst vanish from my thought: entranced in prayer   15
I worshipped the Invisible alone.

Yet, like some sweet beguiling melody,
So sweet, we know not we are listening to it,
Thou, the meanwhile, wast blending with my Thought,
Yea, with my Life and Life's own secret joy: 20
Till the dilating Soul, enrapt, transfused,
Into the mighty vision passing—there
As in her natural form, swelled vast to Heaven!

Awake, my soul! not only passive praise
Thou owest! not alone these swelling tears,   25
Mute thanks and secret ecstasy! Awake,
Voice of sweet song! Awake, my heart, awake!
Green vales and icy cliffs, all join my Hymn.

Thou first and chief, sole sovereign of the Vale!
O struggling with the darkness all the night,   30

And visited all night by troops of stars,
Or when they climb the sky or when they sink:
Companion of the morning-star at dawn,
Thyself Earth's rosy star, and of the dawn
Co-herald: wake, O wake, and utter praise!   35
Who sank thy sunless pillars deep in Earth?
Who filled thy countenance with rosy light?
Who made thee parent of perpetual streams?

     And you, ye five wild torrents fiercely glad!
Who called you forth from night and utter death,   40
From dark and icy caverns called you forth,
Down those precipitous, black, jaggéd rocks,
For ever shattered and the same for ever?
Who gave you your invulnerable life,
Your strength, your speed, your fury, and your joy,   45
Unceasing thunder and eternal foam?
And who commanded (and the silence came),
Here let the billows stiffen, and have rest?

     Ye Ice-falls! ye that from the mountain's brow
Adown enormous ravines slope amain—   50
Torrents, methinks, that heard a mighty voice,
And stopped at once amid their maddest plunge!
Motionless torrents! silent cataracts!
Who made you glorious as the Gates of Heaven
Beneath the keen full moon? Who bade the sun   55
Clothe you with rainbows? Who, with living flowers
Of loveliest blue, spread garlands at your feet?—
God! let the torrents, like a shout of nations,
Answer! and let the ice-plains echo, God!
God! sing ye meadow-streams with gladsome voice!   60
Ye pine-groves, with your soft and soul-like sounds!
And they too have a voice, yon piles of snow,
And in their perilous fall shall thunder, God!

     Ye living flowers that skirt the eternal frost!
Ye wild goats sporting round the eagle's nest!   65
Ye eagles, play-mates of the mountain-storm!
Ye lightnings, the dread arrows of the clouds!
Ye signs and wonders of the element!
Utter forth God, and fill the hills with praise!

Thou too, hoar Mount! with thy sky-pointing peaks, 70
Oft from whose feet the avalanche, unheard,
Shoots downward, glittering through the pure serene
Into the depth of clouds, that veil thy breast—
Thou too again, stupendous Mountain! thou
That as I raise my head, awhile bowed low 75
In adoration, upward from thy base
Slow travelling with dim eyes suffused with tears,
Solemnly seemest, like a vapoury cloud,
To rise before me—Rise, O ever rise,
Rise like a cloud of incense from the Earth! 80
Thou kingly Spirit throned among the hills,
Thou dread ambassador from Earth to Heaven,
Great Hierarch! tell thou the silent sky,
And tell the stars, and tell yon rising sun
Earth, with her thousand voices, praises GOD. 85

1802   *1802*

THE PAINS OF SLEEP

Ere on my bed my limbs I lay,
It hath not been my use to pray
With moving lips or bended knees;
But silently, by slow degrees,
My spirit I to Love compose,   5
In humble trust mine eye-lids close,
With reverential resignation,
No wish conceived, no thought exprest,
Only a sense of supplication;
A sense o'er all my soul imprest   10
That I am weak, yet not unblest,
Since in me, round me, every where
Eternal Strength and Wisdom are.

But yester-night I prayed aloud
In anguish and in agony,   15
Up-starting from the fiendish crowd
Of shapes and thoughts that tortured me:
A lurid light, a trampling throng,
Sense of intolerable wrong,
And whom I scorned, those only strong!   20
Thirst of revenge, the powerless will
Still baffled, and yet burning still!
Desire with loathing strangely mixed
On wild or hateful objects fixed.
Fantastic passions! maddening brawl!   25
And shame and terror over all!
Deeds to be hid which were not hid,
Which all confused I could not know
Whether I suffered, or I did:
For all seemed guilt, remorse or woe,   30
My own or others' still the same
Life-stifling fear, soul-stifling shame.

So two nights passed: the night's dismay
Saddened and stunned the coming day.
Sleep, the wide blessing, seemed to me   35
Distemper's worst calamity.
The third night, when my own loud scream

Had waked me from the fiendish dream,
O'ercome with sufferings strange and wild,
I wept as I had been a child; 40
And having thus by tears subdued
My anguish to a milder mood,
Such punishments, I said, were due
To natures deepliest stained with sin,—
For aye entempesting anew 45
The unfathomable hell within,
The horror of their deeds to view,
To know and loathe, yet wish and do!
Such griefs with such men well agree,
But wherefore, wherefore fall on me?
To be beloved is all I need, 50
And whom I love, I love indeed.

1803 *1816*

SONG

FROM *Zapolya*

A sunny shaft did I behold,
  From sky to earth it slanted:
And poised therein a bird so bold—
  Sweet bird, thou wert enchanted!

He sank, he rose, he twinkled, he trolled   5
  Within that shaft of sunny mist;
His eyes of fire, his beak of gold,
  All else of amethyst!

And thus he sang: "Adieu! adieu!
Love's dreams prove seldom true.   10
The blossoms they make no delay:
The sparkling dew-drops will not stay
  Sweet month of May,
    We must away;
      Far, far away!
        To-day! to-day!"

1815   *1817*

HUNTING SONG

FROM *Zapolya*

Up, up! ye dames, and lasses gay!
To the meadows trip away.
'Tis you must tend the flocks this morn,
And scare the small birds from the corn.
    Not a soul at home may stay: 5
      For the shepherds must go
      With lance and bow
    To hunt the wolf in the woods to-day.

Leave the hearth and leave the house
To the cricket and the mouse: 10
Find grannam out a sunny seat,
With babe and lambkin at her feet.
    Not a soul at home may stay:
      For the shepherds must go
      With lance and bow   15
    To hunt the wolf in the woods to-day.

1815   *1817*

LIMBO

.   .   .   .   .
.   .

The sole true Something—This! In Limbo's Den
It frightens Ghosts, as here Ghosts frighten men.
Thence cross'd unseiz'd—and shall some fated hour
Be pulveris'd by Demogorgon's power,
And given as poison to annihilate souls—   5
Even now it shrinks them—they shrink in as Moles
(Nature's mute monks, live mandrakes of the ground)
Creep back from Light—then listen for its sound;—
See but to dread, and dread they know not why—
The natural alien of their negative eye.   10

'Tis a strange place, this Limbo!—not a Place,
Yet name it so;—where Time and weary Space
Fettered from flight, with night-mare sense of fleeing,
Strive for their last crepuscular half-being;—
Lank Space, and scytheless Time with branny hands   15
Barren and soundless as the measuring sands,
Not mark'd by flit of Shades,—unmeaning they
As moonlight on the dial of the day!
But that is lovely—looks like Human Time,
An Old Man with a steady look sublime,   20
That stops his earthly task to watch the skies;
But he is blind—a Statue hath such eyes;—
Yet having moonward turn'd his face by chance,
Gazes the orb with moon-like countenance,
With scant white hairs, with foretop bald and high,   25
He gazes still,—his eyeless face all eye;—
As 'twere an organ full of silent sight,
His whole face seemeth to rejoice in light!
Lip touching lip, all moveless, bust and limb—
He seems to gaze at that which seems to gaze on him!   30
    No such sweet sights doth Limbo den immure,
Wall'd round, and made a spirit-jail secure,
By the mere horror of blank Naught-at-all,
Whose circumambience doth these ghosts enthral.
A lurid thought is growthless, dull Privation,   35
Yet that is but a Purgatory curse;

Hell knows a fear far worse,
A fear—a future state;—'tis positive Negation!

1817   *1893*

SONG

Though veiled in spires of myrtle-wreath,
Love is a sword which cuts its sheath,
And through the clefts itself has made,
We spy the flashes of the blade!
But through the clefts itself has made   5
We likewise see Love's flashing blade,
By rust consumed, or snapt in twain;
And only hilt and stump remain.

1825?   *1828*

EPIGRAMS AND EPITAPHS

The wit of Samuel Taylor Coleridge tended, on the whole, towards the elephantine. Like many scholars raised in the classical tradition, and bred to parse to the last syllable the nice discriminations of Greek and Latin prose and poetry, he loved few things more than a play on words, found the pedantic pun a good deal to his taste, and enjoyed the manipulation of language in order to unlock its ironic contiguities, its curious verbal accidents, its spurious etymological possibilities. At times he could even be vulgar. But it is of some interest on occasion to watch the great man at play, like Dr. Johnson getting dressed with alacrity to go out for a frisk with his closest cronies. Like Dr. Johnson, whom he resembles in a number of respects including his liking for conversation, Coleridge took pride in his ability to turn a phrase or loose a figurative arrow at a likely target. In the epigrams and most of the epitaphs here reproduced, Coleridge is gamboling. His own epitaph, composed late in life, is however the last and most serious petition he ever made in verse.

[HIPPONA]

Hippona lets no silly flush
Disturb her cheek, nought makes her blush.
Whate'er obscenities you say,
She nods and titters frank and gay.
Oh Shame, awake one honest flush
For this,— that nothing makes her blush.

1799?   *1799*

ON A VOLUNTEER SINGER

Swans sing before they die—'twere no bad thing
Should certain persons die before they sing.

1800?   *1800*

ON THE ABOVE [MAJOR DIEMAN]

As long as ere the life-blood's running,
Say, what can stop a Punster's punning?
He dares bepun even thee, O Death!
To *punish* him, Stop thou his breath.

1800?   *1912*

[WHAT IS AN EPIGRAM?]

What is an Epigram? a dwarfish whole,
Its body brevity, and wit its soul.

1802?   *1802*

FOR A HOUSE-DOG'S COLLAR

When thieves come, I bark: when gallants, I am still—
So perform both my Master's and Mistress's will.

1802?   *1802*

EPITAPH ON A MERCENARY MISER

A poor benighted Pedlar knock'd
    One night at Sell-all's door,
The same who saved old Sell-all's life-
    'Twas but the year before!
And Sell-all rose and let him in,   5
    Not utterly unwilling,
But first he bargain'd with the man,
    And took his only shilling!
That night he dreamt he'd given away his pelf,
Walk'd in his sleep, and sleeping hung himself!   10
And now his soul and body rest below;
    And here they say his punishment and fate is
To lie awake and every hour to know
    How many people read his tombstone GRATIS.

1802?   *1802*

EPITAPH ON HIMSELF

Here sleeps at length poor Col. and without screaming,
Who died, as he had always lived, a-dreaming;
Shot dead, while sleeping, by the Gout within,
Alone, and all unknown, at E'nbro' in an Inn

1803   *1848*

PSYCHE

The butterfly the ancient Grecians made
The soul's fair emblem, and its only name-
But of the soul, escaped the slavish trade
Of mortal life!—For in this earthly frame
Ours is the reptile's lot, much toil, much blame,   5
Manifold motions making little speed,
And to deform and kill the things whereon we feed.

1808   *1817*

[EPITAPH]

An excellent adage commands that we should
Relate of the dead that alone which is good;
But of the great Lord who here lies in lead
We know nothing good but that he is dead.

?   *1809*

[WINE]

In Spain, that land of Monks and Apes,
The thing called Wine doth come from grapes,
But on the noble River Rhine,
The thing called Gripes doth come from Wine!

?   *1871*

ON DONNE'S POETRY

With Donne, whose muse on dromedary trots,
Wreathe iron pokers into true-love knots;
Rhyme's sturdy cripple, fancy's maze and clue,
Wit's forge and fire-blast, meaning's press and screw.

1818?   *1836*

REASON

["*Finally, what is Reason? You have often asked me: and
this is my answer*":—]

Whene'er the mist, that stands 'twixt God and thee,
Defecates to a pure transparency,
That intercepts no light and adds no stain—
There Reason is, and then begins her reign!

But alas!   5
    —"tu stesso, ti fai grosso
   Col falso immaginar, sì che non vedi
   Ciò che vedresti, se l'avessi scosso."

                          Dante, *Paradiso*, Canto i.

1830   *1830*

EPITAPH

Stop, Christian passer-by!—Stop, child of God,
And read with gentle breast. Beneath this sod
A poet lies, or that which once seem'd he.
O, lift one thought in prayer for S. T. C.;
That he who many a year with toil of breath   5
Found death in life, may here find life in death!
Mercy for praise—to be forgiven for fame
He ask'd, and hoped, through Christ. Do thou the same!

1833   *1834*

Prose

Prose

FROM BIOGRAPHIA LITERARIA

The book that Coleridge called "Autobiographia Literaria, or sketches of my literary life and opinions" appeared in the summer of 1817. Although the volume is scarcely the imaginative entity which one might have expected from a critic who constantly preached the virtues of organic unity, and although much of it is now of merely historical interest, the best of *Biographia Literaria* is extraordinarily good. Indeed, Stopford Brooke once remarked that while Coleridge's contributions to esthetic theory are small—perhaps no more than a dozen or a score of pages gleaned from the whole—these pages deserve to be printed in letters of pure gold.

It is as well, therefore, to read the *Biographia Literaria* selectively, a principle which has been adopted in the following excerpts. The introductory Chapters I and II display Coleridge's characteristic method and pretty well set the tone for the whole disquisition. Chapter IV begins discussion of the "new school of poetry" with special attention to Wordsworth, a topic to which Coleridge reverts later on. Chapter V offers a short history of associationism, the more valuable in that Coleridge counted heavily on the laws of association in the composition of his own poetry. Chapter XIII, after a heavy beginning, comes round to the famous distinction between primary and secondary Imagination, and discriminates both from Fancy. Chapter XIV, a golden sequence, provides an account of the inception of *Lyrical Ballads* and the (Coleridgean) theory which lay behind that work; while Chapter XVII offers a superb critique of Wordsworth's views on poetic language as set forth in the second (1800) edition of *Lyrical Ballads.*

Something of the book's diversity and formlessness is indicated by a brief account of what happens in the omitted chapters. Chapter III centers, more or less, on the poetry of Southey. Coleridge devotes Chapters VI–VII to a not-very-wholehearted refutation of Hartleian theory; the eighth and ninth chapters provide ranging commentary on the philosophic systems of Descartes, Spinoza, Leibnitz, Bruno, Böhme, Fichte, Schelling, and Kant. Chapters X–XII are digressive and anecdotal in the extreme, as if the contents of a desk drawer had been emptied onto paper. Yet Chapters XV–XVI, on Shakespeare's narrative poems and on the differences between present and past poets are brief but valuable. Chapters XVIII–XXII continue discursively the critique of Wordsworth's poetry, except for XXI, which contains a digression on the *Edinburgh Review* and reasonably kindred matters.

In short, the only real unity to be found in this remarkable volume is that provided by the impress of Coleridge's inimitable critical personality. Yet its very diversity is of such a sort that it should not be missed by any who would truly know what manner of critic he was.

CHAPTER I

The motives of the present work—Reception of the Author's first publication—The discipline of his taste at school—The effect of contemporary writers on youthful minds—Bowles's sonnets—Comparison between the Poets before and since Mr. Pope.

It has been my lot to have had my name introduced, both in conversation, and in print, more frequently than I find it easy to explain, whether I consider the fewness, unimportance, and limited circulation of my writings, or the retirement and distance in which I have lived, both from the literary and political world. Most often it has been connected with some charge which I could not acknowledge, or some principle which I had never entertained. Nevertheless, had I had no other motive or incitement, the reader would not have been troubled with this exculpation. What my additional purposes were, will be seen in the following pages. It will be found, that the least of what I have written concerns myself personally. I have used the narration chiefly for the purpose of giving a continuity to the work, in part for the sake of the miscellaneous reflections suggested to me by particular events, but still more as introductory to the statement of my principles in Politics, Religion, and Philosophy, and an application of the rules, deduced from philosophical principles, to poetry and criticism. But of the objects, which I proposed to myself, it was not the least important to effect, as far as possible, a settlement of the long continued controversy concerning the true nature of poetic diction; and at the same time to define with the utmost impartiality the real *poetic* character of the poet, by whose writings this controversy was first kindled, and has been since fuelled and fanned.

In 1794, when I had barely passed the verge of manhood, I published a small volume of juvenile poems. They were received with a degree of favor, which, young as I was, I well know was bestowed on them not so much for any positive merit, as because they were considered buds of hope, and promises of better works to come. The critics of that day, the most flattering equally with the severest, concurred in objecting to them obscurity, a general turgidness of diction, and a profusion of new coined double epithets. The first is the fault which a writer is the least able to detect in his own compositions: and my mind was not then sufficiently disciplined to receive the authority of others, as a substitute for my own conviction. Satisfied that the thoughts, such as they were, could not have been expressed otherwise, or at least more perspicuously, I forgot to enquire, whether the thoughts themselves did not demand a degree of attention unsuitable to the nature and objects of poetry. This remark however applies chiefly, though not exclusively, to the *Religious Musings*. The remainder of the charge I admitted to its full extent, and not without sincere acknowledgments both to my private and public censors for their friendly admonitions. In the after editions, I pruned the double epithets with no sparing hand, and used my best efforts to tame the swell and glitter both of thought and diction; though in truth, these parasite plants of youthful poetry had insinuated themselves into my longer poems with such intricacy of union, that I was often obliged to omit disentangling the weed, from the fear of snapping the flower. From that period to the date of the present work I have published nothing, with my name, which could by any possibility have come before the board of anonymous criticism. Even the three or four poems, printed with the works of a friend, as far as they were censured at all, were charged with the same or similar defects, though I am persuaded not with equal justice: with an EXCESS OF ORNAMENT, in addition to STRAINED AND ELABORATE DICTION. (*Vide the criticisms on the "Ancient Mariner" in the* Monthly *and* Critical Reviews *of the first volume of the* Lyrical Ballads.) May I be permitted to add, that, even at the early period of my juvenile poems, I saw and admitted the superiority of an austerer and more natural style, with an insight not less clear, than I at present possess. My judgement was stronger, than were my powers of realizing its dictates; and the faults of my language, though indeed partly owing to a wrong choice of subjects, and the desire of giving a poetic colouring to abstract and metaphysical truths, in which a new world then seemed to open upon me, did yet, in part likewise, originate in unfeigned diffidence of my own comparative talent.—During several years of my youth and early manhood, I reverenced those, who had reintroduced the manly simplicity of the Greek, and of our own elder poets, with such enthusiasm as made the hope seem presumptuous of writing successfully in the same style. Perhaps a similar process has happened to others; but my earliest poems were marked by an ease and simplicity, which I have studied, perhaps with inferior success, to impress on my later compositions.

At school I enjoyed the inestimable advantage of a very sensible, though at the same time a very severe master. He early moulded my taste to the preference of Demosthenes to Cicero, of Homer and Theocritus to Virgil, and again of Virgil to Ovid. He habituated me to compare Lucretius, (in such extracts as I then read) Terence, and above all the chaster poems of Catullus, not only with the Roman poets of the, so called, silver and brazen ages; but with even those of the Augustan era: and on grounds of plain sense and universal logic to see and assert the superiority of the former in the truth and nativeness, both of their thoughts and diction. At the same time that we were studying the Greek Tragic Poets, he made us read Shakespeare and Milton as lessons: and they were the lessons too, which required most time and trouble to *bring up*, so as to escape his censure. I learnt from him, that Poetry, even that of the loftiest and, seemingly, that of the wildest odes, had a logic of its own, as severe as that of science; and more difficult, because more subtle, more complex, and dependent on more, and more fugitive causes. In the truly great poets, he would say, there is a reason assignable, not only for every word, but for the position of every word; and I well remember that, availing himself of the synonimes to the Homer of Didymus, he made us attempt to show, with regard to each, *why* it would not have answered the same purpose; and *wherein* consisted the peculiar fitness of the word in the original text.

In our own English compositions, (at least for the last three years of our school education,) he showed no mercy to phrase, metaphor, or image, unsupported by a sound sense, or where the same sense might have been conveyed with equal force and dignity in plainer words. Lute, harp, and lyre, muse, muses, and inspirations, Pegasus, Parnassus, and Hippocrene were all an abomination to him. In fancy I can almost hear him now, exclaiming *"Harp? Harp? Lyre? Pen and ink, boy, you mean! Muse, boy, Muse? Your Nurse's daughter, you mean! Pierian spring? Oh aye! the cloister-pump, I suppose!"* Nay, certain introductions, similes, and examples, were placed by name on a list of interdiction. Among the similes, there was, I remember, that of the Manchineel fruit, as suiting equally well with too many subjects; in which however it yielded the palm at once to the example of Alexander and Clytus, which was equally good and apt, whatever might be the theme. Was it ambition? Alexander and Clytus!—Flattery? Alexander and Clytus!—Anger? Drunkenness? Pride? Friendship? Ingratitude? Late repentance? Still, still Alexander and Clytus! At length, the praises of agriculture having been exemplified in the sagacious observation, that, had Alexander been holding the plough, he would not have run his friend Clytus through with a spear, this tried and serviceable old friend was banished by public edict in secula seculorum. I have sometimes ventured to think, that a list of this kind, or an index expurgatorius of certain well known and ever returning phrases, both introductory, and transitional, including a large assortment of modest egoisms, and flattering illeisms, &c., &c., might be hung up in our law-courts, and both houses of parliament, with great advantage to the public, as an important saving of national time, an incalculable relief to his Majesty's ministers, but above all, as insuring the thanks of country attornies, and their clients, who have private bills to carry through the house.

Be this as it may, there was one custom of our master's, which I cannot pass over in silence, because I think it imitable and worthy of imitation. He would often permit our exercises, under some pretext of want of time, to accumulate, till each lad had four or five to be looked over. Then placing the whole number *abreast* on his desk, he would ask the writer, why this or that sentence might not have found as appropriate a place under this or that other thesis: and if no satisfying answer could be returned, and two faults of the same kind were found in one exercise, the irrevocable verdict followed, the exercise was torn up, and another on the same subject to be produced, in addition to the tasks of the day. The reader will, I trust, excuse this tribute of recollection to a man, whose severities, even now, not seldom furnish the dreams, by which the blind fancy would fain interpret to the mind the painful sensations of distempered sleep; but neither lessen nor dim the deep sense of my moral and intellectual obligations. He sent us to the University excellent Latin and Greek scholars, and tolerable Hebraists. Yet our classical knowledge was the least of the good gifts, which we derived from his zealous and conscientious tutorage. He is now gone to his final reward, full of years, and full of honors, even of those honors, which were dearest to his heart, as gratefully bestowed by that school, and still binding him to the interests of that school, in which he had been himself educated, and to which during his whole life he was a dedicated thing.

From causes, which this is not the place to investigate, no models of past times, however perfect, can have the same vivid effect on the youthful mind, as the productions of contemporary genius. The Discipline, my mind had undergone, "Ne falleretur rotundo sono et versuum cursu, concinnis et floribus; sed ut inspiceret quidnam subesset, quæ sedes, quod firmamentum, quis fundus verbis; an figuræ essent mera ornatura et orationis fucus; vel sanguinis e materiæ ipsius corde effluentis rubor quidam nativus et incalescentia genuina"; removed all obstacles to the appreciation of excellence in style without diminishing my delight. That I was thus prepared for the perusal of Mr. Bowles's sonnets and earlier poems, at once increased *their* influence, and *my* enthusiasm. The great works of past ages seem to a young man things of another race, in respect to which his faculties must remain passive and submiss, even as to the stars and mountains. But the writings of a contemporary, perhaps not many years older than himself, surrounded by the same circumstances, and disciplined by the same manners, possess a *reality* for him, and inspire an actual friendship as of a man for a man. His very admiration is the wind which fans and feeds his hope. The poems themselves assume the properties of flesh and blood. To recite, to extol, to contend for them is but the payment of a debt due to one, who exists to receive it.

There are indeed modes of teaching which have produced, and are producing, youths of a very different stamp; modes of teaching, in comparison with which we have been called on to despise our great public schools, and universities

in whose halls are hung
Armoury of the invincible knights of old—

modes, by which children are to be metamorphosed into prodigies. And prodigies with a vengeance have I known thus produced! Prodigies of self-conceit, shallowness, arrogance, and infidelity! Instead of storing the memory, during the period when the memory is the predominant faculty, with facts for the after exercise of the judgement; and instead of awakening by the noblest models the fond and unmixed LOVE and ADMIRATION, which is the natural and graceful temper of early youth; *these* nurselings of improved pedagogy are taught to dispute and decide; to suspect all, but their own and their lecturer's wisdom; and to hold nothing sacred from their contempt, but their own contemptible arrogance: boy-graduates in all the technicals, and in all the dirty passions and impudence of anonymous criticism. . . .

I had just entered on my seventeenth year, when the sonnets of Mr. Bowles, twenty in number, and just then published in a quarto pamphlet, were first made known and presented to me, by a schoolfellow who had quitted us for the University, and who, during the whole time that he was in our first form (or in our school language a GRECIAN,) had been my patron and protector. I refer to Dr. Middleton, the truly learned, and every way excellent Bishop of Calcutta. . . .

It was a double pleasure to me, and still remains a tender recollection, that I should have received from a friend so revered the first knowledge of a poet, by whose works, year after year, I was so enthusiastically delighted and inspired. My earliest acquaintances will not have forgotten the undisciplined eagerness and impetuous zeal, with which I laboured to make proselytes, not only of my companions, but of all with whom I conversed, of whatever rank, and in whatever place. As my school finances did not permit me to purchase copies, I made, within less than a year and a half, more than forty transcriptions, as the best presents I could offer to those, who had in any way won my regard. And with almost equal delight did I receive the three or four following publications of the same author.

Though I have seen and known enough of mankind to be well aware, that I shall perhaps stand alone in my creed, and that it will be well, if I subject myself to no worse charge than that of singularity; I am not therefore deterred from avowing, that I regard, and ever have regarded the obligations of intellect among the most sacred of the claims of gratitude. A valuable thought, or a particular train of thoughts, gives me additional pleasure, when I can safely refer and attribute it to

the conversation or correspondence of another. My obligations
to Mr. Bowles were indeed important, and for radical good. At
a very premature age, even before my fifteenth year, I had be-
wildered myself in metaphysicks, and in theological controversy.
Nothing else pleased me. History, and particular facts, lost all
interest in my mind. Poetry (though for a school-boy of that
age, I was above par in English versification, and had already
produced two or three compositions which, I may venture to
say, without reference to my age, were somewhat above medi-
ocrity, and which had gained me more credit than the sound,
good sense of my old master was at all pleased with,) poetry
itself, yea, novels and romances, became insipid to me. In my
friendless wanderings on our *leave-days,* (for I was an orphan,
and had scarcely any connections in London,) highly was I
delighted, if any passenger, especially if he were drest in black,
would enter into conversation with me. For I soon found the
means of directing it to my favorite subjects

> Of providence, fore-knowledge, will, and fate,
> Fix'd fate, free will, fore-knowledge absolute,
> And found no end in wandering mazes lost.

This preposterous pursuit was, beyond doubt, injurious both
to my natural powers, and to the progress of my education. It
would perhaps have been destructive, had it been continued;
but from this I was auspiciously withdrawn, partly indeed by
an accidental introduction to an amiable family, chiefly however, by the genial influence of a style of poetry, so tender and
yet so manly, so natural and real, and yet so dignified and
harmonious, as the sonnets &c. of Mr. Bowles! Well were it for
me, perhaps, had I never relapsed into the same mental disease;
if I had continued to pluck the flower and reap the harvest
from the cultivated surface, instead of delving in the unwhole-
some quicksilver mines of metaphysic depths. But if in after
time I have sought a refuge from bodily pain and mismanaged
sensibility in abstruse researches, which exercised the strength
and subtlety of the understanding without awakening the
feelings of the heart; still there was a long and blessed interval,
during which my natural faculties were allowed to expand, and
my original tendencies to develope themselves: my fancy, and
the love of nature, and the sense of beauty in forms and sounds.

The second advantage, which I owe to my early perusal, and
admiration of these poems, (to which let me add, though

known to me at a somewhat later period, the "Lewsdon Hill"
of Mr. CROW) bears more immediately on my present subject.
Among those with whom I conversed, there were, of course, very
many who had formed their taste, and their notions of poetry,
from the writings of Mr. Pope and his followers: or to speak
more generally, in that school of French poetry, condensed and
invigorated by English understanding, which had predominated
from the last century. I was not blind to the merits of the
school, yet as from inexperience of the world, and consequent
want of sympathy with the general subjects of these poems,
they gave me little pleasure, I doubtless undervalued the *kind,*
and with the presumption of youth withheld from its masters
the legitimate name of poets. I saw that the excellence of this
kind consisted in just and acute observations on men and manners in an artificial state of society, as its matter and substance:
and in the logic of wit, conveyed in smooth and strong epigram-
matic couplets, as its *form.* Even when the subject was addressed
to the fancy, or the intellect, as in the *Rape of the Lock,* or the
Essay on Man; nay, when it was a consecutive narration, as in
that astonishing product of matchless talent and ingenuity,
Pope's Translation of the *Iliad;* still a *point* was looked for
at the end of each second line, and the whole was as it were
a sorites, or, if I may exchange a logical for a grammatical
metaphor, a *conjunction disjunctive,* of epigrams. Meantime
the matter and diction seemed to me characterized not so much
by poetic thoughts, as by thoughts *translated* into the language
of poetry. On this last point, I had occasion to render my own
thoughts gradually more and more plain to myself, by frequent
amicable disputes concerning Darwin's BOTANIC GARDEN,
which, for some years, was greatly extolled, not only by the
reading public in general, but even by those, whose genius
and natural robustness of understanding enabled them afterwards to act foremost in dissipating these "painted mists" that
occasionally rise from the marshes at the foot of Parnassus.
During my first Cambridge vacation, I assisted a friend in a
contribution for a literary society in Devonshire: and in this I
remember to have compared Darwin's work to the Russian
palace of ice, glittering, cold and transitory. In the same essay
too, I assigned sundry reasons, chiefly drawn from a comparison
of passages in the Latin poets with the original Greek, from
which they were borrowed, for the preference of Collins' odes to
those of Gray; and of the simile in Shakespeare

> How like a younker or a prodigal,
> The skarfed bark puts from her native bay,
> Hugg'd and embraced by the strumpet wind!
> How like the prodigal doth she return,
> With over-weather'd ribs and ragged sails,
> Lean, rent, and beggar'd by the strumpet wind!

to the imitation in the Bard;

> Fair laughs the morn, and soft the zephyr blows,
> While proudly riding o'er the azure realm
> In gallant trim the gilded vessel goes,
> YOUTH at the prow and PLEASURE at the helm;
> Regardless of the sweeping whirlwind's sway,
> That hush'd in grim repose, expects its evening prey.

(In which, by the bye, the words "realm" and "sway" are rhymes dearly purchased.) I preferred the original on the ground, that in the imitation it depended wholly on the compositor's putting, or not putting, a *small Capital*, both in this, and in many other passages of the same poet, whether the words should be personifications, or mere abstractions. I mention this, because, in referring various lines in Gray to their original in Shakespeare and Milton; and in the clear perception how completely all the propriety was lost in the transfer; I was, at that early period, led to a conjecture, which, many years afterwards was recalled to me from the same thought having been started in conversation, but far more ably, and developed more fully, by Mr. Wordsworth; namely, that this style of poetry, which I have characterised above, as translations of prose thoughts into poetic language, had been kept up by, if it did not wholly arise from, the custom of writing Latin verses, and the great importance attached to these exercises, in our public schools. Whatever might have been the case in the fifteenth century, when the use of the Latin tongue was so general among learned men, that Erasmus is said to have forgotten his native language; yet in the present day it is not to be supposed, that a youth can *think* in Latin, or that he can have any other reliance on the force or fitness of his phrases, but the authority of the writer from whence he has adopted them. Consequently he must first prepare his thoughts, and then pick out, from Virgil, Horace, Ovid, or perhaps more compendiously from his Gradus, halves and quarters of lines, in which to embody them.

I never object to a certain degree of disputatiousness in a

young man from the age of seventeen to that of four or five and twenty, provided I find him always arguing on one side of the question. The controversies, occasioned by my unfeigned zeal for the honor of a favorite contemporary, then known to me only by his works, were of great advantage in the formation and establishment of my taste and critical opinions. In my defence of the lines running into each other, instead of closing at each couplet, and of natural language, neither bookish, nor vulgar, neither redolent of the lamp, nor of the kennel, such as *I will remember thee;* instead of the same thought tricked up in the rag-fair finery of

> ——Thy image on her wing
> Before my FANCY'S eye shall MEMORY bring,

I had continually to adduce the metre and diction of the Greek Poets from Homer to Theocritus inclusive; and still more of our elder English poets from Chaucer to Milton. Nor was this all. But as it was my constant reply to authorities brought against me from later poets of great name, that no authority could avail in opposition to TRUTH, NATURE, LOGIC, and the LAWS of UNIVERSAL GRAMMAR; actuated too by my former passion for metaphysical investigations; I labored at a solid foundation, on which permanently to ground my opinions, in the component faculties of the human mind itself, and their comparative dignity and importance. According to the faculty or source, from which the pleasure given by any poem or passage was derived, I estimated the merit of such poem or passage. As the result of all my reading and meditation, I abstracted two critical aphorisms, deeming them to comprise the conditions and criteria of poetic style; first, that not the poem which we have *read,* but that to which we *return,* with the greatest pleasure, possesses the genuine power, and claims the name of *essential poetry.* Second, that whatever lines can be translated into other words of the same language, without diminution of their significance, either in sense, or association, or in any worthy feeling, are so far vicious in their diction. Be it however observed, that I excluded from the list of worthy feelings, the pleasure derived from mere novelty in the reader, and the desire of exciting wonderment at his powers in the author. Oftentimes since then, in pursuing French tragedies, I have fancied two marks of admiration at the end of each line, as hieroglyphics of the author's own admiration at his own cleverness. Our genuine admiration of a great poet is a continuous *under-current* of feeling; it is everywhere present, but seldom anywhere as a separate excitement. I was wont boldly to affirm, that it would be scarcely more difficult to push a stone out from the pyramids with the bare hand, than to alter a word, or the position of a word, in Milton or Shakespeare, (in their most important works at least,) without making the author say something else, or something worse, than he does say. One great distinction, I appeared to myself to see plainly, between, even the characteristic faults of our elder poets, and the false beauty of the moderns. In the former, from DONNE to COWLEY, we find the most fantastic out-of-the-way thoughts, but in the most pure and genuine mother English; in the latter, the most obvious thoughts, in language the most fantastic and arbitrary. Our faulty elder poets sacrificed the passion and passionate flow of poetry, to the subtleties of intellect, and to the starts of wit; the moderns to the glare and glitter of a perpetual, yet broken and heterogeneous imagery, or rather to an amphibious something, made up, half of image, and half of abstract meaning. The one sacrificed the heart to the head; the other both heart and head to point and drapery.

The reader must make himself acquainted with the general style of composition that was at that time deemed poetry, in order to understand and account for the effect produced on me by the SONNETS, the MONODY at MATLOCK, and the HOPE, of Mr. Bowles; for it is peculiar to original genius to become less and less *striking*, in proportion to its success in improving the taste and judgement of its contemporaries. The poems of WEST, indeed, had the merit of chaste and manly diction, but they were cold, and, if I may so express it, only *dead-coloured;* while in the best of Warton's there is a stiffness, which too often gives them the appearance of imitations from the Greek. Whatever relation therefore of cause or impulse Percy's collection of Ballads may bear to the most *popular* poems of the present day; yet in the more sustained and elevated style, of the then living poets, Bowles and Cowper were, to the best of my knowledge, the first who combined natural thoughts with natural diction; the first who reconciled the heart with the head. . . .

CHAPTER II

Supposed irritability of men of Genius—Brought to the test of facts—Causes and Occasions of the charge—Its Injustice.

I have often thought, that it would be neither uninstructive nor unamusing to analyze, and bring forward into distinct consciousness, that complex feeling, with which readers in general take part against the author, in favor of the critic; and the readiness with which they apply to *all* poets the old sarcasm of Horace upon the scribblers of his time: "Genus irritabile vatum." A debility and dimness of the imaginative power, and a consequent necessity of reliance on the immediate impressions of the senses, do, we well know, render the mind liable to superstition and fanaticism. Having a deficient portion of internal and proper warmth, minds of this class seek in the crowd *circum fana* for a warmth in common, which they do not possess singly. Cold and phlegmatic in their own nature, like damp hay, they heat and inflame by co-acervation; or like bees they become restless and irritable through the increased temperature of collected multitudes. Hence the German word for fanaticism, (such at least was its original import,) is derived from the swarming of bees, namely, Schwärmen, Schwärmerei. The passion being in an inverse proportion to the insight, *that* the more vivid, as *this* the less distinct; anger is the inevitable consequence. The absence of all foundation within their own minds for that, which they yet believe both true and indispensable for their safety and happiness, cannot but produce an uneasy state of feeling, an involuntary sense of fear from which nature has no means of rescuing herself but by anger. Experience informs us that the first defence of weak minds is to recriminate.

> There's no Philosopher but sees,
> That rage and fear are one disease,
> Tho' that may burn, and this may freeze,
> They're both alike the ague.
>
> *Mad Ox.*

But where the ideas are vivid, and there exists an endless power of combining and modifying them, the feelings and affections blend more easily and intimately with these ideal creations than with the objects of the senses; the mind is affected by thoughts, rather than by things; and only then feels the requisite interest even for the most important events and accidents, when by means of meditation they have passed into *thoughts.* The sanity of the mind is between superstition with fanaticism on the one hand, and enthusiasm with indifference and a diseased slowness to action on the other. For the conceptions of the mind may be so vivid and adequate, as to preclude that impulse to the realizing of them, which is strongest and most restless in those, who possess more than mere *talent,* (or the faculty of appropriating and applying the knowledge of others,) yet still want something of the creative, and self-sufficing power of absolute *Genius.* For this reason therefore, they are men of *commanding* genius. While the former rest content between thought and reality, as it were in an intermundium of which their own living spirit supplies the *substance,* and their imagination the ever-varying *form;* the latter must impress their preconceptions on the world without, in order to present them back to their own view with the satisfying degree of clearness, distinctness, and individuality. These in tranquil times are formed to exhibit a perfect poem in palace, or temple, or landscape-garden; or a tale of romance in canals that join sea with sea, or in walls of rock, which, shouldering back the billows, imitate the power, and supply the benevolence of nature to sheltered navies; or in aqueducts that, arching the wide vale from mountain to mountain, give a Palmyra to the desert. But alas! in times of tumult they are the men destined to come forth as the shaping spirit of Ruin, to destroy the wisdom of ages in order to substitute the fancies of a day, and to change kings and kingdoms, as the wind shifts and shapes the clouds. The records of biography seem to confirm this theory. The men of the greatest genius, as far as we can judge from their own works or from the accounts of their contemporaries, appear to have been of calm and tranquil temper in all that related to themselves. In the inward assurance of permanent fame, they seem to have been either indifferent or resigned, with regard to immediate reputation. Through all the works of Chaucer there reigns a chearfulness, a manly hilarity, which makes it almost impossible to doubt a correspondent habit of feeling in the author himself. Shakespeare's evenness and sweetness of temper were almost proverbial in his own age. That this did not arise from ignorance of his own comparative greatness, we have abundant proof in his Sonnets, which could scarcely have been known to Mr. Pope, when he asserted that our great bard "grew immortal in his own despite." . . .

In Spenser, indeed, we trace a mind constitutionally tender, delicate, and, in comparison with his three great compeers, I had almost said, *effeminate;* and this additionally saddened by the unjust persecution of Burleigh, and the severe calamities, which overwhelmed his latter days. These causes have diffused over all his compositions "a melancholy grace," and have drawn forth occasional strains, the more pathetic from their gentleness. But no where do we find the least trace of irritability, and still less of quarrelsome or affected contempt of his censurers.

The same calmness, and even greater self-possession, may be affirmed of Milton, as far as his poems, and poetic character are concerned. He reserved his anger for the enemies of religion, freedom, and his country. My mind is not capable of forming a more august conception, than arises from the contemplation of this great man in his latter days: poor, sick, old, blind, slandered, persecuted,

> Darkness before, and danger's voice behind,—

in an age in which he was as little understood by the party, *for* whom, as by that, *against* whom he had contended; and among men before whom he strode so far as to *dwarf* himself by the distance; yet still listening to the music of his own thoughts, or if additionally cheered, yet cheered only by the prophetic faith of two or three solitary individuals, he did nevertheless

> ————Argue not
> Against Heaven's hand or will, nor bate a jot
> Of heart or hope; but still bore up and steer'd
> Right onward.

From others only do we derive our knowledge that Milton, in his latter day, had his scorners and detractors; and even in his day of youth and hope, that he had enemies would have been unknown to us, had they not been likewise the enemies of his country.

I am well aware, that in advanced stages of literature, when there exist many and excellent models, a high degree of talent, combined with taste and judgement, and employed in works of imagination, will acquire for a man the *name* of a great genius; though even that *analogon* of genius, which, in certain states of society, may even render his writings more popular than the absolute reality could have done, would be sought for in vain in the mind and temper of the author himself. Yet even in instances of this kind, a close examination will often detect, that the irritability, which has been attributed to the author's *genius* as its cause, did really originate in an ill conformation of body, obtuse pain, or constitutional defect of pleasurable sensation. What is charged to the *author,* belongs to the *man,* who would probably have been still more impatient, but for the humanizing influences of the very pursuit, which yet bears the blame of his irritability.

How then are we to explain the easy credence generally given to this charge, if the charge itself be not, as I have endeavoured to show, supported by experience? This seems to me of no very difficult solution. In whatever country literature is widely diffused, there will be many who mistake an intense desire to possess the reputation of poetic genius, for the actual powers, and original tendencies which constitute it. But men, whose dearest wishes are fixed on objects wholly out of their own power, become in all cases more or less impatient and prone to anger. Besides, though it may be paradoxical to assert, that a man can know one thing and believe the opposite, yet assuredly a vain person may have so habitually indulged the wish, and persevered in the attempt, to appear what he is not, as to become himself one of his own proselytes. Still, as this counterfeit and artificial persuasion must differ, even in the person's own feelings, from a real sense of inward power, what can be more natural, than that this difference should betray itself in suspicious and jealous irritability? Even as the flowery sod, which covers a hollow, may be often detected by its shaking and trembling. . . .

For myself, if from my own feelings, or from the less suspicious test of the observations of others, I had been made aware of any literary testiness or jealousy; I trust, that I should have been, however, neither silly nor arrogant enough to have burthened the imperfection on GENIUS. But an experience (and I should not need documents in abundance to prove my words, if I added) a tried experience of twenty years, has taught me, that the original sin of my character consists in a careless indifference to public opinion, and to the attacks of those who influence it; that praise and admiration have become yearly less and less desirable, except as marks of sympathy; nay that it is difficult and distressing to me, to think with any interest even about the sale and profit of my works, important as, in my present circumstances, such considerations must needs be. Yet it never occurred to me to believe or fancy, that the quantum of intellectual power bestowed on me by nature or education was in any way connected with this habit of my feelings; or that it needed any other parents or fosterers than constitutional indolence, aggravated into languor by ill-health; the accumulating embarrassments of procrastination; the mental cowardice, which is the inseparable companion of procrastination, and which makes us anxious to think and converse on any thing rather than on what concerns ourselves; in fine, all those close vexations, whether chargeable on my faults or my fortunes, which leave me but little grief to spare for evils comparatively distant and alien.

Indignation at literary wrongs I leave to men born under happier stars. I cannot *afford it*. But so far from condemning those who can, I deem it a writer's duty, and think it creditable to his heart, to feel and express a resentment proportioned to the grossness of the provocation, and the importance of the object. There is no profession on earth, which requires an attention so early, so long, or so unintermitting as that of poetry; and indeed as that of literary composition in general, if it be such as at all satisfies the demands both of taste and of sound logic. How difficult and delicate a task even the mere mechanism of verse is, may be conjectured from the failure of those, who have attempted poetry late in life. Where then a man has, from his earliest youth, devoted his whole being to an object, which by the admission of all civilized nations in all ages is honorable as a pursuit, and glorious as an attainment; what of all that relates to himself and his family, if only we except his moral character, can have fairer claims to his protection, or more authorize acts of self-defence, than the elaborate products of his intellect and intellectual industry? Prudence itself would command us to *show*, even if defect or diversion of natural sensibility had prevented us from *feeling*, a due interest and qualified anxiety for the offspring and representatives of our nobler being. I know it, alas! by woeful experience! I have laid too many eggs in the hot sands of this wilderness, the world, with ostrich carelessness and ostrich oblivion. The greater part indeed have been trod under foot, and are forgotten; but yet no small number have crept forth into life, some to furnish feathers for the caps of others, and still more to plume the shafts in the quivers of my enemies, of them that unprovoked have lain in wait against my soul.

Sic vos, non vobis, mellificatis, apes!

*   *   *   *   *

CHAPTER IV

The Lyrical Ballads *with the preface—Mr. Wordsworth's earlier poems—On fancy and imagination—The investigation of the distinction important to the fine arts.*

I have wandered far from the object in view, but as I fancied to myself readers who would respect the feelings that had tempted me from the main road; so I dare calculate on not a few, who will warmly sympathize with them. At present it will be sufficient for my purpose, if I have proved, that Mr. Southey's writings no more than my own furnished the original occasion to this fiction of a *new school* of poetry, and to the clamors against its supposed founders and proselytes.

As little do I believe that "Mr. WORDSWORTH's Lyrical Ballads" were in *themselves* the cause. I speak exclusively of the two volumes so entitled. A careful and repeated examination of these confirms me in the belief, that the omission of less than an hundred lines would have precluded nine-tenths of the criticism on this work. I hazard this declaration, however, on the supposition, that the reader has taken it up, as he would have done any other collection of poems purporting to derive their subjects or interests from the incidents of domestic or ordinary life, intermingled with higher strains of meditation which the poet utters in his own person and character; with the proviso, that they were perused without knowledge of, or reference to, the author's peculiar opinions, and that the reader had not had his attention previously directed to those peculiarities. In these, as was actually the case with Mr. Southey's earlier works, the lines and passages which might have offended the general taste, would have been considered as mere inequalities, and attributed to inattention, not to perversity of judgement.

The men of business who had passed their lives chiefly in cities, and who might therefore be expected to derive the highest pleasure from acute notices of men and manners conveyed in easy, yet correct and pointed language; and all those who, reading but little poetry, are most stimulated with that species of it, which seems most distant from prose, would probably have passed by the volume altogether. Others more catholic in their taste, and yet habituated to be most pleased when most excited, would have contented themselves with deciding, that the author had been successful in proportion to the elevation of his style and subject. Not a few perhaps, might by their admiration of "the lines written near Tintern Abbey," those "left upon a Seat under a Yew Tree," the "old Cumberland beggar," and "Ruth," have been gradually led to peruse with kindred feeling the "Brothers," the "Hart leap well," and whatever other poems in that collection may be described as holding a middle place between those written in the highest and those in the humblest style; as for instance between the "Tintern Abbey," and "The Thorn," or the "Simon Lee." Should their taste submit to no further change, and still remain unreconciled to the colloquial phrases, or the imitations of them, that are, more or less, scattered through the class last mentioned; yet even from the small number of the latter, they would have deemed them but an inconsiderable subtraction from the merit of the whole work; or, what is sometimes not unpleasing in the publication of a new writer, as serving to ascertain the natural tendency, and consequently the proper direction of the author's genius.

In the critical remarks, therefore, prefixed and annexed to the *Lyrical Ballads,* I believe that we may safely rest, as the true origin of the unexampled opposition which Mr. Wordsworth's writings have been since doomed to encounter. The humbler passages in the poems themselves were dwelt on and cited to justify the rejection of the theory. What in and for themselves would have been either forgotten or forgiven as imperfections, or at least comparative failures, provoked direct hostility when announced as intentional, as the result of choice after full deliberation. Thus the poems, admitted by *all* as excellent, joined with those which had pleased the far *greater* number, though they formed two-thirds of the whole work, instead of being deemed (as in all right they should have been, even if we take for granted that the reader judged aright) an atonement for the few exceptions, gave wind and fuel to the animosity against both the poems and the poet. In all per-

plexity there is a portion of fear, which predisposes the mind
to anger. Not able to deny that the author possessed both
genius and a powerful intellect, they felt *very positive,* but
were not *quite certain,* that he might not be in the right, and
they themselves in the wrong; an unquiet state of mind, which
seeks alleviation by quarrelling with the occasion of it, and by
wondering at the perverseness of the man, who had written a
long and argumentative essay to persuade them, that

> Fair is foul, and foul is fair;

in other words, that they had been all their lives admiring
without judgement, and were now about to censure without
reason.

That this conjecture is not wide from the mark, I am induced
to believe from the noticeable fact, which I can state on my own
knowledge, that the same general censure should have been
grounded by almost every different person on some different
poem. Among those, whose candour and judgement I estimate
highly, I distinctly remember six who expressed their objections
to the *Lyrical Ballads* almost in the same words, and altogether
to the same purport, at the same time admitting, that several
of the poems had given them great pleasure; and, strange as it
might seem, the composition which one cited as execrable, another quoted as his favorite. I am indeed convinced in my own
mind, that could the same experiment have been tried with
these volumes, as was made in the well known story of the picture, the result would have been the same; the parts which had
been covered by the number of the black spots on the one day,
would be found equally *albo lapide notatæ* on the succeeding.

However this may be, it is assuredly hard and unjust to fix the
attention on a few separate and insulated poems with as much
aversion, as if they had been so many plague-spots on the whole
work, instead of passing them over in silence, as so much blank
paper, or leaves of a bookseller's catalogue; especially, as no
one pretends to have found any immorality or indelicacy; and
the poems, therefore, at the worst, could only be regarded as
so many light or inferior coins in a roleau of gold, not as so
much alloy in a weight of bullion. A friend whose *talents* I
hold in the highest respect, but whose *judgement* and strong
sound sense I have had almost continued occasion to *revere,*
making the usual complaints to me concerning both the style
and subjects of Mr. Wordsworth's minor poems; I admitted

that there were some few of the tales and incidents, in which I could not myself find a sufficient cause for their having been recorded in metre. I mentioned the "Alice Fell" as an instance; "nay," replied my friend with more than usual quickness of manner, "I cannot agree with you *there!* that, I own, *does* seem to me a remarkably pleasing poem." In the *Lyrical Ballads,* (for my experience does not enable me to extend the remark equally unqualified to the two subsequent volumes,) I have heard at different times, and from different individuals every single poem *extolled* and *reprobated,* with the exception of those of loftier kind, which as was before observed, seem to have won universal praise. This fact of itself would have made me diffident in my censures, had not a still stronger ground been furnished by the strange contrast of the heat and long continuance of the opposition, with the nature of the faults stated as justifying it. The seductive faults, the dulcia vitia of Cowley, Marini, or Darwin might reasonably be thought capable of corrupting the public judgement for half a century, and require a twenty years' war, campaign after campaign, in order to dethrone the usurper and re-establish the legitimate taste. But that a downright simpleness, under the affectation of simplicity, prosaic words in feeble metre, silly thoughts in childish phrases, and a preference of mean, degrading, or at best trivial associations and characters, should succeed in forming a school of imitators, a company of almost *religious* admirers, and this too among young men of ardent minds, liberal education, and not

with academic laurels unbestowed;

and that this bare and bald *counterfeit* of poetry, which is characterized as *below* criticism, should for nearly twenty years have well-nigh *engrossed* criticism, as the main, if not the only, *butt* of review, magazine, pamphlet, poem, and paragraph;— this is indeed matter of wonder! . . .

During the last year of my residence at Cambridge, I became acquainted with Mr. Wordsworth's first publication entitled "Descriptive Sketches"; and seldom, if ever, was the emergence of an original poetic genius above the literary horizon more evidently announced. In the form, style, and manner of the whole poem, and in the structure of the particular lines and periods, there is an harshness and acerbity connected and combined with words and images all a-glow, which might recall those products of the vegetable world, where gorgeous blossoms

rise out of the hard and thorny rind and shell, within which the
rich fruit was elaborating. The language was not only peculiar
and strong, but at times knotty and contorted, as by its own
impatient strength; while the novelty and struggling crowd of
images, acting in conjunction with the difficulties of the style,
demanded always a greater closeness of attention, than poetry,
(at all events, than descriptive poetry) has a right to claim.
It not seldom therefore justified the complaint of obscurity. In
the following extract I have sometimes fancied, that I saw an
emblem of the poem itself, and of the author's genius as it was
then displayed.

> 'Tis storm; and hid in mist from hour to hour,
> All day the floods a deepening murmur pour;
> The sky is veiled, and every cheerful sight:
> Dark is the region as with coming night;
> And yet what frequent bursts of overpowering light!
> Triumphant on the bosom of the storm,
> Glances the fire-clad eagle's wheeling form;
> Eastward, in long perspective glittering, shine
> The wood-crowned cliffs that o'er the lake recline;
> Wide o'er the Alps a hundred streams unfold,
> At once to pillars turn'd that flame with gold;
> Behind his sail the peasant strives to shun
> The West, that burns like one dilated sun
> Where in a mighty crucible expire
> The mountains, glowing hot, like coals of fire.

The poetic PSYCHE, in its process to full development, under-
goes as many changes as its Greek name-sake, the butterfly. And
it is remarkable how soon genius clears and purifies itself from
the faults and errors of its earliest products; faults which, in its
earliest compositions, are the more obtrusive and confluent, because as heterogeneous elements, which had only a temporary
use, they constitute the very *ferment*, by which themselves are
carried off. Or we may compare them to some diseases, which
must work on the humours, and be thrown out on the surface,
in order to secure the patient from their future recurrence. I
was in my twenty-fourth year, when I had the happiness of
knowing Mr. Wordsworth personally, and while memory lasts,
I shall hardly forget the sudden effect produced on my mind, by
his recitation of a manuscript poem, which still remains unpublished, but of which the stanza, and tone of style, were the
same as those of the "Female Vagrant," as originally printed in
the first volume of the *Lyrical Ballads*. There was here no mark

of strained thought, or forced diction, no crowd or turbulence of imagery; and, as the poet hath himself well described in his lines "on re-visiting the Wye," manly reflection, and human associations had given both variety, and an additional interest to natural objects, which in the passion and appetite of the first love they had seemed to him neither to need or permit. The occasional obscurities, which had risen from an imperfect controul over the resources of his native language, had almost wholly disappeared, together with that worse defect of arbitrary and illogical phrases, at once hackneyed, and fantastic, which hold so distinguished a place in the *technique* of ordinary poetry, and will, more or less, alloy the earlier poems of the truest genius, unless the attention has been specifically directed to their worthlessness and incongruity. I did not perceive anything particular in the mere style of the poem alluded to during its recitation, except indeed such difference as was not separable from the thought and manner; and the Spenserian stanza, which always, more or less, recalls to the reader's mind Spenser's own style, would doubtless have authorized, in my then opinion, a more frequent descent to the phrases of ordinary life, than could without an ill effect have been hazarded in the heroic couplet. It was not however the freedom from false taste, whether as to common defects, or to those more properly his own, which made so unusual an impression on my feelings immediately, and subsequently on my judgement. It was the union of deep feeling with profound thought; the fine balance of truth in observing, with the imaginative faculty in modifying the objects observed; and above all the original gift of spreading the tone, the *atmosphere,* and with it the depth and height of the ideal world around forms, incidents, and situations, of which, for the common view, custom had bedimmed all the lustre, had dried up the sparkle and the dew drops. "To find no contradiction in the union of old and new; to contemplate the ANCIENT of days and all his works with feelings as fresh, as if all had then sprang forth at the first creative fiat; characterizes the mind that feels the riddle of the world, and may help to unravel it. To carry on the feelings of childhood into the powers of manhood; to combine the child's sense of wonder and novelty with the appearances, which every day for perhaps forty years had rendered familiar;

> With sun and moon and stars throughout the year,
> And man and woman;

this is the character and privilege of genius, and one of the
marks which distinguish genius from talents. And therefore is it
the prime merit of genius and its most unequivocal mode of
manifestation, so to represent familiar objects as to awaken in
the minds of others a kindred feeling concerning them and that
freshness of sensation which is the constant accompaniment of
mental, no less than of bodily, convalescence. Who has not a
thousand times seen snow fall on water? Who has not watched
it with a new feeling, from the time that he has read Burns'
comparison of sensual pleasure

> To snow that falls upon a river
> A moment white—then gone for ever!

In poems, equally as in philosophic disquisitions, genius produces the strongest impressions of novelty, while it rescues the
most admitted truths from the impotence caused by the very
circumstance of their universal admission. Truths of all others
the most awful and mysterious, yet being at the same time of
universal interest, are too often considered as *so* true, that they
lose all the life and efficiency of truth, and lie bed-ridden in the
dormitory of the soul, side by side with the most despised and
exploded errors."—*The Friend*, p. 76, No. 5.

This excellence, which in all Mr. Wordsworth's writings is
more or less predominant, and which constitutes the character
of his mind, I no sooner felt, than I sought to understand.
Repeated meditations led me first to suspect, (and a more intimate analysis of the human faculties, their appropriate marks,
functions, and effects matured my conjecture into full conviction,) that fancy and imagination were two distinct and widely
different faculties, instead of being, according to the general
belief, either two names with one meaning, or, at furthest, the
lower and higher degree of one and the same power. It is not,
I own, easy to conceive a more opposite translation of the
Greek *Phantasia* than the Latin *Imaginatio;* but it is equally
true that in all societies there exists an instinct of growth, a
certain collective, unconscious good sense working progressively
to desynonymize those words originally of the same meaning,
which the conflux of dialects had supplied to the more homo-
geneous languages, as the Greek and German: and which the
same cause, joined with accidents of translation from original
works of different countries, occasion in mixt languages like our
own. The first and most important point to be proved is, that

two conceptions perfectly distinct are confused under one and the same word, and (this done) to appropriate that word exclusively to one meaning, and the synonyme (should there be one) to the other. But if (as will be often the case in the arts and sciences) no synonyme exists, we must either invent or borrow a word. In the present instance the appropriation has already begun, and been legitimated in the derivative adjective: Milton had a highly *imaginative,* Cowley a very *fanciful* mind. If therefore I should succeed in establishing the actual existences of two faculties generally different, the nomenclature would be at once determined. To the faculty by which I had characterized Milton, we should confine the term *imagination;* while the other would be contra-distinguished as *fancy.* Now were it once fully ascertained, that this division is no less grounded in nature, than that of delirium from mania, or Otway's

Lutes, lobsters, seas of milk, and ships of amber,

from Shakespear's

What! have his daughters brought him to this pass?

or from the preceding apostrophe to the elements; the theory of the fine arts, and of poetry in particular, could not, I thought, but derive some additional and important light. It would in its immediate effects furnish a torch of guidance to the philosophical critic; and ultimately to the poet himself. In energetic minds, truth soon changes by domestication into power; and from directing in the discrimination and appraisal of the product, becomes influencive in the production. To admire on principle, is the only way to imitate without loss of originality.

It has been already hinted, that metaphysics and psychology have long been my hobby-horse. But to have a hobby-horse, and to be vain of it, are so commonly found together, that they pass almost for the same. I trust therefore, that there will be more good humour than contempt, in the smile with which the reader chastises my self-complacency, if I confess myself uncertain, whether the satisfaction from the perception of a truth new to myself may not have been rendered more poignant by the conceit, that it would be equally so to the public. There was a time, certainly, in which I took some little credit to myself, in the belief that I had been the first of my countrymen, who had pointed out the diverse meaning of which the two terms were capable, and analyzed the faculties to which they should be appropriated. Mr. W. Taylor's recent volume of synonymes I have not yet seen; but his specification of the terms in question has been clearly shown to be both insufficient and erroneous by Mr. Wordsworth in the Preface added to the late collection of his *Lyrical Ballads and Other Poems.* The explanation which Mr. Wordsworth has himself given will be found to differ from mine, chiefly perhaps, as our objects are different. It could scarcely indeed happen otherwise, from the advantage I have enjoyed of frequent conversation with him on a subject to which a poem of his own first directed my attention, and my conclusions concerning which, he had made more lucid to myself by many happy instances drawn from the operation of natural objects on the mind. But it was Mr. Wordsworth's purpose to consider the influences of fancy and imagination as they are manifested in poetry, and from the different effects to conclude their diversity in kind; while it is my object to investigate the seminal principle, and then from the kind to deduce the degree. My friend has drawn a masterly sketch of the branches with their *poetic fruitage.* I wish to add the trunk, and even the roots as far as they lift themselves above ground, and are visible to the naked eye of our common consciousness.

Yet even in this attempt I am aware, that I shall be obliged to draw more largely on the reader's attention, than so immethodical a miscellany can authorize; when in such a work (the *Ecclesiastical Polity*) of such a mind as Hooker's, the judicious author, though no less admirable for the perspicuity than for the port and dignity of his language; and though he wrote for men of learning in a learned age; saw nevertheless occasion to anticipate and guard against "complaints of obscurity," as often as he was about to trace his subject "to the highest well-spring and fountain." Which, (continues he) "because men are not accustomed to, the pains we take are more needful a great deal, than acceptable; and the matters we handle, seem by reason of newness (till the mind grow better acquainted with them) dark and intricate." I would gladly therefore spare both myself and others this labor, if I knew how without it to present an intelligible statement of my poetic creed; not as my *opinions,* which weigh for nothing, but as deductions from established premises conveyed in such a form, as is calculated either to effect a fundamental conviction, or to receive a fundamental confutation. If I may dare once more adopt the words of Hooker, "they, unto whom we shall seem tedious, are in no wise injured by us, because it is in their own hands to spare that labor, which they are not willing to endure." Those at least, let me be permitted to add, who have taken so much pains to render me ridiculous for a perversion of taste, and have supported the charge by attributing strange notions to me on no other authority than their own conjectures, owe it to themselves as well as to me not to refuse their attention to my own statement of the theory, which I *do* acknowledge; or shrink from the trouble of examining the grounds on which I rest it, or the arguments which I offer in its justification.

CHAPTER V

On the law of association—Its history traced from Aristotle to Hartley.

There have been men in all ages, who have been impelled as by an instinct to propose their own nature as a problem, and who devote their attempts to its solution. The first step was to construct a table of distinctions, which they seem to have formed on the principle of the absence or presence of the WILL. Our various sensations, perceptions, and movements were classed as active or passive, or as media partaking of both. A still finer distinction was soon established between the voluntary and the spontaneous. In our perceptions we seem to ourselves merely passive to an external power, whether as a mirror reflecting the landscape, or as a blank canvas on which some unknown hand paints it. For it is worthy of notice, that the latter, or the system of idealism may be traced to sources equally remote with the former, or materialism; and Berkeley can boast an ancestry at least as venerable as Gassendi or Hobbs. These conjectures, however, concerning the mode in which our perceptions originated, could not alter the natural difference of *things* and *thoughts*. In the former, the cause appeared wholly external, while in the latter, sometimes our will interfered as the producing or determining cause, and sometimes our nature seemed to act by a mechanism of its own, without any conscious effort of the will, or even against it. Our inward experiences were thus arranged in three separate classes, the passive sense, or what the school-men call the merely receptive quality of the mind; the voluntary; and the spontaneous, which holds the middle place between both. But it is not in human nature to meditate on any mode of action, without enquiring after the law that governs it; and in the explanation of the spontaneous movements of our being, the metaphysician took the lead of the anatomist and natural philosopher. In Egypt, Palestine, Greece, and India the analysis of the mind had reached its noon and manhood, while experimental research was still in its dawn and infancy. For many, very many centuries, it has been difficult to advance a new truth, or even a new error, in the philosophy of the intellect or morals. With regard, however, to the laws that direct the spontaneous movements of thought and the principle of their intellectual mechanism there exists, it has been asserted, an important exception most honorable to the moderns, and in the merit of which our own country claims the largest share. Sir James Mackintosh, (who amid the variety of his talents and attainments is not of less repute for the depth and accuracy of his philosophical enquiries than for the eloquence with which he is said to render their most difficult results perspicuous, and the driest attractive,) affirmed in the lectures, delivered by him in Lincoln's Inn Hall, that the law of association as established in the contemporaneity of the original impressions, formed the basis of all true psychology; and any ontological or metaphysical science, not contained in such (i. e. empirical) psychology, was but a web of abstractions and generalizations. Of this prolific truth, of this great fundamental law, he declared Hobbs to have been the original *discoverer*, while its full application to the whole intellectual system we owed to David Hartley; who stood in the same relation to Hobbs as Newton to Kepler; the law of association being that to the mind, which gravitation is to matter.

Of the former clause in this assertion, as it respects the comparative merits of the ancient metaphysicians, including their commentators, the school-men, and of the modern French and British philosophers from Hobbs to Hume, Hartley, and Condillac, this is not the place to speak. So wide indeed is the chasm between this gentleman's philosophical creed and mine, that so far from being able to join hands, we could scarcely make our voices intelligible to each other: and to *bridge* it over, would require more time, skill, and power than I believe myself to possess. But the latter clause involves for the greater part a mere question of fact and history, and the accuracy of the statement is to be tried by documents rather than reasoning.

First, then, I deny Hobbs's claim in toto: for he had been

anticipated by Des Cartes, whose work "De Methodo," preceded Hobbs's "De Natura Humana," by more than a year. But what is of much more importance, Hobbs builds nothing on the principle which he had announced. He does not even announce it, as differing in any respect from the general laws of material motion and impact: nor was it, indeed, possible for him so to do, compatibly with his system, which was exclusively material and mechanical. Far otherwise is it with Des Cartes; greatly as he too in his after writings (and still more egregiously his followers De la Forge, and others) obscured the truth by their attempts to explain it on the theory of nervous fluids, and material configurations. But, in his interesting work, "De Methodo," Des Cartes relates the circumstance which first led him to meditate on this subject, and which since then has been often noticed and employed as an instance and illustration of the law. A child who with its eyes bandaged had lost several of his fingers by amputation, continued to complain for many days successively of pains, now in this joint and now in that, of the very fingers which had been cut off. Des Cartes was led by this incident to reflect on the uncertainty with which we attribute any particular place to any inward pain or uneasiness, and proceeded after long consideration to establish it as a general law; that contemporaneous impressions, whether images or sensations, recall each other mechanically. On this principle, as a ground work, he built up the whole system of human language, as one continued process of association. He showed in what sense not only general terms, but generic images (under the name of abstract ideas) actually existed, and in what consists their nature and power. As one word may become the general exponent of many, so by association a simple image may represent a whole class. But in truth Hobbs himself makes no claims to any discovery, and introduces this law of association, or (in his own language) *discursûs mentalis*, as an admitted fact, in the *solution* alone of which, this by causes purely physiological, he arrogates any originality. His system is briefly this; whenever the senses are impinged on by external objects, whether by the rays of light reflected from them, or by effluxes of their finer particles, there results a correspondent motion of the innermost and subtlest organs. This motion constitutes a *representation,* and there remains an *impression* of the same, or a certain disposition to repeat the same motion. Whenever we feel several objects at the same time, the *impressions* that are left, (or in the language of Mr. Hume, the *ideas,*) are linked together. Whenever therefore any one of the movements, which constitute a complex impression, is renewed through the senses, the others succeed mechanically. It follows of necessity therefore that Hobbs as well as Hartley and all others who derive association from the connection and interdependence of the supposed matter, the movements of which constitute our thoughts, *must* have reduced all its forms to the one law of time. But even the merit of announcing this law with philosophic precision cannot be fairly conceded to him. For the objects of any two ideas need not have co-existed in the same sensation in order to become mutually associable. The same result will follow when one only of the two ideas has been represented by the senses, and the other by the memory.

Long however before either Hobbs or Des Cartes the law of association had been defined, and its important functions set forth by Melanchthon, Ammerbach, and Ludovicus Vives; more especially by the last. Phantasia, it is to be noticed, is employed by Vives to express the mental power of comprehension, or the *active* function of the mind; and imaginatio for the receptivity (vis receptiva) of impressions, or for the *passive* perception. The power of combination he appropriates to the former: "quæ singula et simpliciter acceperat imaginatio, ea conjungit et disjungit phantasia." And the law by which the thoughts are spontaneously presented follows thus: "quæ simul sunt a phantasia comprehensa, si alterutrum occurrat, solet secum alterum repræsentare." To time therefore he subordinates all the other exciting causes of association. The soul proceeds "a causa ad effectum, ab hoc ad instrumentum, a parte ad totum"; thence to the place, from place to person, and from this to whatever preceded or followed, all as being parts of a total impression, each of which may recall the other. The apparent springs "Saltus vel transitus etiam longissimos," he explains by the same thought having been a component part of two or more total impressions. Thus "ex Scipione venio in cogitationem potentiæ Turcicæ, propter victorias ejus in eâ parte Asiæ in qua regnabat Antiochus."

But from Vives I pass at once to the source of his doctrines, and (as far as we can judge from the remains yet extant of Greek philosophy) as to the first, so to the fullest and most perfect enunciation of the associative principle, viz. to the writings of Aristotle; and of these in particular to the books "De Anima," "De Memoria," and that which is entitled in the old translations "Parva Naturalia." In as much as later writers have either deviated from, or added to his doctrines, they appear to me to have introduced either error or groundless supposition.

In the first place it is to be observed, that Aristotle's positions on this subject are unmixed with fiction. The wise Stagyrite speaks of no successive particles propagating motion like billiard balls, (as Hobbs) ; nor of nervous or animal spirits, where inanimate and irrational solids are thawed down, and distilled, or filtrated by ascension, into living and intelligent fluids, that etch and re-etch engravings on the brain, (as the followers of Des Cartes, and the humoral pathologists in general) ; nor of an oscillating ether which was to effect the same service for the nerves of the brain considered as solid fibres, as the animal spirits perform for them under the notion of hollow tubes (as *Hartley* teaches) —nor finally, (with yet more recent dreamers) of chemical compositions by elective affinity, or of an electric light at once the immediate object and the ultimate organ of inward vision, which rises to the brain like an Aurora Borealis, and there disporting in various shapes (as the balance of plus and minus, or negative and positive, is destroyed or re-established) images out both past and present. Aristotle delivers a just *theory* without pretending to an *hypothesis;* or in other words a comprehensive survey of the different facts, and of their relations to each other without *supposition,* i.e. a fact *placed under* a number of facts, as their common support and explanation; though in the majority of instances these hypotheses or suppositions better deserve the name of ὑποποιήσεις, or *suffictions*. He uses indeed the word κινήσεις, to express what we call representations or ideas, but he carefully distinguishes them from material motion, designating the latter always by annexing the words ἐν τόπῳ, or κατὰ τόπον. On the contrary, in his treatise "De Anima," he excludes place and motion from all the operations of thought, whether representations or volitions, as attributes utterly and absurdly heterogeneous.

The *general law* of association, or, more accurately, the *common condition* under which all exciting causes act, and in which they may be generalized, according to Aristotle is this. Ideas by having been together acquire a power of recalling each other; or every partial representation awakes the total representation of which it had been a part. In the practical determination of this common principle to particular recollections, he admits five agents or occasioning causes: 1st, connection in time, whether simultaneous, preceding, or successive; 2nd, vicinity or connection in space; 3rd, interdependence or necessary connection, as cause and effect; 4th, likeness; and 5th, contrast. As an additional solution of the occasional seeming chasms in the continuity of reproduction he proves, that movements or ideas possessing one or the other of these five characters had passed through the mind as intermediate links, sufficiently clear to recall other parts of the same total impressions with which they had co-existed, though not vivid enough to excite that degree of attention which is requisite for distinct recollection, or as we may aptly express it, *after-consciousness*. In association then consists the whole mechanism of the reproduction of impressions, in the Aristotelian Psychology. It is the universal law of the *passive* fancy and *mechanical* memory; that which supplies to all other faculties their objects, to all thought the elements of its materials.

In consulting the excellent commentary of St. Thomas Aquinas on the Parva Naturalia of Aristotle, I was struck at once with its close resemblance to Hume's Essay on association. The main thoughts were the same in both, the *order* of the thoughts was the same, and even the illustrations differed only by Hume's occasional substitution of more modern examples. I mentioned the circumstances to several of my literary acquaintances, who admitted the closeness of the resemblance, and that it seemed too great to be explained by mere coincidence; but they thought it improbable that Hume should have held the pages of the angelic Doctor worth turning over. But some time after Mr. Payne, of the King's mews, shewed Sir James Mackintosh some odd volumes of St. Thomas Aquinas, partly perhaps from having heard that Sir James (then Mr.) Mackintosh had in his lectures passed a high encomium on this canonized philosopher, but chiefly from the fact, that the volumes had belonged to Mr. Hume, and had here and there marginal marks and notes of reference in his own hand writing. Among these volumes was that which contains the *Parva Naturalia,* in the old Latin version, swathed and swaddled in the commentary afore mentioned!

It remains then for me, first to state wherein Hartley differs from Aristotle; then, to exhibit the grounds of my conviction, that he differed only to err; and next as the result, to shew, by what influences of the choice and judgement the associative power becomes either memory or fancy; and, in conclusion, to appropriate the remaining offices of the mind to the reason,

and the imagination. With my best efforts to be as perspicuous
as the nature of language will permit on such a subject, I
earnestly solicit the good wishes and friendly patience of my
readers, while I thus go "sounding on my dim and perilous
way."

*   *   *   *   *   *

CHAPTER XIII

On the imagination, or esemplastic power.

O Adam, One Almighty is, from whom
All things proceed, and up to him return,
If not depraved from good: created all
Such to perfection, one first nature all,
Indued with various forms, various degrees
Of substance, and, in things that live, of life;
But more refin'd, more spirituous and pure,
As nearer to him plac'd, or nearer tending,
Each in their several active spheres assign'd,
Till body up to spirit work, in bounds
Proportion'd to each kind. So from the root
Springs lighter the green stalk, from thence the leaves
More airy: last the bright consummate flower
Spirits odorous breathes. Flowers and their fruit,
Man's nourishment, by gradual scale sublim'd,
To *vital* spirits aspire: to *animal:*
To *intellectual!*—give both life and sense,
Fancy and understanding; whence the soul
REASON receives, and reason is her *being,*
Discursive or intuitive.

                                        Paradise Lost, Book v.

*   *   *   *   *   *

. . . Now the transcendental philosophy demands; first, that
two forces should be conceived which counteract each other by
their essential nature; not only not in consequence of the
accidental direction of each, but as prior to all direction, nay,
as the primary forces from which the conditions of all possible

directions are derivative and deducible: secondly, that these forces should be assumed to be both alike infinite, both alike indestructible. The problem will then be to discover the result or product of two such forces, as distinguished from the result of those forces which are finite, and derive their difference solely from the circumstance of their direction. When we have formed a scheme or outline of these two different kinds of force, and of their different results by the process of discursive reasoning, it will then remain for us to elevate the Thesis from notional to actual, by contemplating intuitively this one power with its two inherent indestructible yet counteracting forces, and the results or generations to which their inter-penetration gives existence, in the living principle and in the process of our own self-consciousness. By what instrument this is possible the solution itself will discover, at the same time that it will reveal to and for whom it is possible. Non omnia possumus omnes. There is a philosophic no less than a poetic genius, which is differenced from the highest perfection of talent, not by degree but by kind.

The counteraction then of the two assumed forces does not depend on their meeting from opposite directions; the power which acts in them is indestructible; it is therefore inexhaustibly re-ebullient; and as something must be the result of these two forces, both alike infinite, and both alike indestructible; and as rest or neutralization cannot be this result; no other conception is possible, but that the product must be a tertium aliquid, or finite generation. Consequently this conception is necessary. Now this tertium aliquid can be no other than an inter-penetration of the counteracting powers, partaking of both. . . .

The IMAGINATION then, I consider either as primary, or secondary. The primary IMAGINATION I hold to be the living Power and prime Agent of all human Perception, and as a repetition in the finite mind of the eternal act of creation in the infinite I AM. The secondary Imagination I consider as an echo of the former, co-existing with the conscious will, yet still as identical with the primary in the *kind* of its agency, and differing only in *degree,* and in the *mode* of its operation. It dissolves, diffuses, dissipates, in order to re-create; or where this process is rendered impossible, yet still at all events it struggles to idealize and to unify. It is essentially *vital,* even as all objects (*as* objects) are essentially fixed and dead.

FANCY, on the contrary, has no other counters to play with,

but fixities and definites. The Fancy is indeed no other than a mode of Memory emancipated from the order of time and space; while it is blended with, and modified by that empirical phenomenon of the will, which we express by the word CHOICE. But equally with the ordinary memory the Fancy must receive all its materials ready made from the law of association. . . .

CHAPTER XIV

Occasion of the Lyrical Ballads, *and the objects originally proposed—Preface to the second edition—The ensuing controversy, its causes and acrimony—Philosophic definitions of a poem and poetry with scholia.*

During the first year that Mr. Wordsworth and I were neighbours, our conversations turned frequently on the two cardinal points of poetry, the power of exciting the sympathy of the reader by a faithful adherence to the truth of nature, and the power of giving the interest of novelty by the modifying colors of imagination. The sudden charm, which accidents of light and shade, which moon-light or sun-set diffused over a known and familiar landscape, appeared to represent the practicability of combining both. These are the poetry of nature. The thought suggested itself (to which of us I do not recollect) that a series of poems might be composed of two sorts. In the one, the incidents and agents were to be, in part at least, supernatural; and the excellence aimed at was to consist in the interesting of the affections by the dramatic truth of such emotions, as would naturally accompany such situations, supposing them real. And real in *this* sense they have been to every human being who, from whatever source of delusion, has at any time believed himself under supernatural agency. For the second class, subjects were to be chosen from ordinary life; the characters and incidents were to be such, as will be found in every village and its vicinity, where there is a meditative and feeling mind to seek after them, or to notice them, when they present themselves.

In this idea originated the plan of the *Lyrical Ballads;* in which it was agreed, that my endeavours should be directed to persons and characters supernatural, or at least romantic; yet so

as to transfer from our inward nature a human interest and a
semblance of truth sufficient to procure for these shadows of
imagination that willing suspension of disbelief for the moment, which constitutes poetic faith. Mr. Wordsworth, on the
other hand, was to propose to himself as his object, to give the
charm of novelty to things of every day, and to excite a feeling
analogous to the supernatural, by awakening the mind's attention from the lethargy of custom, and directing it to the
loveliness and the wonders of the world before us; an inexhaustible treasure, but for which, in consequence of the film
of familiarity and selfish solicitude we have eyes, yet see not,
ears that hear not, and hearts that neither feel nor understand.

With this view I wrote "The Ancient Mariner," and was
preparing among other poems, "The Dark Ladie," and the
"Christabel," in which I should have more nearly realized my
ideal, than I had done in my first attempt. But Mr. Wordsworth's industry had proved so much more successful, and the
number of his poems so much greater, that my compositions,
instead of forming a balance, appeared rather an interpolation
of heterogeneous matter. Mr. Wordsworth added two or three
poems written in his own character, in the impassioned, lofty,
and sustained diction, which is characteristic of his genius. In
this form the *Lyrical Ballads* were published; and were presented by him, as an *experiment,* whether subjects, which from
their nature rejected the usual ornaments and extra-colloquial
style of poems in general, might not be so managed in the
language of ordinary life as to produce the pleasureable interest,
which it is the peculiar business of poetry to impart. To the
second edition he added a preface of considerable length; in
which, notwithstanding some passages of apparently a contrary
import, he was understood to contend for the extension of this
style to poetry of all kinds, and to reject as vicious and inde-
fensible all phrases and forms of style that were not included
in what he (unfortunately, I think, adopting an equivocal expression) called the language of *real* life. From this preface,
prefixed to poems in which it was impossible to deny the presence of original genius, however mistaken its direction might
be deemed, arose the whole long-continued controversy. For
from the conjunction of perceived power with supposed heresy
I explain the inveteracy and in some instances, I grieve to say,
the acrimonious passions, with which the controversy has been
conducted by the assailants.

Had Mr. Wordsworth's poems been the silly, the childish

things, which they were for a long time described as being; had
they been really distinguished from the compositions of other
poets merely by meanness of language and inanity of thought;
had they indeed contained nothing more than what is found
in the parodies and pretended imitations of them; they must
have sunk at once, a dead weight, into the slough of oblivion,
and have dragged the preface along with them. But year after
year increased the number of Mr. Wordsworth's admirers. They
were found too not in the lower classes of the reading public,
but chiefly among young men of strong sensibility and meditative minds; and their admiration (inflamed perhaps in some
degree by opposition) was distinguished by its intensity, I
might almost say, by its *religious* fervor. These facts, and the
intellectual energy of the author, which was more or less consciously felt, where it was outwardly and even boisterously
denied, meeting with sentiments of aversion to his opinions,
and of alarm at their consequences, produced an eddy of
criticism, which would of itself have borne up the poems by the
violence, with which it whirled them round and round. With
many parts of this preface, in the sense attributed to them, and
which the words undoubtedly seem to authorize, I never concurred; but on the contrary objected to them as erroneous in
principle, and as contradictory (in appearance at least) both to
other parts of the same preface, and to the author's own practice in the greater number of the poems themselves. Mr. Wordsworth in his recent collection has, I find, degraded this
prefatory disquisition to the end of his second volume, to be
read or not at the reader's choice. But he has not, as far as I
can discover, announced any change in his poetic creed. At all
events, considering it as the source of a controversy, in which
I have been honored more than I deserve by the frequent conjunction of my name with his, I think it expedient to declare
once for all, in what points I coincide with his opinions, and
in what points I altogether differ. But in order to render myself
intelligible I must previously, in as few words as possible, explain my ideas, first, of a POEM; and secondly, of POETRY itself,
in *kind*, and in *essence*.

The office of philosophical *disquisition* consists in just *distinction;* while it is the privilege of the philosopher to preserve
himself constantly aware, that distinction is not division. In
order to obtain adequate notions of any truth, we must intel-
lectually separate its distinguishable parts; and this is the technical *process* of philosophy. But having so done, we must then

restore them in our conceptions to the unity, in which they actually co-exist; and this is the *result* of philosophy. A poem contains the same elements as a prose composition; the difference therefore must consist in a different combination of them, in consequence of a different object being proposed. According to the difference of the object will be the difference of the combination. It is possible, that the object may be merely to facilitate the recollection of any given facts or observations by artificial arrangement; and the composition will be a poem, merely because it is distinguished from prose by metre, or by rhyme, or by both conjointly. In this, the lowest sense, a man might attribute the name of a poem to the well-known enumeration of the days in the several months;

> Thirty days hath September,
> April, June, and November, &c.

and others of the same class and purpose. And as a particular pleasure is found in anticipating the recurrence of sounds and quantities, all compositions that have this charm super-added, whatever be their contents, *may* be entitled poems.

So much for the superficial *form*. A difference of object and contents supplies an additional ground of distinction. The immediate purpose may be the communication of truths; either of truth absolute and demonstrable, as in works of science; or of facts experienced and recorded, as in history. Pleasure, and that of the highest and most permanent kind, may *result* from the *attainment* of the end; but it is not itself the immediate end. In other works the communication of pleasure may be the immediate purpose; and though truth, either moral or intellectual, ought to be the *ultimate* end, yet this will distinguish the character of the author, not the class to which the work belongs. Blest indeed is that state of society, in which the immediate purpose would be baffled by the perversion of the proper ultimate end; in which no charm of diction or imagery could exempt the Bathyllus even of an Anacreon, or the Alexis of Virgil, from disgust and aversion!

But the communication of pleasure may be the immediate object of a work not metrically composed; and that object may have been in a high degree attained, as in novels and romances. Would then the mere superaddition of metre, with or without rhyme, entitle *these* to the name of poems? The answer is, that nothing can permanently please, which does not contain in itself the reason why it is so, and not otherwise. If metre be superadded, all other parts must be made consonant with it. They must be such, as to justify the perpetual and distinct attention to each part, which an exact correspondent recurrence of accent and sound are calculated to excite. The final definition then, so deduced, may be thus worded. A poem is that species of composition, which is opposed to works of science, by proposing for its *immediate* object pleasure, not truth; and from all other species (having *this* object in common with it) it is discriminated by proposing to itself such delight from the *whole*, as is compatible with a distinct gratification from each component *part*.

Controversy is not seldom excited in consequence of the disputants attaching each a different meaning to the same word; and in few instances has this been more striking, than in disputes concerning the present subject. If a man chooses to call every composition a poem, which is rhyme, or measure, or both, I must leave his opinion uncontroverted. This distinction is at least competent to characterize the writer's intention. If it were subjoined, that the whole is likewise entertaining or affecting, as a tale, or as a series of interesting reflections, I of course admit this as another fit ingredient of a poem, and an additional merit. But if the definition sought for be that of a *legitimate* poem, I answer, it must be one, the parts of which mutually support and explain each other; all in their proportion harmonizing with, and supporting the purpose and known influences of metrical arrangement. The philosophic critics of all ages coincide with the ultimate judgement of all countries, in equally denying the praises of a just poem, on the one hand, to a series of striking lines or distiches, each of which, absorbing the whole attention of the reader to itself, disjoins it from its context, and makes it a separate whole, instead of an harmonizing part; and on the other hand, to an unsustained composition, from which the reader collects rapidly the general result, unattracted by the component parts. The reader should be carried forward, not merely or chiefly by the mechanical impulse of curiosity, or by a restless desire to arrive at the final solution; but by the pleasureable activity of mind excited by the attractions of the journey itself. Like the motion of a serpent, which the Egyptians made the emblem of intellectual power; or like the path of sound through the air; at every step he pauses and half recedes, and from the retrogressive movement collects the force which again carries him onward. "Præcipitandus est *liber* spiritus," says Petronius Arbiter most happily. The epithet, *liber,* here balances the preceding verb; and it is not easy to conceive more meaning condensed in fewer words.

But if this should be admitted as a satisfactory character of a poem, we have still to seek for a definition of poetry. The writings of PLATO, and Bishop TAYLOR, and the *Theoria Sacra* of BURNET, furnish undeniable proofs that poetry of the highest kind may exist without metre, and even without the contradistinguishing objects of a poem. The first chapter of Isaiah (indeed a very large portion of the whole book) is poetry in the most emphatic sense; yet it would be not less irrational than strange to assert, that pleasure, and not truth, was the immediate object of the prophet. In short, whatever *specific* import we attach to the word, poetry, there will be found involved in it, as a necessary consequence, that a poem of any length neither can be, or ought to be, all poetry. Yet if an harmonious whole is to be produced, the remaining parts must be preserved *in keeping* with the poetry; and this can be no otherwise effected than by such a studied selection and artificial arrangement, as will partake of *one,* though not *peculiar* property of poetry. And this again can be no other than the property of exciting a more continuous and equal attention than the language of prose aims at, whether colloquial or written.

My own conclusions on the nature of poetry, in the strictest use of the word, have been in part anticipated in the preceding disquisition on the fancy and imagination. What is poetry? is so nearly the same question with, what is a poet? that the answer to the one is involved in the solution of the other. For it is a distinction resulting from the poetic genius itself, which sustains and modifies the images, thoughts, and emotions of the poet's own mind.

The poet, described in *ideal* perfection, brings the whole soul of man into activity, with the subordination of its faculties to each other, according to their relative worth and dignity. He diffuses a tone and spirit of unity, that blends, and (as it were) *fuses,* each into each, by that synthetic and magical power, to which we have exclusively appropriated the name of imagination. This power, first put in action by the will and understanding, and retained under their irremissive, though gentle and unnoticed, controul (*laxis effertur habenis*) reveals itself in the balance or reconciliation of opposite or discordant qualities: of sameness, with difference; of the general, with the concrete; the idea, with the image; the individual, with the representative; the sense of novelty and freshness, with old and familiar objects; a more than usual state of emotion, with more than usual order; judgement ever awake and steady self-possession, with enthusiasm and feeling profound or vehement; and while it blends and harmonizes the natural and the artificial, still subordinates art to nature; the manner to the matter; and our admiration of the poet to our sympathy with the poetry. "Doubtless," as Sir John Davies observes of the soul (and his words may with slight alteration be applied, and even more appropriately, to the poetic IMAGINATION),

> Doubtless this could not be, but that she turns
> Bodies to spirit by sublimation strange,
> As fire converts to fire the things it burns,
> As we our food into our nature change.
>
> From their gross matter she abstracts their forms,
> And draws a kind of quintessence from things;
> Which to her proper nature she transforms,
> To bear them light on her celestial wings.
>
> Thus does she, when from individual states
> She doth abstract the universal kinds;
> Which then re-clothed in divers names and fates
> Steal access through our senses to our minds.

Finally, GOOD SENSE is the BODY of poetic genius, FANCY its DRAPERY, MOTION its LIFE, and IMAGINATION the SOUL that is everywhere, and in each; and forms all into one graceful and intelligent whole.

*   *   *   *   *

CHAPTER XVII

Examination of the tenets peculiar to Mr. Wordsworth—Rustic life (above all, low and rustic life) especially unfavorable to the formation of a human diction—The best parts of language the product of philosophers, not of clowns or shepherds—Poetry essentially ideal and generic—The language of Milton as much the language of real life, yea, incomparably more so than that of the cottager.

As far then as Mr. Wordsworth in his preface contended, and most ably contended, for a reformation in our poetic diction, as far as he has evinced the truth of passion, and the *dramatic* propriety of those figures and metaphors in the original poets, which, stripped of their justifying reasons, and converted into mere artifices of connection or ornament, constitute the characteristic falsity in the poetic style of the moderns; and as far as he has, with equal acuteness and clearness, pointed out the process by which this change was effected, and the resemblances between that state into which the reader's mind is thrown by the pleasureable confusion of thought from an unaccustomed train of words and images; and that state which is induced by the natural language of empassioned feeling; he undertook a useful task, and deserves all praise, both for the attempt and for the execution. The provocations to this remonstrance in behalf of truth and nature were still of perpetual recurrence before and after the publication of this preface. I cannot likewise but add, that the comparison of such poems of merit, as have been given to the public within the last ten or twelve years, with the majority of those produced previously to the appearance of that preface, leave no doubt on my mind, that Mr. Wordsworth is fully justified in believing his efforts to have been by no means ineffectual. Not only in the verses of those who have professed their admiration of his genius, but even of those who have distinguished themselves by hostility to his theory, and depreciation of his writings, are the impressions of his principles plainly visible. It is possible, that with these principles others may have been blended, which are not equally evident; and some which are unsteady and subvertible from the narrowness or imperfection of their basis. But it is more than possible, that these errors of defect or exaggeration, by kindling and feeding the controversy, may have conduced not only to the wider propagation of the accompanying truths, but that, by their frequent presentation to the mind in an excited state, they may have won for them a more permanent and practical result. A man will borrow a part from his opponent the more easily, if he feels himself justified in continuing to reject a part. While there remain important points in which he can still feel himself in the right, in which he still finds firm footing for continued resistance, he will gradually adopt those opinions, which were the least remote from his own convictions, as not less congruous with his own theory than with that which he reprobates. In like manner with a kind of instinctive prudence, he will abandon by little and little his weakest posts, till at length he seems to forget that they had ever belonged to him, or affects to consider them at most as accidental and "petty annexments," the removal of which leaves the citadel unhurt and unendangered.

My own differences from certain supposed parts of Mr. Wordsworth's theory ground themselves on the assumption, that his words had been rightly interpreted, as purporting that the proper diction for poetry in general consists altogether in a language taken, with due exceptions, from the mouths of men in real life, a language which actually constitutes the natural conversation of men under the influence of natural feelings. My objection is, first, that in *any* sense this rule is applicable only to *certain* classes of poetry; secondly, that even to these classes it is not applicable, except in such a sense, as hath never by any one (as far as I know or have read) been denied or doubted; and lastly, that as far as, and in that degree in which it is *practicable,* yet as a *rule* it is useless, if not injurious, and therefore either need not, or ought not to be practised. The poet informs his reader, that he had generally chosen *low and rustic* life; but not *as* low and rustic, or in order to repeat that pleasure of doubtful moral effect, which persons of elevated rank and of superior refinement oftentimes derive from a happy *imitation* of the rude unpolished manners and discourse of their inferiors. For the pleasure so derived may be traced to three exciting causes. The first is the naturalness, in *fact,* of the things represented. The second is the apparent naturalness of the *representation,* as raised and qualified by an imperceptible infusion of the author's own knowledge and talent, which infusion does, indeed, constitute it an *imitation* as distinguished from a mere *copy.* The third cause may be found in the reader's conscious feeling of his superiority awakened by the contrast presented to him; even as for the same purpose the kings and great barons of yore retained sometimes *actual* clowns and fools, but more frequently shrewd and witty fellows in that *character.* These, however, were not Mr. Wordsworth's objects. *He* chose low and rustic life, "because in that condition the essential passions of the heart find a better soil, in which they can attain their maturity, are less under restraint, and speak a plainer and more emphatic language; because in that condition of life our elementary feelings coexist in a state of greater simplicity, and consequently may be more accurately contemplated, and more forcibly communicated; because the manners of rural life germinate from those elementary feelings; and from the necessary character of rural occupations are more easily comprehended, and are more durable; and lastly, because.

in that condition the passions of men are incorporated with the beautiful and permanent forms of nature."

Now it is clear to me, that in the most interesting of the poems, in which the author is more or less dramatic, as "the Brothers," "Michael," "Ruth," "the Mad Mother," &c., the persons introduced are by no means taken *from low or rustic life* in the common acceptation of those words; and it is not less clear, that the sentiments and language, as far as they can be conceived to have been really transferred from the minds and conversation of such persons, are attributable to causes and circumstances not necessarily connected with "their occupations and abode." The thoughts, feelings, language, and manners of the shepherd-farmers in the vales of Cumberland and Westmoreland, as far as they are actually adopted in those poems, may be accounted for from causes, which will and do produce the same results in *every* state of life, whether in town or country. As the two principal I rank that INDEPENDENCE, which raises a man above servitude, or daily toil for the profit of others, yet not above the necessity of industry and a frugal simplicity of domestic life; and the accompanying unambitious, but solid and religious, EDUCATION, which has rendered few books familiar, but the Bible, and the liturgy or hymn book. To this latter cause, indeed, which is so far *accidental*, that it is the blessing of particular countries and a particular age, not the product of particular places or employments, the poet owes the show of probability, that his personages might really feel, think, and talk with any tolerable resemblance to his representation. It is an excellent remark of Dr. Henry More's (Enthusiasmus triumphatus, Sec. xxxv.), that "a man of confined education, but of good parts, by constant reading of the Bible will naturally form a more winning and commanding rhetoric than those that are learned; the intermixture of tongues and of artificial phrases debasing *their* style."

It is, moreover, to be considered that to the formation of healthy feelings, and a reflecting mind, *negations* involve impediments not less formidable than sophistication and vicious intermixture. I am convinced, that for the human soul to prosper in rustic life a certain vantage-ground is pre-requisite. It is not every man that is likely to be improved by a country life or by country labors. Education, or original sensibility, or both, must pre-exist, if the changes, forms, and incidents of nature are to prove a sufficient stimulant. And where these are not sufficient, the mind contracts and hardens by want of stimulants: and the man becomes selfish, sensual, gross, and hard-hearted. Let the management of the POOR LAWS in Liverpool, Manchester, or Bristol be compared with the ordinary dispensation of the poor rates in agricultural villages, where the *farmers* are the overseers and guardians of the poor. If my own experience have not been particularly unfortunate, as well as that of the many respectable country clergymen with whom I have conversed on the subject, the result would engender more than scepticism concerning the desireable influences of low and rustic life in and for itself. Whatever may be concluded on the other side, from the stronger local attachments and enterprising spirit of the Swiss, and other mountaineers, applies to a particular mode of pastoral life, under forms of property that permit and beget manners truly republican, not to rustic life in general, or to the absence of artificial cultivation. On the contrary the mountaineers, whose manners have been so often eulogized, are in general better educated and greater readers than men of equal rank elsewhere. But where this is not the case, as among the peasantry of North Wales, the ancient mountains, with all their terrors and all their glories, are pictures to the blind, and music to the deaf.

I should not have entered so much into detail upon this passage, but here seems to be the point, to which all the lines of difference converge as to their source and centre. (I mean, as far as, and in whatever respect, my poetic creed *does* differ from the doctrines promulged in this preface.) I adopt with full faith the principle of Aristotle, that poetry as poetry is essentially *ideal,* that it avoids and excludes all *accident;* that its apparent individualities of rank, character, or occupation must be *representative* of a class; and that the *persons* of poetry must be clothed with *generic* attributes, with the *common* attributes of the class: not with such as one gifted individual might *possibly* possess, but such as from his situation it is most probable beforehand that he *would* possess. If my premises are right and my deductions legitimate, it follows that there can be no *poetic* medium between the swains of Theocritus and those of an imaginary golden age.

The characters of the vicar and the shepherd-mariner in the poem of "THE BROTHERS," that of the shepherd of Greenhead Ghyll in the "MICHAEL," have all the verisimilitude and representative quality, that the purposes of poetry can require. They are persons of a known and abiding class, and their manners

and sentiments the natural product of circumstances common
to the class. Take "MICHAEL" for instance:

> An old man stout of heart, and strong of limb:
> His bodily frame had been from youth to age
> Of an unusual strength: his mind was keen,
> Intense, and frugal, apt for all affairs,
> And in his shepherd's calling he was prompt
> And watchful more than ordinary men.
> Hence he had learnt the meaning of all winds,
> Of blasts of every tone; and oftentimes
> When others heeded not, he heard the South
> Make subterraneous music, like the noise
> Of bagpipers on distant Highland hills.
> The shepherd, at such warning, of his flock
> Bethought him, and he to himself would say,
> The winds are now devising work for me!
> And truly at all times the storm, that drives
> The traveller to a shelter, summon'd him
> Up to the mountains. He had been alone
> Amid the heart of many thousand mists,
> That came to him and left him on the heights.
> So liv'd he, till his eightieth year was pass'd.
> And grossly that man errs, who should suppose
> That the green vallies, and the streams and rocks,
> Were things indifferent to the shepherd's thoughts.
> Fields, where with chearful spirits he had breath'd
> The common air; the hills, which he so oft
> Had climb'd with vigorous steps; which had impress'd
> So many incidents upon his mind
> Of hardship, skill or courage, joy or fear;
> Which, like a book, preserved the memory
> Of the dumb animals, whom he had sav'd,
> Had fed or shelter'd, linking to such acts,
> So grateful in themselves, the certainty
> Of honorable gain; these fields, these hills
> Which were his living being, even more
> Than his own blood—what could they less? had laid
> Strong hold on his affections, were to him
> A pleasureable feeling of blind love,
> The pleasure which there is in life itself.

On the other hand, in the poems which are pitched at a lower
note, as the "HARRY GILL," "IDIOT BOY," the *feelings* are those
of human nature in general; though the poet has judiciously
laid the *scene* in the country, in order to place *himself* in the
vicinity of interesting images, without the necessity of ascribing

a sentimental perception of their beauty to the persons of his drama. In the "Idiot Boy," indeed, the mother's character is not so much a real and native product of a "situation where the essential passions of the heart find a better soil, in which they can attain their maturity and speak a plainer and more emphatic language," as it is an impersonation of an instinct abandoned by judgement. Hence the two following charges seem to me not wholly groundless: at least, they are the only plausible objections, which I have heard to that fine poem. The one is, that the author has not, in the poem itself, taken sufficient care to preclude from the reader's fancy the disgusting images of *ordinary morbid idiocy,* which yet it was by no means his intention to represent. He has even by the "burr, burr, burr," uncounteracted by any preceding description of the boy's beauty, assisted in recalling them. The other is, that the idiocy of the *boy* is so evenly balanced by the folly of the *mother,* as to present to the general reader rather a laughable burlesque on the blindness of anile dotage, than an analytic display of material affection in its ordinary workings.

In the "Thorn" the poet himself acknowledges in a note the necessity of an introductory poem, in which he should have pourtrayed the character of the person from whom the words of the poem are supposed to proceed: a superstitious man moderately imaginative, of slow faculties and deep feelings, "a captain of a small trading vessel, for example, who, being past the middle age of life, had retired upon an annuity, or small independent income, to some village or country town of which he was not a native, or in which he had not been accustomed to live. Such men having nothing to do become credulous and talkative from indolence." But in a poem, still more in a lyric poem (and the NURSE in Shakespeare's Romeo and Juliet alone prevents me from extending the remark even to dramatic *poetry,* if indeed the Nurse itself can be deemed altogether a case in point) it is not possible to imitate truly a dull and garrulous discourser, without repeating the effects of dullness and garrulity. However this may be, I dare assert, that the parts (and these form the far larger portion of the whole) which might as well or still better have proceeded from the poet's own imagination, and have been spoken in his own character, are those which have given, and which will continue to give, universal delight; and that the passages exclusively appropriate to the supposed narrator, such as the last couplet of the third stanza; the seven last lines of the tenth; and the five following stanzas, with the exception of the four admirable lines at the commencement of the fourteenth, are felt by many unprejudiced and unsophisticated hearts, as sudden and unpleasant sinkings from the height to which the poet had previously lifted them, and to which he again re-elevates both himself and his reader.

If then I am compelled to doubt the theory, by which the choice of *characters* was to be directed, not only *a priori*, from grounds of reason, but both from the few instances in which the poet himself *need* be supposed to have been governed by it, and from the comparative inferiority of those instances; still more must I hesitate in my assent to the sentence which immediately follows the former citation; and which I can neither admit as particular fact, or as general rule. "The language too of these men is adopted (purified indeed from what appear to be its real defects, from all lasting and rational causes of dislike or disgust) because such men hourly communicate with the best objects from which the best part of language is originally derived; and because, from their rank in society and the sameness and narrow circle of their intercourse, being less under the action of social vanity, they convey their feelings and notions in simple and unelaborated expressions." To this I reply; that a rustic's language, purified from all provincialism and grossness, and so far reconstructed as to be made consistent with the rules of grammar (which are in essence no other than the laws of universal logic, applied to psychological materials) will not differ from the language of any other man of commonsense, however learned or refined he may be, except as far as the notions, which the rustic has to convey, are fewer and more indiscriminate. This will become still clearer, if we add the consideration (equally important though less obvious) that the rustic, from the more imperfect developement of his faculties, and from the lower state of their cultivation, aims almost solely to convey *insulated facts*, either those of his scanty experience or his traditional belief; while the educated man chiefly seeks to discover and express those *connections* of things, or those relative *bearings* of fact to fact, from which some more or less general law is deducible. For *facts* are valuable to a wise man, chiefly as they lead to the discovery of the indwelling *law*, which is the true *being* of things, the sole solution of their modes of existence, and in the knowledge of which consists our dignity and our power.

As little can I agree with the assertion, that from the objects with which the rustic hourly communicates the best part of language is formed. For first, if to communicate with an object implies such an acquaintance with it, as renders it capable of being discriminately reflected on; the distinct knowledge of an uneducated rustic would furnish a very scanty vocabulary. The few things, and modes of action, requisite for his bodily conveniences, would alone be individualized; while all the rest of nature would be expressed by a small number of confused general terms. Secondly, I deny that the words and combinations of words derived from the objects, with which the rustic is familiar, whether with distinct or confused knowledge, can be justly said to form the *best* part of language. It is more than probable, that many classes of the brute creation possess discriminating sounds, by which they can convey to each other notices of such objects as concern their food, shelter, or safety. Yet we hesitate to call the aggregate of such sounds a language, otherwise than metaphorically. The best part of human language, properly so called, is derived from reflection on the acts of the mind itself. It is formed by a voluntary appropriation of fixed symbols to internal acts, to processes and results of imagination, the greater part of which have no place in the consciousness of uneducated man; though in civilized society, by imitation and passive remembrance of what they hear from their religious instructors and other superiors, the most uneducated share in the harvest which they neither sowed or reaped. If the history of the phrases in hourly currency among our peasants were traced, a person not previously aware of the fact would be surprised at finding so large a number, which three or four centuries ago were the exclusive property of the universities and the schools; and, at the commencement of the Reformation, had been transferred from the school to the pulpit, and thus gradually passed into common life. The extreme difficulty, and often the impossibility, of finding words for the simplest moral and intellectual processes of the languages of uncivilized tribes has proved perhaps the weightiest obstacle to the progress of our most zealous and adroit missionaries. Yet these tribes are surrounded by the same nature as our peasants are; but in still more impressive forms; and they are, moreover, obliged to *particularize* many more of them. When, therefore, Mr. Wordsworth adds, "accordingly, such a language" (meaning, as before, the language of rustic life purified from provincialism) "arising out of repeated experience and regular feelings, is a more permanent, and a far more

philosophical language, than that which is frequently substituted for it by poets, who think they are conferring honor
upon themselves and their art in proportion as they indulge
in arbitrary and capricious habits of expression:" it may be
answered, that the language, which he has in view, can be
attributed to rustics with no greater right, than the style of
Hooker or Bacon to Tom Brown or Sir Roger L'Estrange.
Doubtless, if what is peculiar to each were omitted in each,
the result must needs be the same. Further, that the poet, who
uses an illogical diction, or a style fitted to excite only the low
and changeable pleasure of wonder by means of groundless
novelty, substitutes a language of *folly* and *vanity*, not for that
of the *rustic*, but for that of *good sense* and *natural feeling*.

Here let me be permitted to remind the reader, that the
positions, which I controvert, are contained in the sentences—
"a selection of the REAL *language of men;"*—*"the language of
these men"* (i.e. men in low and rustic life) *"I propose to myself to imitate, and, as far as is possible, to adopt the very language of men."* *"Between the language of prose and that of
metrical composition, there neither is, nor can be any essential
difference."* It is against these exclusively that my opposition is
directed.

I object, in the very first instance, to an equivocation in the
use of the word "real." Every man's language varies, according
to the extent of his knowledge, the activity of his faculties, and
the depth or quickness of his feelings. Every man's language
has, first, its *individualities;* secondly, the common properties
of the *class* to which he belongs; and thirdly, words and phrases
of *universal* use. The language of Hooker, Bacon, Bishop
Taylor, and Burke differs from the common language of the
learned class only by the superior number and novelty of the
thoughts and relations which they had to convey. The language
of Algernon Sidney differs not at all from that, which every
well-educated gentleman would wish to write, and (with due
allowances for the undeliberateness, and less connected train,
of thinking natural and proper to conversation) such as he
would wish to talk. Neither one nor the other differ half so
much from the general language of cultivated society, as the
language of Mr. Wordsworth's homeliest composition differs
from that of a common peasant. For "real" therefore, we must
substitute *ordinary*, or *lingua communis*. And this, we have
proved, is no more to be found in the phraseology of low and
rustic life than in that of any other class. Omit the peculiarities

of each, and the result of course must be common to all. And assuredly the omissions and changes to be made in the language of rustics, before it could be transferred to any species of poem, except the drama or other professed imitation, are at least as numerous and weighty, as would be required in adapting to the same purpose the ordinary language of tradesmen and manufacturers. Not to mention, that the language so highly extolled by Mr. Wordsworth varies in every county, nay in every village, according to the accidental character of the clergyman, the existence or non-existence of schools; or even, perhaps, as the exciseman, publican, or barber, happen to be, or not to be, zealous politicians, and readers of the weekly newspaper *pro bono publico*. Anterior to cultivation, the lingua communis of every country, as Dante has well observed, exists every where in parts, and no where as a whole.

Neither is the case rendered at all more tenable by the addition of the words, *in a state of excitement*. For the nature of a man's words, where he is strongly affected by joy, grief, or anger, must necessarily depend on the number and quality of the general truths, conceptions and images, and of the words expressing them, with which his mind had been previously stored. For the property of passion is not to *create;* but to set in increased activity. At least, whatever new connections of thoughts or images, or (which is equally, if not more than equally, the appropriate effect of strong excitement) whatever generalizations of truth or experience, the heat of passion may produce; yet the terms of their conveyance must have pre-existed in his former conversations, and are only collected and crowded together by the unusual stimulation. It is indeed very possible to adopt in a poem the unmeaning repetitions, habitual phrases, and other blank counters, which an unfurnished or confused understanding interposes at short intervals, in order to keep hold of his subject, which is still slipping from him, and to give him time for recollection; or in mere aid of vacancy, as in the scanty companies of a country stage the same player pops backwards and forwards, in order to prevent the appearance of empty spaces, in the procession of Macbeth, or Henry VIIIth. But what assistance to the poet, or ornament to the poem, these can supply, I am at a loss to conjecture. Nothing assuredly can differ either in origin or in mode more widely from the *apparent* tautologies of intense and turbulent feeling,

in which the passion is greater and of longer endurance than
to be exhausted or satisfied by a single representation of the
image or incident exciting it. Such repetitions I admit to be a
beauty of the highest kind; as illustrated by Mr. Wordsworth
himself from the song of Deborah. *"At her feet he bowed, he
fell, he lay down; at her feet he bowed, he fell; where he bowed,
there he fell down dead."*

*   *   *   *   *   *

1815   *1817*

CRITICAL ESSAYS

Coleridge's criticism, broadly speaking, is of two sorts: theoretical and practical. In the present collection his theoretical work is well represented by such essays as those on taste, beauty, allegory, style, and the definition of poetry. In his examination of world classics like the *Divine Comedy, Don Quixote, Hamlet,* or the fourth voyage of Swift's Gulliver, Coleridge displays his bent for practical criticism—that is, the close interpretation of particular texts, the kind of exegetical commentary which the so-called "new critics" have made fashionable in our own time. As the acknowledged paternal great-grandfather of much modern criticism, Coleridge the Commentator is usually revealing and frequently brilliant. If we look back for examples of the two kinds to the *Biographia Literaria,* the distinction between Imagination and Fancy in Chapter XIII very well represents the theoretical critic in action, while the critique of Wordsworth's poetical practice which begins at Chapter XVII reminds us of those presiding powers of taste and judgment in which Coleridge excelled whenever he set his mind to a problem of evaluation, whenever he conquered his bodily pain or his mental lethargy for long enough to set pen to paper in serious discourse.

Much of his best work was done on the plays of William Shakespeare. Professor Thomas M. Raysor, editor of the two-volume *Coleridge's Shakespearean Criticism,* believes that there was an observable connection between the personal life of the critic and the kind of interpretation which he offered both in lectures and in letterpress. "The unhappiness," says Raysor, "which turned inward his superb analytical powers and forced him to explore his own soul as few men ever have, created an introspective psychologist of supreme genius, and gave him the basis for a knowledge of human motives which no English critic has ever surpassed. In rich ethical reflectiveness, in delicate sensitiveness of poetic imagination, and above all in profound insight into human nature, Coleridge is a critic worthy of his high place at the head of English criticism of Shakespeare."

It may well be, therefore, that Coleridge's journey to hell and back, intolerable as it was to his soul and grievous as its effects were on his bodily health, yet made him aware, as few others have been, of certain of the more profound connections between private psychology and public art. Despite his ingrained tendencies to gab and to digress, to procrastinate like a Hamlet or pace the nocturnal ramparts like a ghost in torment, he managed to turn the flashlight of introspection into the darker corners of his capacious mind, with what results we see in the essays which follow.

ON TASTE

THE same arguments that decide the question, whether taste has any fixed principles, may probably lead to a determination of what those principles are. First, then, what is taste in its metaphorical sense, or, which will be the easiest mode of arriving at the same solution, what is there in the primary sense of the word, which may give to its metaphorical meaning an import different from that of sight or hearing, on the one hand, and of touch or smell on the other? And this question seems the more natural, because in correct language we confine beauty, the main subject of taste, to objects of sight and combinations of sounds, and never, except sportively or by abuse of words, speak of a beautiful flavor or a beautiful scent.

Now the analysis of our senses in the commonest books of anthropology has drawn our attention to the distinction between the perfectly organic, and the mixed senses;—the first presenting objects, as distinct from the perception,—the last as blending the perception with the sense of the object. Our eyes and ears— (I am not now considering what is or is not the case really, but only that of which we are regularly conscious as appearances) —our eyes most often appear to us perfect organs of the sentient principle, and wholly in action, and our hearing so much more so than the three other senses, and in all the ordinary exertions of that sense, perhaps, equally so with the sight, that all languages place them in one class, and express their different modifications by nearly the same metaphors. The three remaining senses appear in part passive, and combine with the perception of the outward object a distinct sense of our own life. Taste, therefore, as opposed to vision and sound, will teach us to expect in its metaphorical use a certain reference of any given object to our own being, and not merely a distinct notion of the object as in itself, or in its independent properties. From the sense of touch, on the other hand, it is distinguishable by adding to this reference to our vital being some degree of enjoyment, or—the contrary—some perceptible impulse from pleasure or pain to complacency or dislike. The sense of smell, indeed, might perhaps have furnished a metaphor of the same import with that of taste; but the latter was naturally chosen by the majority of civilized nations on account

of the greater frequency, importance, and dignity of its employment or exertion in human nature.

By taste, therefore, as applied to the fine arts, we must be
supposed to mean an intellectual perception of any object
blended with a distinct reference to our own sensibility of
pain or pleasure, or *vice versa*, a sense of enjoyment or dislike
co-instantaneously combined with, and appearing to proceed
from, some intellectual perception of the object;—intellectual
perception, I say; for otherwise it would be a definition of taste
in its primary rather than in its metaphorical sense. Briefly,
taste is a metaphor taken from one of our mixed senses, and
applied to objects of the more purely organic senses, and of our
moral sense, when we would imply the co-existence of immediate personal dislike or complacency. In this definition of taste,
therefore, is involved the definition of fine arts, namely, as being
such, the chief and discriminative purpose of which it is to
gratify the taste,—that is, not merely to connect, but to combine
and unite, a sense of immediate pleasure in ourselves with the
perception of external arrangement.

The great question, therefore, whether taste in any one of
the fine arts has any fixed principle or ideal, will find its solution in the ascertainment of two facts:—first, whether in every
determination of the taste concerning any work of the fine arts,
the individual does not, with or even against the approbation
of his general judgement, involuntarily claim that all other
minds ought to think and feel the same; whether the common
expressions, "I dare say I may be wrong, but that is my particular taste," are uttered as an offering of courtesy, as a
sacrifice to the undoubted fact of our individual fallibility, or
are spoken with perfect sincerity, not only of the reason, but
of the whole feeling, with the same entireness of mind and
heart, with which we concede a right to every person to differ
from another in his preference of bodily tastes and flavors. If we
should find ourselves compelled to deny this, and to admit that,
notwithstanding the consciousness of our liability to error, and
in spite of all those many individual experiences which may
have strengthened the consciousness, each man does at the
moment so far legislate for all men, as to believe of necessity
that he is either right or wrong, and that if it be right for him,
it is universally right,—we must then proceed to ascertain:—
secondly, whether the source of these phenomena is at all to
be found in those parts of our nature, in which each intellect
is representative of all,—and whether wholly or partially. No

person of common reflection demands even in feeling, that what
tastes pleasant to him ought to produce the same effect on all
living beings; but every man does and must expect and demand
the universal acquiescence of all intelligent beings in every
conviction of his understanding.

1810   *1836*

ON POETRY AND RELIGION

It is impossible to pay a higher compliment to poetry, than
to consider the effects it produces in common with religion, yet
distinct (as far as distinction can be, where there is no division)
in those qualities which religion exercises and diffuses over all
mankind, as far as they are subject to its influence.

I have often thought that religion (speaking of it only as it
accords with poetry, without reference to its more serious impressions) is the poetry of mankind, both having for their objects:—

1. To generalise our notions; to prevent men from confining
their attention solely, or chiefly, to their own narrow sphere of
action, and to their own individual circumstances. By placing
them in certain awful relations it merges the individual man in
the whole species, and makes it impossible for any one man
to think of his future lot, or indeed of his present condition,
without at the same time comprising in his view his fellow-
creatures.

2. That both poetry and religion throw the object of deepest
interest to a distance from us, and thereby not only aid our
imagination, but in a most important manner subserve the interest of our virtues; for that man is indeed a slave, who is a
slave to his own senses, and whose mind and imagination cannot carry him beyond the distance which his hand can touch,
or even his eye can reach.

3. The grandest point of resemblance between them is, that
both have for their object (I hardly know whether the English
language supplies an appropriate word) the perfecting, and
the pointing out to us the indefinite improvement of our
nature, and fixing our attention upon that. They bid us, while
we are sitting in the dark at our little fire, look at the mountain-
tops, struggling with darkness, and announcing that light which

shall be common to all, in which individual interests shall resolve into one common good, and every man shall find in his fellow man more than a brother.

Such being the case, we need not wonder that it has pleased Providence, that the divine truths of religion should have been revealed to us in the form of poetry; and that at all times poets, not the slaves of any particular sectarian opinions, should have joined to support all those delicate sentiments of the heart (often when they were most opposed to the reigning philosophy of the day) which may be called the feeding streams of religion.

I have heard it said that an undevout astronomer is mad. In the strict sense of the word, every being capable of understanding must be mad, who remains, as it were, fixed in the ground on which he treads—who, gifted with the divine faculties of indefinite hope and fear, born with them, yet settles his faith upon that, in which neither hope nor fear has any proper field for display. Much more truly, however, might it be said that, an undevout poet is mad: in the strict sense of the word, an undevout poet is an impossibility. . . .

1811–1812   *1836*

ON BEAUTY

The only necessary, but this the absolute necessary, prerequisite to a full insight into the grounds of the beauty in the objects of sight, is—the directing of the attention to the action of those thoughts in our own mind which are not consciously distinguished. Every man may understand this, if he will but recall the state of his feelings in endeavouring to recollect a name, which he is quite sure that he remembers, though he cannot force it back into consciousness. This region of unconscious thoughts, oftentimes the more working the more indistinct they are, may, in reference to this subject, be conceived as forming an ascending scale from the most universal associations of motion with the functions and passions of life,—as when, on passing out of a crowded city into the fields on a day in June, we describe the grass and king-cups as nodding their heads and dancing in the breeze,—up to the half perceived, yet not fixable, resemblance of a form to some particular object of a diverse class, which resemblance we need only increase but a little, to destroy, or at least injure, its beauty-enhancing effect, and to make it a fantastic intrusion of the accidental and the arbitrary, and consequently a disturbance of the beautiful. This might be abundantly exemplified and illustrated from the paintings of Salvator Rosa.

I am now using the term beauty in its most comprehensive sense, as including expression and artistic interest,—that is, I consider not only the living balance, but likewise all the accompaniments that even by disturbing are necessary to the renewal and continuance of the balance. And in this sense I proceed to show, that the beautiful in the object may be referred to two elements,—lines and colors; the first belonging to the shapely (*forma, formalis, formosuṣ*), and in this, to the law, and the reason; and the second, to the lively, the free, the spontaneous, and the self-justifying. As to lines, the rectilineal are in themselves the lifeless, the determined *ab extra*, but still in immediate union with the cycloidal, which are expressive of function. The curve line is a modification of the force from without by the force from within, or the spontaneous. These are not arbitrary symbols, but the language of nature, universal and intuitive, by virtue of the law by which man is impelled to explain visible motions by imaginary causative powers analogous to his own acts, as the Dryads, Hamadryads, Naiads, &c.

The better way of applying these principles will be by a brief and rapid sketch of the history of the fine arts,—in which it will be found, that the beautiful in nature has been appropriated to the works of man, just in proportion as the state of the mind in the artists themselves approached to the subjective beauty. Determine what predominance in the minds of the men is preventive of the living balance of excited faculties, and you will discover the exact counterpart in the outward products. Egypt is an illustration of this. Shapeliness is intellect without freedom; but colors are significant. The introduction of the arch is not less an epoch in the fine than in the useful arts.

Order is beautiful arrangement without any purpose *ab extra;*—therefore there is a beauty of order, or order may be contemplated exclusively as beauty.

The form given in any empirical intuition,—the stuff, that is, the quality of the stuff, determines the agreeable: but when a thing excites us to receive it in such and such a mould, so that its exact correspondence to that mould is what occupies the mind,— this is taste or the sense of beauty. Whether dishes full of painted wood or exquisite viands were laid out on a table in the same arrangement, would be indifferent to the taste, as in ladies' patterns; but surely the one is far more agreeable than the other. Hence observe the disinterestedness of all taste; and hence also a sensual perfection with intellect is occasionally possible without moral feeling. So it may be in music and painting, but not in poetry. How far it is a real preference of the refined to the gross pleasures, is another question, upon the supposition that pleasure, in some form or other, is that alone which determines men to the objects of the former;—whether experience does not show that if the latter were equally in our power, occasioned no more trouble to enjoy, and caused no more exhaustion of the power of enjoying them by the enjoyment itself, we should in real practice prefer the grosser pleasure. It is not, therefore, any excellence in the quality of the refined pleasures themselves, but the advantages and facilities in the means of enjoying them, that give them the pre-eminence.

This is, of course, on the supposition of the absence of all moral feeling. Suppose its presence, and then there will accrue an excellence even to the quality of the pleasures themselves; not only, however, of the refined, but also of the grosser kinds,— inasmuch as a larger sweep of thoughts will be associated with each enjoyment, and with each thought will be associated a number of sensations; and so, consequently, each pleasure will become more the pleasure of the whole being. This is one of the earthly rewards of our being what we ought to be, but which would be annihilated, if we attempted to be it for the sake of this increased enjoyment. Indeed it is a contradiction to suppose it. Yet this is the common *argumentum in circulo*, in which the eudæmonists flee and pursue.

1818   *1836*

ON POESY OR ART

Man communicates by articulation of sounds, and paramountly by the memory in the ear; nature by the impression of bounds and surfaces on the eye, and through the eye it gives significance and appropriation, and thus the conditions of memory, or the capability of being remembered, to sounds, smells, &c. Now Art, used collectively for painting, sculpture, architecture and music, is the mediatress between, and reconciler of, nature and man. It is, therefore, the power of humanizing nature, of infusing the thoughts and passions of man into every thing which is the object of his contemplation; color, form, motion, and sound, are the elements which it combines, and it stamps them into unity in the mould of a moral idea.

The primary art is writing;—primary, if we regard the purpose abstracted from the different modes of realizing it, those steps of progression of which the instances are still visible in the lower degrees of civilization. First, there is mere gesticulation; then rosaries or *wampum*; then picture-language; then hieroglyphics, and finally alphabetic letters. These all consist of a translation of man into nature, of a substitution of the visible for the audible.

The so-called music of savage tribes as little deserves the name of art for the understanding, as the ear warrants it for music. Its lowest state is a mere expression of passion by sounds which the passion itself necessitates;—the highest amounts to no more than a voluntary reproduction of these sounds in the absence of the occasioning causes, so as to give the pleasure of contrast,—for example, by the various outcries of battle in the song of security and triumph. Poetry also is purely human; for all its materials are from the mind, and all its products are for the mind. But it is the apotheosis of the former state, in which by excitement of the associative power passion itself imitates order, and the order resulting produces a pleasureable passion, and thus it elevates the mind by making its feelings the object of its reflexion. So likewise, whilst it recalls the sights and sounds that had accompanied the occasions of the original passions, poetry impregnates them with an interest not their own by means of the passions, and yet tempers the passion by the calming power which all distinct images exert on the human soul. In this way poetry is the preparation for art, inasmuch as it avails itself of the forms of nature to recall, to express, and to modify the thoughts and feelings of the mind. Still, however, poetry can only act through the intervention of articulate speech, which is so peculiarly human, that in all languages it constitutes the ordinary phrase by which man and nature are contradistinguished. It is the original force of the word "brute," and even "mute" and "dumb" do not convey the absence of sound but the absence of articulated sounds.

As soon as the human mind is intelligibly addressed by an outward image exclusively of articulate speech, so soon does art commence. But please to observe that I have laid particular stress on the words "human mind,"—meaning to exclude thereby all results common to man and all other sentient creatures, and consequently confining myself to the effect produced by the congruity of the animal impression with the reflective powers of the mind; so that not the thing presented, but that which is re-presented by the thing, shall be the source of the pleasure. In this sense nature itself is to a religious observer the art of God; and for the same cause art itself might be defined as of a middle quality between a thought and a thing, or, as I said before, the union and reconciliation of that which is nature with that which is exclusively human. It is the figured language of thought, and is distinguished from nature by the unity of all the parts in one thought or idea. Hence nature itself would give us the impression of a work of art, if we could see the thought which is present at once in the whole and in every part; and a work of art will be just in proportion as it adequately conveys the thought, and rich in proportion to the variety of parts which it holds in unity.

If, therefore, the term "mute" be taken as opposed not to sound but to articulate speech, the old definition of painting will in fact be the true and best definition of the Fine Arts in general, that is, *muta poesis,* mute poesy, and so of course poesy. And, as all languages perfect themselves by a gradual process of desynonymizing words originally equivalent, I have cherished the wish to use the word "poesy" as the generic or common term, and to distinguish that species of poesy which is not *muta poesis* by its usual name "poetry"; while of all the other species which collectively form the Fine Arts, there would remain this as the common definition,—that they all, like poetry, are to express intellectual purposes, thoughts, conceptions, and sentiments which have their origin in the human mind,—not, however, as poetry does, by means of articulate speech, but as nature or the divine art does, by form, color, magnitude, proportion, or by sound, that is, silently or musically.

Well! it may be said—but who has ever thought otherwise? We all know that art is the imitatress of nature. And, doubtless, the truths which I hope to convey would be barren truisms, if all men meant the same by the words "imitate" and "nature." But it would be flattering mankind at large, to presume that such is the fact. First, to imitate. The impression on the wax is not an imitation, but a copy, of the seal; the seal itself is an imitation. But, further, in order to form a philosophic conception, we must seek for the kind, as the heat in ice, invisible

light, &c., whilst, for practical purposes, we must have reference
to the degree. It is sufficient that philosophically we understand that in all imitation two elements must coexist, and not
only coexist, but must be perceived as coexisting. These two
constituent elements are likeness and unlikeness, or sameness
and difference, and in all genuine creations of art there must be
a union of these disparates. The artist may take his point of
view where he pleases, provided that the desired effect be
perceptibly produced,—that there be likeness in the difference,
difference in the likeness, and a reconcilement of both in one.
If there be likeness to nature without any check of difference,
the result is disgusting, and the more complete the delusion,
the more loathsome the effect. Why are such simulations of nature, as waxwork figures of men and women, so disagreeable?
Because, not finding the motion and the life which we expected,
we are shocked as by a falsehood, every circumstance of detail,
which before induced us to be interested, making the distance
from truth more palpable. You set out with a supposed reality
and are disappointed and disgusted with the deception; whilst,
in respect to a work of genuine imitation, you begin with an
acknowledged total difference, and then every touch of nature
gives you the pleasure of an approximation to truth. The fundamental principle of all this is undoubtedly the horror of falsehood and the love of truth inherent in the human breast. The
Greek tragic dance rested on these principles, and I can deeply
sympathize in imagination with the Greeks in this favorite part
of their theatrical exhibitions, when I call to mind the pleasure
I felt in beholding the combat of the Horatii and Curiatii most
exquisitely danced in Italy to the music of Cimarosa.

Secondly, as to nature. We must imitate nature! yes, but what
in nature,—all and every thing? No, the beautiful in nature.
And what then is the beautiful? What is beauty? It is, in the
abstract, the unity of the manifold, the coalescence of the
diverse; in the concrete, it is the union of the shapely
(*formosum*) with the vital. In the dead organic it depends on
regularity of form, the first and lowest species of which is the
triangle with all its modifications, as in crystals, architecture,
&c.; in the living organic it is not mere regularity of form, which
would produce a sense of formality; neither is it subservient to
any thing beside itself. It may be present in a disagreeable
object, in which the proportion of the parts constitutes a whole;
it does not arise from association, as the agreeable does, but
sometimes lies in the rupture of association; it is not different

to different individuals and nations, as has been said, nor is it connected with the ideas of the good, or the fit, or the useful. The sense of beauty is intuitive, and beauty itself is all that inspires pleasure without, and aloof from, and even contrarily to, interest.

If the artist copies the mere nature, the *natura naturata,* what idle rivalry! If he proceeds only from a given form, which is supposed to answer to the notion of beauty, what an emptiness, what an unreality there always is in his productions, as in Cipriani's pictures! Believe me, you must master the essence, the *natura naturans,* which presupposes a bond between nature in the higher sense and the soul of man.

The wisdom in nature is distinguished from that in man by the co-instantaneity of the plan and the execution; the thought and the product are one, or are given at once; but there is no reflex act, and hence there is no moral responsibility. In man there is reflexion, freedom, and choice; he is, therefore, the head of the visible creation. In the objects of nature are presented, as in a mirror, all the possible elements, steps, and processes of intellect antecedent to consciousness, and therefore to the full development of the intelligential act; and man's mind is the very focus of all the rays of intellect which are scattered throughout the images of nature. Now so to place these images, totalized, and fitted to the limits of the human mind, as to elicit from, and to superinduce upon, the forms themselves the moral reflexions to which they approximate, to make the external internal, the internal external, to make nature thought, and thought nature,—this is the mystery of genius in the Fine Arts. Dare I add that the genius must act on the feeling, that body is but a striving to become mind,—that it is mind in its essence!

In every work of art there is a reconcilement of the external with the internal; the conscious is so impressed on the unconscious as to appear in it; as compare mere letters inscribed on a tomb with figures themselves constituting the tomb. He who combines the two is the man of genius; and for that reason he must partake of both. Hence there is in genius itself an unconscious activity; nay, that is the genius in the man of genius. And this is the true exposition of the rule that the artist must first eloign himself from nature in order to return to her with full effect. Why this? Because if he were to begin by mere painful copying, he would produce masks only, not forms breathing life. He must out of his own mind create forms

according to the severe laws of the intellect, in order to gen-
erate in himself that co-ordination of freedom and law, that
involution of obedience in the prescript, and of the prescript
in the impulse to obey, which assimilates him to nature, and
enables him to understand her. He merely absents himself for a
season from her, that his own spirit, which has the same ground
with nature, may learn her unspoken language in its main
radicals, before he approaches to her endless compositions of
them. Yes, not to acquire cold notions—lifeless technical rules—
but living and life-producing ideas, which shall contain their
own evidence, the certainty that they are essentially one with
the germinal causes in nature,—his consciousness being the
focus and mirror of both,—for this does the artist for a time
abandon the external real in order to return to it with a complete sympathy with its internal and actual. For of all we see,
hear, feel and touch the substance is and must be in ourselves;
and therefore there is no alternative in reason between the
dreary (and thank heaven! almost impossible) belief that every
thing around us is but a phantom, or that the life which is in
us is in them likewise; and that to know is to resemble, when we
speak of objects out of ourselves, even as within ourselves to
learn is, according to Plato, only to recollect;—the only effective
answer to which, that I have been fortunate to meet with, is
that which Pope has consecrated for future use in the line—

"And coxcombs vanquish Berkeley with a grin!"

The artist must imitate that which is within the thing, that
which is active through form and figure, and discourses to us
by symbols—the *Natur-geist,* or spirit of nature, as we unconsciously imitate those whom we love; for so only can he hope to
produce any work truly natural in the object and truly human
in the effect. The idea which puts the form together cannot
itself be the form. It is above form, and is its essence, the
universal in the individual, or the individuality itself,—the
glance and the exponent of the indwelling power.

Each thing that lives has its moment of self-exposition, and
so has each period of each thing, if we remove the disturbing
forces of accident. To do this is the business of ideal art,
whether in images of childhood, youth, or age, in man or in
woman. Hence a good portrait is the abstract of the personal;
it is not the likeness for actual comparison, but for recollection.
This explains why the likeness of a very good portrait is not

always recognized; because some persons never abstract, and amongst these are especially to be numbered the near relations and friends of the subject, in consequence of the constant pressure and check exercised on their minds by the actual presence of the original. And each thing that only appears to live has also its possible position of relation to life, as nature herself testifies, who where she cannot be, prophesies her being in the crystallized metal, or the inhaling plant.

The charm, the indispensable requisite, of sculpture is unity of effect. But painting rests in a material remoter from nature, and its compass is therefore greater. Light and shade give external, as well as internal, being even with all its accidents, whilst sculpture is confined to the latter. And here I may observe that the subjects chosen for works of art, whether in sculpture or painting, should be such as really are capable of being expressed and conveyed within the limits of those arts. Moreover they ought to be such as will affect the spectator by their truth, their beauty, or their sublimity, and therefore they may be addressed to the judgement, the senses, or the reason. The peculiarity of the impression which they may make, may be derived either from color and form, or from proportion and fitness, or from the excitement of the moral feelings; or all these may be combined. Such works as do combine these sources of effect must have the preference in dignity.

Imitation of the antique may be too exclusive, and may produce an injurious effect on modern sculpture;—ist, generally, because such an imitation cannot fail to have a tendency to keep the attention fixed on externals rather than on the thought within;—2ndly, because, accordingly, it leads the artist to rest satisfied with that which is always imperfect, namely, bodily form, and circumscribes his views of mental expression to the ideas of power and grandeur only;—3rdly, because it induces an effort to combine together two incongruous things, that is to say, modern feelings in antique forms;—4thly, because it speaks in a language, as it were, learned and dead, the tones of which, being unfamiliar, leave the common spectator cold and unimpressed;—and lastly, because it necessarily causes a neglect of thoughts, emotions and images of profounder interest and more exalted dignity, as motherly, sisterly, and brotherly love, piety, devotion, the divine become human,—the Virgin, the Apostle, the Christ. The artist's principle in the statue of a great man should be the illustration of departed merit; and I cannot but think that a skilful adoption of modern habiliments would, in many instances, give a variety and force of effect which a bigoted adherence to Greek or Roman costume precludes. It is, I believe, from artists finding Greek models unfit for several important modern purposes, that we see so many allegorical figures on monuments and elsewhere. Painting was, as it were, a new art, and being unshackled by old models it chose its own subjects, and took an eagle's flight. And a new field seems opened for modern sculpture in the symbolical expression of the ends of life, as in Guy's monument, Chantrey's children in Worcester Cathedral, &c.

Architecture exhibits the greatest extent of the difference from nature which may exist in works of art. It involves all the powers of design, and is sculpture and painting inclusively. It shows the greatness of man, and should at the same time teach him humility.

Music is the most entirely human of the fine arts, and has the fewest *analoga* in nature. Its first delightfulness is simple accordance with the ear; but it is an associated thing, and recalls the deep emotions of the past with an intellectual sense of proportion. Every human feeling is greater and larger than the exciting cause,—a proof, I think, that man is designed for a higher state of existence; and this is deeply implied in music, in which there is always something more and beyond the immediate expression.

With regard to works in all the branches of the fine arts, I may remark that the pleasure arising from novelty must of course be allowed its due place and weight. This pleasure consists in the identity of two opposite elements, that is to say—sameness and variety. If in the midst of the variety there be not some fixed object for the attention, the unceasing succession of the variety will prevent the mind from observing the difference of the individual objects; and the only thing remaining will be the succession, which will then produce precisely the same effect as sameness. This we experience when we let the trees or hedges pass before the fixed eye during a rapid movement in a carriage, or, on the other hand, when we suffer a file of soldiers or ranks of men in procession to go on before us without resting the eye on any one in particular. In order to derive pleasure from the occupation of the mind, the principle of unity must always be present, so that in the midst of the multeity the centripetal force be never suspended, nor the sense be fatigued by the predominance of the centrifugal force. This unity in multeity I have elsewhere stated as the principle of beauty. It is equally the source of pleasure in variety, and in fact a higher term including both. What is the seclusive or distinguishing term between them?

Remember that there is a difference between form as proceeding, and shape as superinduced;—the latter is either the death or the imprisonment of the thing;—the former is its self-witnessing and self-effected sphere of agency. Art would or should be the abridgment of nature. Now the fulness of nature is without character, as water is purest when without taste, smell, or color; but this is the highest, the apex only,—it is not the whole. The object of art is to give the whole *ad hominem*; hence each step of nature hath its ideal, and hence the possibility of a climax up to the perfect form of a harmonized chaos.

To the idea of life victory or strife is necessary; as virtue consists not simply in the absence of vices, but in the overcoming of them. So it is in beauty. The sight of what is subordinated and conquered heightens the strength and the pleasure; and this should be exhibited by the artist either inclusively in his figure, or else out of it, and beside it to act by way of supplement and contrast. And with a view to this, remark the seeming identity of body and mind in infants, and thence the loveliness of the former; the commencing separation in boyhood, and the struggle of equilibrium in youth: thence onward the body is first simply indifferent; then demanding the translucency of the mind not to be worse than indifferent; and finally all that presents the body as body becoming almost of an excremental nature.

1818   *1836*

ON THE GOTHIC LITERATURE AND ART

In my last lecture I stated that the descendants of Japhet and Shem peopled Europe and Asia, fulfilling in their distribution the prophecies of Scripture, while the descendants of Ham passed into Africa, there also actually verifying the interdiction pronounced against them. The Keltic and Teutonic nations occupied that part of Europe, which is now France, Britain, Germany, Sweden, Denmark, &c. They were in general a hardy race, possessing great fortitude, and capable of great endurance.

The Romans slowly conquered the more southerly portion of their tribes, and succeeded only by their superior arts, their policy, and better discipline. After a time, when the Goths,—to use the name of the noblest and most historical of the Teutonic tribes,—had acquired some knowledge of these arts from mixing with their conquerors, they invaded the Roman territories. The hardy habits, the steady perseverance, the better faith of the enduring Goth, rendered him too formidable an enemy for the corrupt Roman, who was more inclined to purchase the subjection of his enemy, than to go through the suffering necessary to secure it. The conquest of the Romans gave to the Goths the Christian religion as it was then existing in Italy; and the light and graceful building of Grecian, or Roman-Greek order, became singularly combined with the massy architecture of the Goths, as wild and varied as the forest vegetation which it resembled. The Greek art is beautiful. When I enter a Greek church, my eye is charmed, and my mind elated; I feel exalted, and proud that I am a man. But the Gothic art is sublime. On entering a cathedral, I am filled with devotion and with awe; I am lost to the actualities that surround me, and my whole being expands into the infinite; earth and air, nature and art, all swell up into eternity, and the only sensible impression left is, 'that I am nothing!' This religion, while it tended to soften the manners of the Northern tribes, was at the same time highly congenial to their nature. The Goths are free from the stain of hero worship. Gazing on their rugged mountains, surrounded by impassable forests, accustomed to gloomy seasons, they lived in the bosom of nature, and worshipped an invisible and unknown deity. Firm in his faith, domestic in his habits, the life of the Goth was simple and dignified, yet tender and affectionate.

The Greeks were remarkable for complacency and completion; they delighted in whatever pleased the eye; to them it was not enough to have merely the idea of a divinity, they must have it placed before them, shaped in the most perfect symmetry, and presented with the nicest judgment; and if we look upon any Greek production of art, the beauty of its parts, and the harmony of their union, the complete and complacent effect of the whole, are the striking characteristics. It is the same in their poetry. In Homer you have a poem perfect in its form, whether originally so, or from the labour of after critics, I know not; his descriptions are pictures brought vividly before you, and as far as the eye and understanding are concerned, I am indeed gratified. But if I wish my feelings to be affected, if I wish my heart to be touched, if I wish to melt into sentiment and tenderness, I must turn to the heroic songs of the Goths, to the poetry of the middle ages. The worship of statues in Greece had, in a civil sense, its advantage, and disadvantage; advantage in promoting statuary and the arts; disadvantage, in bringing their gods too much on a level with human beings, and thence depriving them of their dignity, and gradually giving rise to scepticism and ridicule. But no statue, no artificial emblem, could satisfy the Northman's mind; the dark wild imagery of nature, which surrounded him, and the freedom of his life, gave his mind a tendency to the infinite, so that he found rest in that which presented no end, and derived satisfaction from that which was indistinct.

We have few and uncertain vestiges of Gothic literature till the time of Theodoric, who encouraged his subjects to write, and who made a collection of their poems. These consisted chiefly of heroic songs, sung at the Court; for at that time this was the custom. Charlemagne, in the beginning of the ninth century, greatly encouraged letters, and made a further collection of the poems of his time, among which were several epic poems of great merit; or rather in strictness there was a vast cycle of heroic poems, or minstrelsies, from and out of which separate poems were composed. The form of poetry was, however, for the most part, the metrical romance and heroic tale. Charlemagne's army, or a large division of it, was utterly destroyed in the Pyrenees, when returning from a successful attack on the Arabs of Navarre and Arragon; yet the name of Roncesvalles became famous in the songs of the Gothic poets. The Greeks and Romans would not have done this; they would not have recorded in heroic verse the death and defeat of their fellow-countrymen. But the Goths, firm in their faith, with a constancy not to be shaken, celebrated those brave men who died for their religion and their country! What though they had been defeated, they died without fear, as they had lived without reproach; they left no stain on their names, for they fell fighting for their God, their liberty, and their rights; and the song that sang that day's reverse animated them to future victory and certain vengeance.

I must now turn to our great monarch, Alfred, one of the most august characters that any age has ever produced; and when I picture him after the toils of government and the dangers of battle, seated by a solitary lamp, translating the holy scriptures into the Saxon tongue,—when I reflect on his moderation in success, on his fortitude and perseverance in difficulty and defeat, and on the wisdom and extensive nature of his legislation, I am really at a loss which part of this great man's character most to admire. Yet above all, I see the grandeur, the freedom, the mildness, the domestic unity, the universal character of the middle ages condensed into Alfred's glorious institution of the trial by jury. I gaze upon it as the immortal symbol of that age;—an age called indeed dark;—but how could that age be considered dark, which solved the difficult problem of universal liberty, freed man from the shackles of tyranny, and subjected his actions to the decision of twelve of his fellow countrymen? The liberty of the Greeks was a phenomenon, a meteor, which blazed for a short time, and then sank into eternal darkness. It was a combination of most opposite materials, slavery and liberty. Such can neither be happy nor lasting. The Goths on the other hand said, You shall be our Emperor; but we must be Princes on our own estates, and over them you shall have no power! The Vassals said to their Prince, We will serve you in your wars, and defend your castle; but we must have liberty in our own circle, our cottage, our cattle, our proportion of land. The Cities said, We acknowledge you for our Emperor; but we must have our walls and our strongholds, and be governed by our own laws. Thus all combined, yet all were separate; all served, yet all were free. Such a government could not exist in a dark age. Our ancestors may not indeed have been deep in the metaphysics of the schools; they may not have shone in the fine arts; but much knowledge of human nature, much practical wisdom, must have existed amongst them, when this admirable constitution was formed; and I believe it is a decided truth, though certainly an awful lesson, that nations are not the most happy at the time when literature and the arts flourish the most among them.

The translations I had promised in my syllabus I shall defer to the end of the course, when I shall give a single lecture of recitations illustrative of the different ages of poetry. There is one Northern tale I will relate, as it is one from which Shakespeare derived that strongly marked and extraordinary scene between Richard III. and the Lady Anne. It may not be equal to that in strength and genius, but it is, undoubtedly, superior in decorum and delicacy.

A Knight had slain a Prince, the lord of a strong castle, in combat. He afterwards contrived to get into the castle, where he obtained an interview with the Princess's attendant, whose life he had saved in some encounter; he told her of his love for her mistress, and won her to his interest. She then slowly and gradually worked on her mistress's mind, spoke of the beauty of his person, the fire of his eyes, the sweetness of his voice, his valour in the field, his gentleness in the court; in short, by watching her opportunities, she at last filled the Princess's soul with this one image; she became restless; sleep forsook her; her curiosity to see this Knight became strong; but her maid still deferred the interview, till at length she confessed she was in love with him;—the Knight is then introduced, and the nuptials are quickly celebrated.

In this age there was a tendency in writers to the droll and the grotesque, and in the little dramas which at that time existed, there were singular instances of these. It was the disease of the age. It is a remarkable fact that Luther and Melancthon, the great religious reformers of that day, should have strongly recommended for the education of children, dramas, which at present would be considered highly indecorous, if not bordering on a deeper sin. From one which they particularly recommended, I will give a few extracts; more I should not think it right to do. The play opens with Adam and Eve washing and dressing their children to appear before the Lord, who is coming from heaven to hear them repeat the Lord's Prayer, Belief, &c. In the next scene the Lord appears seated like a schoolmaster, with the children standing round, when Cain, who is behind hand, and a sad pickle, comes running in with a bloody nose and his hat on. Adam says, "What, with your hat on!" Cain then goes up to shake hands with the Almighty, when Adam says (giving him a cuff), "Ah, would you give your left hand to the Lord?" At length Cain takes his place in the class, and it becomes his turn to say the Lord's Prayer. At this time the Devil (a constant attendant at that time) makes his appearance, and getting behind Cain, whispers in his ear; instead of the Lord's Prayer, Cain gives it so changed by the transposition of the words, that the meaning is reversed; yet this is so artfully done by the author, that it is exactly as an obstinate child would answer, who knows his lesson, yet does not choose to say it. In the last scene, horses in rich trappings and carriages covered with gold are introduced, and the good children are to ride in them and be Lord Mayors, Lords, &c.; Cain and the bad ones are to be made cobblers and tinkers, and only to associate with such.

This, with numberless others, was written by Hans Sachs. Our simple ancestors, firm in their faith, and pure in their morals, were only amused by these pleasantries, as they seemed to them, and neither they nor the reformers feared their having any influence hostile to religion. When I was many years back in the north of Germany, there were several innocent superstitions in practice. Among others at Christmas, presents used to be given to the children by the parents, and they were delivered on Christmas day by a person who personated, and was supposed by the children to be, Christ: early on Christmas morning he called, knocking loudly at the door, and (having received his instructions) left presents for the good and a rod for the bad. Those who have since been in Germany have found this custom relinquished; it was considered profane and irrational. Yet they have not found the children better, nor the mothers more careful of their offspring; they have not found their devotion more fervent, their faith more strong, nor their morality more pure.

1818   *1836*

ON ALLEGORY

Substitute a simile for the thing it resembles, instead of annexing it, and it becomes a metaphor: thus if in speaking of the Duke of Wellington's campaign in Portugal against Massena we should say, "At length he left his mountain strongholds and fell on the rear of the retreating army, as a cloud from the hill tops," it is a simile; if more briefly we say, "At length the cloud descended from its hill and discharged itself in thunder and lightning on the plain," it becomes a metaphor, and a metaphor is a fragment of an allegory. But if it be asked, how do you define an allegory so as to distinguish it from a fable, I can reply only by a confession of my ignorance and inability. The fact is, that allegory must be used in two senses —the one including, while the other is defined by excluding, fable. Fable is a shorter and simpler sort of allegory—this is the past sense—and again whatever of this kind is not a fable, not only is, but is called, an allegory. So a pony is a smaller sort of horse: and horses that are not ponies are called horses. A shrub is a smaller sort of tree: and we are in no risk of being misunderstood when we say, the laurel is but a shrub in this country, but in the south of Europe it is a tree. It may indeed

be justly said, that in a fable no allegoric agent or image should
be used which has not had some one paramount quality universally attributed to it beforehand, while in an allegory the resemblance may have been presented for the first time by the writer.
This is the true cause why animals, the heathen gods, and trees,
the properties of which are recalled by their very names, are
almost the only proper *dramatis personae* of a fable. A bear, a
fox, a tiger, a lion, Diana, an oak, a willow, are *every man's*
metaphor for clumsiness, cunning, ferocious or magnanimous
courage, chastity, unbendingness, and flexibility, and it would
be a safe rule that what would not be at once and generally
intelligible in a metaphor may be introduced in an allegory,
but ought not to be in a fable. This, however, is one of the
conditions of a good fable rather than a definition of a fable
generally, and fortunately the difficulty of defining a thing
or term is almost always in an inverse proportion to the
necessity. Linnaeus found no difficulty in establishing discriminating characters of the different tribes of apes, but very
great in scientific contra-distinctions between the genera man
and ape; but it is to be hoped that he had not met with many
individuals of either kind that had produced any practical
hesitation in determining his judgment.

We may then safely define allegoric writing as the employment of one set of agents and images with actions and accompaniments correspondent, so as to convey, while in disguise,
either moral qualities or conceptions of the mind that are not
in themselves objects of the senses, or other images, agents,
actions, fortunes, and circumstances, so that the difference is
everywhere presented to the eye or imagination while the likeness is suggested to the mind; and this connectedly so that the
parts combine to form a consistent whole. Whatever composition answering to this definition is not a fable, is entitled an
allegory—of which [what] may be called picture allegories, or
real or supposed pictures interpreted and moralized, and satirical allegories, we have several instances among the classics—as
the Tablet of Cebes, the Choice of Hercules, and Simonides'
origin of women—but of narrative or epic allegories scarce any,
the multiplicity of their gods and goddesses precluding it—unless we choose rather to say that all the machinery of their
poets is allegorical. Of a people who raised altars to fever, to
sport, to fright, etc., it is impossible to determine how far they
meant a personal power or a personification of a power. This
only is certain, that the introduction of these agents could not

have the same unmixed effect as the same agents used allegor-
ically produce on our minds, but something more nearly
resembling the effect produced by the introduction of characteristic saints in the Roman Catholic poets, or of Moloch, Belial,
and Mammon in the second Book of *Paradise Lost* compared
with his Sin and Death.

The most beautiful allegory ever composed, the Tale of
Cupid and Psyche, tho' composed by an heathen, was subsequent to the general spread of Christianity, and written by
one of those philosophers who attempted to Christianize a sort
of Oriental and Egyptian Platonism enough to set it up against
Christianity; but the first allegory completely modern in its
form is the *Psychomachia* or *Battle of the Soul* by Prudentius, a
Christian poet of the fifth century—facts that fully explain both
the origin and nature of narrative allegory, as a substitute for
the mythological imagery of polytheism, and differing from it
only in the more obvious and intentional distinction of the
sense from the symbol, and the known unreality of the latter—
so as to be a kind of intermediate step between actual persons
and mere personifications. But for this very cause it is incapable
of exciting any lively interest for any length of time, for if the
allegoric personage be strongly individualized so as to interest
us, we cease to think of it as allegory; and if it does not interest
us, it had better be away. The dullest and most defective parts
of Spenser are those in which we are compelled to think of his
agents as allegories—and how far the Sin and Death of Milton
are exceptions to this censure, is a delicate problem which I
shall attempt to solve in another lecture; but in that admirable
allegory, the first Part of *Pilgrim's Progress*, which delights
every one, the interest is so great that [in] spite of all the
writer's attempts to force the allegoric purpose on the reader's
mind by his strange names—Old Stupidity of the Tower of
Honesty, etc., etc.—his piety was baffled by his genius, and the
Bunyan of Parnassus had the better of Bunyan of the con-
venticle; and with the same illusion as we read any tale known
to be fictitious, as a novel, we go on with his characters as real
persons, who had been nicknamed by their neighbours. But the
most decisive verdict against narrative allegory is to be found
in Tasso's own account of what he would have the reader
understand by the persons and events of his *Jerusalem*. Apollo
be praised! not a thought like it would ever enter of its own
accord into any mortal mind; and what is an additional good
feature, when put there, it will not stay, having the very

opposite quality that snakes have—they come out of their holes into open view at the sound of sweet music, while the allegoric meaning slinks off at the very first notes, and lurks in murkiest oblivion—and utter invisibility.

1818   *1836*

ON DREAMS AND APPARITIONS

. . . I have thought it a mistake, tho' a very general one, that in ordinary dreams we judge the objects to be real. The fact is that we simply do not determine that they are unreal; and the sensations, which they seem to occasion, are in truth the causes and occasions of the images—of which there are two obvious proofs: first, that the strangest and most sudden transformations do not produce any sensation of surprise; and the second, that [in dreaming of] the most dreadful images, which during the dream were accompanied with agonies of terror, we merely wake or even turn round on the other side, and off fly both image and agony, which would be impossible if the sensations were produced by the images. This has always appeared to me absolute demonstration of the true nature of ghosts and apparitions, such of the tribe as were not pure lies. Fifty years ago, and to this day in the ruder parts of Great Britain and Ireland, in almost every kitchen, and in many parlours, you might meet persons who would assure you in the most solemn manner, so that you could not doubt of their *veracity* at least, that they had seen an apparition of such and such a person—in many cases, that the apparition had spoken to them; and they describe themselves as in an agony of terror. "But how were you in health the hour after?"—"Oh, there was nothing the matter with my health." Now take the other class of facts, in which real ghosts have appeared. I mean tricks and dressed up figures for the purpose of passing for an apparition. In every instance I have known or heard of (and I have collected very many) the consequence has been either sudden death, or fits, or idiocy, or mania, or a brain fever. Whence comes the difference? Evidently from this—that in the one case the whole of the nervous system has been by slight internal causes, gradually and all together, brought into a certain state, the sensation of which is extravagantly exaggerated during sleep, and of which the images are the mere effects and exponents, as the motions of the weathercock are of the wind; while in the other case, the image, rushing thro' the senses upon a nervous system wholly unprepared, actually causes the sensation, which is sometimes powerful enough to produce a total check, and almost always lesion or inflammation. Who has not witnessed the difference in shock when we have leaped down half a dozen steps intentionally, and that of having missed a single stair? How comparatively severe the latter is! To return, however, to dreams, I not only believe, from the reasons given, but have more than once actually experienced, that the most fearful forms, when produced simply by association, instead of causing pain, produce no other effect than the same would do if they had passed thro' my mind as thoughts, while I was composing a fairy tale. The whole depends on the wise and gracious law in our nature that the actual bodily sensations called forth according to the law of association by thoughts and images of the mind, never greatly transcend the limits of pleasurable feeling in a tolerably healthy frame, unless where an act of judgment supervenes and interprets them as purporting instant danger to ourselves, as for instance in the case of the King in *Hamlet*.

The fact really is, as to apparitions, that the terror produces the image instead of the contrary; for *in omnem actum perceptionis influit imaginatio,* as says Wolfe.

O, strange is the self-power of the imagination—when painful sensations have made it their interpreter, or returning gladsomeness or convalescence has made its chilled and evanished figures and landscape bud, blossom, and live in scarlet, green, and snowy white (like the fire-screen inscribed with the nitrate and muriate of cobalt,) —strange is the power to represent the events and circumstances, even to the anguish or the triumph of the *quasi*-credent soul, while the necessary conditions, the only possible causes of such contingencies, are known to be in fact quite hopeless;—yea, when the pure mind would recoil from the eve-lengthened shadow of an approaching hope, as from a crime;—and yet the effect shall have place, and substance, and living energy, and, on a blue islet of ether, in a whole sky of blackest cloudage, shine like a firstling of creation!

To return, however, to apparitions, and by way of an amusing illustration of the nature and value of even contemporary testimony upon such subjects, I will present you with a passage, literally translated by my friend, Mr. Southey, from the well-known work of Bernal Dias, one of the companions of Cortes, in the conquest of Mexico:

> Here it is that Gomara says, that Francisco de Morla rode forward on a dappled grey horse, before Cortes and the cavalry came up, and that the apostle St. Iago, or St. Peter, was there. I must say that all our works and victories are by the hand of our Lord Jesus Christ, and that in this battle there were for each of us so many Indians, that they could have covered us with handfuls of earth, if it had not been that the great mercy of God helped us in every thing. And it may be that he of whom Gomara speaks, was the glorious Santiago or San Pedro, and I, as a sinner, was not worthy to see him; but he whom I saw there and knew, was Francisco de Morla on a chestnut horse, who came up with Cortes. And it seems to me that now while I am writing this, the whole war is represented before these sinful eyes, just in the manner as we then went through it. And though I, as an unworthy sinner, might not deserve to see either of these glorious apostles, there were in our company above four hundred soldiers, and Cortes, and many other knights; and it would have been talked of and testified, and they would have made a church, when they peopled the town, which would have been called Santiago de la Vittoria, or San Pedro de la Vittoria, as it is now called, Santa Maria de la Vittoria. And if it was, as Gomara says, bad Christians must we have been, when our Lord God sent us his holy apostles, not to acknowledge his great mercy, and venerate his church daily. And would to God, it had been, as the Chronicler says!—but till I read his Chronicle, I never heard such a thing from any of the conquerors who were there.

Now, what if the odd accident of such a man as Bernal Dias' writing a history had not taken place! Gomara's account, the account of a contemporary, which yet must have been read by scores who were present, would have remained uncontradicted. I remember the story of a man, whom the devil met and talked with, but left at a particular lane;—the man followed him with his eyes, and when the devil got to the turning or bend of the lane, he vanished! The devil was upon this occasion drest in a blue coat, plush waistcoat, leather breeches and boots, and talked and looked just like a common man, except as to a particular lock of hair which he had. "And how do you know then that it was the devil?" —"How do I know," replied the fellow,—"why, if it had not been the devil, being drest as he was, and looking as he did, why should I have been sore stricken with fright, when I first saw him? and why should I be in such a tremble all the while he talked? And, moreover, he had a particular sort of a kind of a lock, and when I groaned and said, upon every question he asked me, Lord have mercy upon me! or, Christ have mercy upon me! it was plain enough that he did not like it, and so he left me!"—The man was quite sober when he related this story; but as it happened to him on his return from market, it is probable that he was then muddled. As for myself, I was actually seen in Newgate in the winter of 1798;—the person who saw me there, said he had asked my name of Mr. A. B. a known acquaintance of mine, who told him that it was young Coleridge, who had married the eldest Miss——. "Will you go to Newgate, Sir?" said my friend; "for I assure you that Mr. C. is now in Germany." "Very willingly," replied the other, and away they went to Newgate, and sent for A. B. "Coleridge," cried he, "in Newgate! God forbid!" I said, "young Col—— who married the eldest Miss——." The names were something similar. And yet this person had himself really seen me at one of my lectures.

I remember, upon the occasion of my inhaling the nitrous oxide at the Royal Institution, about five minutes afterwards, a gentleman came from the other side of the theatre and said to me,—"Was it not ravishingly delightful, Sir?"—"It was highly pleasurable, no doubt."—"Was it not very like sweet music?"—"I cannot say I perceived any analogy to it."—"Did you not say it was very like Mrs. Billington singing by your ear?"—"No, Sir, I said that while I was breathing the gas, there was a singing in my ears."

1818   *1836*

ON THE ALCHEMISTS

There have been very strange and incredible stories told of and by the alchemists. Perhaps in some of them there may have been a specific form of mania, originating in the constant intension of the mind on an imaginary end, associated with an immense variety of means, all of them substances not familiar to men in general, and in forms strange and unlike to those of ordinary nature. Sometimes, it seems as if the alchemists wrote like the Pythagoreans on music, imagining a metaphysical and inaudible music as the basis of the audible. It is clear that by sulphur they meant the solar rays or light, and by mercury the principle of ponderability, so that their theory was the same with that of the Heraclitic physics, or the modern German *Naturphilosophie,* which deduces all things from light and gravitation, each being bipolar; gravitation = north and south, or attraction and repulsion; light = east and west, or contraction and dilation; and gold being the tetrad, or interpenetration of both, as water was the dyad of light, and iron the dyad of gravitation.

It is, probably, unjust to accuse the alchemists generally of dabbling with attempts at magic in the common sense of the term. The supposed exercise of magical power always involved some moral guilt, directly or indirectly, as in stealing a piece of meat to lay on warts, touching humours with the hand of an executed person, &c. Rites of this sort and other practices of sorcery have always been regarded with trembling abhorrence by all nations, even the most ignorant, as by the Africans, the Hudson's Bay people and others. The alchemists were, no doubt, often considered as dealers in art magic, and many of them were not unwilling that such a belief should be prevalent; and the more earnest among them evidently looked at their association of substances, fumigations, and other chemical operations as merely ceremonial, and seem, therefore, to have had a deeper meaning, that of evoking a latent power. It would be profitable to make a collection of all the cases of cures by magical charms and incantations; much useful information might, probably, be derived from it; for it is to be observed that such rites are the form in which medical knowledge would be preserved amongst a barbarous and ignorant people.

1818   *1836*

ON THE DEFINITION OF POETRY

Poetry is not the proper antithesis to prose, but to science. Poetry is opposed to science, and prose to metre. The proper and immediate object of science is the acquirement, or communication, of truth; the proper and immediate object of poetry is the communication of immediate pleasure. This definition is useful; but as it would include novels and other works of fiction, which yet we do not call poems, there must be some additional character by which poetry is not only divided from opposites, but likewise distinguished from disparate, though similar, modes of composition. Now how is this to be effected?

In animated prose, the beauties of nature, and the passions and accidents of human nature, are often expressed in that natural language which the contemplation of them would suggest to a pure and benevolent mind; yet still neither we nor the writers call such a work a poem, though no work could deserve that name which did not include all this, together with something else. What is this? It is that pleasurable emotion, that peculiar state and degree of excitement, which arises in the poet himself in the act of composition;—and in order to understand this, we must combine a more than ordinary sympathy with the objects, emotions, or incidents contemplated by the poet, consequent on a more than common sensibility, with a more than ordinary activity of the mind in respect of the fancy and the imagination. Hence is produced a more vivid reflection of the truths of nature and of the human heart, united with a constant activity modifying and correcting these truths by that sort of pleasurable emotion which the exercise of all our faculties gives in a certain degree; but which can only be felt in perfection under the full play of those powers of mind, which are spontaneous rather than voluntary, and in which the effort required bears no proportion to the activity enjoyed. This is the state which permits the production of a highly pleasurable whole, of which each part shall also communicate for itself a distinct and conscious pleasure; and hence arises the definition, which I trust is now intelligible, that poetry, or rather a poem, is a species of composition, opposed to science, as having intellectual pleasure for its object, and as attaining its end by the use of language natural to us in a state of excitement,—but distinguished from other species of composition, not excluded by the former criterion, by permitting a pleasure from the whole consistent with a consciousness of pleasure from the component parts;—and the perfection of which is, to communicate from each part the greatest immediate pleasure compatible with the largest sum of pleasure on the whole. This, of course, will vary with the different modes of poetry;—and that splendor of particular lines, which would be worthy of admiration in an impassioned elegy, or a short indignant satire, would be a blemish and proof of vile taste in a tragedy or an epic poem.

It is remarkable, by the way, that Milton in three incidental words has implied all which for the purposes of more distinct apprehension, which at first must be slow-paced in order to be distinct, I have endeavored to develop in a precise and strictly adequate definition. Speaking of poetry, he says, as in a parenthesis, "which is simple, sensuous, passionate." How awful is the power of words!—fearful often in their consequences when merely felt, not understood; but most awful when both felt and understood!—Had these three words only been properly understood by, and present in the minds of, general readers, not only almost a library of false poetry would have been either precluded or stillborn, but, what is of more consequence, works truly excellent and capable of enlarging the understanding, warming and purifying the heart, and placing in the centre of the whole being the germs of noble and manlike actions, would have been the common diet of the intellect instead. For the first condition, simplicity,—while, on the one hand, it distinguishes poetry from the arduous processes of science, laboring towards an end not yet arrived at, and supposes a smooth and finished road, on which the reader is to walk onward easily, with streams murmuring by his side, and trees and flowers and human dwellings to make his journey as delightful as the object of it is desirable, instead of having to toil with the pioneers, and painfully make the road on which others are to travel,—precludes, on the other hand, every affectation and morbid peculiarity;—the second condition, sensuousness, insures that framework of objectivity, that definiteness and articulation of imagery, and that modification of the images themselves, without which poetry becomes flattened into mere didactics of practice, or evaporated into a hazy, unthoughtful daydreaming; and the third condition, passion, provides that neither thought nor imagery shall be simply objective, but that the *passio vera* of humanity shall warm and animate both.

To return, however, to the previous definition, this most general and distinctive character of a poem originates in the poetic genius itself; and though it comprises whatever can with any propriety be called a poem (unless that word be a mere lazy synonyme for a composition in metre), it yet becomes a just, and not merely discriminative, but full and adequate, definition of poetry in its highest and most peculiar sense, only so far as the distinction still results from the poetic genius, which sustains and modifies the emotions, thoughts, and vivid representations of the poem by the energy without effort of the poet's own mind,—by the spontaneous activity of his imagination and fancy, and by whatever else with these reveals itself in the balancing and reconciling of opposite or discordant qualities, sameness with difference, a sense of novelty and freshness with old or customary objects, a more than usual state of emotion with more than usual order, self-possession and judgment with enthusiasm and vehement feeling,—and which, while it blends and harmonizes the natural and the artificial, still subordinates art to nature, the manner to the matter, and our admiration of the poet to our sympathy with the images, passions, characters, and incidents of the poem:—

> Doubtless, this could not be, but that she turns
> Bodies to *spirit* by sublimation strange,
> As fire converts to fire the things it burns—
> As we our food into our nature change!
>
> From their gross matter she abstracts *their* forms,
> And draws a kind of quintessence from things,
> Which to her proper nature she transforms
> To bear them light on her celestial wings!
>
> *Thus* doth she, when from *individual states*
> She doth abstract the universal kinds,
> *Which then reclothed in divers names and fates*
> *Steal access thro' our senses to our minds.*

1818   *1836*

ON STYLE

I have, I believe, formerly observed with regard to the character of the governments of the East, that their tendency was despotic, that is, towards unity; whilst that of the Greek governments, on the other hand, leaned to the manifold and the popular, the unity in them being purely ideal, namely of all as an identification of the whole. In the northern or Gothic nations the aim and purpose of the government were the preservation of the rights and interests of the individual in conjunction with those of the whole. The individual interest was sacred. In the character and tendency of the Greek and Gothic languages there is precisely the same relative difference. In Greek the sentences are long, and the structure architectural, so that each part or clause is insignificant when compared with the whole. The result is every thing, the steps and processes nothing. But in the Gothic and, generally, in what we call the modern, languages, the structure is short, simple, and complete in each part, and the connection of the parts with the sum total of the

discourse is maintained by the sequency of the logic, or the
community of feelings excited between the writer and his
readers. As an instance equally delightful and complete, of what
may be called the Gothic structure as contra-distinguished
from that of the Greeks, let me cite a part of our famous
Chaucer's character of a parish priest as he should be. Can it
ever be quoted too often?

> A good man thér was of religiöun
> That was a pouré Parsone of a toun,
> But riche he was of holy thought and werk;
> He was alsó a lerned man, a clerk,
> That Cristés gospel trewély wolde preche;
> His párishens devoutly wolde he teche;
> Benigne he was, and wonder diligent,
> And in adverste ful patient,
> And swiche he was ypreved often sithes;
> Ful loth were him to cursen for his tithes,
> But rather wolde he yeven out of doute
> Unto his pouré párishens aboute
> Of hís offríng, and eke of his substánce;
> He coude in litel thing have suffisance:
> Wide was his parish, and houses fer asonder,
> But he ne left nought for no rain ne thonder,
> In sikenesse and in mischief to visíte
> The ferrest in his parish moche and lite
> Upon his fete, and in his hand a staf:
> This noble ensample to his shepe he yaf,
> That first he wrought, and afterward he taught,
> Out of the gospel he the wordés caught,
> And this figúre he added yet thereto,
> That if gold rusté, what should iren do.
>
>   He setté not his benefice to hire,
> And lette his shepe accombred in the mire,
> And ran untó Londón untó Seint Poules,
> To seken him a chantérie foɪ soules,
> Or with a brotherhede to be withold,
> But dwelt at home, and kepte wel his fold,
> So that the wolf ne made it not miscarie:
> He was a shepherd and no mercenarie;
> And though he holy were and vertuous,
> He was to sinful men not dispitous,
> Ne of his speché dangerous ne digne,
> But in his teching discrete and benigne,
> To drawen folk to heven with fairénesse,
> By good ensample was his besinesse;
> But it were any persone obstinat,

What so he were of high or low estat,
Him wolde he snibben sharply for the nones:
A better preest I trowe that no wher non is;
He waited after no pompe ne reverence,
He maked him no spiced conscience,
But Cristés love and his apostles' twelve
He taught, but first he folwed it himselve.

Such change as really took place in the style of our literature after Chaucer's time is with difficulty perceptible, on account of the dearth of writers, during the civil wars of the fifteenth century. But the transition was not very great; and accordingly we find in Latimer and our other venerable authors about the time of Edward VI, as in Luther, the general characteristics of the earliest manner;—that is, every part popular, and the discourse addressed to all degrees of intellect;—the sentences short, the tone vehement, and the connection of the whole produced by honesty and singleness of purpose, intensity of passion, and pervading importance of the subject.

Another and a very different species of style is that which was derived from, and founded on, the admiration and cultivation of the classical writers, and which was more exclusively addressed to the learned class in society. I have previously mentioned Boccaccio as the original Italian introducer of this manner, and the great models of it in English are Hooker, Bacon, Milton, and Taylor, although it may be traced in many other authors of that age. In all these the language is dignified but plain, genuine English, although elevated and brightened by superiority of intellect in the writer. Individual words themselves are always used by them in their precise meaning, without either affectation or slipslop. The letters and state papers of Sir Francis Walsingham are remarkable for excellence in style of this description. In Jeremy Taylor the sentences are often extremely long, and yet are generally so perspicuous in consequence of their logical structure, that they require no perusal to be understood; and it is for the most part the same in Milton and Hooker.

Take the following sentence as a specimen of the sort of style to which I have been alluding:—

Concerning Faith, the principal object whereof is that eternal verity which hath discovered the treasures of hidden wisdom in Christ; concerning Hope, the highest object whereof is that everlasting goodness which in Christ doth quicken the dead; concerning Charity, the

final object whereof is that incomprehensible beauty which shineth
in the countenance of Christ, the Son of the living God: concerning
these virtues, the first of which beginning here with a weak apprehension of things not seen, endeth with the intuitive vision of God
in the world to come; the second beginning here with a trembling
expectation of things far removed, and as yet but only heard of,
endeth with real and actual fruition of that which no tongue can
express; the third beginning here with a weak inclination of heart
towards him unto whom we are not able to approach, endeth with
endless union, the mystery whereof is higher than the reach of the
thoughts of men; concerning that Faith, Hope, and Charity, without which there can be no salvation, was there ever any mention
made saving only in that Law which God himself hath from Heaven
revealed? There is not in the world a syllable muttered with certain
truth concerning any of these three, more than hath been super-
naturally received from the mouth of the eternal God.

Eccles. Pol. i. s. 11.

The unity in these writers is produced by the unity of the
subject, and the perpetual growth and evolution of the
thoughts, one generating, and explaining, and justifying, the
place of another, not, as it is in Seneca, where the thoughts,
striking as they are, are merely strung together like beads,
without any causation or progression. The words are selected
because they are the most appropriate, regard being had to
the dignity of the total impression, and no merely big phrases
are used where plain ones would have sufficed, even in the most
learned of their works.

There is some truth in a remark, which I believe was made
by Sir Joshua Reynolds, that the greatest man is he who forms
the taste of a nation, and that the next greatest is he who cor-
rupts it. The true classical style of Hooker and his fellows was
easily open to corruption; and Sir Thomas Brown it was, who,
though a writer of great genius, first effectually injured the literary taste of the nation by his introduction of learned words,
merely because they were learned. It would be difficult to describe Brown adequately; exuberant in conception and conceit,
dignified, hyperlatinistic, a quiet and sublime enthusiast; yet a
fantast, a humorist, a brain with a twist; egotistic like Mon-
taigne, yet with a feeling heart and an active curiosity, which,
however, too often degenerates into a hunting after oddities. In
his *Hydriotaphia,* and, indeed, almost all his works, the entireness of his mental action is very observable; he metamorphoses
every thing, be it what it may, into the subject under consideration. But Sir Thomas Brown with all his faults had a genuine

idiom; and it is the existence of an individual idiom in each, that makes the principal writers before the Restoration the great patterns or integers of English style. In them the precise intended meaning of a word can never be mistaken; whereas in the latter writers, as especially in Pope, the use of words is for the most part purely arbitrary, so that the context will rarely show the true specific sense, but only that something of the sort is designed. A perusal of the authorities cited by Johnson in his dictionary under any leading word, will give you a lively sense of this declension in etymological truth of expression in the writers after the Restoration, or perhaps, strictly, after the middle of the reign of Charles II.

The general characteristic of the style of our literature down to the period which I have just mentioned, was gravity, and in Milton and some other writers of his day there are perceptible traces of the sternness of republicanism. Soon after the Restoration a material change took place, and the cause of royalism was graced, sometimes disgraced, by every shade of lightness of manner. A free and easy style was considered as a test of loyalty, or at all events, as a badge of the cavalier party; you may detect it occasionally even in Barrow, who is, however, in general remarkable for dignity and logical sequency of expression; but in L'Estrange, Collyer, and the writers of that class, this easy manner was carried out to the utmost extreme of slang and ribaldry. Yet still the works, even of these last authors, have considerable merit in one point of view; their language is level to the understandings of all men; it is an actual transcript of the colloquialism of the day, and is accordingly full of life and reality. Roger North's life of his brother, the Lord Keeper, is the most valuable specimen of this class of our literature; it is delightful, and much beyond any other of the writings of his contemporaries.

From the common opinion that the English style attained its greatest perfection in and about Queen Anne's reign I altogether dissent; not only because it is in one species alone in which it can be pretended that the writers of that age excelled their predecessors; but also because the specimens themselves are not equal, upon sound principles of judgment, to much that had been produced before. The classical structure of Hooker— the impetuous, thought-agglomerating flood of Taylor—to these there is no pretence of a parallel; and for mere ease and grace, is Cowley inferior to Addison, being as he is so much more thoughtful and full of fancy? Cowley, with the omission of a quaintness here and there, is probably the best model of style for modern imitation in general. Taylor's periods have been frequently attempted by his admirers; you may, perhaps, just catch the turn of a simile or single image, but to write in the real manner of Jeremy Taylor would require as mighty a mind as his. Many parts of Algernon Sidney's treatises afford excellent exemplars of a good modern practical style; and Dryden in his prose works is a still better model, if you add a stricter and purer grammar. It is, indeed, worthy of remark that all our great poets have been good prose writers, as Chaucer, Spenser, Milton; and this probably arose from their just sense of metre. For a true poet will never confound verse and prose; whereas it is almost characteristic of indifferent prose writers that they should be constantly slipping into scraps of metre. Swift's style is, in its line, perfect; the manner is a complete expression of the matter, the terms appropriate, and the artifice concealed. It is simplicity in the true sense of the word.

After the Revolution, the spirit of the nation became much more commercial than it had been before; a learned body, or clerisy, as such, gradually disappeared, and literature in general began to be addressed to the common miscellaneous public. That public had become accustomed to, and required, a strong stimulus; and to meet the requisitions of the public taste, a style was produced which by combining triteness of thought with singularity and excess of manner of expression, was calculated at once to soothe ignorance and to flatter vanity. The thought was carefully kept down to the immediate apprehension of the commonest understanding, and the dress was as anxiously arranged for the purpose of making the thought appear something very profound. The essence of this style consisted in a mock antithesis, that is, an opposition of mere sounds, in a rage for personification, the abstract made animate, far-fetched metaphors, strange phrases, metrical scraps, in every thing, in short, but genuine prose. Style is, of course, nothing else but the art of conveying the meaning appropriately and with perspicuity, whatever that meaning may be, and one criterion of style is that it shall not be translatable without injury to the meaning. Johnson's style has pleased many from the very fault of being perpetually translatable; he creates an impression of cleverness by never saying any thing in a common way. The best specimen of this manner is in Junius, because his antithesis is less merely verbal than Johnson's. Gibbon's manner is the worst of all; it has every fault of which this peculiar style is capable. Tacitus is an example of it in Latin; in coming from Cicero you feel the *falsetto* immediately.

In order to form a good style, the primary rule and condition is, not to attempt to express ourselves in language before we thoroughly know our own meaning:—when a man perfectly understands himself, appropriate diction will generally be at his command either in writing or speaking. In such cases the thoughts and the words are associated. In the next place preciseness in the use of terms is required, and the test is whether you can translate the phrase adequately into simpler terms, regard being had to the feeling of the whole passage. Try this upon Shakespeare, or Milton, and see if you can substitute other simpler words in any given passage without a violation of the meaning or tone. The source of bad writing is the desire to be something more than a man of sense,—the straining to be thought a genius; and it is just the same in speech-making. If men would only say what they have to say in plain terms, how much more eloquent they would be! Another rule is to avoid converting mere abstractions into persons. I believe you will very rarely find in any great writer before the Revolution the possessive case of an inanimate noun used in prose instead of the dependent case, as 'the watch's hand,' for 'the hand of the watch.' The possessive or Saxon genitive was confined to persons, or at least to animated subjects. And I can not conclude this Lecture without insisting on the importance of accuracy of style as being near akin to veracity and truthful habits of mind; he who thinks loosely will write loosely, and, perhaps, there is some moral inconvenience in the common forms of our grammars which give our children so many obscure terms for material distinctions. Let me also exhort you to careful examination of what you read, if it be worth any perusal at all; such an examination will be a safeguard from fanaticism, the universal origin of which is in the contemplation of phenomena without investigation into their causes.

1818   *1836*

ON SHAKSPEARE'S JUDGMENT

Thus then Shakspeare appears, from his Venus and Adonis and Rape of Lucrece alone, apart from all his great works, to have possessed all the conditions of the true poet. Let me now proceed to destroy, as far as may be in my power, the popular notion that he was a great dramatist by mere instinct, that he grew immortal in his own despite, and sank below men of second or third-rate power, when he attempted aught beside the drama—even as bees construct their cells and manufacture their honey to admirable perfection; but would in vain attempt to build a nest. Now this mode of reconciling a compelled sense of inferiority with a feeling of pride, began in a few pedants, who having read that Sophocles was the great model of tragedy, and Aristotle the infallible dictator of its rules, and finding that the Lear, Hamlet, Othello, and other master-pieces were neither in imitation of Sophocles, nor in obedience to Aristotle,—and not having (with one or two exceptions) the courage to affirm, that the delight which their country received from generation to generation, in defiance of the alterations of circumstances and habits, was wholly groundless,—took upon them, as a happy medium and refuge, to talk of Shakspeare as a sort of beautiful *lusus naturæ,* a delightful monster,—wild, indeed, and without taste or judgment, but like the inspired idiots so much venerated in the East, uttering, amid the strangest follies, the sublimest truths. In nine places out of ten in which I find his awful name mentioned, it is with some epithet of "wild," "irregular," "pure child of nature," &c. If all this be true, we must submit to it; though to a thinking mind it can not but be painful to find any excellence, merely human, thrown out of all human analogy, and thereby leaving us neither rules for imitation, nor motives to imitate;—but if false, it is a dangerous falsehood;—for it affords a refuge to secret self-conceit,—enables a vain man at once to escape his reader's indignation by general swoln panegyrics, and merely by his *ipse dixit* to treat, as contemptible, what he has not intellect enough to comprehend, or soul to feel, without assigning any reason, or referring his opinion to any demonstrative principle; thus leaving Shakspeare as a sort of grand Lama, adored indeed, and his very excrements prized as relics, but with no authority or real influence. I grieve that every late voluminous edition of his works would enable me to substantiate the present charge with a variety of facts, one tenth of which would of themselves exhaust the time allotted to me. Every critic, who has or has not made a collection of black-letter books—in itself a useful and respectable amusement,—puts on the seven-league boots of self-opinion, and strides at once from an illustrator into a supreme judge, and blind and deaf, fills his three-ounce phial at the waters of

Niagara; and determines positively the greatness of the cataract to be neither more nor less than his three-ounce phial has been able to receive.

I think this a very serious subject. It is my earnest desire—my passionate endeavor,—to enforce at various times, and by various arguments and instances, the close and reciprocal connection of just taste with pure morality. Without that acquaintance with the heart of man, or that docility and childlike gladness to be made acquainted with it, which those only can have, who dare look at their own hearts—and that with a steadiness which religion only has the power of reconciling with sincere humility;—without this, and the modesty produced by it, I am deeply convinced that no man, however wide his erudition, however patient his antiquarian researches, can possibly understand, or be worthy of understanding, the writings of Shakspeare.

Assuredly that criticism of Shakspeare will alone be genial which is reverential. The Englishman, who, without reverence, a proud and affectionate reverence, can utter the name of William Shakspeare, stands disqualified for the office of critic. He wants one at least of the very senses, the language of which he is to employ, and will discourse at best, but as a blind man, while the whole harmonious creation of light and shade with all its subtle interchange of deepening and dissolving colors rises in silence to the silent *fiat* of the uprising Apollo. However inferior in ability I may be to some who have followed me, I own I am proud that I was the first in time who publicly demonstrated to the full extent of the position, that the supposed irregularity and extravagances of Shakspeare were the mere dreams of a pedantry that arraigned the eagle because it had not the dimensions of the swan. In all the successive courses of lectures delivered by me, since my first attempt at the Royal Institution, it has been, and it still remains, my object, to prove that in all points from the most important to the most minute, the judgment of Shakspeare is commensurate with his genius—nay, that his genius reveals itself in his judgment, as in its most exalted form. And the more gladly do I recur to this subject from the clear conviction, that to judge aright, and with distinct consciousness of the grounds of our judgment, concerning the works of Shakspeare, implies the power and the means of judging rightly of all other works of intellect, those of abstract science alone excepted.

It is a painful truth that not only individuals, but even whole nations, are ofttimes so enslaved to the habits of their education and immediate circumstances, as not to judge disinterestedly even on those subjects, the very pleasure arising from which consists in its disinterestedness, namely, on subjects of taste and polite literature. Instead of deciding concerning their own modes and customs by any rule of reason, nothing appears rational, becoming, or beautiful to them, but what coincides with the peculiarities of their education. In this narrow circle, individuals may attain to exquisite discrimination, as the French critics have done in their own literature; but a true critic can no more be such without placing himself on some central point, from which he may command the whole, that is, some general rule, which, founded in reason, or the faculties common to all men, must therefore apply to each—than an astronomer can explain the movements of the solar system without taking his stand in the sun. And let me remark, that this will not tend to produce despotism, but, on the contrary, true tolerance, in the critic. He will, indeed, require, as the spirit and substance of a work, something true in human nature itself, and independent of all circumstances; but in the mode of applying it, he will estimate genius and judgment according to the felicity with which the imperishable soul of intellect, shall have adapted itself to the age, the place, and the existing manners. The error he will expose, lies in reversing this, and holding up the mere circumstances as perpetual to the utter neglect of the power which can alone animate them. For art can not exist without, or apart from, nature; and what has man of his own to give to his fellow-man, but his own thoughts and feelings, and his observations, so far as they are modified by his own thoughts or feelings?

Let me, then, once more submit this question to minds emancipated alike from national, or party, or sectarian prejudice:— Are the plays of Shakspeare works of rude uncultivated genius, in which the splendor of the parts compensates, if aught can compensate, for the barbarous shapelessness and irregularity of the whole? Or is the form equally admirable with the matter, and the judgment of the great poet, not less deserving our wonder than his genius?—Or, again, to repeat the question in other words:—Is Shakspeare a great dramatic poet on account only of those beauties and excellences which he possesses in common with the ancients, but with diminished claims to our love and honor to the full extent of his differences from them?— Or are these very differences additional proofs of poetic wisdom, at once results and symbols of living power as contrasted with lifeless mechanism—of free and rival originality as contra-distinguished from servile imitation, or, more accurately, a blind copying of effects, instead of a true imitation of the essential principles?—Imagine not that I am about to oppose genius to rules. No! the comparative value of these rules is the very cause to be tried. The spirit of poetry, like all other living powers, must of necessity circumscribe itself by rules, were it only to unite power with beauty. It must embody in order to reveal itself; but a living body is of necessity an organized one; and what is organization but the connection of parts in and for a whole, so that each part is at once end and means?—This is no discovery of criticism;—it is a necessity of the human mind; and all nations have felt and obeyed it, in the invention of metre, and measured sounds, as the vehicle and *involucrum* of poetry— itself a fellow-growth from the same life—even as the bark is to the tree!

(g) No work of true genius dares want its appropriate form, neither indeed is there any danger of this. As it must not, so genius can not, be lawless; [for it is even this that constitutes it genius—the power of acting creatively under laws of its own origination.] How then comes it that not only single *Zoili,* but whole nations have combined in unhesitating condemnation of our great dramatist, as a sort of African nature, rich in beautiful monsters—as a wild heath where islands of fertility look the greener from the surrounding waste, where the loveliest plants now shine out among unsightly weeds, and now are choked by their parasitic growth, so intertwined that we can not disentangle the weed without snapping the flower?—In this statement I have had no reference to the vulgar abuse of Voltaire, save as far as his charges are coincident with the decisions of Shakspeare's own commentators and (so they would tell you) almost idolatrous admirers. The true ground of the mistake lies in the confounding mechanical regularity with organic form. The form is mechanic, when on any given material we impress a pre-determined form, not necessarily arising out of the properties of the material;—as when to a mass of wet clay we give whatever shape we wish it to retain when hardened. The organic form, on the other hand, is innate; it shapes, as it develops, itself from within, and the fulness of its development is one and the same with the perfection of its outward form. Such as the life is, such is the form. Nature, the prime genial artist, inexhaustible in diverse powers, is equally inexhaustible

in forms;—each exterior is the physiognomy of the being within
—its true image reflected and thrown out from the concave
mirror;—and even such is the appropriate excellence of her
chosen poet, of our own Shakspeare—himself a nature human-
ized, a genial understanding directing self-consciously a power
and an implicit wisdom deeper even than our consciousness.

I greatly dislike beauties and selections in general; but as
proof positive of his unrivalled excellence, I should like to try
Shakspeare by this criterion. Make out your amplest catalogue
of all the human faculties, as reason or the moral law, the will,
the feeling of the coincidence of the two (a feeling *sui generis et
demonstratio demonstrationum*) called the conscience, the understanding or prudence, wit, fancy, imagination, judgment—
and then of the objects on which these are to be employed, as
the beauties, the terrors, and the seeming caprices of nature, the
realities and the capabilities, that is, the actual and the ideal,
of the human mind, conceived as an individual or as a social
being, as in innocence or in guilt, in a play-paradise, or in a
war-field of temptation;—and then compare with Shakspeare
under each of these heads all or any of the writers in prose
and verse that have ever lived! Who, that is competent to judge,
doubts the result?—And ask your own hearts—ask your own common-sense—to conceive the possibility of this man being—I say
not, the drunken savage of that wretched socialist, whom
Frenchmen, to their shame, have honored before their elder
and better worthies—but the anomalous, the wild, the irregular,
genius of our daily criticism! What! are we to have miracles
in sport?—Or, I speak reverently, does God choose idiots by
whom to convey divine truths to man?

1818   *1836*

ON HAMLET

Hamlet was the play, or rather Hamlet himself was the character, in the intuition and exposition of which I first made my
turn for philosophical criticism, and especially for insight into
the genius of Shakspeare, noticed. This happened first among
my acquaintances, as Sir George Beaumont will bear witness;
and subsequently, long before Schlegel had delivered at Vienna
the lectures on Shakspeare, which he afterwards published, I
had given on the same subject eighteen lectures substantially

the same, proceeding from the very same point of view, and deducing the same conclusions, so far as I either then agreed, or now agree, with him. I gave these lectures at the Royal Institution, before six or seven hundred auditors of rank and eminence, in the spring of the same year, in which Sir Humphrey Davy, a fellow-lecturer, made his great revolutionary discoveries in chemistry. Even in detail the coincidence of Schlegel with my lectures was so extraordinary, that all who at a later period heard the same words, taken by me from my notes of the lectures at the Royal Institution, concluded a borrowing on my part from Schlegel. Mr. Hazlitt, whose hatred of me is in such an inverse ratio to my zealous kindness towards him, as to be defended by his warmest admirer, Charles Lamb— (who, God bless him! besides his characteristic obstinacy of adherence to old friends, as long at least as they are at all down in the world, is linked as by a charm to Hazlitt's conversation) —only as 'frantic;'—Mr. Hazlitt, I say, himself replied to an assertion of my plagiarism from Schlegel in these words;—"That is a lie; for I myself heard the very same character of Hamlet from Coleridge before he went to Germany, and when he had neither read nor could read a page of German!" Now Hazlitt was on a visit to me at my cottage at Nether Stowey, Somerset, in the summer of the year 1798, in the September of which year I first was out of sight of the shores of Great Britain. Recorded by me, S. T. Coleridge, 7th January, 1819.

The seeming inconsistencies in the conduct and character of Hamlet have long exercised the conjectural ingenuity of critics; and, as we are always loth to suppose that the cause of defective apprehension is in ourselves, the mystery has been too commonly explained by the very easy process of setting it down as in fact inexplicable, and by resolving the phenomenon into a misgrowth or *lusus* of the capricious and irregular genius of Shakspeare. The shallow and stupid arrogance of these vulgar and indolent decisions I would fain do my best to expose. I believe the character of Hamlet may be traced to Shakspeare's deep and accurate science in mental philosophy. Indeed, that this character must have some connection with the common fundamental laws of our nature may be assumed from the fact, that Hamlet has been the darling of every country in which the literature of England has been fostered. In order to understand him, it is essential that we should reflect on the constitution of our own minds. Man is distinguished from the brute animals in proportion as thought prevails over sense: but

in the healthy processes of the mind, a balance is constantly
maintained between the impressions from outward objects and
the inward operations of the intellect:—for if there be an overbalance in the contemplative faculty, man thereby becomes the
creature of mere meditation, and loses his natural power of
action. Now one of Shakspeare's modes of creating characters
is, to conceive any one intellectual or moral faculty in morbid
excess, and then to place himself, Shakspeare, thus mutilated
or diseased, under given circumstances. In Hamlet he seems to
have wished to exemplify the moral necessity of a due balance
between our attention to the objects of our senses, and our
meditation on the workings of our minds,—an *equilibrium* between the real and the imaginary worlds. In Hamlet this balance is disturbed: his thoughts, and the images of his fancy,
are far more vivid than his actual perceptions, and his very
perceptions, instantly passing through the *medium* of his con-
templations, acquire, as they pass, a form and a color not
naturally their own. Hence we see a great, an almost enormous, intellectual activity, and a proportionate aversion to real
action, consequent upon it, with all its symptoms and accompanying qualities. This character Shakspeare places in circumstances, under which it is obliged to act on the spur of the
moment:—Hamlet is brave and careless of death; but he
vacillates from sensibility, and procrastinates from thought,
and loses the power of action in the energy of resolve. Thus it
is that this tragedy presents a direct contrast to that of Macbeth; the one proceeds with the utmost slowness, the other with
a crowded and breathless rapidity.

The effect of this overbalance of the imaginative power is
beautifully illustrated in the everlasting broodings and superflu-
ous activities of Hamlet's mind, which, unseated from its
healthy relation, is constantly occupied with the world within,
and abstracted from the world without,—giving substance to
shadows, and throwing a mist over all common-place actualities.
It is the nature of thought to be indefinite;—definiteness belongs
to external imagery alone. Hence it is that the sense of sublimity arises, not from the sight of an outward object, but from
the beholder's reflection upon it;—not from the sensuous impression, but from the imaginative reflex. Few have seen a celebrated waterfall without feeling something akin to disappointment: it is only subsequently that the image comes back full
into the mind, and brings with it a train of grand or beautiful
associations. Hamlet feels this; his senses are in a state of trance,

and he looks upon external things as hieroglyphics. His soliloquy—

> Oh! that this too, too solid flesh would melt, &c.

springs from that craving after the indefinite—for that which is not—which most easily besets men of genius; and the self-delusion common to this temper of mind is finely exemplified in the character which Hamlet gives of himself:—

> —It can not be
> But I am pigeon-livered, and lack gall
> To make oppression bitter.

He mistakes the seeing his chains for the breaking of them, delays action till action is of no use, and dies the victim of mere circumstance and accident.

There is a great significancy in the names of Shakspeare's plays. In the Twelfth Night, Midsummer Night's Dream, As You Like It, and Winter's Tale, the total effect is produced by a co-ordination of the characters as in a wreath of flowers. But in Coriolanus, Lear, Romeo and Juliet, Hamlet, Othello, &c., the effect arises from the subordination of all to one, either as the prominent person, or the principal object. Cymbeline is the only exception; and even that has its advantages in preparing the audience for the chaos of time, place, and costume, by throwing the date back into a fabulous king's reign.

But as of more importance, so more striking, is the judgment displayed by our truly dramatic poet, as well as poet of the drama, in the management of his first scenes. With the single exception of Cymbeline, they either place before us at one glance both the past and the future in some effect, which implies the continuance and full agency of its cause, as in the feuds and party-spirit of the servants of the two houses in the first scene of Romeo and Juliet; or in the degrading passion for shows and public spectacles, and the overwhelming attachment for the newest successful war-chief in the Roman people, already become a populace, contrasted with the jealousy of the nobles in Julius Cæsar;—or they at once commence the action so as to excite a curiosity for the explanation in the following scenes, as in the storm of wind and waves, and the boatswain in the Tempest, instead of anticipating our curiosity, as in most other first scenes, and in too many other first acts;—or they act, by contrast of diction suited to the characters, at once to heighten the effect, and yet to give a naturalness to the language and rhythm of the principal personages, either as that of Prospero and Miranda by the appropriate lowness of the style,—or as in King John, by the equally appropriate stateliness of official harangues or narratives, so that the after blank verse seems to belong to the rank and quality of the speakers, and not to the poet;—or they strike at once the key-note, and give the predominant spirit of the play, as in the Twelfth Night and in Macbeth;—or finally, the first scene comprises all these advantages at once, as in Hamlet.

Compare the easy language of common life, in which this drama commences, with the direful music and wild wayward rhythm and abrupt lyrics of the opening of Macbeth. The tone is quite familiar;—there is no poetic description of night, no elaborate information conveyed by one speaker to another of what both had immediately before their senses— (such as the first distich in Addison's Cato, which is a translation into poetry of 'Past four o'clock and a dark morning!') ;—and yet nothing bordering on the comic on the one hand, nor any striving of the intellect on the other. It is precisely the language of sensation among men who feared no charge of effeminacy for feeling what they had no want of resolution to bear. Yet the armor, the dead silence, the watchfulness that first interrupts it, the welcome relief of the guard, the cold, the broken expressions of compelled attention to bodily feelings still under control—all excellently accord with, and prepare for, the after gradual rise into tragedy;—but, above all, into a tragedy, the interest of which is as eminently *ad et apud intra,* as that of Macbeth is directly *ad extra.*

In all the best attested stories of ghosts and visions, as in that of Brutus, of Archbishop Cranmer, that of Benvenuto Cellini recorded by himself, and the vision of Galileo communicated by him to his favorite pupil Torricelli, the ghost-seers were in a state of cold or chilling damp from without, and of anxiety inwardly. It has been with all of them as with Francisco on his guard,—alone, in the depth and silence of the night;—' 'twas bitter cold, and they were sick at heart, and *not a mouse stirring.'* The attention to minute sounds,—naturally associated with the recollection of minute objects, and the more familiar and trifling, the more impressive from the unusualness of their producing any impression at all—gives a philosophic pertinency to this last image; but it has likewise its dramatic use and purpose. For its commonness of ordinary conversation tends to pro-

duce the sense of reality, and at once hides the poet, and yet
approximates the reader or spectator to that state in which the
highest poetry will appear, and in its component parts, though
not in the whole composition, really is, the language of nature.
If I should not speak it, I feel that I should be thinking it;—the
voice only is the poet's,—the words are my own. That Shakspeare meant to put an effect in the actor's power in the very
first words—"Who's there?"—is evident from the impatience expressed by the startled Francisco in the words that follow—
"Nay, answer me: stand and unfold yourself." A brave man is
never so peremptory, as when he fears that he is afraid. Observe
the gradual transition from the silence and the still recent habit
of listening in Francisco's—"I think I hear them"—to the more
cheerful call out, which a good actor would observe, in the—
"Stand ho! Who is there?" Bernardo's inquiry after Horatio,
and the repetition of his name and in his own presence indicate a respect or an eagerness that implies him as one of the
persons who are in the foreground; and the skepticism attributed to him,—

> Horatio says, 'tis but our fantasy;
> And will not let belief take hold of him—

prepares us for Hamlet's after-eulogy on him as one whose
blood and judgment were happily commingled. The actor
should also be careful to distinguish the expectation and gladness of Bernardo's 'Welcome, Horatio!' from the mere courtesy
of his 'Welcome, good Marcellus!'

Now observe the admirable indefiniteness of the first opening
out of the occasion of all this anxiety. The preparation inform-
ative of the audience is just as much as was precisely necessary, and no more;—it begins with the uncertainty appertain-
ing to a question:—

> *Mar.* What! has *this thing* appeared again to-night?—

Even the word 'again' has its *credibilizing* effect. Then Horatio,
the representative of the ignorance of the audience, not himself, but by Marcellus to Bernardo, anticipates the common
solution—' 'tis but our fantasy!' upon which Marcellus rises into

> This dreaded sight, twice seen of us—

which immediately afterwards becomes 'this apparition,' and

that, too, an intelligent spirit, that is, to be spoken to! Then comes the confirmation of Horatio's disbelief;—

> Tush! tush! 'twill not appear!—

and the silence, with which the scene opened, is again restored in the shivering feeling of Horatio sitting down, at such a time, and with the two eye-witnesses, to hear a story of a ghost, and that, too, of a ghost which had appeared twice before at the very same hour. In the deep feeling which Bernardo has of the solemn nature of what he is about to relate, he makes an effort to master his own imaginative terrors by an elevation of style,— itself a continuation of the effort,—and by turning off from the apparition, as from something which would force him too deeply into himself, to the outward objects, the realities of nature, which had accompanied it:—

> *Ber.* Last night of all,
> When yon same star, that's westward from the pole,
> Had made his course to illume that part of heaven
> Where now it burns, Marcellus and myself,
> The bell then beating one—

This passage seems to contradict the critical law that what is told, makes a faint impression compared with what is beholden; for it does indeed convey to the mind more than the eye can see; whilst the interruption of the narrative at the very moment when we are most intensely listening for the sequel, and have our thoughts diverted from the dreaded sight in expectation of the desired, yet almost dreaded, tale—this gives all the suddenness and surprise of the original appearance;—

> *Mar.* Peace, break thee off; look, where it comes again!—

Note the judgment displayed in having the two persons present, who, as having seen the Ghost before, are naturally eager in confirming their former opinions,—whilst the skeptic is silent, and after having been twice addressed by his friends, answers with two hasty syllables—'Most like,'—and a confession of horror:—

> It harrows me with fear and wonder.

O heaven! words are wasted on those who feel, and to those

who do not feel the exquisite judgment of Shakspeare in this
scene, what can be said?—Hume himself could not but have had
faith in this Ghost dramatically, let his anti-ghostism have been
as strong as Samson against other ghosts less powerfully raised.

Act i. sc. 1.

> *Mar.* Good now, sit down, and tell me, he that knows
> Why this same strict and most observant watch, &c.

How delightfully natural is the transition to the retrospective
narrative! And observe, upon the Ghost's reappearance, how
much Horatio's courage is increased by having translated the
late individual spectator into general thought and past experience,—and the sympathy of Marcellus and Bernardo with
his patriotic surmises in daring to strike at the Ghost; whilst in
a moment, upon its vanishing the former solemn awe-stricken
feeling returns upon them:—

> We do it wrong, being so majestical,
> To offer it the show of violence.—

Ib. Horatio's speech:—

> I have heard,
> The cock, that is the trumpet to the morn,
> Doth with his lofty and shrill sounding throat
> Awake the god of day, &c.

No Addison could be more careful to be poetical in diction than
Shakspeare in providing the grounds and sources of its propriety. But how to elevate a thing almost mean by its familiarity, young poets may learn in this treatment of the cock-crow.

Ib. Horatio's speech:—

> And, by my advice,
> Let us impart what we have seen to-night
> Unto young Hamlet; for, upon my life,
> The spirit, dumb to us, will speak to him.

Note the unobtrusive and yet fully adequate mode of intro-
ducing the main character, 'young Hamlet,' upon whom is
transferred all the interest excited for the acts and concerns
of the king his father.

Ib. sc. 2. The audience are now relieved by a change of
scene to the royal court, in order that Hamlet may not have

to take up the leavings of exhaustion. In the king's speech, observe the set and pedantically antithetic form of the sentences when touching that which galled the heels of conscience,—the strain of undignified rhetoric,—and yet in what follows concerning the public weal, a certain appropriate majesty. Indeed was he not a royal brother?—

Ib.   King's speech:—

> And now, Laertes, what's the news with you? &c.

Thus with great art Shakspeare introduces a most important, but still subordinate character first, Laertes, who is yet thus graciously treated in consequence of the assistance given to the election of the late king's brother instead of his son by Polonius.

Ib.

> *Ham.* A little more than kin, and less than kind.
> *King.* How is it that the clouds still hang on you?
> *Ham.* Not so, my lord, I am too much i' the sun.

Hamlet opens his mouth with a playing on words, the complete absence of which throughout characterizes Macbeth. This playing on words may be attributed to many causes or motives, as either to an exuberant activity of mind, as in the higher comedy of Shakspeare generally;—or to an imitation of it as a mere fashion, as if it were said—'Is not this better than groaning?'—or to a contemptuous exultation in minds vulgarized and overset by their success, as in the poetic instance of Milton's Devils in the battle;—or it is the language of resentment, as is familiar to every one who has witnessed the quarrels of the lower orders, where there is invariably a profusion of punning invective, whence, perhaps, nicknames have in a considerable degree sprung up;—or it is the language of suppressed passion, and especially of a hardly smothered personal dislike. The first and last of these combine in Hamlet's case; and I have little doubt that Farmer is right in supposing the equivocation carried on in the expression 'too much i' the sun,' or son.

Ib.

> *Ham.* Ay, madam, it is common

Here observe Hamlet's delicacy to his mother, and how the suppression prepares him for the overflow in the next speech, in

which his character is more developed by bringing forward his
aversion to externals, and which betrays his habit of brooding
over the world within him, coupled with a prodigality of beautiful words, which are the half-embodyings of thought, and are
more than thought, and have an outness, a reality *sui generis,*
and yet contain their correspondence and shadowy affinity to
the images and movements within. Note also Hamlet's silence
to the long speech of the king which follows, and his respectful,
but general, answer to his mother.

Ib.   Hamlet's first soliloquy:—

> O, that this too too solid flesh would melt,
> Thaw, and resolve itself into a dew! &c.

This *tædium vitæ* is a common oppression on minds cast in
the Hamlet mould, and is caused by disproportionate mental
exertion, which necessitates exhaustion of bodily feeling. Where
there is a just coincidence of external and internal action,
pleasure is always the result; but where the former is deficient,
and the mind's appetency of the ideal is unchecked, realities
will seem cold and unmoving. In such cases, passion combines
itself with the indefinite alone. In this mood of his mind the
relation of the appearance of his father's spirit in arms is made
all at once to Hamlet:—it is—Horatio's speech, in particular—a
perfect model of the true style of dramatic narrative;—the
purest poetry, and yet in the most natural language, equally
remote from the inkhorn and the plough.

1819   *1836*

ON DANTE AND THE *DIVINE COMEDY*

BORN AT FLORENCE, 1265—DIED 1321

. . . The *Divina Commedia* is a system of moral, political, and
theological truths, with arbitrary personal exemplifications,
which are not, in my opinion, allegorical. I do not even feel
convinced that the punishments in the Inferno are strictly
allegorical. I rather take them to have been in Dante's mind
quasi-allegorical, or conceived in analogy to pure allegory.

I have said, that a combination of poetry with doctrines, is

one of the characteristics of the Christian muse; but I think
Dante has not succeeded in effecting this combination nearly
so well as Milton.

This comparative failure of Dante, as also some other peculiarities of his mind, *in malam partem,* must be immediately
attributed to the state of North Italy in his time, which is
vividly represented in Dante's life; a state of intense demo-
cratical partizanship, in which an exaggerated importance was
attached to individuals, and which whilst it afforded a vast
field for the intellect, opened also a boundless arena for the
passions, and in which envy, jealousy, hatred, and other malignant feelings, could and did assume the form of patriotism, even
to the individual's own conscience.

All this common, and, as it were, natural partizanship was
aggravated and coloured by the Guelf and Ghibelline factions;
and, in part explanation of Dante's adherence to the latter, you
must particularly remark, that the Pope had recently territorial-
ized his authority to a great extent, and that this increase of
territorial power in the church, was by no means the same
beneficial movement for the citizens of free republics, as the
parallel advance in other countries was for those who groaned
as vassals under the oppression of the circumjacent baronial
castles.

By way of preparation to a satisfactory perusal of the *Divina
Commedia,* I will now proceed to state what I consider to be
Dante's chief excellences as a poet. And I begin with

1. Style—the vividness, logical connexion, strength and energy
of which cannot be surpassed. In this I think Dante superior to
Milton; and his style is accordingly more imitable than Milton's,
and does to this day exercise a greater influence on the literature of his country. You cannot read Dante without feeling a
gush of manliness of thought within you. Dante was very
sensible of his own excellence in this particular, and speaks of
poets as guardians of the vast armory of language, which is the
intermediate something between matter and spirit. Indeed there
was a passion and a miracle of words in the twelfth and thirteenth centuries, after the long slumber of language in
barbarism, which gave an almost romantic character, a virtuous
quality and power, to what was read in a book, independently
of the thoughts or images contained in it. This feeling is very
often perceptible in Dante.

II. The Images in Dante are not only taken from obvious nature, and are all intelligible to all, but are ever conjoined with the universal feeling received from nature, and therefore affect the general feelings of all men. And in this respect, Dante's excellence is very great, and may be contrasted with the idiosyncracies of some meritorious modern poets, who attempt an eruditeness, the result of particular feelings. Consider the simplicity, I may say plainness, of the following simile, and how differently we should in all probability deal with it at the present day:

> Quale i fioretti dal notturno gelo
> Chinati e chiusi, poi che 'l sol gl' imbianca,
> Si drizzan tutti aperti in loro stelo,—
> Tal mi fec' io di mia virtute stanca:
>> Inferno, canto 2, v. 127-31

As florets, by the frosty air of night
Bent down and clos'd, when day has blanch'd their leaves,
Rise all unfolded on their spiry stems,—
So was my fainting vigour new restor'd.

CARY

III. Consider the wonderful profoundness of the whole third canto of the Inferno; and especially of the inscription over Hell gate: "Per me si va," etc. which can only be explained by a meditation on the true nature of religion; that is,—reason *plus* the understanding. I say profoundness rather than sublimity; for Dante does not so much elevate your thoughts as send them down deeper. In this canto all the images are distinct, and even vividly distinct; but there is a total impression of infinity; the wholeness is not in vision or conception, but in an inner feeling of totality, and absolute being.

IV. In picturesqueness, Dante is beyond all other poets, modern or ancient, and more in the stern style of Pindar, than of any other. Michel Angelo is said to have made a design for every page of the *Divina Commedia*. As superexcellent in this respect, I would note the conclusion of the third canto of the Inferno [and canto 22, v. 127–144].

V. Very closely connected with this picturesqueness, is the topographic reality of Dante's journey through Hell. You should note and dwell on this as one of his great charms, and which gives a striking peculiarity to his poetic power. He thus takes the thousand delusive forms of a nature worse than chaos, having no reality but from the passions which they excite, and compels them into the service of the permanent. . . .

VI. For Dante's power,—his absolute mastery over, although rare exhibition of, the pathetic, I can do no more than refer to the passages on Francesca di Rimini (Inferno, canto 5, v. 73 to the end) and on Ugolino (Inferno, canto 33, v. 1 to 75). They are so well known, and rightly so admired, that it would be pedantry to analyze their composition; but you will note that the first is the pathos of passion, the second that of affection; and yet even in the first, you seem to perceive that the lovers have sacrificed their passion to the cherishing of a deep and rememberable impression.

VII. As to going into the endless subtle beauties of Dante, that is impossible; but I cannot help citing the first triplet of the twenty-ninth canto of the Inferno:

> *La molta gente e le diverse piaghe*
> *'Avean le luci mie sì inebriate,*
> *Che dello stare a piangere eran vaghe.*

> So were mine eyes inebriate with the view
> Of the vast multitude, whom various wounds
> Disfigur'd, that they long'd to stay and weep.
>
> CARY

Nor have I now room for any specific comparison of Dante with Milton. But if I had, I would institute it upon the ground of the last canto of the Inferno from the first to the sixty-ninth line, and from the 106th to the end. And in this comparison I should notice Dante's occasional fault of becoming grotesque from being too graphic without imagination; as in his Lucifer compared with Milton's Satan. Indeed he is sometimes horrible rather than terrible,—falling into the μισητόν instead of the δεινόν of Longinus; in other words, many of his images excite bodily disgust, and not moral fear. But here, as in other cases, you may perceive that the faults of great authors are generally excellencies carried to an excess.

1818   *1836*

ON CERVANTES AND *DON QUIXOTE*

Born at Madrid, 1547;—Shakspeare, 1564; both put off mortality on the same day, the 23rd of April, 1616,—the one in the sixty-ninth, the other in the fifty-second, year of his life. The resemblance in their physiognomies is striking, but with a predominance of acuteness in Cervantes, and of reflection in Shakspeare, which is the specific difference between the Spanish and English characters of mind.

I. The nature and eminence of Symbolical writing;—

II. Madness, and its different sorts, (considered without pretension to medical science) ;—

To each of these, or at least to my own notions respecting them, I must devote a few words of explanation, in order to render the after critique on Don Quixote, the master work of Cervantes' and his country's genius easily and throughout intelligible. This is not the least valuable, though it may most often be felt by us both as the heaviest and least entertaining portion of these critical disquisitions: for without it, I must have foregone one at least of the two appropriate objects of a Lecture, that of interesting you during its delivery, and of leaving behind in your minds the germs of after-thought, and the materials for future enjoyment. To have been assured by several of my intelligent auditors that they have reperused Hamlet or Othello with increased satisfaction in consequence of the new points of view in which I had placed those characters—is the highest compliment I could receive or desire; and should the address of this evening open out a new source of pleasure, or enlarge the former in your perusal of Don Quixote, it will compensate for the failure of any personal or temporary object.

I. The Symbolical cannot, perhaps, be better defined in distinction from the Allegorical, than that it is always itself a part of that, of the whole of which it is the representative.—"Here comes a sail,"—(that is, a ship) is a symbolical expression. "Behold our lion!" when we speak of some gallant soldier, is allegorical. Of most importance to our present subject is this point, that the latter (the allegory) cannot be other than spoken consciously;—whereas in the former (the symbol) it is very possible that the general truth represented may be working unconsciously in the writer's mind during the construction of the symbol;—and it proves itself by being produced out of his own mind,—as the Don Quixote out of the perfectly sane mind of Cervantes, and not by outward observation, or historically. The advantage of symbolical writing over allegory is, that it presumes no disjunction of faculties, but simple predominance.

II. Madness may be divided as—
   1. hypochondriasis; or, the man is out of his senses.
   2. derangement of the understanding; or, the man is out of his wits.
   3. loss of reason.
   4. frenzy, or derangement of the sensations.

Cervantes's own preface to Don Quixote is a perfect model of the gentle, every where intelligible, irony in the best essays of the Tatler and the Spectator. Equally natural and easy, Cervantes is more spirited than Addison; whilst he blends with the terseness of Swift, an exquisite flow and music of style, and above all, contrasts with the latter by the sweet temper of a superior mind, which saw the follies of mankind, and was even at the moment suffering severely under hard mistreatment; and yet seems everywhere to have but one thought as the under-song—"Brethren! with all your faults I love you still!"—or as a mother that chides the child she loves, with one hand holds up the rod, and with the other wipes off each tear as it drops!

Don Quixote was neither fettered to the earth by want, nor holden in its embraces by wealth;—of which, with the temperance natural to his country, as a Spaniard, he had both far too little, and somewhat too much, to be under any necessity of thinking about it. His age too, fifty, may be well supposed to prevent his mind from being tempted out of itself by any of the lower passions;—while his habits, as a very early riser and a keen sportsman, were such as kept his spare body in serviceable subjection to his will, and yet by the play of hope that accompanies pursuit, not only permitted, but assisted, his fancy in shaping what it would. Nor must we omit his meagreness and entire featureliness, face and frame, which Cervantes gives us at once: "It is said that his surname was *Quixada* or *Quesada*," &c. —even in this trifle showing an exquisite judgment;—just once insinuating the association of *lantern-jaws* into the reader's mind, yet not retaining it obtrusively like the names in old farces and in the Pilgrim's Progress,—but taking for the regular appellative one which had the no meaning of a proper name in real life, and which yet was capable of recalling a number of very different, but all pertinent, recollections, as old armour, the precious metals hidden in the ore, &c. Don Quixote's leanness and featureliness are happy exponents of the excess of the formative or imaginative in him, contrasted with Sancho's plump rotundity, and recipiency of external impression.

He has no knowledge of the sciences or scientific arts which give to the meanest portions of matter an intellectual interest, and which enable the mind to decypher in the world of the senses the invisible agency—that alone, of which the world's phenomena are the effects and manifestations,—and thus, as in a mirror, to contemplate its own reflex, its life in the powers, its imagination in the symbolic forms, its moral instincts in the final causes, and its reason in the laws of material nature: but—estranged from all the motives to observation from self-interest—the persons that surround him too few and too familiar to enter into any connection with his thoughts, or to require any adaptation of his conduct to their particular characters or relations to himself—his judgment lies fallow, with nothing to excite, nothing to employ it. Yet,—and here is the point, where genius even of the most perfect kind, allotted but to few in the course of many ages, does not preclude the necessity in part, and in part counterbalance the craving by sanity of judgment, without which genius either cannot be, or cannot at least manifest itself,—the dependency of our nature asks for some confirmation from without, though it be only from the shadows of other men's fictions.

Too uninformed, and with too narrow a sphere of power and opportunity to rise into the scientific artist, or to be himself a patron of art, and with too deep a principle and too much innocence to become a mere projector, Don Quixote has recourse to romances:—

His curiosity and extravagant fondness herein arrived at that pitch, that he sold many acres of arable land to purchase books of knight-errantry, and carried home all he could lay hands on of that kind! C. 1.

The more remote these romances were from the language of common life, the more akin on that very account were they to the shapeless dreams and strivings of his own mind;—a mind, which possessed not the highest order of genius which lives in an atmosphere of power over mankind, but that minor kind which, in its restlessness, seeks for a vivid representative of its own wishes, and substitutes the movements of that objective puppet for an exercise of actual power in and by itself. The more wild and improbable these romances were, the more were they akin to his will, which had been in the habit of acting as an unlimited monarch over the creations of his fancy! Hence observe how the startling of the remaining common sense, like a glimmering before its death, in the notice of the impossible-improbable of Don Belianis, is dismissed by Don Quixote as impertinent:—

He had some doubt as to the dreadful wounds which Don Belianis gave and received: for he imagined, that notwithstanding the most expert surgeons had cured him, his face and whole body must still be full of seams and scars. Nevertheless he commended in his author the concluding his book with a promise of that unfinishable adventure! C. 1.

Hence also his first intention to turn author; but who, with such a restless struggle within him, could content himself with writing in a remote village among apathists and ignorants? During his colloquies with the village priest and the barber surgeon, in which the fervour of critical controversy feeds the passion and gives reality to its object—what more natural than that the mental striving should become an eddy?—madness may perhaps be defined as the circling in a stream which should be progressive and adaptive: Don Quixote grows at length to be a man out of his wits; his understanding is deranged; and hence without the least deviation from the truth of nature, without losing the least trait of personal individuality, he becomes a substantial living allegory, or personification of the reason and the moral sense, divested of the judgment and the understanding. Sancho is the converse. He is the common sense without reason or imagination; and Cervantes not only shows the excellence and power of reason in Don Quixote, but in both him and Sancho the mischiefs resulting from a severance of the two main constituents of sound intellectual and moral action. Put him and his master together, and they form a perfect intellect; but they are separated and without cement; and hence each having a need of the other for its own completeness, each has at times a mastery over the other. For the common sense, although it may see the practical inapplicability of the dictates of the imagination or abstract reason, yet cannot help submitting to them. These two characters possess the world, alternately and interchangeably the cheater and the cheated. To impersonate them, and to combine the permanent with the individual, is one of the highest creations of genius, and has been achieved by Cervantes and Shakspeare, almost alone.

Observations on particular passages,

B. I. c. 1. But not altogether approving of his having broken it to pieces with so much ease, to secure himself from the like danger for the future, he made it over again, fencing it with small bars of iron within, in such a manner, *that he rested satisfied of its strength; and without caring to make a fresh experiment on it, he approved and looked upon it as a most excellent helmet.*

His not trying his improved scull-cap is an exquisite trait of human character, founded on the oppugnancy of the soul in such a state to any disturbance by doubt of its own broodings. Even the long deliberation about his horse's name is full of meaning;—for in these day-dreams the greater part of the history passes and is carried on in words, which look forward to other words as what will be said of them.

Ib. Near the place where he lived, there dwelt a very comely country lass, with whom he had formerly been in love; though, as it is supposed, she never knew it, nor troubled herself about it

The nascent love for the country lass, but without any attempt at utterance, or an opportunity of knowing her, except as the hint—the ὅτι ἔστι—of the inward imagination, is happily conceived in both parts;—first, as confirmative of the shrinking back of the mind on itself, and its dread of having a cherished image destroyed by its own judgment; and secondly, as showing

how necessarily love is the passion of novels. Novels are to love
as fairy tales to dreams. I never knew but two men of taste and
feeling who could not understand why I was delighted with the
Arabian Nights' Tales, and they were likewise the only persons
in my knowledge who scarcely remembered having ever
dreamed.

1818   *1836*

ON SWIFT AND THE HOUYHNHNMS

BORN IN DUBLIN, 1667.—DIED 1745.

In Swift's writings there is a false misanthropy grounded
upon an exclusive contemplation of the vices and follies of
mankind, and this misanthropic tone is also disfigured or
brutalized by his obtrusion of physical dirt and coarseness. I
think Gulliver's Travels the great work of Swift. In the voyages
to Lilliput and Brobdingnag he displays the littleness and
moral contemptibility of human nature; in that to the Houyhnhnms he represents the disgusting spectacle of man with the
understanding only, without the reason or the moral feeling,
and in his horse he gives the misanthropic ideal of man—that
is, a being virtuous from rule and duty, but untouched by the
principle of love.

GULLIVER'S TRAVELS

The great defect of the Houyhnhnms is not its misanthropy,
and those who apply this word to it must really believe that
the essence of human nature, that the *anthropos misoumenos,*
consists in the shape of the body. Now, to shew the falsity of
this was Swift's great object: he would prove to our feelings and
imagination, and thereby teach *practically* that it is reason and
conscience which give all the loveliness and dignity not only to
man, but to the shape of man; that deprived of these, and yet
retaining the understanding, he would be the most loathsome
and hateful of all animals; that his understanding would manifest itself only as malignant cunning, his free will as obstinacy
and unteachableness. And how true a picture this is every mad-

house may convince any man; a brothel where highwaymen meet will convince every philosopher. But the defect of the work is its inconsistency; the Houyhnhnms are not rational creatures, *i.e.*, creatures of perfect reason; they are not progressive; they have servants without any reason for their natural inferiority or any explanation how the difference acted [?]; and, above all, they—*i.e.*, Swift himself—has a perpetual affectation of being wiser than his Maker (see postscript[1]), and of eradicating what God gave to be subordinated and used; *ex. gr.*, the maternal and paternal affection (σουργή). There is likewise a true Yahooism in the constant denial of the existence of love, as not identical with friendship, and yet distinct always and very often divided from lust. The best defence is that it is a satire; still, it would have been felt a thousand times more deeply if reason had been truly portrayed, and a finer imagination would have been evinced if the author had shewn the effects of the possession of reason and the moral sense on the outward form and gestures of the horses. In short, critics in general complain of the Yahoos; I complain of the Houyhnhnms.

As to the wisdom of adopting this mode of proving the great truths here exemplified, that is another question, which no feeling mind will find a difficulty in answering who has read and understood the Paradise scenes in "Paradise Lost," and compared the moral effect on his heart and his virtuous aspirations of Milton's Adam with Swift's horses; but different men have different turns of genius; Swift's may be good, tho' very inferior to Milton's; they do not stand in each other's way.

A case in point, and besides utterly inconsistent with the boasted reason of the Houyhnhnm, may be seen, p. 194, 195 [chap. iv.], where the horse discourses on the human frame with the grossest prejudices that could possibly be inspired by vanity and self-opinion. That reason which commands man to admire the fitness of the horse and stag for superior speed, of the bird for flight, &c., &c.,—must it not have necessitated the rational horse to have seen and acknowledged the admirable aptitude of the human hand, compared with his own fetlocks, of the human limbs for climbing, for the management of tools, &c.? In short, compare the *effect* of the satire, when it is founded in truth and good sense (chapt. v., for instance), with the wittiest of those passages which have their only support in spleen and want of reverence for the original frame of man, and the feelings of the reader will be his faithful guide in the

reperusal of the work, which I still think the highest effort of
Swift's genius, unless we should except the "Tale of the Tub."
Then I would put Lilliput; next Brobdingnag; and Laputa I
would expunge altogether. It is a wretched abortion, the product of spleen and ignorance and self-conceit.

1818   *1896*

LETTERS, 1785–1819

The best possible picture of Coleridge's arresting personality emerges from his letters. Here, as in his notebooks, he seems almost infinitely various: the poet, the philosopher, the metaphysician, the logician, the bumbling husband, the loving father, the perpetual valetudinarian, the warm friend to scores of contemporaries. As the novelist Virginia Woolf once noted, the reading of Coleridge is a constant surprise, for "anything may tumble out of that great maw: the subtlest criticism, the wildest jest, the exact condition of his intestines." And one might add: the highest piety, the deepest sense of personal guilt, the written record of the most indubitable suffering.

Coleridge's correspondents were many. The twenty-five people to whom the present letters were addressed are here briefly identified. Ann Coleridge was the poet's mother, Derwent his son, George his elder brother, and Sara (Mrs. S. T. Coleridge) was his wife. Lady Beaumont was wife to Sir George Beaumont (1753–1827), art patron, landscape painter, and benefactor of the Wordsworth family, whom the Beaumonts came to know through Coleridge. Lord Byron (1788–1824) was the famous poet who attacked Coleridge in *English Bards and Scotch Reviewers* (1809) but came to be on good terms with the author of *Christabel*. Joseph Cottle (1770–1835) was the Bristol bookseller who published Coleridge's early poems and *Lyrical Ballads* (1798). After Coleridge's death he brought out a valuable memoir on their friendship. John Prior Estlin (1747–1817) was a Unitarian preacher, also of Bristol. Mary Evans was sister of Tom Evans, one of Coleridge's schoolmates at Christ's Hospital. Their widowed mother lived in Piccadilly and was kind to the young Coleridge; but his passion for Mary was not reciprocated. Benjamin Flower (1755–1829) was a publisher-journalist of Cambridge and brought out Coleridge's and Southey's tragedy, *The Fall of Robespierre*. Dr. and Mrs. James Gillman lodged Coleridge in their capacious house at Highgate for the last eighteen years of his life. William Godwin (1756–1836) was a philosopher and novelist, father-in-law of the poet Shelley, and author of the renowned *Political Justice* (1793). Sara Hutchinson, sister of the Mary Hutchinson who became Mrs. William Wordsworth, was the girl for whom Coleridge conceived a hopeless passion and to whom he addressed the early version of *Dejection: An Ode.* Charles Lloyd, Sr. was father of the poet Charles Lloyd (1775–1839) who lodged with the Coleridges for a time in 1796. The Lloyds were a Quaker family of Birmingham. Charles Mathews (1776–1835) was a comic actor, working in the Bristol Theatre when Coleridge wrote to him. Coleridge first met John J. Morgan in Bristol in 1795 and subsequently lived with the Morgans for considerable periods of time. Thomas Poole of Stowey, near Bridgwater in Somerset, was a tanner by trade who helped the young Coleridge through many difficult times. Robert Southey (1774–1843), the poet, was Coleridge's brother-in-law. Daniel Stuart (1766–1846) was editor and publisher of the *Morning Post,* to which Coleridge made many contributions. Josiah Wade was a Bristol businessman who became a good friend to Coleridge. Josiah and Thomas Wedgwood of the famous eighteenth-century family of pottery-makers were patrons to Coleridge, settling an annuity upon him. Thomas (1771–1805) was one of the earliest photographers. The poet Wordsworth (1770–1850) and his sister Dorothy were Coleridge's closest associates in 1798–99 and for many subsequent years.

The fifty-one letters here reprinted follow the authoritative text established by Earl Leslie Griggs in his *Letters of Samuel Taylor Coleridge,* four volumes, Oxford, Clarendon Press, 1956 and 1959. For convenience of reference, Professor Griggs's numbering of the letters has been retained.

1. *To his Mother*

February 4, 1785 [London, Christ's Hospital]
Dear Mother,—I received your letter with pleasure on the second instant, and should have had it sooner, but that we had not a holiday before last Tuesday, when my brother delivered it me. I also with gratitude received the two handkerchiefs and the half-a-crown from Mr. Badcock, to whom I would be glad if you would give my thanks. I shall be more careful of the somme, as I now consider that were it not for my kind friends I should be as destitute of many little necessaries as some of my schoolfellows are; and Thank God and my relations for them! My brother Luke saw Mr. James Sorrel, who gave my brother a half-a-crown from Mrs. Smerdon, but mentioned not a word of the plumb cake, and said he would call again. Return my most respectful thanks to Mrs. Smerdon for her kind favour. My aunt was so kind as to accommodate me with a box. I suppose my sister Anna's beauty has many admirers. My brother Luke says that Burke's Art of Speaking would be of great use to me. If Master Sam and Harry Badcock are not gone out of (Ottery), give my kindest love to them. Give my compliments to Mr. Blake and Miss Atkinson, Mr. and Mrs. Smerdon, Mr. and Mrs. Clapp, and all other friends in the country. My uncle, aunt, and cousins join with myself and Brother in love to my sisters, and hope they are well, as I, your dutiful son,

S. Coleridge, am at present.
P.S. Give my kind love to Molly.

8. *To George Coleridge*

October 16th [1791]
Dear Brother
Here I am—videlicet—Jesus College. I had a tolerable Journey—went by a night-coach packed up with five more—one of whom had a long, broad, red, hot face—four feet by three. I very luckily found Middleton at Pembroke—who (after Breakfast &c) conducted me to Jesus. Dr Pearce is in Cornwall and not expected to return to Cambridge till the Summer: and what is still more extraordinary—(and (n. b.) rather shameful) neither of the Tutors are here. I *keep* (as the phrase is) in an absent member's rooms, till one of the aforesaid duetto return to ap-

point me my own. The Letter, which Mr Corp wrote directed
to the Bursar (n.b. Mr Corp behaved very civil) attains or
attaches, as you would say, no more to the Bursar, than the Bed
maker. The Tutor is the Letteree in this case. I accordingly did
not deliver it—but reserve it for the proper man. Neither Lectures, or Chapel—or any thing—is begun. The College very thin
—and Middleton has not the least acquaintance with any of
Jesus, except a very blackguardly fellow, whose phisiog: I did
not like. So I sit down to dinner in the Hall in silence—except
the noise of suction, which accompanies my eating—and rise-up
ditto. I then walk off to Pembroke and sit with my friend
Middleton.

I am very disagreeably situated on account of Mr B's plan of
suspending the ten pound. I might daily by means of Middleton and his friends buy furniture, which will be necessary, at
half the price, which I can have it when the bills are sent in to
[the] College Tutor. If I had that money I could save near ten
pound of the twenty allowed by the Hospital. Besides one feels
cold and naked and shivering, and gelid, and chilly and such
like synonimes—without a little money in one's pocket. N.B. I
am the first, on whom Boyer has ventured to try this famous
experiment—and if you do not think, *you* can let me have it
consistently with your trust—I shall write a nasty letter to him.
The burthen of it will be—Mr Boyer, you have no order from
Committee or Court for this plan—and if you had, they have no
right to issue such an order. The money was hardly and dearly
earned by that ignominious custom of begging—and even
though the donors had a power of retracting their gift, I
received nothing but sixpences from [the] Governors. This may
be strange language to [a] man, who like Boyer is so used to
admire the influence of Committees and contemplate with awe
the omnipotence of general courts—it is true though—and therefore I shall write it at him, only in more energetic language.

Pray let me hear from you—Le Grice will send a parcel in two
or three days—By these parcels my letters to and from you will
be [conveyed]—My respects to Mr and Mrs Sparrow—I shall
write to Mr Sparrow, after my examination &c—N.B. I am
queerly off about the Rustat Scholarship—Believe me,

             with sincere affection and | gratitude | Your's ever
                                                   S T Coleridge

13. *To Mary Evans*

13th Feb: [1792]
Ten of the most talkative young ladies now in London—!!!!!
Now by the most accurate calculation of the specific quantities
of sounds a female tongue, *when it exerts itself to the utmost,*
equals the noise of 18 sign posts, which the wind swings backwards and forwards in full creak. If then 1 equals 18, 10 must
equal 180——consequently the circle at Jermyn street unitedly
must have produced a noise equal to that of 180 old crazy sign
posts inharmoniously agitated, as aforesaid. Well! to be sure
there are few disagreeables, for which the pleasure of Mary
and Anne Evans' company would not amply compensate—but
faith! I feel myself half-inclined to thank God, that I was 52
miles off during this *clattering clapperation* of tongues. Do you
keep Ale at Jermyn Street?—if so, I hope, it is not *soured.*

Such, my dear Mary, were the reflections that instantly suggested themselves to me on reading the former part of your
letter—believe me however, that my gratitude keeps pace with
my sense of your exertions—as I can most feelingly conceive the
difficulty of writing amid that second edition of Babel with
additions. That your Health is restored gives me sincere delight.
May the giver of all pleasure and pain preserve it so!—I am likewise glad to hear, that your *hand* is *rewhiten'd,* though I cannot
help smiling at a certain young Lady's *effrontery* in having
boxed a young Gentleman's ears, till her own hand became
black and blue, and then attributing those unseemly marks to
the poor unfortunate object of her resentment. *You are at
liberty to say what you please.*

It has been confidently affirmed by most excellent judges
(tho' the best may be mistaken) that I have grown very handsome lately.—Pray—that I may have grace not to be vain.—Yet
ah! who can read the stories of Pamela, or Joseph Andrews, or
Susannah and the three elders—and not perceive what a dangerous snare Beauty is—. Beauty is like the grass, that groweth
up in the Morning, and is withered before night. Mary! Anne!
Do not be vain of your beauty!!!!!——
I keep a Cat. Amid the strange collection of strange animals,
with which I am surrounded, I think it necessary to have some
meek well-looking being, that I may keep my social affections
alive. Puss like her master is a very gentle brute, and I behave
to her with all possible politeness.—Indeed—a Cat is a very

worthy animal—To be sure, I have known some very malicious
Cats in my life time—but then they were old—and besides, they
had not nearly so many legs as you, my sweet Pussy. I wish,
Puss! I could break you of that indecorous habit of turning
your back front to the fire—It is not frosty Weather now.

N.B. If ever, Mary, you should feel yourself inclined to visit
me at Cambridge, pray do not suffer the consideration of my
having a Cat to deter you. *Indeed* I will keep her *chained up*
all the while, you stay.

I was in company the other day with a very dashing literary
Lady. After my departure a friend of mine asked her her
opinion of me. She answered—'The best I can say of him is, that
He is a very gentle Bear.['] What think you of this character?

What a lovely anticipation of Spring the last three or four
days have afforded! Nature has not been very profuse of her
ornaments to the country about Cambridge—yet the clear
rivulet, that runs thro' the grove adjacent to our College, and
the numberless little birds (particularly Robins) that are singing away,—and above all—the little Lambs, each by the side of
it's Mother—recall the most pleasing ideas of pastoral simplicity, and almost sooth one's soul into congenial innocence.
Amid these delightful scenes, of which the uncommon flow of
Health, I at present possess, permits me the full enjoyment, I
should not deign to think of London, were it not for a little
family whom, I trust, I need not name. What bird of the Air
whispers me, that You too will soon enjoy the same and more
delightful pleasures in a much more delightful country? What
we strongly wish, we are very apt to believe—at present my
presentiments on that head amount to Confidence.

Last Sunday Middleton and I set off at one [o']clock on a
ramble—We sauntered on, chatting and contemplating, till to
our great surprize we came to a Village seven miles from Cambridge—And here at a farm house we drank Tea—the rusticity
of the habitation and the inhabitants was charming—we had
cream to our Tea, which tho' not brought in *a lordly dish*,
Sisera would have jumped at. Being here informed that we
could return to Cambridge another way, over a common,
for the sake of diversifying our walk we chose this road—'if
road it might be call'd, where road was none'—tho'—we were
not unapprized of it's difficulties. The fine Weather deceived
us. We forgot, that it was a summer day in warmth only, and
not in length—but we were soon reminded of it. For on the
pathless solitude of this common the night overtook us: we must

have been four miles distant from Cambridge. The night, tho'
calm, was as dark as the place was dreary—here steering our
course by our imperfect conceptions of the point, in which *we
conjectured* Cambridge to lie, we wandered on 'with cautious
steps and slow.['] We feared the bog, the stump, and the fen:
we feared the Ghosts of the night—at least, those material and
knock me down Ghosts, the apprehension of which causes you,
Mary (valorous girl, that you are!) always to peep under your
bed of a night. As we were thus creeping forwards like the two
children in the wood, we spy'd something white moving across
the common—This we made up to—tho' contrary to our *supposed* destination.—It proved to be a man with a white bundle.
We enquired our Way, and luckily he was going to Cambridge—
he informed us, that we had gone half a mile out of our way,
and that in five minutes more we must have arrived at a deep
quagmire grassed over. What an escape! The Man was as glad
of our company as we of his—for, it seemed, the poor fellow was
afraid of Jack o' lantherns—the superstition of this county attributing a kind of fascination to those wandering vapours, so
that whoever fixes his eyes on them is forced by some irre-
sistable impulse to follow them. He entertained us with many
a dreadful tale—. By nine o'clock we arrived at Cambridge—
betired, and bemudded. I never recollect to have been so much
fatigued.

Do you spell the word—*scarsely*? When Momus, the fault-
finding God, endeavoured to discover some imperfection in
Venus, he could only censure the creaking of her Slipper. I too,
Momuslike, can only fall foul on a single s. Yet will not my dear
Mary be angry with me, or think the remark trivial, when she
considers, that half a grain is of consequence in the weight of a
diamond.

I had entertained hopes, that you would *really* have sent me
a piece of sticking plaister—which would have been very convenient at that time, I having cut my finger. I hate to *buy* sticking plaister, etc. What is the use of a man's knowing you Girls,
if he cannot *chouse* you out of such little things, as that? Do not
your fingers, Mary, feel an odd kind of titillation to be about
my ears for my impudence?

On Saturday night as I was sitting by myself all alone I heard
a creaking sound, something like the noise which a crazy chair
would make, if pressed by the tremendous weight of Mrs Bar-
low's extremities. I cast my eyes around—and what should I
behold, but a *Ghost* rising out of the floor! A deadly paleness

instantly overspread my body, which retained no other symptom of Life, but it's violent trembling: my hair (as is usual in frights of this nature) stood upright by many degrees stiffer than the Oaks of the Mountains, yea, stiffer than Mr —; yet was it rendered *oily pl[ian]t* by the profuse perspiration, that burst from every pore. The Spirit advanced with a book in his hand, and having first dissipated my terrors, said as follows: I am the Ghost of Gray—there lives a young Lady (then he mentioned *your* name) of whose judgment I entertain so high an opinion, that *her* approbation of my Works would make the turf lie lighter on me: present her with this book—and transmit it to her as soon as possible—adding my Love to her. And as for you, O Young Man (*now* he addressed himself to me) write no more verses—in the first place, your poetry is vile stuff; and secondly (here he sighed almost to bursting) all Poets go to —ll, we are so intolerably addicted to the Vice of Lying!—He vanished—and convinced me of the truth of his last dismal account by the sulphureous stink, which he left behind him.

His first mandate I have obeyed, and, I hope, you will receive *safe* your ghostly admirer's present—but so far have I been from obeying his second injunction, that I never had the scribblomania stronger on me, than for these last three or four days— nay, not content with suffering it myself, I must pester those, I love best, with the blessed effects of my disorder. Besides two *things,* which you will find in the next sheet, I cannot forbear filling the remainder of *this* sheet with an Odeling—tho' I know and approve your aversion to *mere prettiness,* and tho' my tiny love ode possesses no other property in the world. Let then it's *shortness* recommend it to your perusal—*by the by,* the *only* thing, in which it resembles you: for Wit, Sense, Elegance, or Beauty it has none.

An Ode in the manner of Anacreon

As late in wreaths gay flowers I bound,
Beneath some roses Love I found,
And by his little frolic pinion
As quick as thought I seiz'd the minion,
Then in my Cup the prisoner threw,
And drank him in it's sparkling dew:
And sure I feel my angry Guest
Flutt'ring his Wings within my breast!

Are you quite asleep, dear Mary? Sleep on—but when you

awake, read the following productions—and then, I'll be bound,
you will sleep again sounder than ever.

A Wish written in Jesus Wood Feb: 10th 1792

Lo! thro' the dusky silence of the groves,
Thro' vales irriguous, and thro' green retreats,
With languid murmur creeps the placid stream
  And works it's secret way!

Awhile meand'ring round it's native fields
It rolls the playful wave, and winds it's flight:
Then downward flowing with awaken'd speed
  Embosoms in the Deep!

Thus thro' it's silent tenor may my Life
Smooth it's meek stream, by sordid Wealth unclogg'd,
Alike unconscious of forensic storms,
  And Glory's blood stain'd palm!

And when dark Age shall close Life's little day,
Satiate of sport, and weary of it's toils,
E'en thus may slumbrous Death my decent limbs
  Compose with icy hand!

A lover's complaint to his Mistress, who deserted him in quest
of a more wealthy Husband in the East Indies:

The dubious light sad glimmers o'er the sky:
'Tis Silence all. By lonely anguish torn
With wandering feet to gloomy groves I fly,
And wakeful Love still tracks my course forlorn.

Ah, will you, cruel Julia! will you go?
And trust you to the Ocean's dark dismay?
Shall the wide wat'ry world between us flow?
And Winds unpitying snatch my Hopes away?

Thus could you sport with my too easy heart?
Yet tremble, lest not unavenged I grieve!
The Winds may learn your own delusive art,
And faithless Ocean smile—but to deceive.

If I have written too long a letter, give me an hint—& I will
avoid a repetition of the offence.

As a compensation for the above written rhymes (which if
you ever condescend to read a second time, pray, let it be by the
light of their own flames) in my next letter I will send some
delicious poetry lately published by the exquisite Bowles.

To morrow morning I fill the rest of this sheet with a letter to
Anne—and now, Good Night, dear Sister! and peaceful slumbers await us both!

S T Coleridge—11 o'clock.

91. *To Thomas Poole*

Wednesday Evening. [7 October 1795]

My dear Sir—God bless you!—or rather, God be praised for
that he *has* blessed you—!——

On Sunday Morning I was *married*—at St Mary's, Red Cliff—
poor Chatterton's Church— / The thought gave me a tinge of
melancholy to the solemn Joy, which I felt—united to the
woman, whom I love best of all created Beings.—We are settled
—nay—quite domesticated at Clevedon—Our comfortable
Cot!—!—

Mrs Coleridge—Mrs COLERIDGE!!—I like to *write* the name—
well—as I was saying—Mrs Coleridge desires her affectionate
regards to you—I talked of you on my wedding night——God
bless you!—I hope that some ten years hence you will believe
and know of my affection towards you what I will not now
profess.

The prospect around us is perhaps more *various* than any in
the kingdom—Mine Eye gluttonizes.——The Sea—the distant
Islands!—the opposite Coasts!—I shall assuredly write Rhymes—
let the nine Muses prevent it, if they can—/.

Cruickshanks, I find, is married to Miss Buclé—. I am happy
to hear it—he will surely, I hope, make a good husband to a
woman, to whom *he* would be a villain who should make a bad
one——.

I have given up all thoughts of the Magazine—for various
Reason[s]. Imprimis—I must be connected with R. Southey in
it, which I could not be with comfort to my feelings. Secundò—
It is a thing of monthly *Anxiety* & quotidian Bustle—Tertiò—It
would cost Cottle an 100 pounds in buying Paper &c all on an
uncertainty—Quartò—To publish a Magazine for *one* year
would be nonsense—and if I pursue what I mean to pursue—
my school plan—I could not publish it for more than one year—.
Quintò—Cottle has entered into an engagement to give me a
guinea & a half for every hundred Lines of Poetry, I write—
which will be perfectly sufficient for my maintenance, I only
amusing myself on Mornings—and all my prose works he is

eager to purchase. Sextò—In the course of half-a year I mean to return to Cambridge (having previously taken my name off from the university controll) and taking Lodgings there for myself and wife finish my great work of Imitations in 2 vols—My former works may, I hope, prove somewhat of genius and erudition—this will be better—it will shew great Industry, and manly consistency—at the end of it I shall publish proposals for School &c—/ .

[Cottle] has spent a day with me—and takes this letter to Bristol—my next will be long and full of SOMETHING—this is inanity & egotism. Pray, let me hear from you—directing the letter to Mr Cottle's—who will forward it—My respectful & grateful remembrance to your Mother—& believe me, dear Poole! your affectionate & mindful—*Friend*—shall I so soon dare to say?—Believe me, my *heart* prompts it—.

S. T. Coleridge

124. *To Thomas Poole*

May 5th 1796

My very dear Friend

The Heart is a little relieved, when vexation converts itself into anger. But from this privelege I am utterly precluded by my own epistolary 'sins & negligences.'—Yet in very truth thou must be an hard-hearted fellow to let me trot for four weeks together every Thursday to the Bear Inn—to receive *no* letter. I have sometimes thought that Milton did not deliver my last parcel—; but he assures me he did.——

This morning I received a truly fraternal letter from Richard Poole of Sherbourne—containing good & acceptable advice.— He deems my religious Musings too *metaphysical for common readers*. I answer—the Poem was not written for common Readers. In so miscellaneous a collection as I have presented to the Public, Singula cuique should be the Motto.—There are however instances of vicious affectation in the phraseology of that poem—'Unshudder'd, unaghasted' for instance.——Good Writing is produced more effectually by rapidly glancing thro' language as it already exists, than by an hasty recourse to the *Mint* of Invention. The 'Religious Musings' has more *mind* than the Introduction of B. IId of *Joan of Arc,* but it's versification is not equally rich: it has more passages of sublimity, but it has not that diffused air of severe Dignity which characterizes *my*

Epic Slice. Have I estimated my own performances rightly?——

My house is at present a house of Mourning. My Wife's Mother has *lived dying* these last six weeks, and she is not yet dead—& the Husband of my Wife's Sister, Robert Lovell, (author of the two Sonnets in No. 5) died on Tuesday Morning of a putrid fever, & has left an Infant & a Widow. All Monday Night I sate up *with her*—she was removed to the Kitchen, the furthest room in the House from her Husband's Bed-chamber—there being a Courtyard between the two.—It was, you know, a very windy night—but his loud, deep, unintermitted groans mingled audibly with the wind, & whenever the wind dropt, they were very horrible to hear, & drove my poor young Sister-in law frantic. I prayed by her with fervor & very frequently—it soothed her with almost miraculous consolation—At one o'clock the Clock in the Kitchen went down—'Ah!' (said She) 'it is stopt—Now it clicked & told the hour & did all it's Maker willed it to do—and now it is stopped.'—(A long pause) 'O God! O God! my poor Love will stop'—.—Here her agonies became wild —I hastened out, knocked up a Chairman, & had her conveyed to my House——He died ten o'clock that morning——She is quite calm, & perpetually questions me concerning the Resurrection.—Her Husband when I first knew him was an Atheist—he became a Deist—& a month before he fell ill publickly professed himself a convert to Christianity.[1] I look back on my conversations with him with great & solacing Pleasure.—She will, I believe, be protected by her father-in-law, who is a wealthy Quaker—

With regard to my own affairs they are as bad, as the most Trinitarian Anathemizer, or rampant Philo-despot could wish in the moment of cursing—After No. 12, I shall cease to cry the state of the political atmosphere—It is not pleasant, Thomas Poole! to have worked 14 weeks for nothing—*for nothing*—nay— to have given the Public in addition to that toil five & 40 pounds!—When I began the Watchman, I had forty pounds worth of paper *given me*—yet *with this* I shall not have received a farthing at the end of the Quarter of the Year—To be sure, I

---

[1] While these volumes were in the press, the following fragment to an unknown correspondent came to light and is now in the editor's possession:

May 3rd 1796 Oxford Street, Bristol

. . . agonies are heart-rending:—she is removed to my House—
About a month ago R. Lovell openly professed
himself a convert to Christianity.——
Southey has spent the last half year in Spain
with his uncle—he is expected home weekly.——
God bless you, my dear Sir! & S. T. Coleridge

E. L. Griggs

have been somewhat fleeced & overreached by my London Publisher——In short, my tradesmen's Bill[s] for the Watchman, including what Paper I have sought since the seventh number,
the Printing, &c—amount to exactly five pounds more than the
whole amount of my receipts——Meantime Mrs Coleridge asks
about baby-linen & anticipates the funeral expences of her poor
Mother——

O Watch Man! thou hast watched in vain—said the Prophet
Ezekiel, when, I suppose, he was taking a prophetic glimpse of
my sorrow-sallowed Cheeks.—

My Plans are reduced to two—. The first impracticable—the
second not likely to succeed—

Plan the first is as follows.

Plan 1st.—I am studying German, & in about six weeks shall be
able to read that language with tolerable fluency. Now I have
some thoughts of making a proposal to Robinson, the great
London Bookseller, of translating all the works [of] Schiller,
which would make a portly Quarto, on the conditions that he
should pay my Journey & wife's to & from Jena, a cheap German University where Schiller resides—& allow me two guineas
each Quarto Sheet—which would maintain me—. If I could
realize this scheme, I should there study Chemistry & Anatomy,
[and] bring over with me all the works of Semler & Michaelis,
the German Theologians, & of Kant, the great German Metaphysician. On my return I would commence a School for 8
young men at 100 guineas each—proposing to *perfect* them in
the following studies in order as follows——

1. Man as Animal: including the complete knowledge of Anatomy, Chemistry, Mechanics & Optics.—
2. Man as an *Intellectual* Being: including the ancient Metaphysics, the systems of Locke & Hartley,—of the Scotch Philosophers—& the new Kantian S[ystem—]
3. Man as a Religious Being: including an historic summary of
all Religions & the arguments for and against Natural &
Revealed Religion. Then proceeding from the individual to the
aggregate of Individuals & disregarding all chronology except
that of mind I should perfect them 1. in the History of Savage
Tribes. 2. of semi-barbarous nations. 3 of nations emerging from
semi-barbarism. 4. of civilized states. 5 of luxurious states. 6 of
revolutionary states.—7.—of Colonies.—During these studies I
should intermix the knowledge of languages and instruct my

scholars in Belles Lettres & the principles of composition.—
Now seriously—do you think that one of my Scholars thus perfected would make a better Senator than perhaps any one Member in either of our Houses?——

Bright Bubbles of the aye-ebullient brain!

Gracious Heaven! that a scheme so big with advantage to this
Kingdom, therefore to Europe, therefore to the World should
be demolishable by one monosyllable from a Bookseller's
Mouth!

No!——Genii &c—

My second Plan is to become a Dissenting Parson & abjure
Politics & carnal literature. Preaching for Hire is not right;
because it must prove a strong temptation to continue to profess
what I had ceased to believe, *if ever* maturer Judgment with
wider & deeper reading should lessen or destroy my faith in
Christianity. But tho' not right in itself, it may become right
by the greater wrongness of the only Alternative—the remaining
in neediness & Uncertainty. That in the one case I should
[be e]xposed to temptation, is a mere *contingency*: that under
necessitous circ[umstances] I am exposed to great & frequent
temptatio[ns is] a melancholy certainty.—

Write, my dear Poole! or I will crib all the rampant Billings-
gate of Burke to abuse you—

Count Rumford is being reprinted——

God bless you &
S. T. Coleridge—

P.S.—I open the parcel which was to have gone for you—& which
Milton promised to call for at Mr Cottle's—but did not—A
rascal! So I must send this Letter by post—& defer the Watch-
men till next Thursday.—Pray, write me by Milton—pray do—
May 6th.

143. *To Charles Lamb*

[28 September 1796]

Your letter, my friend, struck me with a mighty horror. It
rushed upon me and stupefied my feelings. You bid me write
you a religious letter. I am not a man who would attempt to
insult the greatness of your anguish by any other consolation.

Heaven knows that in the easiest fortunes there is much dissatisfaction and weariness of spirit; much that calls for the exercise of patience and resignation; but in storms like these, that shake the dwelling and make the heart tremble, there is no middle way between despair and the yielding up of the whole spirit unto the guidance of faith. And surely it is a matter of joy that your faith in Jesus has been preserved; the Comforter that should relieve you is not far from you. But as you are a Christian, in the name of that Saviour, who was filled with bitterness and made drunken with wormwood, I conjure you to have recourse in frequent prayer to 'his God and your God;' the God of mercies, and father of all comfort. Your poor father is, I hope, almost senseless of the calamity; the unconscious instrument of Divine Providence knows it not, and your mother is in heaven. It is sweet to be roused from a frightful dream by the song of birds and the gladsome rays of the morning. Ah, how infinitely more sweet to be awakened from the blackness and amazement of a sudden horror by the glories of God manifest and the hallelujahs of angels.

As to what regards yourself, I approve altogether of your abandoning what you justly call vanities. I look upon you as a man called by sorrow and anguish and a strange desolation of hopes into quietness, and a soul set apart and made peculiar to God! We cannot arrive at any portion of heavenly bliss without in some measure imitating Christ; and they arrive at the largest inheritance who imitate the most difficult parts of his character, and, bowed down and crushed underfoot, cry in fulness of faith, 'Father, thy will be done.'

I wish above measure to have you for a little while here; no visitants shall blow on the nakedness of your feelings; you shall be quiet, and your spirit may be healed. I see no possible objection, unless your father's helplessness prevent you, and unless you are necessary to him. If this be not the case, I charge you write me that you will come.

I charge you, my dearest friend, not to dare to encourage gloom or despair. You are a temporary sharer in human miseries that you may be an eternal partaker of the Divine nature. I charge you, if by any means it be possible, come to me.

I remain your affectionate
S. T. Coleridge

151. *To Thomas Poole*

Saturday night.   November 5th—[1796]

Thanks, my heart's warm thanks to you, my beloved Friend! for your tender letter—indeed I did not deserve so kind a one— but by this time you have received my last.—

To live in a beautiful country & to inure myself as much as possible to the labors of the field, have been for this year past my dream of the day, my Sigh at midnight—but to enjoy these blessings *near you,* to see you daily, to tell you all my thoughts in their first birth, and to hear your's, to be mingling identities with you, as it were;—the vision-weaving *Fancy* has indeed often pictured such things, but *Hope* never dared whisper a promise!—Disappointment! Disappointment! dash not from my trembling hand this bowl, which almost touches my lips! Envy me not this immortal Draught, and I will forgive thee all thy persecutions—forgive thee! impious!—I will *bless thee,* black-vested Minister of Optimism! Stern Pioneer of Happiness!— Thou hast been *'the Cloud'* before me from the day that I left the flesh-pots of Egypt & was led thro' the way of a wilderness— the *cloud,* that hast been guiding me to a land flowing with milk & honey—the milk of Innocence, the honey of Friendship! I wanted such a letter as your's—: for I am very unwell. On Wednesday night I was seized with an intolerable pain from my right temple to the tip of my right shoulder, including my right eye, cheek, jaw, & that side of the throat——I was nearly frantic—and ran about the House naked, endeavouring by every means to excite sensations in different parts of my body, & so to weaken the enemy by creating a division. It continued from one in the morning till half past 5, & left me pale & fainty.—It came on fitfully but not so violently, several times on Thursday —and began severer threats towards night, but I took between 60 & 70 drops of Laudanum, and *sopped* the Cerberus just as his mouth began to open. On Friday it only *niggled*; as if the Chief had departed as from a conquered place, and merely left a small garrison behind, or as if he evacuated the Corsica, & a few straggling pains only remained; but *this morning* he returned in full force, & his Name is Legion!—Giant-fiend of an hundred hands! with a shower of arrowy Death-pangs he transpierced me, & then he became a Wolf & lay gnawing my bones.——I am not mad, most noble Festus!—but in sober sadness I have suffered this day more bodily pain than I had before a conception of—. My right cheek has certainly been placed with admirable exactness under the focus of some invisible Burning-Glass, which concentrated all the Rays of a Tartarean Sun.—My medical attendant decides it to be altogether nervous, and that it originates either in severe application, or excessive anxiety.— My beloved Poole! in excessive anxiety, I believe, it might originate!——I have a blister under my right-ear, and I take 25 drops of Laudanum every five hours: the ease & *spirits* gained by which have enabled me to write you this flighty, but not exaggerating, account——. With a gloomy wantonness of Imagination I had been coquetting with the hideous *Possibles* of Disappointment—I drank fears, like wormwood; yea, made myself drunken with bitterness! for my ever-shaping & distrustful mind still mingled gall-drops, till out of the cup of Hope *I almost poisoned* myself with Despair!

Your letter is dated November 2nd—I wrote to you November 1st—Your Sister was married on that day—& on that day several times I felt my heart overflowed with such tendernesses for her, as made me repeatedly ejaculate prayers in her behalf!—Such things are strange—it may be superstition to think about such correspondences; but it is a superstition which softens the heart & leads to no evil.—We will call on your dear Sister as soon as I am quite well—& in the mean time I will write a few Lines to her. I am anxious beyond measure to be in the country as soon as possible—I would it were possible to get a temporary residence till Adscombe is ready for us.—I would, that it could be, that we could have three Rooms in Bill Poole's large House for the winter——Will you try to look out for a fit servant for us—simple of heart, *physiognomically* handsome, & scientific in vaccimulgence? That last word is a new one; but soft in sound, and full of expression. Vaccimulgence!—I am pleased with the word.—Write to me all things about yourself—where I can not advise, I can console—and communication, which doubles joy, halves Sorrow.——

Tell me whether you think it at all possible to make any terms with William Poole—you know, I would not wish to touch with the edge of the Nail of my great toe the line which should be but half a barley corn out of the circle of the most trembling Delicacy!—I will write Cruikshanks tomorrow, if God permit me!—God bless & protect you, Friend! Brother! Beloved!

S. T. Coleridge

Sara's best love & Lloyd's——David Hartley is well, saving

that he is sometimes inspired by the God Eolus, & like Isaiah,
his 'bowells, sound like an Harp'! (My filial Love to your dear
Mother / —love to Ward— / Little Tommy! I often think of
thee!)

154. To Charles Lloyd, Senior

Monday, November 14th [1796]
Dear Sir,—I received your letter, and thank you for that
interest which you take in my welfare. The reasons which you
urge against my present plan are mostly well-founded; but they
would apply equally against any other scheme of life which *my*
Conscience would permit me to adopt. I might have a situation
as a Unitarian minister, I might have lucrative offices as an
active Politician; but on both of these the Voice within puts a
firm and unwavering negative. Nothing remains for me but
schoolmastership in a large town or my present plan. To the
success of both, and indeed even to my *subsisting* in either,
health and the possession of my faculties are necessary Requisites. While I possess these Requisites, *I know*, I can maintain
myself and family in the COUNTRY; the task of educating children suits not the activity of my mind, and the anxieties and
confinement incident to it, added to the living in a town or
city, would to a moral certainty ruin that Health and those
faculties which, as I said before, are necessary to my gaining my
livelihood in *any* way. Undoubtedly, without fortune, or trade,
or profession it is *impossible* that I should be in any situation
in which I must not be dependent on my own health and exertions for the bread of my family. I do not regret it—it will make
me *feel* my dependence on the Almighty, and it will prevent
my affections from being made earthly altogether. I praise God
in all things, and feel that to His grace alone it is owing that I
am *enabled* to praise Him in all things. You think my scheme
monastic rather than Christian. Can he be deemed monastic
who is married, and employed in rearing his children?—who
personally preaches the truth to his friends and neighbours, and
who endeavours to instruct tho' Absent by the Press? In what
line of Life could I be more *actively* employed? and what titles,
that are dear and venerable, are there which I shall not possess,
God permit[ting] my present resolutions to be realised? Shall
I not be an Agriculturist, an Husband, a Father, and a *Priest*
after the order of *Peace*? an *hireless* Priest? 'Christianity teaches

us to let our lights shine before men.' It does so—but it likewise bids us say, Our Father, lead us not [into] temptation! which how can he say with a safe conscience who voluntarily places himself in those circumstances in which, if he believe Christ, he must acknowledge that it would be easier for a Camel to go thro' the eye of a needle than for HIM to enter into the Kingdom of Heaven? Does not that man *mock* God who daily prays against temptations, yet daily places himself in the midst of the most formidable? I meant to have written a few lines only respecting myself, because I have much and weighty matter to write concerning my friend, Charles Lloyd; but I have been seduced into many words from the importance of the general truths on which I build my conduct.

While your Son remains with me, he will, of course, be acquiring that knowledge and those powers of Intellect which are necessary as the *foundation* of excellence in all professions, rather than the immediate science of *any*. *Languages* will engross one or two hours in every day: the *elements* of Chemistry, Geometry, Mechanics, and Optics the remaining hours of study. After tolerable proficiency in these, we shall proceed to the study of *Man* and of *Men*—I mean, Metaphysics and History—and finally, to a thorough examination of the Jewish and Christian Dispensations, their doctrines and evidences: an examination necessary for all men, but peculiarly so to your son, if he be destined for a medical man. A Physician who should be even a Theist, still more a *Christian*, would be a rarity indeed. I do not know *one*—and I know a *great many* Physicians. They are *shallow* Animals: having always employed their minds about Body and Gut, they imagine that in the whole system of things there is nothing but Gut and Body. . . .

['Here followed an account of Charles Lloyd's health, which was just then so "unsatisfactory" as to shut out anything but amusement. In his anxiety, Coleridge called in Dr. Beddoes.']

I chose Dr. Beddoes, because he is a *philosopher*, and the knowledge of *mind* is essentially requisite in order to the well-treating of your Son's distemper. . . . Such is Dr. Beddoes's *written* opinion. But he *told* me, that your Son's cure must be effected by Sympathy and Calmness—by being in company with some one before whom he *thought aloud* on all subjects, and by being in situations perfectly according with the tenderness of his Disposition. . . .

I hope your Health is confirmed, and that your Wife and children are well. Present my well-wishes. You are blessed with children who are *pure in Heart*—add to this Health, Competence, Social Affections, and Employment, and you have a complete idea of Human Happiness.

Believe me, | With esteem and friendly-heartedness, |
Your obliged
S. T. Coleridge.

161. *To Benjamin Flower*

Sunday Night. [11 December 1796]
My much esteemed Friend

I truly sympathize with you in your severe Loss, and pray to God that he may give you a sanctified use of your Affliction. The death of a young person of high hopes and opening faculties impresses me less gloomily, than the Departure of the Old. To my more natural Reason, the former *appears* like a *transition*; there seems an *incompleteness* in the life of such a person, contrary to the general order of nature; and it makes the heart say, 'this is not all.' But when an old man sinks into the grave, we have seen the bud, the blossom, and the fruit; and the unassisted mind droops in melancholy, as if *the Whole* had come and gone.—But God hath been merciful to us, and strengthened our eyes thro' faith, and Hope may cast her anchor in a certain bottom, and the young and old may rejoice before God and the Lamb, weeping as tho' they wept not, and crying in the Spirit of faith, Art thou not from everlasting, O Lord God my Holy One? We shall not die!——I have known affliction, yea, my friend! I have been myself sorely afflicted, and have rolled my dreary eye from earth to Heaven, and found no comfort, till it pleased the Unimaginable High & Lofty One to make my Heart more tender in regard of religious feelings. My philosophical refinements, & metaphysical Theories lay by me in the hour of anguish, as toys by the bedside of a Child deadly-sick. May God continue his visitations to my soul, bowing it down, till the pride & Laodicean self-confidence of human Reason be utterly done away; and I cry with deeper & yet deeper feelings, O my Soul! thou art wretched, and miserable, & poor, and blind, and naked!——The young Lady, who in a fit of frenzy killed her own mother, was the Sister of my dearest Friend, and herself dear to me as an only Sister. She is recovered, and is acquainted with what she has done, and is very calm. She was a truly pious young woman; and her Brother, whose soul is almost wrapped up in her, hath had his heart purified by this horror of desolation, and prostrates his Spirit at the throne of God in believing Silence. The Terrors of the Almighty are the whirlwind, the earthquake, and the Fire that precede the still small voice of his Love. The pestilence of our lusts must be scattered, the strong-layed Foundations of our Pride blown up, & the stubble & chaff of our Vanities burnt, ere we can give ear to the inspeaking Voice of Mercy, 'Why *will* ye die?'——

My answer to Godwin will be a six shilling Octavo; and is designed to shew not only the absurdities and wickedness of *his* System, but to detect what appear to me the defects of all the systems of morality before & since Christ, & to shew that wherein they have been right, they have exactly coincided with the Gospel, and that each has erred exactly where & in proportion as, he has deviated from that perfect canon. My last Chapter will attack the credulity, superstition, calumnies, and hypocrisy of the present race of Infidels. Many things have fallen out to retard the work; but I hope, that it will appear shortly after Christmas, at the farthest. I have endeavoured to make it a cheap book; and it will contain as much matter as is usually sold for eight shillings. I perceive, that in the New Monthly Magazine the Infidels have it all hollow. How our ancestors would have lifted up their hands at th[at] modest proposal for making experiments in favor of Idolatry!

Before the 24th of this month I will send you my *poetic endeavor*—it shall be as good as I can make it. The following Lines are at your service, if you approve of them.

LINES to a Young Man of Fortune who abandoned himself to an indolent and causeless Melancholy.

> Hence that fantastic Wantonness of Woe,
> O Youth to partial Fortune vainly dea[r!]
> To plunder'd WANT's half-shelter'd Hovel go,
> Go, and some hunger-bitten Infant hear
> Moan haply in a dying Mother's Ear;
> Or when the cold and dismal fog-damps brood
> O'er the rank Church-yard with sear elm-leaves strew'd
> Pace round some WIDOW's grave, whose dearer Part
> Was slaughter'd where o'er his uncoffin'd limbs
> The flocking Flesh-birds scream'd! Then, while thy Heart
> Groans, and thine eyes a fiercer Sorrow dims,
> Know (and the Truth shall kindle thy young Mind)
> What Nature makes thee mourn, she bids thee heal:
> O Abject! if to sickly Dreams resign'd

All effortless thou leave Earth's common weal
A prey to the thron'd Murderers of Mankind!
Bristol, Dec. 11th.

S. T. COLERIDGE.

Do you keep a Shop in Cambridge?——I seldom see *any*
paper. Indeed, I am out of heart with the French. In one of
the numbers of my Watchman I wrote 'a remonstrance to the
French Legislators': it contain'd *my* politics, & the splendid
Victories of the French since that time have produced no
alterations in them. I am tired of reading butcheries and altho'
I should be unworthy the name of Man, if I did not feel my
Head & Heart awefully interested in the final Event, yet, I
confess, my Curiosity is worn out with regard to the particulars
of the Process.—The paper, which contained an account of the
departure of your friend, had in it a Sonnet written during a
Thunder-storm. In thought & diction it was sublime & fearfully
impressive. I do not remember to have ever read so fine a
Sonnet—Surely, I thought, this burst from no common feelings
agitated by no common sorrow!—Was it your's?—

A young man of fortune, (his name, Gurney) wrote & published a book of horrible Blasphemies, asserting that our blessed
Lord deserved his fate more than any malefactor ever did
Tyburn (I pray heaven, I may incur no Guilt by transcribing
it!) —& after a fulsome panegyric adds that the name of *Godwin*
will soon supersede that of Christ.—Godwin wrote a letter to
this Man, thanking him for his *admirable* work, & soliciting the
honor of his personal friendship!!!—

With affectionate Esteem | Your's sincerely
S. T. Coleridge

At the close of this week I go with my Wife & Baby to Stowey,
near Bridgewater, Somersetshire: where you will for the future
direct to me. Whenever there is any thing particular, I shall be
thankful for your Paper.

S. T. C.

162. *To Thomas Poole*

[Endorsed 12 December 1796]

You tell me, my dear Poole! that my residence near you
would give you great pleasure; and I am sure, that if you had

any objections on your own account to my settling near Stowey, you would have mentioned them to me. Relying on this, I assure you that a Disappointment would try my philosophy. Your Letter did indeed give me unexpected and most acute pain. I will *make* the Cottage do. We want but three rooms.—If Cruikshanks have promised more than his circumstances enable him to perform, I am sure, that I can get the other purchased by my friends in Bristol—I mean, the place at Adscombe. I wrote him pressingly on this head some ten days ago; but he has returned me no answer. Lloyd has obtained his Father's permission & will return to me. He is willing to be his own Servant. As to Acton, 'tis out of the Question.—In Bristol I have Cottle & Estlin (for Mr Wade is going away) willing & eager to serve me—but how they can serve me more effectually at Acton, than at Stowey, I cannot divine. If I live at Stowey, you indeed *can* serve me effectually, by assisting me in the acquirement of agricultural practice.—If you can instruct me to manage an acre and a half of Land, and to raise on it with my own hands all kinds of vegetables, and grain, enough for myself & my Wife, and sufficient to feed a pig or two with the refuse, I hope, that you will have served me *most* effectually, by placing me out of the necessity of being served. I receive about forty guineas yearly from the Critical Review & New Monthly magazine. It is hard if by my greater works I do not get twenty more. I know how little the human mind requires when it is tranquil—and in proportion, as I should find it difficult to simplify my wants, it becomes my duty to simplify them. For there must be a vice in my nature, which woe be to me if I do not cure. The less meat I eat, the more healthy I am; and strong Liquors of any kind always & perceptibly injure me.—Sixteen shillings would cover all the weekly expences of my Wife, infant, and myself—this I say from my Wife's own calculation.

But whence this sudden revolution in your opinions, my dear Poole? You saw the Cottage, that was to be our temporary residence, and thought, we might be *happy* in it—and now you hurry to tell me, that we shall not even be *comfortable* in it.— You tell me, I shall be too far from my *friends*—i.e. Cottle & Estlin—for I have no other in Bristol—in the name of Heaven, *what can* Cottle or Estlin do for me? Or indeed what can any body [do] for me?—They do nothing who do not teach me how to be independent of any except the Almighty Dispenser of Sickness & Health!—And too far from the Press——With the printing of the Review & Magazine I have no concern—and if I

publish any work on my own account, I will send a fair &
faultless Copy, and Cottle promises to correct the Press for me.—
Mr King's Family may be very worthy sort of people, for aught
I know; but assuredly I can employ my time wiselier, than to
gabble with my tongue to Beings, with whom neither my Head
or Heart can commune.—My habits & feelings have suffered a
total alteration. I *hate* company except of my dearest friends;
and systematically avoid it, and when in it keep silence as far
as social Humanity will permit me. Lloyd's Father in a letter
to me yesterday enquired, how I should live without any companions?——I answered him, not an hour before I received your
letter——'I shall have six companions—My Sara, my Babe, my
own shaping and disquisitive mind, my Books, my beloved
Friend, Thomas Poole, & lastly, Nature, looking at me with a
thousand looks of Beauty, and speaking to me in a thousand
melodies of Love. If I were capable of being tired with all
these, I should then detect a Vice in my Nature, and would
fly to habitual Solitude to eradicate it.'—Yes! my friend! while
I opened your letter, my heart was glowing with enthusiasm
towards you—how little did I expect that I should find you
earnestly & vehemently persuading me to prefer Acton to
Stowey, and in return for the loss of *your* Society recommending
Mr King's Family as 'very pleasant Neighbours'! Neighbours!—
Can mere Juxta-position form a neighbourhood? As well should
the Louse in my Head call himself my friend, and the Flea in
my Bosom style herself my Love!——

On Wednesday Week we must leave our House: so that if you
continue to dissuade me from settling near Stowey, I scarcely
know what I shall do.—Surely, my beloved Friend! there must
be some reason, which you have not yet told me, which urged
You to send this hasty and heart-chilling Letter! I suspect that
something has passed between your Sister & dear Mother—(in
whose illness I sincerely sympathize with you.) ——

I have never considered my settlement at Stowey in any other
Relation than it's advantages to myself, and they would be great
indeed. My objects (assuredly, wise ones) were to learn agriculture (& where should I get instruction except at Stowey)
and to be where [I] can communicate in a literary way?——

I must conclude—I pray you let me hear from [you] immediately—

God bless you &
S. T. Coleridge.

173. *To John Prior Estlin*

[January 1797]

My dear Friend

I was indeed greatly rejoiced at the first sight of a letter from you; but it's contents were painful. Dear, dear Mrs Estlin!—Sara burst into an agony of tears, that she HAD been so ill.—Indeed, indeed, we hover about her—& think, & talk of her, with many an interjection of prayer.—I do not wonder that you have acquired a distaste to London—your associations must be painful indeed.—But God be praised! you shall look back on those sufferings, as the vexations of a dream! Our friend, T. Poole, particularly requests me to mention how deeply he condoles with you in Mrs Estlin's illness, how fervently he thanks God for her recovery.—I assure you he was extremely affected.——We are all remarkably well—& the child grows fat & strong. Our House is better than we expected—there is a comfortable bedroom & sitting room for C. Lloyd, & another for us—a room for Nanny, a kitchen, and outhouse. Before our door a clear brook runs of very soft water; and in the back yard is a nice *Well* of fine spring water. We have a very pretty garden, and large enough to find us vegetables & employment. And I am already an expert Gardener—& both my Hands can exhibit a callum, as testimonials of their Industry. We have likewise a sweet Orchard; & at the end of it T. Poole has made a gate, which leads into his garden—& from thence either thro' the tan yard into his house, or else thro' his orchard over a fine meadow into the garden of a Mr Cruikshanks, an old acquaintance, who married on the same day as I, & has got a little girl a little younger than David Hartley. Mrs Cruikshanks is a sweet little woman, of the same size as my Sara—& they are extremely cordial. T. Poole's Mother behaves to *us,* as a kind & tender Mother—She is very fond indeed of my Wife.—So that, you see, I ought to be happy —& thank God, I am so.——

I may expect your sermon I suppose, in the course of a fortnight—Will you send me introductory Letter[s] to Mr Howell of Bridgewater & Toulmin of Taunton? I have fifty things to write—but the carrier is at the door——To poor John give our love——and our kind love to Miss Estlin—& to all friends—To Mrs Estlin my heart is so full, that I know not what to write——

Believe me with gratitude, with filial respect, & fraternal affection

> Your sincere *friend*
> S. T. Coleridge.

179. *To Thomas Poole*

Sunday   March 1797

My dear Poole

My Father, (Vicar of, and Schoolmaster at, Ottery St. Mary, Devon) was a profound Mathematician, and well-versed in the Latin, Greek, & Oriental Languages. He published, or rather attempted to publish, several works: 1st, Miscellaneous Dissertations arising from the 17th and 18th Chapters of the Book of Judges; II. Sententiae excerptae, for the use of his own School; 3rd (& his best work) a Critical Latin Grammar; in the preface to which he proposes a bold Innovation in the names of the Cases. My father's new nomenclature was not likely to become popular, altho' it must be allowed to be both sonorous and expressive—exempli gratiâ—he calls the ablative the Quippe-quare-quale-quia-quidditive Case!—My Father made the world his confidant with respect to his Learning & ingenuity: & the world seems to have kept the secret very faithfully.—His various works, uncut, unthumbed, have been preserved free from all pollution, except that of his Family's Tails.—This piece of good-luck promises to be hereditary: for all *my* compositions have the same amiable *home-staying* propensity.—The truth is, My Father was not a first-rate Genius—he was however a first-rate Christian. I need not detain you with his Character—in learning, good-heartedness, absentness of mind, & excessive ignorance of the world, he was a perfect *Parson Adams.*—My Mother was an admirable Economist, and managed exclusively.—My eldest Brother's name was John: he went over to the East Indies in the Company's Service; he was a successful Officer, & a brave one, I have heard: he died of a consumption there about 8 years ago. My second Brother was called William —he went to Pembroke College, Oxford; and afterwards was assistant to Mr Newcome's School, at Hackney. He died of a putrid fever the year before my Father's death, & just as he was on the eve of marriage with Miss Jane Hart, the eldest Daughter of a very wealthy Druggist in Exeter.—My third Brother, James, has been in the army since the age of sixteen—has married a woman of fortune—and now lives at Ottery St Mary, a respectable Man. My Brother Edward, the wit of the Family, went to Pembroke College; & afterwards, to Salisbury, as assistant to Dr Skinner: he married a woman 20 years older than his Mother. She is dead: & he now lives at Ottery St Mary, an idle Parson. My fifth Brother, George, was educated at Pembroke College, Oxford; and from thence went to Mr Newcome's, Hackney, on the death of William. He stayed there fourteen [ten] years: when the living of Ottery St Mary was given him—there he now has a fine school, and has lately married Miss Jane Hart; who with beauty, & wealth, had remained a faithful Widow to the memory of William for 16 years.—My Brother George is a man of reflective mind & elegant Genius. He possesses Learning in a greater degree than any of the Family, excepting myself. His manners are grave, & hued over with a tender sadness. In his moral character he approaches every way nearer to Perfection than any man I ever yet knew—indeed, he is worth the whole family in a Lump. My sixth Brother, Luke (indeed the seventh, for one Brother, the second, died in his Infancy, & I had forgot to mention him) was bred as a medical Man—he married Miss Sara Hart: and died at the age of 22 [25], leaving one child, a lovely Boy, still alive. My Brother Luke was a man of uncommon Genius,—a severe student, & a good man.——The 8th Child was a Sister, Anne—she died a little after my Brother Luke—aged 21.

> Rest, gentle Shade! & wait thy Maker's will;
> Then rise *unchang'd,* and be an Angel still!

The 9th Child was called Francis: he went out as a Midshipman, under Admiral Graves—his Ship lay on the Bengal Coast —& he accidentally met his Brother John—who took him to Land, & procured him a Commission in the Army.—He shot himself (having been left carelessly by his attendant) in a delirious fever brought on by his excessive exertions at the siege of Seringapatam: at which his conduct had been so gallant, that Lord Cornwallis payed him a high compliment in the presence of the army, & presented him with a valuable gold Watch, which my Mother now has.—All my Brothers are remarkably handsome; but they were as inferior to Francis as I am to them. He went by the name of 'the handsome Coleridge.' The tenth & last Child was S. T. Coleridge, the subject of these Epistles: born (as I told you in my last) October 20th, 1772.

From October 20th, 1772 to October 20th, 1773.——Christened
Samuel Taylor Coleridge—my Godfather's name being Samuel
Taylor Esq. I had another Godfather, his name was Evans: &
two Godmothers; both called 'Monday' [Mundy].—

From October 20th, 1773 to October 20th 1774.——In this
year I was carelessly left by my Nurse—ran to the Fire, and
pulled out a live coal—burnt myself dreadfully—while my hand
was being Drest by a Mr Young, I spoke for the first time (so
my Mother informs me) & said—'Nasty Doctor Young'!—The
snatching at fire, & the circumstance of my first words expressing
hatred to professional men, are they at all *ominous?* This Year,
I went to School—My Schoolmistress, the very image of Shen-
stone's, was named, Old Dame Key—she was nearly related to
Sir Joshua Renyolds [*sic*].—

From October 20th 1774 to October 1775. I was inoculated;
which I mention, because I distinctly remember it: & that my
eyes were bound—at which I manifested so much obstinate
indignation, that at last they removed the bandage—and un-
affrighted I looked at the lancet & suffered the scratch.—At the
close of this Year I could read a Chapter in the Bible.

Here I shall end; because the remaining years of my Life
all assisted to form *my particular mind*—the three first years had
nothing in them that seems to relate to it.

[Signature cut off]

184. *To Joseph Cottle*

[Early April 1797]

My dearest Cottle

I love and respect you as a brother, and my memory deceives
me woefully, if I have not evidenced by the animated tone of
my conversation, when we have been *tête-à-tête,* how much
your company interested me. But when last in Bristol the day
I meant to have devoted to you was such a day of sadness,
that I could *do nothing.*—On the Saturday, the Sunday, and the
ten days after my arrival at Stowey I felt a depression too
dreadful to be described

> So much I felt my genial spirits droop!
> My hopes all flat, nature within me seem'd
> In all her functions weary of herself.

Wordsworth's conversation, &c roused me somewhat; but even now I am not the man I have been—and I think never shall. A sort of calm hopelessness diffuses itself over my heart.—Indeed every mode of life which has promised me bread and cheese, has been, one after another torn away from me—but God remains. I have no immediate pressing distress, having received ten pounds from Lloyd's father at Birmingham.—I employ myself now on a book of Morals in answer to Godwin, and on my Tragedy. David Hartley is well, and grows.—Sara is well and desires a sister's love to you.

Tom Poole desires to be kindly remembered to you. I see they have reviewed Southey's Poems and my Ode in the Monthly Review. Notwithstanding the Reviews, I, who in the sincerity of my heart am *jealous* for Robert Southey's fame, regret the publication of that volume. Wordsworth complains, with justice, that Southey writes *too much at his ease*—that he seldom 'feels his burthened breast

Heaving beneath th' incumbent Deity.'

He certainly will make literature more *profitable to him* from the fluency with which he writes, and the facility with which he pleases himself. But I fear, that to posterity his wreath will look unseemly—here an ever living amaranth, and close by its side some weed of an hour, sere, yellow, and shapeless—his exquisite beauties will lose half their effect from the bad company they keep. Besides I am fearful that he will begin to rely too much on *story* and *event* in his poems, to the neglect of those *lofty imaginings,* that are peculiar to, and definitive of, the poet. The *story* of Milton might be told in two pages—it is this which distinguishes an *Epic Poem* from a *Romance in metre.* Observe the march of Milton—his severe application, his laborious polish, his deep metaphysical researches, his prayers to God before he began his great poem, all that could lift and swell his intellect, became his daily food. I should not think of devoting less than 20 years to an Epic Poem. Ten to collect materials and warm my mind with universal science. I would be a tolerable Mathematician, I would thoroughly know Mechanics, Hydrostatics, Optics, and Astronomy, Botany, Metallurgy, Fossilism, Chemistry, Geology, Anatomy, Medicine—then the *mind of man*—then the *minds of men*—in all Travels, Voyages and Histories. So I would spend ten years—the next five to the composition of the poem—and the five last to the correction of it.

So I would write haply not unhearing of that divine and rightly-whispering Voice, which speaks to mighty minds of predestinated Garlands, starry and unwithering. God love you,

S. T. Coleridge.

195. *To Joseph Cottle*

[*Circa* 3 July 1797]

My dear friend

These are the errors, or the alterations—Now, I conceive, that as the volumes are bound, you might employ a boy for sixpence or a shilling to go thro' them & with a fine pen, and dainty ink, make the alterations in each volume—I am confident, it would not cost more than printing the errata,—and then the Errata may remain, as it is *now already* printed.—*I wish, it could be so*: for really, nobody scarcely does look at the table of Errata—the Volume is a most beautiful one——you have determined that the three Bards shall walk up Parnassus, or the Hill of Fame, in their best Bib & Tucker. Give my Love to your Brother Amos—I condole with him—but it is the fortune of War—the finest poem, I ever wrote, lost the prize—& that which gained it, was contemptible—but an ode may *sometimes* be too bad for the prize; but VERY OFTEN *too good*.

Wordsworth & his exquisite Sister are with me—She is a woman indeed!—in mind, I mean, & heart—for her person is such, that if you expected to see a pretty woman, you would think her ordinary—if you expected to find an ordinary woman, you would think her pretty!—But her manners are simple, ardent, impressive—.

> In every motion her most innocent soul
> Outbeams so brightly, that who saw would say,
> Guilt was a thing impossible in her.—

Her information various—her eye watchful in minutest observation of nature—and her taste a perfect electrometer—it bends, protrudes, and draws in, at subtlest beauties & most recondite faults.——She with her Brother desire their kindest respects to you—If you can pick up a Hamlet, an Othello, & a Romeo & Juliet, separately, in *numbers,* or an odd volume—Wordsworth would thank you to get it for him——

T. Poole will be collecting the names of the persons, who want my poems here—when I have got them, I will send the Number & you will put it to Poole's account—For myself I want one, for C. Lamb *one,* for Wordsworth in *your* name *one,* for my Brother *one,* and one I shall send with a sonnet to Dr *Parr*—

God love you | & your ever affectionate

S. T. Coleridge

208. *To Thomas Poole*

October 9th, 1797

My dearest Poole

From March to October—a long silence! but [as] it is possible, that I may have been preparing materials for future letters, the time cannot be considered as altogether subtracted from you.

From October 1775 to October 1778.

These three years I continued at the reading-school—because I was too little to be trusted among my Father's School-boys—. After breakfast I had a halfpenny given me, with which I bought three cakes at the Baker's close by the school of my old mistress—& these were my dinner on every day except Saturday & Sunday—when I used to dine at home, and wallowed in a beef & pudding dinner.—I am remarkably fond of Beans & Bacon—and this fondness I attribute to my father's having given me a penny for having eat a large quantity of beans, one Saturday—for the other boys did not like them, and as it was an economic food, my father thought, that my attachment & penchant for it ought to be encouraged.——My Father was very fond of me, and I was my mother's darling—in consequence, I was very miserable. For Molly, who had nursed my Brother Francis, and was immoderately fond of him, hated me because my mother took more notice of me than of Frank—and Frank hated me, because my mother gave me now & then a bit of cake, when he had none—quite forgetting that for one bit of cake which I had & he had not, he had twenty sops in the pan & pieces of bread & butter with sugar on them from Molly, from whom I received only thumps & ill names.—So I became fretful, & timorous, & a tell-tale—& the School-boys drove me from play, & were always tormenting me—& hence I took no pleasure in boyish sports—but read incessantly. My Father's Sister kept an *everything* Shop at Crediton—and there I read thro' all the gilt-cover little books that could be had at that time, & likewise all the uncovered tales of Tom Hickathrift, Jack the Giant-killer, &c & &c &c &c —/—and I used to lie by the wall, and *mope*—and my spirits used to come upon me suddenly, & in a flood—& then I was accustomed to run up and down the church-yard, and act over all I had been reading on the docks, the nettles, and the rank-grass.—At six years old I remember to have read Belisarius, Robinson Crusoe, & Philip Quarle [Quarll]—and then I found the Arabian Nights' entertainments—one tale of which (the tale of a man who was compelled to seek for a pure virgin) made so deep an impression on me (I had read it in the evening while my mother was mending stockings) that I was haunted by spectres, whenever I was in the dark—and I distinctly remember the anxious & fearful eagerness, with which I used to watch the window, in which the books lay—& whenever the Sun lay upon them, I would seize it, carry it by the wall, & bask, & read—. My Father found out the effect, which these books had produced—and burnt them.—So I became a *dreamer*—and acquired an indisposition to all bodily activity—and I was fretful, and inordinately passionate, and as I could not play at any thing, and was slothful, I was despised & hated by the boys; and because I could read & spell, & had, I may truly say, a memory & understanding forced into almost an unnatural ripeness, I was flattered & wondered at by all the old women—& so I became very vain, and despised most of the boys, that were at all near my own age—and before I was eight years old, I was a *character*—sensibility, imagination, vanity, sloth, & feelings of deep & bitter contempt for almost all who traversed the orbit of my understanding, were even then prominent & manifest.

From October 1778 to 1779.—That which I began to be from 3 to 6, I continued from 6 to 9.—In this year I was admitted into the grammer school, and soon outstripped all of my age.—I had a dangerous putrid fever this year—My Brother George lay ill of the same fever in the next room.——My poor Brother Francis, I remember, stole up in spite of orders to the contrary, & sate by my bedside, & read Pope's Homer to me—Frank had a violent love of beating me—but whenever that was superseded by any humour or circumstance, he was always very fond of me—& used to regard me with a strange mixture of admiration & contempt—strange it was not—: for he hated books, and

loved climbing, fighting, playing, & robbing orchards, to distraction.—

My mother relates a story of me, which I repeat here—because
it must be regarded as my first piece of wit.—During my fever I
asked why Lady Northcote (our neighbour) did not come & see
me.—My mother said, She was afraid of catching the fever—I
was piqued & answered—Ah—Mamma! the four Angels round
my bed an't afraid of catching it.—I suppose, you know the old
prayer—

> Matthew! Mark! Luke! & John!
> God bless the bed which I lie on.
> Four Angels round me spread,
> Two at my foot & two at my bed [head]—

This prayer I said nightly—& most firmly believed the truth of
it.—Frequently have I, half-awake & half-asleep, my body diseased & fevered by my imagination, seen armies of ugly Things
bursting in upon me, & these four angels keeping them off.—In
my next I shall carry on my life to my Father's Death.—

God bless you, my dear Poole! | & your affectionate
S. T. Coleridge.

210. *To Thomas Poole*

[Endorsed Octr 16th, (17) 97]

Dear Poole

From October 1779 to Oct. 1781.——I had asked my mother
one evening to cut my cheese *entire,* so that I might toast it:
this was no easy matter, it being a *crumbly* cheese—My mother
however did it— / I went into the garden for some thing or
other, and in the mean time my Brother Frank *minced* my
cheese, 'to disappoint the favorite'. I returned, saw the exploit,
and in an agony of passion flew at Frank—he pretended to
have been seriously hurt by my blow, flung himself on the
ground, and there lay with outstretched limbs——I hung over
him moaning & in a great fright—he leaped up, & with a horse-
laugh gave me a severe blow in the face—I seized a knife, and
was running at him, when my Mother came in & took me by
the arm—/ I expected a flogging—& struggling from her I ran
away, to a hill at the bottom of which the Otter flows—about
one mile from Ottery.—There I stayed; my rage died away; but
my obstinacy vanquished my fears—& taking out a little shilling

book which had, at the end, morning & evening prayers, I very
devoutly repeated them—thinking *at the same time* with inward
& gloomy satisfaction, how miserable my Mother must be!—I
distinctly remember my feelings when I saw a Mr Vaughan
pass over the Bridge, at about a furlong's distance—and how I
watched the Calves in the fields beyond the river. It grew dark—
& I fell asleep—it was towards the latter end of October—& it
proved a dreadful stormy night— / I felt the cold in my sleep,
and dreamt that I was pulling the blanket over me, & actually
pulled over me a dry thorn bush, which lay on the hill—in my
sleep I had rolled from the top of the hill to within three yards
of the River, which flowed by the unfenced edge of the bottom.
—I awoke several times, and finding myself wet & stiff, and cold,
closed my eyes again that I might forget it.——In the mean time
my Mother waited about half an hour, expecting my return,
when the *Sulks* had evaporated—I not returning, she sent into
the Church-yard, & round the town—not found!—Several men &
all the boys were sent to ramble about & seek me—in vain! My
Mother was almost distracted—and at ten o'clock at night I was
cry'd by the crier in Ottery, and in two villages near it—with a
reward offered for me.—No one went to bed—indeed, I believe,
half the town were up all one night! To return to myself—
About five in the morning or a little after, I was broad awake;
and attempted to get up & walk—but I could not move—I saw
the Shepherds & Workmen at a distance—& cryed but so faintly,
that it was impossible to hear me 30 yards off——and there I
might have lain & died—for I was now almost given over, the
ponds & even the river near which I was lying, having been
dragged.—But by good luck Sir Stafford Northcote, who had
been out all night, resolved to make one other trial, and came
so near that he heard my crying—He carried me in his arms, for
near a quarter of a mile; when we met my father & Sir Stafford's
Servants.—I remember, & never shall forget, my father's face as
he looked upon me while I lay in the servant's arms—so calm,
and the tears stealing down his face: for I was the child of his
old age.——My Mother, as you may suppose, was outrageous
with joy—in rushed a *young Lady,* crying out—'I hope, you'll
whip him, Mrs Coleridge!'—This woman still lives at Ottery—
& neither Philosophy or Religion have been able to conquer
the antipathy which I *feel* towards her, whenever I see her.—I
was put to bed—& recovered in a day or so—but I was certainly
injured—For I was weakly, & subject to the ague for many years
after—.—

My Father (who had so little of parental ambition in him, that he had destined his children to be Blacksmiths &c, & had accomplished his intention but for my Mother's pride & spirit of aggrandizing her family) my father had however resolved, that I should be a Parson. I read every book that came in my way without distinction—and my father was fond of me, & used to take me on his knee, and hold long conversations with me. I remember, that at eight years old I walked with him one winter evening from a farmer's house, a mile from Ottery——& he told me the names of the stars—and how Jupiter was a thousand times larger than our world—and that the other twinkling stars were Suns that had worlds rolling round them—& when I came home, he shewed me how they rolled round— / . I heard him with a profound delight & admiration; but without the least mixture of wonder or incredulity. For from my early reading of Faery Tales, & Genii &c &c—my mind had been habituated *to the Vast*——& I never regarded *my senses* in any way as the criteria of my belief. I regulated all my creeds by my conceptions not by my *sight*—even at that age. Should children be permitted to read Romances, & Relations of Giants & Magicians, & Genii?——I know all that has been said against it; but I have formed my faith in the affirmative.—I know no other way of giving the mind a love of 'the Great', & 'the Whole'.—Those who have been led to the same truths step by step thro' the constant testimony of their senses, seem to me to want a sense which I possess—They contemplate nothing but *parts*—and all *parts* are necessarily little—and the Universe to them is but a mass of *little things*.—It is true, that the mind *may* become credulous & prone to superstition by the former method—but are not the Experimentalists credulous even to madness in believing any absurdity, rather than believe the grandest truths, if they have not the testimony of their own senses in their favor? —I have known some who have been *rationally* educated, as it is styled. They were marked by a microscopic acuteness; but when they looked at great things, all became a blank & they saw nothing—and denied (very illogically) that any thing could be seen; and uniformly put the negation of a power for the possession of a power—& called the want of imagination Judgment, & the never being moved to Rapture Philosophy!——

Towards the latter end of September 1781 my Father went to Plymouth with my Brother Francis, who was to go as Midshipman under Admiral Graves; the Admiral was a friend of my Father's.—My Father settled my Brother; & returned Oct. 4th,

1781—. He arrived at Exeter about six o'clock—& was pressed to take a bed there by the Harts—but he refused—and to avoid their intreaties he told them—that he had never been superstitious—but that the night before he had had a dream which had made a deep impression. He dreamt that Death had appeared to him, as he is commonly painted, & touched him with his Dart. Well he returned home—& all his family, I excepted, were up. He told my mother his dream—; but he was in high health & good spirits—& there was a bowl of Punch made—& my Father gave a long & particular account of his Travel, and that he had placed Frank under a religious Captain &c—/ At length, he went to bed, very well, & in high Spirits.—A short time after he had lain down he complained of a pain in his bowells, which he was subject to, from the wind—my mother got him some peppermint water—and after a pause, he said—'I am much better now, my dear!'—and lay down again. In a minute my mother heard a noise in his throat—and spoke to him—but he did not answer—and she spoke repeatedly in vain. Her *shriek* awaked me—& I said, 'Papa is dead.'—I did not know [of] my Father's return, but I knew that he was expected. How I came to think of his Death, I cannot tell; but so it was.—Dead he was—some said it was the Gout in the Heart—probably, it was a fit of Apoplexy / —He was an Israelite without guile; simple, generous, and, taking some scripture texts in their literal sense, he was conscientiously indifferent to the good & the evil of this world.—

God love you & S. T. Coleridge

225. *To William Wordsworth*

Tuesday Morning. Jan. [23,] 1798

My dear Wordsworth

You know, of course, that I have accepted the magnificent liberality of Josiah & Thomas Wedgewood. I accepted it on the presumption that I had talents, honesty, & propensities to perseverant effort. If I have hoped wisely concerning myself, I have acted justly. But dismissing severer thoughts, believe me, my dear fellow! that of the pleasant ideas, which accompanied this unexpected event, it was not the least pleasant nor did it pass thro' my mind the last in the procession, that I should at least be able to trace the spring & early summer of Alfoxden with you; & that wherever your after residence may be, it is probable that you will be within the reach of my Tether, lengthened as it now is.——The country round Shrewsbury is rather tame—My imagination has cloathed it with all it's summer attributes; but I still can see in it no possibility beyond that of *Beauty*.—The Society here were sufficiently eager to have me, as their Minister, and, I think, would have behaved kindly & respectfully—but I perceive clearly, that without great courage & perseverance in the use of the monosyllable, *No*! I should have been plunged in a very Maelstrom of visiting—whirled round, and round, and round, never changing yet always moving.—Visiting with all it's pomps & vanities is the mania of the place; & many of the congregation are both rich & expensive.—I met a young man, a Cambridge undergraduate—talking of plays &c, he told that an acquaintance of his was printing a translation of one of Kotzebu's Tragedies, entitled, Beniowski——The name startled me, and upon examination I found that the story of my 'Siberian Exiles' has been already dramatized.—If Kotzebu has exhibited no greater genius in it than in his Negro slaves, I shall consider this as an unlucky circumstance—but the young man speaks enthusiastically of it's merits. I have just read the Castle Spectre—& shall bring it home with me.—I will begin with it's defects, in order that my 'But' may have a charitable transition.—1. Language—2. Character. 3. Passion. 4. Sentiment. 5. Conduct——1. Of styles some are pleasing, durably and on reflection—some only in transition—and some are not pleasing at all—And to this latter class belongs the Castle Spectre. There are no felicities in the humourous passages; and in the serious ones it is Schiller Lewis-ized—i.e. a flat, flabby, unimaginative Bombast oddly sprinkled with colloquialisms. 2.—No character at all. The author in a postscript lays claim to *novelty* in *one* of his characters—that of Hassan.—Now Hassan is a negro, who *had* a warm & benevolent heart; but having been kidnapped from his country & barbarously used by the Christians, becomes a Misanthrope.—This is all!!——3. Passion—horror! agonizing pangs of Conscience! Dreams full of hell, serpents, & skeletons! starts & attempted murders &c &c &c; but, positively, not *one* line that marks even a superficial knowledge of human feelings, could I discover. 4. Sentiments are moral & humourous. There is a book called the Frisky Songster, at the end of which are two chapters—the first containing *Frisky* Toasts & Sentiments—the second, *Moral* Toasts:—and from these chapters I suspect, that Mr Lewis has stolen all his sentimentality, moral & humourous. A very fat Friar, renowned for Gluttony & Lubricity, furnishes abundance of jokes (all of them abdominal vel si quid infra) Jokes that would have stunk, had they been fresh; and alas! they have the very saeva mephitis of *antiquity* on them.—BUT—5—the Conduct of the Piece is, I think, *good*—except that the first act is *wholly* taken up with explanation & narration.——This Play proves how accurately you conjectured concerning *theatric* merit. The merit of the Castle Spectre consists wholly in it's *situations*. These are all borrowed, and all absolutely *pantomimical;* but they are admirably managed for stage effect. There is not much bustle; but *situations* for ever. The whole plot, machinery, & incident are borrowed—the play is a mere patchwork of plagiarisms—but they are very well worked up, & for stage effect make an excellent *whole*.—There is a pretty little Ballad-song introduced—and Lewis, I think, has great & peculiar excellence in these compositions. The simplicity & naturalness is his own, & not imitated; for it is made to subsist in congruity with a language perfectly modern—the language of his own times, in the same way that the language of the writer of 'Sir Cauline' was the language of *his* times. This, I think, a rare merit: at least, I find, *I* cannot attain this innocent nakedness, except by *assumption*—I resemble the Dutchess of Kingston, who masqueraded in the character of 'Eve before the Fall' in flesh-coloured Silk.——This play struck me with utter hopelessness—it would be [easy] to produce these situations, but not in a play so for[cibly] as to admit the permanent & closest beauties of style, passion & character. To admit pantomimic tricks the plot itself must be pantomimic—Harlequin cannot be had unaccompanied by the Fool.——

I hope to be with you by the middle of next week—I must stay over next Sunday, as Mr Row is obliged to go to Bristol to seek a House. He & his Family are honest, sensible, pleasant people. My kind Love to Dorothy—& believe me | with affectionate esteem |

Your's sincerely
S. T. Coleri[dge]

234. *To Thomas Poole*

[Endorsed Feby 19th 1798]
From October 1781 to October 1782.

After the death of my father we, of course, changed houses, & I remained with my mother till the spring of 1782, and was a day-scholar to Parson Warren, my Father's successor— / He was a booby, I believe; and I used to delight my poor mother by relating little instances of his deficiency in grammar knowledge —every detraction from his merits seemed an oblation to the memory of my Father, especially as Parson Warren did certainly *pulpitize* much better.—Somewhere, I think, about April 1792, [1782] Judge Buller, who had been educated by my Father, sent for me, having procured a Christ's Hospital Presentation.—I accordingly went to London, and was received by my mother's Brother, Mr Bowden, a Tobacconist & (at the same [time]) clerk to an Underwriter. My Uncle lived at the corner of the Stock exchange, & carried on his shop by means of a confidential Servant, who, I suppose, fleeced him most unmercifully.— He was a widower, & had one daughter who lived with a Miss Cabriere, an old Maid of great sensibilities & a taste for literature——Betsy Bowden had obtained an unlimited influence over her mind, which she still retains—Mrs Holt (for this is her name now) was, when I knew her, an ugly & an artful woman & not the kindest of Daughters—but indeed, my poor Uncle would have wearied the patience & affection of an Euphrasia. —He was generous as the air & a man of very considerable talents—but he was a Sot.—He received me with great affection, and I stayed ten weeks at his house, during which time I went occasionally to Judge Buller's. My Uncle was very proud of me, & used to carry me from Coffee-house to Coffee-house, and Tavern to Tavern, where I drank, & talked & disputed, as if I had been a man— /. Nothing was more common than for a large party to exclaim in my hearing, that I *was a prodigy*, &c &c &c—so that, while I remained at my Uncle's, I was most completely spoilt & pampered, both mind & body. At length the time came, & I donned the *Blue* coat & yellow stockings, & was sent down to Hertford, a town 20 miles from London, where there are about 300 of the younger Blue coat boys—At Hertford I was very happy, on the whole; for I had plenty to eat & drink, & pudding & vegetables almost every day. I stayed there six weeks; and then was drafted up to the great school at London, where I arrived in September, 1792 [1782]—and was placed in the second ward, then called Jefferies's ward; & in the under Grammar School. There are twelve Wards, or dormitories, of unequal sizes, beside the Sick Ward, in the great School—& they contained, all together, 700 boys; of whom I think nearly one third were the Sons of Clergymen. There are 5 Schools, a Mathematical, a Grammar, a drawing, a reading, & a writing

School—all very large Buildings.—When a boy is admitted, if he read very badly, he is either sent to Hertford or to the Reading-School—(N.B. Boys are admissible from 7 to 12 years old)—If he learn to read tolerably well before 9, he is drafted into the lower Grammar-school—if not, into the writing-school, as having given proof of unfitness for classical attainment.—If before he is eleven he climbs up to the first form of the lower Grammar-school, he is drafted into the head Grammar School—if not, at 11 years old he is sent into the writing School, where he continues till 14 or 15—and is then either apprenticed, & articled as clerk, or whatever else his turn of mind, or of fortune shall have provided for him. Two or three times a year the Mathematical Master beats up for recruits for the King's boys, as they are called—and all, who like the navy, are drafted into the Mathematical & Drawing Schools—where they continue till 16 or 17, & go out as Midshipmen & Schoolmasters in the Navy.—The Boys, who are drafted into the head Grammar School, remain there till 13—& then if not chosen for the university, go into the writing school. Each dormitory has a Nurse, or Matron—& there is a head Matron to superintend all these Nurses.—The boys were, when I was admitted, under excessive subordination to each other, according to rank in School—& every ward was governed by four Monitors, (appointed by the *Steward,* who was the supreme Governor out of School—our Temporal Lord) and by four *Markers,* who wore silver medals, & were appointed by the head Grammar Master, who was our supreme Spiritual Lord. The same boys were commonly both Monitors & Markers—We read in classes on Sundays to our *Markers,* & were catechized by them, & under their sole authority during prayers, &c—all other authority was in the monitors; but, as I said, the same boys were ordinarily both the one & the other.—Our diet was very scanty—Every morning a bit of dry bread & some bad small beer—every evening a larger piece of bread, & cheese or butter, whichever we liked—For dinner—on Sunday, boiled beef & broth—Monday, Bread & butter, & milk & water—on Tuesday, roast mutton, Wednesday, bread & butter & rice milk, Thursday, boiled beef & broth—Friday, boiled mutton & broth—Saturday, bread & butter, & pease porritch—Our food was portioned—& excepting on Wednesdays I never had a belly full. Our appetites were *damped* never satisfied—and we had no vegetables.—

                                                                S. T. Coleridge

235. *To Joseph Cottle*

Stowey, Wednesday Morning. [7 March 1798]

My dear Cottle

I have been confined to my bed for some days thro' a fever occasioned by the stump of a tooth which baffled chirurgical efforts to eject it; & which by affecting my eye affected my stomach, & thro' that my whole frame. I am better—but still weak in consequence of such long sleeplessness & wearying pains—weak, very weak.—I thank you, my dear Friend! for your late kindness—and in a few weeks will either repay you in money or by verses, as you like.—With regard to Lloyd's verses, it is curious that *I* should be applied to—to be 'PERSUADED to RESIGN,['] and in ho[pe] that I might 'CONSENT to GIVE UP' a number of poem[s] which were published at the earnest request of the author[, who] assured me that the circumstance was 'of no trivial import to his happiness.'——Times change, & people change; but let us keep our souls in quietness!——I have no objection to any disposal of C. Lloyd's poems except that of their being republished with mine. The motto, which I had prefixed 'Duplex &c' from Groscollius has placed me in a ridiculous situation—but it was a foolish & presumptuous start of affectionateness, and I am not unwilling to incur punishments due to my folly.—By past experiences we build up our moral being.——How comes it that I have never heard from dear Mr Estlin, my fatherly & brotherly friend? This idea haunted me during my sleepless nights, till my sides were sore in turning from one to the other, as if I were hoping to turn away from the idea.—The Giant Wordsworth—God love him!—even when I speak in the terms of admiration due to his intellect, I fear lest tho[se] terms should keep out of sight the amiableness of his manners——he has written near 1200 lines of a blank verse, superior, I hesitate not to aver, to any thing in our language which any way resembles it. Poole (whom I feel so consolidated with myself that I seem to have no occasion to speak of him out of myself) thinks of it as likely to benefit mankind much more than any thing, Wordsworth has yet written.——With regard to my poems I shall prefix the Maid of Orleans, 1000 lines —& three blank verse poems, making all three, about 200— / and I shall utterly leave out perhaps a larger quantity of lines: & I should think, it would answer to you in a pecuniary way to print the third Edition *humbly* & cheaply. My alterations in the

Religious Musings will be considerable, & will lengthen the poem.——Oh! Poole desires you *not* to mention his house to any one unless you hear from him again; as since I have been writing a thought has struck us of letting it to an inhabitant of the village—which we should prefer, as we should be certain that his manners would be severe, inasmuch as he would be a Stow-ic.

God bless you & S. T. C.

242. *To Joseph Cottle*

[Early April 1798]

My dear Cottle,

Neither Wordsworth nor myself could have been otherwise than uncomfortable, if any but yourself had received from us the first offer of our Tragedies, and of the volume of Wordsworth's Poems. At the same time, we did not expect that you could with prudence and propriety, advance such a sum, as we should want at the time we specified. In short, we both regard the publication of our Tragedies as an evil. It is not impossible but that in happier times, they may be brought on the stage: and to throw away this chance for a mere trifle, would be to make the present moment act fraudulently and usuriously towards the future time.

My Tragedy employed and strained all my thoughts and faculties for six or seven months: Wordsworth consumed far more time, and far more thought, and far more genius. We consider the publication of them an evil on any terms; but our thoughts were bent on a plan for the accomplishment of which, a certain sum of money was necessary, (the whole) at that particular time, and in order to this we resolved, although reluctantly, to part with our Tragedies: that is, if we could obtain thirty guineas for each, and at less than thirty guineas Wordsworth will not part with the copy-right of his volume of Poems. We shall offer the Tragedies to no one, for we have determined to procure the money some other way. If you choose the volume of Poems, at the price mentioned, to be paid at the time specified, i.e. thirty guineas, to be paid sometime in the last fortnight of July, you may have them; but remember, my dear fellow! I write to you now merely as a bookseller, and intreat you, in your answer, to consider yourself only; as to us, although money is necessary to our plan, [that of visiting Germany] yet the plan is not necessary to our happiness; and if it were, W. would sell his Poems for that sum to some one else, or we could procure the money without selling the poems. So I entreat you, again and again, in your answer, which must be immediate, consider yourself only.

Wordsworth has been caballed against *so long and so loudly,* that he has found it impossible to prevail on the tenant of the Allfoxden estate, to let him the house, after their first agreement is expired, so he must quit it at Midsummer; whether we shall be able to procure him a house and furniture near Stowey, we know not, and yet we must: for the hills, and the woods, and the streams, and the sea, and the shores would break forth into reproaches against us, if we did not strain every nerve, to keep their Poet among them. Without joking, and in serious sadness, Poole and I cannot endure to think of losing him.

At all events, come down, Cottle, as soon as you can, but before Midsummer, and we will procure a horse easy as thy own soul, and we will go on a roam to Linton and Linmouth, which, if thou comest in May, will be in all their pride of woods and waterfalls, not to speak of its august cliffs, and the green ocean, and the vast valley of stones, all which live disdainful of the seasons, or accept new honours only from the winter's snow. At all events come down, and cease not to believe me much and affectionately your friend,

S. T. COLERIDGE

244. *To William Wordsworth*

May 10th, 1798

In stale blank verse a subject stale
I send *per post* my *Nightingale;*
And like an honest bard, dear Wordsworth,
You'll tell me what you think, my Bird's worth.
My opinion's briefly this—
His *bill* he opens not amiss;
And when he has sung a stave or so,
His breast, & some small space below,
So throbs & swells, that you might swear
No vulgar music's working there.

So far, so good; but then, 'od rot him!
There's something falls off at his bottom.
Yet, sure, no wonder it should breed,
That my Bird's Tail's a tail indeed
And makes it's own inglorious harmony
AEolio crepitû, non carmine.

                                                    S. T. COLERIDGE

247. To George Coleridge

                                        May 14th, Monday. 1798

My dear Brother

By an odd jumble of accidents I did not receive the parcel till
within a few days— / My wife was this morning delivered of a
very fine boy—she had a remarkably good time & both she and
the child are as well as can be. May God be praised!——

Believe me, I am truly anxious to hear concerning your little
one; my little Hartley has had an ugly cough & feverish complaint which made me fear the whooping cough; but it was only
the effect of teething, at least, so we hope.——Yesterday I walked
in to Taunton to perform the divine services for poor Dr Toulmin whose daughter in a melancholy derangement suffered
herself to be swallowed up by the tide on the coast between
Sidmouth & Bere. Good old Man! he bears it like one in whom
Christianity is an habit of feeling in a still greater degree than
a conviction of the understanding. He sanctifies his calamity;
but it is plain, that it has cut deep into his heart.—And then
from a Mrs Stone I heard all at once the death of Mr William
Lewis: remembering the man, & remembering the conversation
we had concerning him in the churchyard walk, and considering
as it were in a glance of the imagination his bulk & stature, &
then the horrid manner of his death—it so overpowered me that
I felt as if I had been choked, and then burst into an agony of
tears. I scarcely remember ever to have been so deeply affected.—

I will write again in a few days, and send you the Tragedy, &c
&c—Sheridan has again promised to fit it for the stage & bring
it on, which promise he will as certainly break as

I am

                            your affectionate & grateful | Brother
                                        S. T. Coleridge

250. *To Joseph Cottle*

Monday Morning [28 May 1798]

My dear Cottle

You know what I think of a letter—how impossible it is to *argue* in it. You must therefore take simple statements, & in a week or two I shall see you & endeavor to *reason* with you.

Wordsworth & I have *maturely weigh'd* your proposal, & this is our answer—W. would not object to the publishing of Peter Bell *or* the Salisbury Plain, singly; but to the publishing of *his poems* in two volumes he is decisively repugnant & oppugnant —He deems that they would want variety &c &c—if this apply in his case, it applies with tenfold force to mine.—We deem that the volumes offered to you are to a certain degree *one work,* in *kind tho' not in degree,* as an Ode is one work—& that our different poems are as stanzas, good relatively rather than absolutely:—Mark you, I say *in kind* tho' not in degree.—The extract from my Tragedy will have no sort of reference to my Tragedy, but is a Tale in itself, as the ancient Mariner.—The Tragedy will not be mentioned— / As to the Tragedy, when I consider it [in] reference to Shakespear's & to *one* other Tragedy, it seems a poor thing; & I care little what becomes of it—when I consider [it] in comparison with modern Dramatists, it *rises:* & I think it too bad to be published, too good to be *squandered.*—I think of breaking it up; the planks are sound, & I will build a new ship of old materials.—The dedication to the Wedgewoods would be indelicate & *unmeaning.*—If after 4 or 5 years I shall have finished some work of some importance, which could not have been written but in an unanxious seclusion—to them I will dedicate it, for the Public will have owed the work to them who gave me the power of that unanxious Seclusion.——As to anonymous Publications, depend on it, you are deceived.—Wordsworth's name is nothing—to a large number of persons mine *stinks*——The Essay on Man, Darwin's Botanic Garden, the Pleasures of memory, & many other most popular works were published anonymously.——However, I waive all *reasoning;* & simply state it as an unaltered opinion, that you should proceed as before, with the ancient Mariner.—

The picture shall be sent. For your love-gifts & book-loans accept our hearty love—The Joan of Arc is a divine book.—It opens lovelily——I hope that you will *take off* some half dozen of our poems in great paper, even as the Joan of Arc.——Cottle,

my dear Cottle, I meant to have written you an Essay on the
Metaphysics of Typography; but I have not time.—Take a few
hints without the abstruse reasons for them with which I mean
to favor you—18 lines in a page, the lines closely printed, certainly, *more closely* than those of the Joan— (Oh by all means
closer! W. Wordsworth) *equal ink*; & *large margins*. That is
beauty—it may even under your immediate care mingle the
sublime!——

And now, my dear Cottle! may God love you & me who am
ever with most unauthorish feelings your true friend

S. T. Coleridge

I walked to Linton the day after you left us, & returned on
Saturday.—I walked in one day & returned in one— /

254. *To Mrs. S. T. Coleridge*

I.

Tuesday Night, 9' o clock. Sept. 18th, 1798

Over what place does the Moon hang to your eye, my dearest
Sara? To me it hangs over the left bank of the Elbe; and a long
trembling road of moonlight reaches from thence up to the
stern of our Vessel, & there it ends. We have dropped anchor
in the middle of the Stream, 30 miles from Cuxhaven, where we
arrived this morning at eleven o'clock, after an unusually fine
passage of only 48 hours—.—The Captain agreed to take all the
passengers up to Hamburgh for ten guineas— / my share
amounted only to half a guinea. We shall be there if no fogs
intervene tomorrow morning.—Chester was ill the whole voyage,
Wordsworth shockingly ill, his Sister worst of all—vomiting, &
groaning, unspeakably! And I neither sick or giddy, but gay
as a lark. The sea rolled rather high; but the motion was
pleasant to me. The stink of a sea cabbin in a packet, what
from the bilge water, & what from the crowd of *sick* passengers,
is horrible. I remained chiefly on deck.——We left Yarmouth,
Sunday Morning, Sept. 16th, at eleven o'clock— / Chester
& [the] Wordsworths ill immediately—Our passengers were
‡ Wordsworths, ‡ Chester, S. T. Coleridge, A Dane, Second
Dane, Third Dane, A Prussian, an Hanoverian & ‡ his Serv-

ant, a German Taylor & his ‡ Wife, a French ‡ Emigrant, &
‡ french Servant, ‡ two English Gentlemen, and ‡ a Jew.
—All those with the prefix ‡ were sick; those marked ‡
horribly sick.—The view of Yarmouth from the sea is interesting
—besides, it was English Ground that was flying away from
me.—When we lost sight of land, the moment that we quite
lost sight of it, & the heavens all round me rested upon the
waters, my dear Babies came upon me like a flash of lightning—
I saw their faces so distinctly!—This day enriched me with characters—and I passed it merrily. Each of these characters, I will
delineate to you in my Journal, which you & Poole, alternately,
will receive regularly as soon as I arrive at any settled place—
which will be in a week. Till then I can do little more than give
you notice of my safety, & my faithful affection to you / but the
Journal will commence from the day of my arrival at London, &
give every day's occurrence, &c—I have it written, but I have
neither paper, or time, to transcribe it. I trust nothing to
memory.—The Ocean is a noble Thing by night; a beautiful
white cloud of foam at momently intervals roars & rushes by
the side of the Vessel, and Stars of Flame dance & sparkle &
go out in it—& every now and then light Detachments of Foam
dart away from the Vessel's side with their galaxies of stars,
& scour out of sight, like a Tartar Troop over a Wilderness!—
What these Stars are, I cannot say—the sailors say, that they
are the Fish Spawn which is phosphorescent.— / The noisy Passengers swear in all their languages with drunken Hiccups that
I shall write no more—& I must join them.—Indeed, they present
a rich feast for a Dramatist.——My kind love to dear Mrs Poole
/ with what wings of swiftness would I fly home if I could but
find something in Germany to do her good!——Remember me
affectionately to Ward—& my love to the Chesters, Bessy, Susan
& Julia / & to Cruckshanks, & to Ellen & Mary when you see
them—& to Lavinia Poole, & Harriet & Sophy. And be sure you
give my kind love to Nanny—I associate so much of Hartley's
Infancy with her, so many of his figures, looks, words & antics
with her form, that I can never cease to think of her, poor Girl!
without interest.—Tell my best good Friend, my dear Poole! that
all his manuscripts with Wordsworth's Tragedy are safe in
Josiah Wedgewood's hands—& they will be returned to him
together.—Good night, my dear, dear Sara!—'every night when
I go to bed & every morning when I rise' I will think of you
with a yearning love, & of my blessed Babies!——Once more, my
dear Sara! good night.——

Did you receive my letter, *directed* in a different hand, with the 30£ Bank Note?—The Morning Post & Magazine will come to you as before. If not regularly, Stewart desires that you will write to him.

                                    Wednesday afternoon, 4 o'clock

We are safe in Hamburgh—an ugly City that stinks in every corner, house, & room worse than Cabbin, Sea sickness, or bilge Water!—The Hotels are all crowded—with great difficulty we have procured a very filthy room at a large expence; but we shall move tomorrow.—We get very excellent Claret for a Trifle—a guinea sells at present for more than 23 shillings here.—But for all particulars, I must refer your patience to my Journal—& I must get some proper paper. / I shall have to pay a shilling or eighteen pence with every letter.—N.B.—Johnson, the Book-seller, without any poems sold to him; but purely out of affec-tion conceived for me, & as part of any thing I *might* do for him, gave me an order on Remnant at Hamburgh for 30 pound. ——The Epea Pterocenta, an Essay on Population, and a His-tory of Paraguay, will come down for me directed to Poole / & for Poole's Reading— / Likewise, I have desired Johnson to print in Quarto a little Poem [of mine, one of which Quartos must] be sent to my Brother, [Revd G C Ottery St Mary, car-riage paid——] I pray you, my Love! read Edgeworth's Essay on Education—read it heart & soul—& if you approve of the mode, teach Hartley his Letters—I am very desirous, that you should begin to teach him to read—& they point out some easy modes. ——J. Wedgewood informed me that the Edgeworths were most miserable when Children, & yet the Father, *in his book,* is ever vapouring about their *Happiness!*—!—However there are very good things in the work—& some nonsense!——

Kiss my Hartley, & Bercoo Baby Brodder / Kiss them for their dear Father, whose heart will never be absent from them many hours together!—My dear Sara—I think of you with affection & a desire to be home / & in the full & holiest sense of the word, & after the antique principles of *Religion* unsophisticated by philosophy will be, I trust, your Husband faithful unto Death.

                                    [S T Coleridge]

[Wednesday night 11 o'clock—The sky & colours of the clouds are quite English just as if I were coming out of T Poole's homeward with you in] my arm.

276. *To Mrs. S. T. Coleridge*

Göttingen, bey Hüne in der Wende Strasse.

April 23rd 1799

My dear Sara

Surely it is unnecessary for me to say, how infinitely I languish to be in my native Country & with how many struggles I have remained even so long in Germany!—I received your affecting letter, dated Easter Sunday; and had I followed my impulses, I should have packed up & gone with Wordsworth & his Sister, who passed thro', & only passed thro', this place, two or three days ago.—If they burn with such impatience to return to their native Country, they who are all to each other, what must *I* feel, with every thing pleasant & every thing valuable, & every thing dear to me at a distance—here, where I may truly say, my only amusement is—to labour!—. But it is in the strictest sense of the word impossible that I can collect what I have to collect, in less than six weeks from this day; yet I read & transcribe from 8 to 10 hours every day. Nothing could support me but the knowlege that if I return now, we shall be embarrassed & in debt; & the moral certainty that having done what I am doing, we shall be more than *cleared:* / not to add that so large a work with so great a variety of information from sources so scattered, & so little known even in Germany, will, of course, establish my character—for industry & erudition, certainly; & I would fain hope, for reflection & genius.—This day in June I hope, & trust, that I shall be in England—!—O that the Vessel could but land at Shurton Bars!—Not that I should wish to see you & Poole immediately on my Landing—No!—the sight, the touch of my native Country were sufficient for one *whole Feeling*—one most deep unmingled Emotion! But then & after a lonely walk of the three miles—*then,* first of *all* whom I knew, to see you, & my *Friend!*—It lessens the delight of the thought of my Return, that I must get at you thro' a tribe of *acquaintances, damping* the freshness of one's Joy!—My poor little Baby! —at this moment I see the corner of the Room where his cradle stood—& his cradle too—and I cannot help seeing *him in* the cradle. Little lamb! & the snow would not melt on his limbs! —I have some faint recollection that he had that difficulty of breathing once before I left England—or was it Hartley?—/— 'A child! a child! is born, and the fond heart Dances: and yet the childless are more happy!'—/— In Christmas I saw a custom

which pleased & interested me here—the children make little
Presents to their Parents, & to one another; & the Parents to the
Children. For three or four months before Christmas the Girls
are all busy, & the boys save up their pocket-money, to make or
purchase these presents—What the present is to be, is cautiously
kept secret, & the Girls have a world of contrivances to conceal
it—such as, working when they are out on visits & the others are
not with them, & getting up in the morning long before light,
&c.—Then on the Evening before Christmas Day one of the
parlours is lighted up by the Children, into which the Parents
must not go; a great yew-bough is fastened on the Table at a
little distance from the wall, a multitude of little Tapers are
fastened in the bough, but not so as to burn it till they are
nearly burnt out—& coloured paper &c hangs & flutters from the
twigs.——Under this bough the Children lay out in great neat-
ness the presents they mean for their parents; still concealing
in their pockets what they intend for each other. Then the
Parents are introduced—& each presents his little gift—& then
they bring out the others & present them to each other, with
kisses, & embraces.—Where I saw the Scene, there were 8 or 9
children of different ages; and the eldest Daughter & the
Mother wept aloud for joy & tenderness; & the tears ran
down the face of the Father, & he clasped all his children so
tight to his breast, as if he did it to stifle the Sob that was
rising within him.—I was very much affected. And the
Shadow of the Bough on the wall, on the wall & arching
over on the Ceiling, made a pretty picture—& then the
raptures of the very little ones, when at least [last] the
Twigs & thread leaves began to catch fire, & *snap*—O
that was a delight for them!— / On the next day, in the great
parlour, the Parents lay out on the Tables the presents for the
children / a scene of more sober joy succeeds / as on this day,
after an old custom, the Mother says privately to each of her
Daughters, & the Father to each of his Sons, that which he has
observed most praiseworthy & that which he has observed most
faulty in their conduct—. Formerly, & still in all the little
Towns & villages through the whole of North Germany, these
Presents were sent by all the parents of the village to some one
Fellow who in high Buskins, a white Robe, a Mask, & an enormous Flax Wig personates Knecht Rupert—i.e. the Servant
Rupert. On Christmas night he goes round [to] every house, &
says that Jesus Christ, his Master, sent him there—the Parents
& older children receive him with great pomp of reverence,

while the little ones are most terribly frightened / he then en-
quires for the children, & according to the character which he
hears from the Parent, he gives them the intended Presents, as
if they came out of Heaven from Jesus Christ—or if they should
have been bad children, he gives the Parents a rod, & in the
Name of his Master Jesus recommends them to use it frequently.—About 7 or 8 years old, the children are let into the
secret; & it is curious, how faithfully they all keep it!—There are
a multitude of strange wild superstitions among the Bauers—
these still survive in spite of the efforts of the Clergy who in the
north of Germany, i.e. in the Hanoverian, Saxon, & Prussian
Dominions are almost all Deists. But they make little or no
impressions on the Bauers, who are wonderfully religious &
fantastically superstitious; but not in the least priest-rid.—But
in the Catholic Countries of Germany the difference is vast
indeed!—I met lately an intelligent & calm-minded man who
had spent a considerable time at Marburg, in the Bishoprich of
Paderborn, in Westphalia. He told me, that Bead-prayers to the
Holy Virgin are universal & universally too are magical Powers
attributed to one particular formula of words which are absolutely jargon / at least, the words are to be found in no known
Language. The Peasants believe it however to be a prayer to
the Virgin, & happy is the man among them who is made confident by a Priest that he can repeat it perfectly; for heaven
knows, what terrible calamity might not happen, if any one
should venture to repeat it, & blunder.—Vows, & Pilgrimages
to particular Images, are still common among the Bauers / if
any one die before the performance of his vow, they believe that
he hovers between Heaven & Earth, and at times *hobgoblins* his
relations till they perform it for him. Particular Saints are believed to be eminently favorable to particular Prayers—& he
assured me solemnly that a little before he left Marburg, a *Lady*
of Marburg had prayed, & given money to have *the public
Prayers,* at St Erasmus's Chapel to St Erasmus—for what, think
you?—That the Baby, with which she was then pregnant, might
be a Boy with white Hair & rosy Cheeks.—When their Cows,
Pigs, or Horses are sick they take them to the Dominican Monks
who prescribe *texts out of holy books,* & perform exorcisms.—
When men or women are sick, they give largely to the Convent,
who, on good conditions, dress them in Church-robes, & lay a
particular & highly-venerated Crucifix on their Breasts / & perform a multitude of antic Ceremonies.—In general, my In-
former confessed, that they *cured* the persons—which he seemed

to think extraordinary, but which I think very natural. Yearly
on St Blasius' Day unusual multitudes go to receive the Lord's
Supper; & while they are receiving it, the Monks hold a Blasius
Taper (as it [is] called) before the Forehead of the kneeling
Person, & then pray to St Blasius to drive away all head-achs
for the ensuing year.—Their wishes are often expressed in this
form—'Mary, Mother of God, make her Son *do so and so.*'—
Yet with all this, from every information which I can collect (&
I have had very many opportunities of collating various accounts) the Peasants in the Catholic Countries of Germany, but
especially in Austria, are far better off, & a far happier & livelier
race than those in the Protestant Lands.—/—I fill up the sheet
with scattered information, / put down in the order in which
I happened to see them.—The Peasant children where ever I
have been, are dressed warm & tight; but very ugly the dress
looks; a frock-coat, some of coarse blue cloath, some of Plaid,
buttoned behind—the Row of Buttons running down the Back,
& the seamless buttonless fore-part—'t has an odd look!——When
the Peasants marry, if the Girl is of a good character, the Clergyman gives her a virgin Crown—(a tawdry ugly thing made of
gold & silver Tinsel, like the Royal Crowns in Shape)—this
they wear, with cropped, powdered, & pomatumed Hair— / in
short, the Bride looks Ugliness personified.—While I was at
Ratzeburg, a girl came to beg the Pastor to let her be married
in this crown—& she had had two Bastards!—The Pastor refused,
of course.—I wondered that a reputable Farmer should marry
her; but the Pastor told me that where a female Bauer is
the heiress, her having had a bastard does not much stand in
her way / and yet tho' little or no infamy attaches to it, the
number of Bastards is but small / 2 in 70 has been the average
at Ratzeburg among the Peasants.—By the bye, the Bells in
Germany are not rung as our's with ropes—but two men stand,
one on each side of the Bell—& each pushes the Bell away from
him with his foot.—In the Churches, what is a Baptismal Font
in our churches, is a great Angel with a Bason in his hand;—he
draws up & down with a chain, like a Lamp—. In a particular
part of the Ceremony down comes the great Stone Angel with
the Bason, presents it to the Pastor who having taken *quant.
suff.*, up flies my Angel to his old place in the Ceiling. You cannot conceive, how droll it looked.——The Graves, in the little
village Church yards, are square; and in square or paral-
lelogrammic wooden cases—they look like Boxes without lids
—& Thorns & Briars are woven over them, as is done in some

parts of England. Perhaps, you recollect that beautiful passage
in Jeremy Taylor's Holy Dying / '& the Summer brings briars
to bud on our graves'—.—The Shepherds, with iron-soled boots,
walk before their Sheep (as in the East)—you know, our
Saviour says—My Sheep follow me.—So it is here—the Dog and
[the S]hepherd walk first, the Shepherd with his romantic
fur-C[ap] & general[ly k]nitting a pair of white worsted Gloves—
he walks on, & his dog by him, & then follow the Sheep, winding
along the roads in a beautiful *Stream*! In the fields I observed
a multitude of poles with bands & trusses of Straw tied round
the higher part, & the top—on enquiry we found that they
were put there for the Owls to perch on— / And the Owls?—O—
they catch the Field mice, who do amazing damage in the light
soil all throughout the north of Germany.—/—The Gallows near
Gottingen like that near Ratzeburg is three great Stone Pillars,
square like huge Tall chimneys, & connected with each other
at the top by three iron bars with hooks to them—& near them
is a wooden pillar with a wheel on the top of it, on which the
head is exposed, if the Person instead of being hung is be-
headed.—I was frightened at first to see such a multitude of
bones & Skeletons of Sheep, Oxen, & Horses, & bones, as I
imagined, of Men for many, many yards all round the Gallows—/—I found that in Germany the Hangman is by the laws
of the Empire *infamous*—these Hangmen form a cast—& their
Families always marry with each other &c—and that all dead
Cattle—who have died belong [to] them—& are carried by the
Owners to the Gallows & left [by] them there—When their cattle
are bewitched or otherwise desperately sick, the Peasants take
them, & tie them to the Gallows—Drowned Dogs, & Kittens, &c
are thrown there; in short, the Grass grows rank, & yet the Bones
overtop it.—The fancy of human bones must, I suppose, have
arisen in my ignorance of comparative Anatomy.——

God bless you, my Love!—I will write again speedily.—When
I was at Ratzeburgh, I wrote one wintry night in bed but
never sent you three stanzas which, I dare say, you will think
very silly; & so they are: & yet they were not written without
a yearning, yearning, yearning *Inside*—for my yearning affects
more than my *heart*—I feel it all within me.

1

If I had but two little wings
And were a little feath'ry Bird,

To *you* I'd fly, my Dear!
But Thoughts, like these, are idle Things—
    And I stay here.

2

But in my sleep to *you* I fly,
I'm always with you in my sleep—
    The World is all one's own.
But then one wakes—and where am I?
    All, all alone!

3

Sleep stays not tho' a Monarch bids,
So I love to wake ere break of Day;
    For tho' my Sleep be gone,
Yet while 'tis dark, one shuts one's lids,
    And still dreams *on*!

If Mrs Southey be with you, remember me with all kindness / & thankfulness for their attention to you & Hartley.——To
dear Mrs Poole give my filial love—My love to Ward.—Why
should I write the name of Tom Poole except for the pleasure
of writing it?—It grieves me to the heart that Nanny is not
without [*sic*] you. I cannot bear changes——Death makes
enough!—God bless you, my dear dear Wife, &
        believe me with eagerness to clasp you to my heart, your
                                    faithful Husband
                                    S. T. Coleridge

309. *To Thomas Wedgwood*

                          No / 21, Buckingham Street, Strand.
My dear Sir
    I am sitting by a fire in a rug great Coat. Your Room is
doubtless to a greater degree air-tight than mine; or your notion
of Tartarus would veer round to the Groenlanders' creed. It is
most barbarously cold: and you, I fear, can shield yourself from
it only by perpetual imprisonment. If any place in the southern

Climates were in a state of real quiet & likely to continue so, should you feel no inclination to migrate?—Poor Southey, from over great Industry, as I suspect, the Industry too of solitary Composition, has reduced himself to a terrible state of weakness—& is determined to leave this Country as soon as he has finished the Poem on which he is now employed. 'Tis a melancholy thing—so young a man & one whose Life has ever been so simple and self-denying!—O for Peace & the South of France.—I could almost too wish foı a Bourbon King if it were only that Sieyes & Buonaparte might finish their career in the old orthodox way of Hanging.—Thank God, I have *my Health perfectly* & I am working hard—yet the present state of human affairs presses on me for days together, so as to deprive me of all my chearfulness. It is probable, that a man's private & personal connections & interests ought to be uppermost in his daily & hourly Thoughts, & that the dedication of much hope & fear to subjects which are perhaps disproportionate to our faculties & powers, is a disease. But I have had this disease so long, & my early Education was so undomestic, that I know not how to get rid of it; or even to wish to get rid of it. Life were so flat a thing without Enthusiasm—that if for a moment it leave me, I have a sort of stomach-sensation attached to all my Thoughts, like those which succeed to the pleasurable operation of a dose of Opium. *Now* I make up my mind to a sort of heroism in believing the progressiveness of all nature, during the present melancholy state of Humanity—& on this subject I am now writing / and no work, on which I ever employed myself, makes me so happy while I am writing.—

İ shall remain in London till April—the expences of my last year made it necessary for me to exert my industry; and many other good ends are answered at the same time. Where I next settle, I shall continue; & that must be in a state of retirement & rustication. It is therefore good for me to have a run of society —& that various, & consisting of marked characters!—Likewise by being obliged to write without much elaboration I shall greatly improve myself in naturalness & facility of style / & the particular subjects on which I write for money, are nearly connected with my future schemes.—My mornings I give to compilations, which I am sure cannot be wholly useless—& for which by the beginning of April I shall have earned nearly an 150£—my evenings to the Theatres—as I am to conduct a sort of Dramaturgy, a series of Essays on the Drama, both it's general principles, and likewise in reference to the present

State of the English Theatres. This I shall publish in the Morning Post—the attendance on the Theatres costs me nothing, & Stuart, the Editor, covers my expences in London. Two mornings & one whole day I dedicate to the Essay on the possible Progressiveness of Man & on the principles of Population.—In April I return to my greater work—the Life of Lessing. —My German Chests are arrived; but I have them not yet—but expect them from Stowey daily——when they come, I shall send a little pacquet down to you—.

To pay my Wife's travelling expences & al[so] my first expences in London I borrowed 25£ from my friend Purkis, for which I gave him an order on your Brother, York Street, dating it Jan. 5, 1800.—Will you be so kind as to mention this to him—He will be kind enough to excuse my having done this without having previously written; but I have every reason to believe, that I shall have no occasion to draw again till the year 1801—& I believe, that as I now [stand], I have not anticipated beyond the year; if I have wholly anticipated that.—I shall write to Jos. tomorrow for certain.—

I have seen a good deal of Godwin who has just published a novel. I like him for thinking so well of Davy. He talks of him every where as the most extraordinary human Being, he had ever met with. I cannot say that: for I know one whom I feel to be the superior—; but I never met so extraordinary a young man.—I have likewise dined with Horne Tooke. He is a clearheaded old man, as every man needs must be who attends to the real import of words; but there is a sort of charletannery [sic] in his manner that did not please me. He makes such a mystery & difficulty out of plain & palpable Things—and never tells you any thing without first exciting & detaining your Curiosity. But it were a bad Heart that could not pardon worse faults than these in the Author of the Epea Pteroenta.——

Believe me, my dear Sir! with much affection your's S. T. C.

325. To William Godwin

8, Monday Morning [3 March 1800]

Dear Godwin

The Punch after the Wine made me tipsy last night—this I mention, not that my head aches, or that I felt after I quitted you, any unpleasantness, or titubancy—; but because tipsiness has, and has always, one unpleasant effect—that of making me

talk *very* extravagantly / & as when sober, I talk extravagantly
enough for any *common* Tipsiness, it becomes a matter of
nicety in discrimination to know when I am or am not affected.
—An idea starts up in my hand [head?]—away I follow it thro'
thick & thin, Wood & Marsh, Brake and Briar—with all the
apparent Interest of a man who was defending one of his old
and long-established Principles—Exactly of this kind was the
Conversation, with which I quitted you / I do not believe it
possible for a human Being to have a greater horror of the
Feelings that usually accompany such principles as I then
supported, or a deeper Conviction of their irrationality than
myself—but the whole Thinking of my Life will not bear me up
against the accidental Press & Crowd of my mind, when it is
elevated beyond it's natural Pitch / .—

We shall talk wiselier with the Ladies on Tuesday—God bless
you, & give your dear little ones a kiss a piece for me—

The Agnus Dei & the Virgin Mary desire their kind respects
to *you*, you sad Atheist—!

Your's with affectionate | Esteem
S. T. Coleridge

332. *To Josiah Wedgwood*

Monday, April 21 1800

Mr Wordsworth's Grasmere near Ambleside, Westmoreland
My dear Sir

You may well suppose, what a pain at heart it is to me to
have an explanation to make to *you* concerning money matters.
—So far back as four years ago my Bill to Cottle for various
articles, for cash among the rest, was 20£—Cottle was then in
prosperous & promising circumstances, & gave me to understand
that he should never consider me in his Debt, till I became a
richer man than he—& refused to send me in his Bill. Lately,
poor fellow! his affairs have fallen to rack & ruin / my debt
stood on his Ledger—& he wrote me a very importunate Letter.
He had suffered deeply from the very mean opinion, which I
had frankly expressed to him of his Epic Poem—expressed
wholly as an expedient to prevent him from publishing it at his
own expence—& he made the application not without expressions of a wounded & angry mind. At the time I received his
Letter I knew that within three weeks I should receive more
than the 20£ from the Bookseller—& I sent him therefore a

Draft on you—imagining of course that he would not present it till the expiration of the three weeks, before which time I should have not only advertised you of it, but included the 20£. This indeed was the sole reason of my not doing what, I am now sensible, I should have done—written to you immediately—but in truth, I was sore all over with the apprehension, that you might accuse me of irregularity & a presumption wholly unjustifiable, well knowing that I have already more than overdrawn myself. With an unlucky, but I should hope, not very blameable Cowardice of feeling I felt a repugnance to acquaint you of it without at the same time sending the money. To morrow morning I send off the last sheet of my irksome & soul-wearying Labor, the Translation of Schiller—and as soon as I have received my stipend, I will remit to you.—My dear Sir—how much you have been harrassed by irregular men, what disgust have you associated, of necessity, with them, & the idea of meanness that attaches to the expedients of embarrassment, I well know—and I am sure, the extreme pain & agitation, which your letter gave me, did not seduce me into the slightest censure of you, as unkind——but I anticipate a sort of comfort in knowing that you can understand how much I suffered from pride & far honester feelings than Pride.——

For these last six months I have worked incessantly——and have lived with as much economy as is practicable by any man / but many expences, not expected, & not immediately my own, have still thrown me back. In this engagement of translating the prolix Plays of Schiller I made too a very, very foolish bargain—the Bookseller indeed has given me his word, that in case of their success he will consider [me] as entitled to an additional Remuneration—but of their Success I have no hope— / for I can say with truth, that I could have written a far better play myself in half the time. But with all this I have learnt that I have Industry & Perseverance—and before the end of the year, if God grant me health, I shall have my wings wholly unbirdlim'd.—This is Monday—and I shall be in London the beginning of next week—I pray you, my dear Sir! be so kind as to write to me—for God forbid that so sore an affliction should befall me, as that the connection between us should ever be a source of Doubt to you, or otherwise than honorable to me—.—Believe me

                              most affectionately | & | gratefully | Your's
                                                       S. T. Coleridge

340. *To Thomas Poole*

July 24, 1800

My dear Poole

Within a few days of my arrival at Grasmere I increased the cold, which I had caught at Liverpool, to a rheumatic fever almost, which confined me to my bed for some days, & left me so weak, & listless, that writing was hateful to me——& my eye lids were so swoln, that it was painful too. Had I written to you, I could have written only as a Duty—and with that feeling never will I write to you.—We met at Bristol a pleasant chaise companion who did not leave us till we arrived at Liverpool—we travelled the first day to Tewksbury, the next night we slept at Shrewsbury, having passed thro' Worcester, Kidderminster, Bridgenorth & Colebrook Dale—the next night at Chester, where we stayed a day & a half. It is a walled city, a walk on the walls all around it—the Air of the city is thick enough to be edible, & stinks. From Chester we proceeded, crossing a ferry of 7 miles, to Liverpool.—At Liverpool we took up our quarters with Dr Crompton, who lives at Eton, a noble seat four miles & a half from the town—he received us with joyous hospitality, & Mrs Crompton, who is all I can conceive of an angel, with most affectionate gladness. Here we stayed 8 or 9 days, during which I saw a great deal of Dr Currie, Roscoe, Rathbone (Colebrook Renyolds's Brother-in-law) & other literati. Currie is a genuine philosopher; a man of mild & rather solemn manners—if you had ever seen my Brother George, I would have referred you to him for a striking resemblance of Currie.—I would have you by all means order the late Edition in four Volumes of Burns's Works—the Life is written by Currie, and a masterly specimen of philosophical Biography it is.—Roscoe is a man of the most delightful manners—natural, sweet, & cheerful—zealous in kindness, and a republican with all the feelings of prudence & all the manners of good sense—so that he is beloved by the Aristocrats themselves. He has a nice matronly wife, & 9 fine children.—Rathbone is a quaker, as brimful of enthusiastic goodness as a vessel of mortality can be. He is a man of immense fortune. The union of all these men is most amiable—they truly love each other, a band of Brothers! And yet by their wisdom in keeping back all political trials of power in Liverpool they have stifled party spirit in that city, & enabled themselves to be the founders of a most magnificent Library—

magnificent as a Building, respectable in it's present stock of Books, & magnificent in what it is to be. They have received last week an accession of 3000£, all to be laid out in books of acknowledged reputation—& the yearly income of the foundation is 1000£. The slave-merchants of Liverpool fly over the heads of the slave-merchants of Bristol, as Vultures over carrion crows.—This library is called the Athenaeum. In religion Currie, I suppose, is a philosopher—Roscoe is a pious Deist—Rathbone, I suppose, is the same; or more probably he cloathes his Deism even to his own mind in the language of Scripture—a Christian, as Taylor is a Platonist.—But this is all *guess.*

On this day I arrived at Keswick, & have entered on my habitation. Wordsworth will stay at Grasmere for a year to come at least—it is possible, he may not quit it at all.—He is well, unless when he uses any effort of mind—then he feels a pain in his left side, which threatens to interdict all species of composition to him.——Our goods are all arrived—& now in house.— Of Keswick, & [of] my house, heaven forbid that I shall begin to write at the fag end of such a beggarly sheet of paper as this—. No! as soon as the Stir & Hurry is over I shall open upon you in a sheet that might serve for a sheet!— My address is

Greta Hall, Keswick, Cumberland.

We are very anxious about your mother—I have said to myself, that no news is good news.

My love to Ward.—My eyes still remain so weak that it is disagreeable to me to read over my own letter.—I wish, that Ward would immediately copy for me the third letter which I wrote, descriptive of the Hartz Mountains. I have got the two first; but the last is lost—& I want it *immediately.*—Sheridan has sent me a strange sort of a message about my Tragedy—wishing me to write for the stage, making all his old offers over again, & charging the non-representation of my play on my extreme obstinacy in refusing to have it at all altered!—Did you ever hear of such a damned impudent Dog?—God for ever bless you, my dear Poole—

& your most affectionate | Friend
S. T. Coleridge

341. *To Josiah Wedgwood*

Thursday, July 24, 1800

My dear Sir

I found your letter on my arrival at Grasmere, namely, on the 29th of June—since which time to the present with the exception of the last few days I have been more unwell, than I have ever been since I left School—for many days I was forced to keep my bed, & when released from that worst incarceration, I suffered most grievously from a brace of swoln Eyelids, & a head into which on the least agitation the blood felt as rushing in & flowing back again like the raking of the Tide on a coast of loose stones.—However, thank God! I am now coming about again. That Tom receives such pleasure from natural scenery strikes me as it does you—the total incapability, which I have found in myself to associate any but the most languid feelings with the godlike objects which have surrounded me lately, & the nauseous efforts to *impress* my admiration into the service of nature, has given me a sympathy with his former state of health which I never before could have had.—I wish from the bottom of my soul that he may be enjoying similar pleasures with those which I am now enjoying with all that newness of sensation; that voluptuous correspondence of the blood & flesh about me with breeze & sun-heat; which make convalescence more than repay one for disease.

I parted from Poole with pain & dejection. For him & for myself in him I should have given Stowey a decisive preference—it was likewise so conveniently situated that I was in the *way* of almost all whom I love & esteem. But there was no suitable house, & no prospect of a suitable house—& the utter desolation, which a small & inconvenient house spread thro' my literary efforts & hourly comforts, & the contagious fretfulness of the weaker vessels in my family, I had experienced to a degree which made it a *duty* for me to live in no house, in which I could not command one quiet room. Nor was Stowey without other objections—Mrs Coleridge had scarcely any society there, and inter nos the nearness to Bristol connected me too intimately with all the affairs of her family. Likewise I will say to you what I should not say to another—the antipathy of those of Poole's relations to whom he is most attached (& by the most delicate ties) to me, to my wife, & even to my poor little boy, was excessive—in more than one instance it led his Brother's

Widow into absolute insult to Mrs Coleridge, which perhaps
Poole should have noticed more than he did—perhaps, & more
probably, he could not & ought not to have been otherwise
than passive. However, it required no overstrained sensibility
to make this at times very painful.—These things would have
weighed as nothing, *could* I have remained at Stowey; but now
they come upon me to diminish my regret.—Add to this Poole's
determination to spend a year or two on the continent in case
of a Peace & his Mother's Death—. God in heaven bless her! I
am sure, she will not live long.—This is the first day of my
arrival at Keswick—my house is roomy, situated on an eminence
a furlong from the Town—before it an *enormous* Garden more
than two thirds of which is rented as a Garden for sale articles,
but the walks &c are our's most completely. Behind the house
are shrubberies, & a declivity planted with flourishing trees of
15 years' growth or so, at the bottom of which is a most delightful shaded walk by the River Greta, a quarter of a mile in
length. The room in which I sit, commands from one window
the Basenthwaite Lake, Woods, & Mountains, from the opposite
the Derwentwater & fantastic mountains of Borrowdale—
straight before me is a wilderness of mountains, catching &
streaming lights or shadows at all times—behind the house &
entering into all our views is Skiddaw.—My acquaintance here
are pleasant—& at some distance is Sir Guilfrid Lawson's Seat
with a very large & expensive Library to which I have every
reason to hope that I shall have free access.—But when I have
been settled here a few days longer, I will write you a minute
account of my situation.—Wordsworth lives 12 miles distant—
in about a year's time he will probably settle at Keswick likewise.—It is no small advantage here that for two thirds of the
year we are in complete retirement—the other third is alive &
swarms with Tourists of all shapes & sizes, & characters—it is
the very place I would recommend to a novelist or farce writer.
—Besides, at that time of the year there is always hope that a
friend may be among the number, & miscellaneous crowd,
whom this place attracts. So much for Keswick at present.

Have you seen my translation of the Wallenstein? It is a dull
heavy play; but I entertain hopes, that you will think the
language for the greater part, natural & good common-sense
English—to which excellence if I can lay fair claim in any book
of poetry or prose, I shall be a very *singular* writer at least.—I
am now working at my introduction to the life of Lessing which
I trust will be in the press before Christmas—that is, the Intro-

duction which will be published first I believe. I shall write again in a few days. Respects to Mrs W. God bless you &

S. T. Coleridge

I have had a sort of a message from Sheridan about my Tragedy.—

I thank you for your kind offer respecting the 20£; but if my health continue, I trust, I shall be able to sail smoothly, without availing myself of it.

362. *To Josiah Wedgwood*

Nov. 1. 1800.—Keswick

My dear Sir

I would fain believe, that the experiment which your Brother has made in the W. Indies, is not wholly a discouraging one. If a warm climate did nothing but only prevented him from growing worse, it surely evidenced *some* power—and perhaps a climate equally favorable in a country of more various interest, Italy or the South of France, may tempt your Brother to make a longer trial. If (disciplining myself into *silent* cheerfulness) I could be of any comfort to him by being his companion & attendant for two or three months, on the supposition that he should wish to travel & was at a loss for a companion more fit, I would go with him with a willing affection. You will easily see, my dear friend, that I say this, only to increase the *Range* of your Brother's choice—for even in *chusing* there is some pleasure.—

There happen frequently little odd coincidences in time, that recall a momentary faith in the notion of sympathies acting in absence. I heard of your Brother's Return for the first time on Monday last (the day on which your Letter is dated) from Stoddart.—Had it rained on my naked Skin, I could not have felt more strangely. The three or 4 hundred miles that are between us, seemed converted into a moral distance; & I knew that the whole of this Silence I was myself accountable for, for I ended my last letter by promising to follow it with a second & longer one before you could answer the first.—But immediately on my arrival in this country I undertook to finish a poem which I had begun, entitled Christabel, for a second volume of the Lyrical Ballads. I tried to perform my promise; but the deep unutterable Disgust, which I had suffered in the translation of that accursed Wallenstein, seemed to have stricken me with barrenness—for I tried & tried, & nothing would come of it. I desisted with a deeper dejection than I am willing to remember. The wind from Skiddaw & Borrodale was often as loud as wind need be—& many a walk in the clouds on the mountains did I take; but all would not do—till one day I dined out at the house of a neighbouring clergyman, & some how or other drank so much wine, that I found some effort & dexterity requisite to balance myself on the hither Edge of Sobriety. The next day, my verse making faculties returned to me, and I proceeded successfully—till my poem grew so long & in Wordsworth's opinion so impressive, that he rejected it from his volume as disproportionate both in size & merit, & as discordant in it's character.—In the meantime, I had gotten myself entangled in the old Sorites of the old Sophist, Procrastination—I had suffered my necessary businesses to accumulate so terribly, that I neglected to write to any one—till the Pain, I suffered from not writing, made me waste as many hours in dreaming about it, as would have sufficed for the Letter-writing of half a Life. But there is something beside Time requisite for the writing of a Letter—at least with me. My situation here is indeed a delightful situation; but I feel what I have lost—feel it deeply—it recurs more often & more painfully, than I had anticipated—indeed, so much so that I scarcely ever feel myself impelled, that is to say, *pleasurably* impelled to write to Poole. I used to feel myself more at home in his great windy Parlour, than in my own cottage. We were well suited for each other—my animal Spirits corrected his inclinations to melancholy; and there was something both in his understanding & in his affection so healthy & manly, that my mind freshened in his company, and my ideas & habits of thinking acquired day after day more of substance & reality.—Indeed, indeed, my dear Sir, with tears in my eyes, and with all my heart & soul I wish it were as easy for us all to meet, as it was when you lived at Upcott.—Yet when I revise the step, I have taken, I know not how I could have acted otherwise than I did act. Every thing, I promised myself in this country, has answered far beyond my expectation. The room in which I write commands six distinct Landscapes—the two Lakes, the Vale, River, & mountains, & mists, & Clouds, & Sunshine make endless combinations, as if heaven & Earth were for ever talking to each other.—Often when in a deep Study I have walked to the window & remained there *looking without seeing,* all at once the Lake of Keswic[k] & the fantastic Mountains of Borrodale at the head of it have entered into my mind with a suddenness, as if I had been snatched out of Cheapside & placed for the first time on the spot where I stood.—And that is a delightful Feeling—these Fits & Trances of *Novelty* received from a long known Object. The river Greta flows behind our house, roaring like an untamed Son of the Hills, then winds round, & *glides* away in the front—so that we live in a penins[ula.]—But besides this etherial Eye-feeding, we have very substantial Conveniences. We are close to the town, where we have a respectable & neighbourly acquainta[nce] and a sensible & truly excellent medical man.—Our Garden is part of a large nursery Garden / which is the same to us & as private as if the whole had been our own, & thus too we have delightful walks without passing our garden gate. My Landlord, who lives in the Sister House (for the two Houses are built so as to look like one great one) is a modest & kind man, & a singular character. By the severest economy he raised himself from a Carrier into the possession of a comfortable Independence—he was always very fond of reading, and has collected nearly 500 volumes of our most esteemed modern Writers, such as Gibbon, Hume, Johnson, &c &c.— / His habits of economy & simplicity remain with him—& yet so very disinterested a man I scarcely ever knew. Lately when I wished to settle with him about the Rent of our House he appeared much affected, told me that my living near him & the having so much of Hartley's company were great comforts to him & his housekeeper—that he had no children to provide for, & did not mean to marry—& in short, that he did not want any rent at all from me.—This of course I laughed him out of; but he absolutely refused to receive any rent for the first half year under the Pretext, that the house was not completely finished.——Hartley quite *lives* at the house—& it [is] as you may suppose no small joy to my wife to have a good affectionate motherly woman divided from her only by a Wall. Eighteen miles from our House lives Sir Guilfred Lawson, who has a princely Library, chiefly of natural History—a kind, & generous, but weak & ostentatious sort of man, who has been abundantly civil to me.—Among other raree shews he keeps a wild beast or two, with some eagles &c——The Master of the Beasts at the Exeter change sent him down a large Bear—with it a long letter [of] directions concerning the food &c of the animal, & many solicitations respecting other agreeable Quadrupeds which he was *desirous* to send to the Baronet at a moderate Price, concluding in this manner—'and remain your Honor's most devoted humble Servant, J.P.—P.S.—*Permit* me,

Sir Guilfred, to send you a Buffalo and a Rhinoceros.'—!——As
neat a Postscript as I ever heard—! the tradesmanlike coolness
with which those pretty little animals occurred to him just
at the finishing of his Letter——!!—

You will in the course of three weeks see the Letters on the
rise & condition of the German Boors. I found it convenient
to make up a volume out of my Journeys &c in North Germany
—& the Letters (your name of course erased) are in the Print-
ers' Hands—/. I was so weary of transcribing & *composing,* that
when I found those more carefully written than the rest, I even
sent them off as they were.—

Poor Alfred! I have not seen it in print—Charles Lamb wrote
me the following account of it—I have just received from Cottle a magnificent Copy of his Guinea Alfred! Four & 20 books
to read in the Dog Days. I got as far as the mad Monk the first
day, & fainted. Mr Cottle's Genius strongly points him to the
very simple *Pastoral,* but his inclinations divert him perpetually
from his calling. He imitates Southey as Row did Shakespeare
with his Good morrow to you, good Master Lieutenant!—Instead of *a* man, *a* woman, *a* daughter he constantly writes 'one,
a man,' 'one, a woman,' 'one, his daughter'—instead of *the* King,
the Hero, he constantly writes 'He, the King'—[']He, the Hero'
—two flowers of Rhetoric palpably from the Joan. But Mr
Cottle soars a higher pitch, and when he *is* original, it is in a
most original way indeed. His terrific Scenes are indefatigable.
Serpents, Asps, Spiders, Ghosts, Dead Bodies, & Stair-cases made
of NOTHING with Adders' Tongues for Bannisters—my God!
what a Brain he must have! he puts as many Plums in his
Pudding as my Grandmother used to do—& then his Emerging
from Hell's Horrors into *Light,* & treading on pure Flats of
this Earth for 23 Books together!—C.L.——

My *littlest* One is a very Stout Boy indeed—he is christened
by the name of 'DERWENT'—a sort of sneaking affection, you see,
for the *poetical* & the *novellish* which I disguised to myself
under the Shew, that my Brothers had so many children, Johns,
James, Georges, &c &c—that a handsome Christian-like name
was not to be had, except by incroaching on the names of my
little Nephews.

If you are at Gunville at Christmas, I hold out Hopes to myself that I shall be able to pass a week with you then.—I mentioned to you at Upcott a kind of a Comedy that I had *committed*—to writing, in part.—This is in the *wind.*

Wordsworth's second Volume of the Ly. Ball. will, I hope &

almost believe, afford you as unmingled pleasure as is in the nature of a collection of very various poems to afford to one individual mind. Sheridan has sent to *him* too, requesting him to write a Tragedy for Drury Lane. But W. will not be diverted by any thing from the prosecution of his Great Work.

I shall request permission to draw upon you shortly for 20£—but if it be in the least inconvenient to you, I pray you, tell me so—for I *can* draw on Longman, who in less than a month will owe me 60£, tho' I would rather not do it.

Southey's Thalaba in 12 books is going to the Press. I hear—his Madoc is to be *nonum-in-annum'd.*—Besides these, I have heard of four other Epic Poems—all in Quarto! a happy age this for tossing off an *Epic* or two!——

Remember me with great affection to your Brother—& present my kindest respects to Mrs Wedgewood.—Your late Governess wanted one thing which, where there is Health, is I think indispensable in the moral character of a young person—a light & chearful Heart—. She interested me a good deal; she appears to me to have been injured by going out of the common way without any of that Imagination, which if it be a Jack o'Lanthorn to lead us out of that way is however at the same time a Torch to light us whither we are going. A whole Essay might be written on the Danger of *thinking* without Images.—

God bless you, my dear Sir, & him who is with grateful and affectionate Esteem

Your's ever
S. T. Coleridge

375. *To Thomas Poole*

Monday Night, Jan. 19, 1801

My dearest Poole

Since I last wrote, I have had a sad time & a painful—a fluid, it seems, had collected between the tunica vaginalis & the left Testicle—in short, 'twas an hydrocele. By the increased weight the spermatic cord was affected, and in consequence the hip & the back, & where ever the spermatic cord passed, were troubled constantly by a *dull* pain and frequently by sharp & shooting Pains—& towards night I had regularly feverish Symptoms. But the sense of Lassitude, if I only sate up in bed, was worst of all—I seem'd to fall in upon myself in ruin, like a column

of sand, that had been informed & animated only by a whirl
blast of the desart—such & so treacherous were my animal spirits
to me.—The Vinegar fomentations & fumigations, &c producing
no effect, we had recourse to an application of Sal Ammoniac
dissolved in verjuice—this promised well at first, but it soon by
the extreme irritation brought on over the whole surface of the
scrotum such a *frantic* Itching, that I have no doubt but that
this & no other is the Torment in Hell, & that Brimstone was
given not [as] a producer, but as a merciful Palliative, of the
Punishment.—This Itching was succeeded by the appearance
of five small but angry Ulcers on the Scrotum / on Wednesday
morning I had *three* Leeches applied, & the wounds by means
of hot cloaths were kept bleeding the whole day—& after this
I applied poultices, of bread grated & mixed up with a strong
solution of Lead.—Since that day I have been (not indeed without sorrowful Relapses at Evening) mending fast—the fever
toward night is almost gone—& the Fluid has been absorbed
& is absorbing apace—and all seems doing well. This day for
the first time I sate up for an hour or two, & do not find myself
the worse.—Our Surgeon & apothecary is an excellent, modest,
truly intelligent man.—

The Lyrical Ballads will be published by the time this Letter
reaches you—for my sake, & Wordsworth's, & your own, you will
purchase not only the new Volume, but likewise the second
Edition of the First Volume, on account of the valuable Preface. By my advice, & at Longman's expence, copies with appropriate Letters were sent to the Dutchess of Devonshire, Sir
Bland Burgess, Mrs Jordan, Mr Fox, Mr Wilberforce, & 2 or 3
others—I dictated all the other Letters while W. wrote one to
Mr Fox. I have had that letter transcribed for you, for it's
excellence—& mine to Wilberforce, because the two contain a
good view of our notions & motives, poetical & political.—I *had
written* to Mr Wedgewood to repay you. I rejoice at your dear
Mothe[r's heal]th. Love to Ward, & congrat. on his Sister's
account. God love you, *dear* Friend—S. T. Coleridge. *Write.*

I have not heard from Mr Wedgewood since I wrote—& am
not a little pinched for money. Last week I payed 25£ to
Phillips, in consequence of an attorney's Letter, the first I ever
received & which amused me infinitely.—I felt like a man of
this World. I had irritated P. by an exceedingly humorous Letter, which I will send you.

Wordsworths left me this morning.—

To William Wilberforce Esqr. M.P.

[Composed by Coleridge for Wordsworth]

Sir,

I composed the accompanying poems under the persuasion, that all which is usually included under the name of action bears the same pro[por]tion (in respect of worth) to the affections, as a language to the thing sign[ified.] When the material forms or intellectual ideas which should be employed to [rep]resent the internal state of feeling, are made to claim attention for their own sake, then commences Lip-worship, or superstition, or disputatiousness, in religion; a passion for gaudy ornament & violent stimulants in morals; & in our literature bombast and vicious refinements, an aversion to the common conversational language of our Countrymen, with an extravagant preference given to *Wit* by some, and to outrageous *incident* by others; while the most sacred affections of the human race seem to lay no hold on our sympathies unless we can contemplate them in the train of some circumstances that excite *curiosity,* or unriddle them from some gaudy phrases that are to attract our wonder for themselves. It was the excellence of our elder Poets to write in such a language as should the *most* rapidly convey their mean[ing,] but the pleasure which I am persuaded the greater number of Read[ers re]ceive from our modern writers in verse & prose, arises from the sense of having overcome a difficulty, of having made a series of lucky guesses, & perhaps, in some degree, of understanding what they are conscious the lower Classes of their Countrymen would not be able to understand. The poems which accompany this letter were written with no idle expectation of the Author's immediate fame or their rapid circulation: had my predominant influences been either the love of praise or the desire of profit, I should have held out to myself other subjects than the affections which walk 'in silence and in a veil' and other rules of poetic diction than the determination to prefer passion to imagery, & (except when the contrary was chosen for dramatic purposes) to express what I meant to express with all possible regard to precision and propriety but with very little attention to what is called *dignity.* In thus stating my opinions I state at the same time my reasons for soliciting your acceptance of these Volumes. In your religious treatise these truths are developed, & applied to the present state of our religion; I have acted on them in a less awful department, but not I trust with less serious convictions. Indeed had I not persuaded myself that in the composition of them I had been a Fellow-labourer with you in the same Vineyard, acting under the perception of some one common truth & attributing to that truth the same importance & necessity; if I had not appeared to myself to have discovered (in my intentions at least) some bond of connection between us; I could not without self-reproof have taken this opportunity of &c &c

W. Wordsworth.

379. To Dorothy Wordsworth

Monday, Feb. 9. 1801

My dearest Rotha

The Hack, Mr Calvert was so kind as to borrow for me, carried me home as pleasantly as the extreme Soreness of my whole frame admitted. I was indeed in the language of Shakespere, not a Man but a Bruise—I went to bed immediately, & rose on Sunday quite restored.—If I do not hear from you any thing to the contrary, I shall walk half way to Grasmere, on Friday Morning—leaving Keswick at ten o'clock precisely—in the hopes of meeting Sara—partly to prevent the necessity of William's walking so far, just as he will have begun to tranquillize, & partly to remove from Mrs Coleridge's mind all uncertainty as to the time of her coming, which if it depended on William's mood of Body, might (unless he went to the injury of his health) be a week, or a fortnight hence——But if Sara should have been so fatigued, as not to be able to take so long a walk without discomfort, on Friday / I shall walk on to Grasmere, & return with her the next day—all this however to be understood with the usual Deo Volente of Health & Weather. The Small Pox is in Keswick—& we are anxious, and eddy-minded about Derwent— /

I had a very long conversation with Hartley about Life, Reality, Pictures, & Thinking, this evening. He sate on my knee for half an hour at least, & was exceedingly serious. I wish to God, you had been with us. Much as you would desire to believe me, I cannot expect that I could communicate to you all that Mrs C. & I felt from his answers—they were so very sensible, accurate, & well worded. I am convinced, that we are under great obligations to Mr Jackson, who, I have no doubt, takes every opportunity of making him observe the differences of Things: for he pointed out without difficulty that there might be five Hartleys, Real Hartley, Shadow Hartley, Picture Hartley, Looking Glass Hartley, and Echo Hartley / and as to the difference between his Shadow & the Reflection in the Looking Glass, he said, the Shadow was black, and he could not see his *eyes* in it. One thing, he said, was very curious—I asked him what he did when he thought of any thing—he answered—I look at it, and then go to sleep. To sleep?—said I—you mean, that you *shut your eyes*. Yes, he replied—I shut my eyes, & put my hands so (covering his eyes) and go to sleep —then I WAKE again, and away I run.——That of shutting his eyes, & covering them was a Recipe I had given him some time ago / but the notion of that state of mind being Sleep is very striking, & he meant more, I suspect, than that People when asleep have their eyes shut—indeed I *know* it from the tone & *leap up* of Voice with which he uttered the word 'WAKE.' To morrow I am to exert my genius in making a paper-balloon / the idea of carrying up a bit of lighted Candle into the clouds makes him almost insane with Pleasure. As I have given you Hartley's Metaphysics I will now give you a literal Translation of page 49 of the celebrated Fichte's Uber den Begriff der Wissenschaftslehre [1794]—if any of *you,* or if either your Host or Hostess, have any propensity to *Doubts,* it will cure them for ever / for the object of the author is to attain absolute certainty. So read it aloud. (N.B. the 'I' means poor Gilbert's *I— das 'Ich'*—) ——'Suppose, that A in the proposition A = A stands not for the I, but for something or other different, then from this proposition you may deduce the condition under which it may be affirmed, that it is established, and *how* we are authorized to conclude, that If A is established, then it is established. Namely: the Proposition, A = A, holds good originally only of the I: it is abstracted from the Proposition in the Science of absolute Knowledge, I am I—the substance therefore or sum total of every Thing, to which it may be legitimately applied, must lie in the I, and be comprehended under it. No A therefore can be aught else than something established in the I, and now therefore the Proposition may stand thus: What is established in the I, is established—if therefore A is established in the I, then it is established (that is to say in so far as it is established, whether as only possible, or as real, or necessary) and then the Proposition is true without possibility of contradic-

tion, if the I is to be I.—Farther, if the I be established, because
it is established, then all, that is established in the I, is established because it is established; and provided only, that A is
indeed a something established in the I, then it is established,
if it is established; and the second Question likewise is solved.'
——Here's a numerous Establishment for you / nothing in
Touchstone ever equalled this—it is not even surpassed by
Creech's account of Space in his notes to Lucretius.—

Remember me & my wife kindly to Mr & Mrs Clarkson—&
give a kiss for me to dear little Tom—God love him!—I gave
H. pictures, nuts, & mince pie, all as a Present from Tommy.——
Heaven bless you, my dear friends!   S. T. C.—

453. *To Sara Hutchinson*

August 10, 1802. Tuesday Evening

My dearest Sara

You will this morning, I trust, have received the Letter
which I left at the Ambleside Post (the first, I came to) on
Sunday Evening. I have half such another, the continuation of
my tour, written; but on my arrival yesterday at my home,
about 8 o'clock in the evening, I found 7 Letters for me / I
opened none for an hour, I was so overglad to see the children
again / and the first, I opened, I was forced to answer directly—
which was as much as I could do, to save the Post—& to day I
have been so busy letter-writing, that I have not time to finish
the Great-sheet Letter—so must send a short one, briefly to say
that I have received your two Letters, one of Monday, Aug. 2.
inclosing the 5£—which I read last night, & had better left it
alone, as I did 5 others—for it kept me awake longer than I
ought to have been—and one this evening. I am well, & have
had a very delightful & feeding Excursion, or rather Circum-
cursion.—When you did not hear from me, & in answer too to a
letter containing a note, you should surely have concluded, my
Darling! that I was not at home: for when do ı neglect these
things to those, I love? Other things, & weighty ones, God help
me! I neglect in abundance / for instance / two little Boxes,
which Dorothy fears, (& with abundant Reason) are lost—&
which contain, besides my cloathes & several very valuable
Books, all my written collections made in Germany—which
taken merely in a pecuniary point of view are not worth less
than 150£ to me.——More Rain coming! I broke off writing to

look at the Sky / it was exactly 35 minutes after 7, which [was] 4 minutes after the real Sunset, and long long after the apparent sun-set behind our Vales—& I saw such a sight as I never before saw. Beyond Bassenthwaite at the end of the view was a Sky of bright yellow-green; but over that & extending all over Bassenthwaite, & almost up to Keswick church a Cloud-Sky of the deepest most fiery Orange—Bassenthwaite Lake look'd like a Lake of 'blood-red Wine'—and the River Greta, in all it's winding, before our house, & the upper part of the Keswick Lake, were fiery red—even as I once saw the Thames when the huge Albion Mills were burning, amid the Shouts of an exulting Mob—but with one foot upon Walla Crag, and the other foot exactly upon Calvert's House at Windy Brow was one great Rainbow, *red* and *all* red, entirely formed by the Clouds——I have now seen all the Rain-bows, that, I suppose, are possible—the Solar Rainbow, with it's many colors, the grey lunar Rainbow, & a fiery red Rainbow, wholly from the Clouds after sunset!—

I seem, I know not why, to be beating off all Reference to Dorothy & William, & their Letters—I heard from Sotheby of their meeting—(tho' I did not read his Letter till after I had read your's—) I wish, I wish, they were back!——When I think of them in Lodgings at Calais, Goslar comes back upon me; & of Goslar I never think but with dejection.—[Dear little Caroline!—Will she be a ward of Annette?—Was the subject too delicate for a Letter?—] I suppose so.——To morrow morning they will leave Calais, if they indeed leave it 10 days after the Date of Dorothy's Letter / so that they will probably be with you, I would fain hope, by Monday next.—I saw old Molly yesterday / She was weakly, but *'mended'* from what she had been / the Rheumatic Pain & weakness had left her Back, & gone into her arms—I slept at Bratha on Sunday Night—& did not go on to Grasmere, tho' I had time enough, and was not over-fatigued; but tho' I have no objection to sleep in a lonely House, I did not like to sleep in *their* lonely House. I called the next day—went into the garden—pulled some Peas, & shelled & drest them, & eat them for my dinner with one rasher of Bacon boiled—but I did not go up stairs, nor indeed any where but the Kitchen. Partly I was very wet & my boots very dirty—& Molly had set the Pride of her Heart upon it's niceness—& still more—I had small desire to go up!

It was very kind in you, my Darlings! to send the 5£; (which I have now sent back) but it was not very wise. I could have easily procured 3 or 4£ from Mr Jackson / but I gave up the Residence at St Bees, because I began to reflect that in the present state of my finances I ought not to *spend* so much money. Thomas Ashburner's call was the *occasion* of my resolve not to go to St Bees; but my own after reflections were the *cause*.—In the course of my Tour (& I was absent 9 days) I gave away to Bairns, & foot-sore Wayfarers four shillings, & some odd pence; & I *spent* nine shillings—sum total, £0″ 13s 0D—but to this must be added the wear & tear of my Boots, which are gone to be mended; & sixpence for a great knee-patch for my Pantaloons, which will not however be worn an hour the shorter time for the said large knee-patch. I have now *no clothes but what are patched at the elbows, & knees, & in the seat*—& I am determined to wear them *out & out*—& to have none till after Christmas.——Hartley is in good spirits; but he does not look well. Derwent too looks less rosy than usual—for we cannot keep him from the Gooseberries—Hartley says—[']He is far over wicked; but it's all owing to Adam, who did the same thing in Paradise.'—Derwent can *repeat* all the Letters; & can point out six or seven / O! that you could see his Darling mouth, when he shouts out Q.—But notwithstanding his *erudition*, he is very backward in his Tongue.—Lloyd's children are nice fair Babies; but there is nothing *lovely* in their countenances or manners.—I have seldom seen children, I was so little inclined to caress—fair & clean, as they were. O how many a cottage Bairn have I kissed or long'd to kiss, whose Cheeks I could scarce see for the healthy dirt—but these I had no wish to kiss!—There is a something in children that makes Love flow out upon them, distinct from beauty, & still more distinct from good-behaviour / I cannot say, God knows! that our children are even decently well-behaved—& Hartley is no beauty—& yet it has been the Lot of the two children to be beloved. They are the general Darlings of the whole Town: & wherever they go, Love is their natural Heritage.

Mrs Coleridge is now pretty well.—

God bless my darling Sara!—& thee, dear Mary! I will finish my long Letter, as soon as possible / but for the next 3 or 4 days I shall be exceedingly busy. Write immediately. Kind Remembrances to Tom & Joanna.—Bless you, my Darling!

&

S. T. Coleridge

I have received a large Wedgewood Jug, & a large Cup, finely embossed with figures, & thick-rimmed with silver, as a present, from—*Lady Rush!* with a *kind Note*.—I had a shrewd suspicion, that I was a favorite.——

Inclosed is the £5, 5s note.—

464. *To Thomas Wedgwood*

Oct. 20, 1802. Greta Hall, Keswick

My dear Sir

This is my Birth-day, my thirtieth. It will not appear wonderful to you therefore, when I tell you that before the arrival of your Letter I had been thinking with a great weight of different feelings concerning you & your dear Brother. For I have good reason to believe, that I should not now have been alive, if in addition to other miseries I had had immediate poverty pressing upon me. I will never again remain silent so long. It has not been altogether Indolence or my habits of Procrastination which have kept me from writing, but an eager wish, I may truly say, a Thirst of Spirit to have something honorable to tell you of myself——at present, I must be content to tell you something cheerful. My Health is very much better. I am stronger in every respect: & am not injured by study or the act of sitting at my writing Desk. But my eyes suffer, if at any time I have been intemperate in the use of Candlelight.— This account supposes another, namely, that my mind is calmer & more at ease.—My dear Sir! when I was last with you at Stowey, my heart was often full, & I could scarcely keep from communicating to you the tale of my domestic distresses. But how could I add to your depression, when you were low? or how interrupt or cast a shade on your good spirits, that were so rare & so precious to you?—After my return to Keswick I was, if possible, more miserable than before. Scarce a day passed without such a scene of discord between me & Mrs Coleridge, as quite incapacitated me for any worthy exertion of my faculties by degrading me in my own estimation. I found my temper injured, & daily more so; the good & pleasurable Thoughts, which had been the support of my moral character, departed from my solitude—I determined to go abroad—but alas! the less I loved my wife, the more dear & necessary did my children seem to me. I found no comfort except in the driest speculations—in the ode to dejection, which you were

pleased with, these Lines in the original followed the line—
My shaping Spirit of Imagination.

> For not to think of what I needs must feel,
> But to be still and patient, all I can,
> And haply by abstruse Research to steal
> From my own Nature all the natural Man—
> This was my sole resource, my only plan,
> And that which suits a part infects the whole
> And now is almost grown the Temper of my Soul

I give you these Lines for the Truth & not for the Poetry—.—
However about two months ago after a violent quarrel I was
taken suddenly ill with spasms in my stomach—I expected to
die—Mrs C. was, of course, shocked & frightened beyond measure—& two days after, I being still very weak & pale as death,
she threw herself upon me, & made a solemn promise of amend-
ment—& she has kept her promise beyond any hope, I could
have flattered myself with: and I have reason to believe, that
two months of tranquillity, & the sight of my now not colourless
& cheerful countenance, have really made her feel as a Wife
ought to feel. If any woman wanted an exact & copious Recipe,
'How to make a Husband compleatly miserable', I could furnish
her with one—with a Probatum est, tacked to it.—Ill tempered
Speeches sent after me when I went out of the House, ill-
tempered Speeches on my return, my friends received with
freezing looks, the least opposition or contradiction occasioning
screams of passion, & the sentiments, which I held most base,
ostentatiously avowed—all this added to the utter negation of
all, which a Husband expects from a Wife—especially, living in
retirement—& the conciousness, that I was myself growing a
worse man / O dear Sir! no one can tell what I have suffered.
I can say with strict truth, that the happiest half-hours, I have
had, were when all of a sudden, as I have been sitting alone
in my Study, I have burst into Tears.——But better days have
arrived, & are still to come. I have had visitations of Hope, that
I may yet be something of which those, who love me, may be
proud.—I cannot write that without recalling dear Poole—I have
heard twice—& written twice—& I fear, that by a strange fatality
one of the Letters will have missed him.—Leslie was here
sometime ago. I was very much pleased with him.—And now
I will tell you what I am doing. I dedicate three days in the
week to the Morning Post / and shall hereafter write for the
far greater part such things as will be of as permanent Interest,

as any thing I can hope to write——& you will shortly see a little Essay of mine justifying the writing in a Newspaper. My Comparison of the French with the Roman Empire was very favorably received.—The Poetry, which I have sent, has been merely the emptying out of my Desk. The Epigrams are wretched indeed; but they answered Stuart's purpose better than better things—/. I ought not to have given any signature to them whatsoever / I never dreamt of acknowledging either them or the Ode to the Rain. As to feeble expressions & unpolished Lines—there is the Rub! Indeed, my dear Sir! I do value your opinion very highly—I should think your judgment on the sentiment, the imagery, the flow of a Poem decisive / at least, if it differed from my own, & after frequent consideration mine remained different—it would leave me at least perplexed. For you are a perfect electrometer in these things— / but in point of poetic Diction I am not so well s[atisf]ied that you do not require a certain *Aloofness* from [the la]nguage of real Life, which I think deadly to Poetry. Very shortly however, I shall present you from the Press with my opinions in full on the subject of Style both in prose & verse—& I am confident of one thing, that I shall convince you that I have thought much & patiently on the subject, & that I understand the whole strength of my Antagonists' Cause.—For I am now busy on the subject—& shall in a very few weeks go to the Press with a Volume on the Prose writings of Hall, Milton, & Taylor—& shall immediately follow it up with an Essay on the writings of Dr Johnson, & Gibbon—. And in these two Volumes I flatter myself, that I shall present a fair History of English Prose.—If my life & health remain, & I do but write half as much and as regularly, as I have done during the last six weeks, these will be finished by January next—& I shall then put together my memorandum Book on the subject of poetry. In both I have sedulously endeavoured to state the Facts, & the Differences, clearly & acutely—& my reasons for the Preference of one style to another are secondary to this.—Of this be assured, that I will never give any thing to the world in propriâ personâ, in my own name, which I have not tormented with the File. I sometimes suspect, that my foul Copy would often appear to general Readers more polished, than my fair Copy—many of the feeble & colloquial Expressions have been industriously substituted for others, which struck me as artificial, & not standing the test— as being neither the language of passion nor distinct Conceptions.—Dear Sir! indulge me with looking still further on to my literary Life. I have since my twentieth year meditated an heroic poem on the Siege of Jerusalem by Titus—this is the Pride, & the Stronghold of my Hope. But I never think of it except in my best moods.—The work, to which I dedicate the ensuing years of my Life, is one which highly pleased Leslie in prospective / & my paper will not let me prattle to you about it.——I have written what you most wished me to write—all about myself—.—Our climate is inclement, & our Houses not as compact as they might be / but it is a stirring climate / & the worse the weather, the more unceasingly entertaining are my Study Windows—& the month, that is to come, is the Glory of the year with us. A very warm Bedroom I can promise you, & one that at the same time commands our finest Lake—& mountain-view. If Leslie could not go abroad with you, & I could in any way mould my manners & habits to suit you, I should of all things like to be your companion. Good nature, an affectionate Disposition, & so thorough a sympathy with the nature of your complaint that I should feel no pain, not the most momentary, in being told by you what your feelings required, at the time in which they required it—this I should bring with me. But I need not say, that you may say to me—'you don't suit me', without inflicting the least mortification.—Of course, this Letter is for your Brother, as for you—but I shall write to him soon. God bless you, & S. T. Coleridge

478. *To Robert Southey*

Christmas Day, 1802

My dear Southey

I arrived at Keswick, with T. Wedgewood, on Friday Afternoon—that is to say, yesterday—& had the comfort to find that Sara was safely brought to bed, the morning before—i.e. Thursday ½ past six, of a healthy—GIRL! I had never thought of a Girl as a possible event—the word[s] child & man child were perfect Synonimes in my feelings—however I bore the sex with great Fortitude—& she shall be called Sara. Both Mrs Coleridge & the Coleridgiella are as well as can be—I left the little one sucking at a great rate. Derwent & Hartley are both well.—

I was at Cote in the beginning of November—and of course had calculated on seeing you & above all on seeing little Edith's physiognomy, among the certain things of my expedition—but I had no sooner arrived at Cote, than I was forced to quit it—

T. Wedgewood having engaged to go into Wales with his Sister—I arrived at Cote in the afternoon, & till late evening did not know or conjecture that we were to go *off* early on the next morning.—I do not say this for you—you must know, how earnestly I yearn to see you—but for Mr Estlin, who expressed himself wounded by the circumstance. When you see him therefore, be so good as to mention this to him.—

I was much affected by Mrs Coleridge's account of your health & eyes. God have mercy on us!—We are all sick, all mad, all slaves!—It is a theory of mine that Virtue & Genius are Diseases of the Hypochondriacal & Scrofulous Genus—& exist in a peculiar state of the Nerves, & diseased Digestion—analogous to the beautiful Diseases, that colour & variegate certain Trees. —However, I add by way of comfort, that it is my Faith that the Virtue & Genius produce the Disease, not the Disease the Virtue &c—tho' when present, it fosters them. Heaven knows! there are fellows who have more vices than scabs, & scabs countless—with fewer Ideas than Plaisters.——

As to my own Health, it is very indifferent. I am exceedingly temperate in every thing—abstain wholly from wine, spirits, or fermented Liquors—almost wholly from Tea—abjure all fermentable & vegetable food—bread excepted—& use *that* sparingly—live almost entirely on Eggs, Fish, Flesh, & Fowl—& thus contrive not to be *ill*—but well I am not—& in this climate never shall be. A deeply ingrained, tho' mild Scrofula, is diffused thro' me: & is a very Proteus. I am fully determined to *try* Teneriffe or Gran Canaria, influenced to prefer them to Madeira solely by the superior cheapness of living. The Climate & Country are heavenly—the Inhabitants Papishes, all of whom I would burn with fire & faggot—for what didn't they do to us Christians under bloody Queen Mary? O the Devil sulphur-roast them—I I would have no mercy on them, unless they drowned all their Priests—& then spite of the Itch (which they have in an inveterate degree, Rich & Poor, Gentle & simple, old & young, Male & female) would shake hands with them unglov'd.——By way of *one* impudent Half-Line in this meek & mild Letter—will you go with me?—'I' & 'you' mean mine & your's—of course.——

Remember, you are to give me Thomas Aquinas & Scotus Erigena.—

God bless you | &
S. T. Coleridge

I can have the best Letters of recommendation.——

My Love & their Sister's to Edith & Mary—& if you see Mrs
Fricker, be so good as to tell her that she will hear from me or
Sara in the course of ten days.——

612. *To Mrs. S. T. Coleridge*

Malta, 12 Decembr, 1804

Dear Sara

I will not occupy much of the short Letter, I have time to
write, in expressing what anguish even to bodily disease I have
suffered by the almost total failure of my Letters from England,
the *certain* Loss of *one* large pacquet sent by me homeward
from Sicily, which was taken by an Algerine & my papers not
improbably at Paris at this time / & no certainty of the other.
A convoy will leave this place in less than a fortnight, when I
shall write at full / this Letter I send to the fleet, in *hope* that
it may come to hand, by a Russian officer of my acquaintance /
I returned or rather was abruptly recalled from Syracuse, Nov.
7th, just as the Carriage was at the door in which I was going
to Messina, & thence to circle the Island / I was there about 3
months, chiefly at Syracuse or within forty miles of it / but I
have been twice on the Top of Mount Etna, & if I had gone on
to Messina, I should have been just in time to have seen the
Eruption of Vesuvius. The fatigue of ascending Etna is the only
thing that has not been exaggerated in it—& of Sicily in general
all is exaggerated grossly except the abominableness of the Government, & the vice & abject wretchedness of the people. I have
been strenuous in awakening our Government to the true character & views of the Court of Naples, for the last 4 months;
yet still I have reason to fear, that the cowardice & ignorance
of Ministers, their improper choice of foreign agents, & a sort of
stupid personal feeling for the King & Queen of Naples will
throw Sicily into the hands of France / if even *at this moment*
it is not done.—My Health is *very greatly* improved in this
heavenly climate / the Trees are loaded with Oranges, now in
the state for plucking—& La Vallette echoes with the cries of
Green Peas / G. Peas cried in *Arabic* in December!—The last
week was very cold & rainy, & I suffered from it / but now it
is exactly like our pleasantest days in Autumn / Were I happy,
I should grow stout; but tho' I am tranquil, I do not know
what it is to have one *happy* moment, or *one* genial Feeling!
Not one—so help me God!—No visitations of mind or of fancy—

but only the same dull gnawing pain at the heart, sometimes indeed, tho' seldom, relieved by a flood of tears when I can say aloud to myself—My Children! my children!

I am still an Inmate of the Palace, tho' I sleep & study in a sort of Garrets in the Treasury, commanding a most magnificent view of open Sea, & lake-like Harbours; as grand & impressive as a view can be without Trees, river, or green fields. I only however stay here till a suite of rooms can be fitted up for me at the Palace / my old ones were given in my absence to Commissioner Otway.—What I am to receive, I scarcely know / I have had 50£; but my various expences in Sicily, bedding, 2 pair of Sheets, mosquito curtain, &c & for clothes (as I dine at the Palace as confidential Secretary of the Government every day) —as well as for the little comforts I must have in my own rooms, & the expence of my servant—&c &c obliged [me] to draw upon Stuart for 50£; which however I hope to replace by the next convoy / at all events I shall send you 50£ to pay my Life-assurance, & your Mother.—Out of this 100£ however which I have spent, you must understand that I have payed Dr Stoddart an old debt of 25£; which reduces it to 75£. I guess that in [a] few days I shall have to receive a 100£, as four m[onths'] Salary—I am constantly & even laboriously emplo[yed] & the confidence placed in me by Sir A. Ball is unlimi[ted.] I am—if I do not cry off myself—to go into Greece in the beginning of January, on a corn-commission for the Island, & from thence thro' Albania along the North[ern] Shore of the Archipelago to Constantinople, then up the Black Sea to the mouth of the Dnieper & into the Crimea / & possibly into the Heart of Russia. Captn Leake is to be with me, if he is not called off by other Duties; but it will be a most anxious business—as I shall have the trust & management of 70, or 80 thousand £, while I shall not have for my toils, & perils more than 3 or 4 hundred £, exclusive of all my expences in travelling &c—On the whole, if I could get off with honor, I would—& shall make the attempt / I undertook it in a fit of Despair, when Life was a burthen to me. If I could make up my mind to stay here, or to follow Sir A.B. in case that circumstances & changes in the political world should lead him to Sardinia, no doubt, I might have about 500£ a year, & live mainly at the Palace / but O God! O God! if that, Sara! which we both know too well, were not unalterably my Lot, how gladly would I prefer the mere necessaries of Life in England, & these obtained by daily Effort! But since my Health has been restored to me, I have felt more than ever how unalterable it is! —Whatever & where ever I am; be assured that my first anxiety & prominent Duty will be to contribute every thing in my power to make you as happy as I can, compatibly with the existence of that Health & Tranquillity (joyless indeed both) on which the very power of doing any thing for you must depend. I hope however to see more clearly the way before me in less than a fortnight.—How I long for Letters from Southey & from Grasmere. O my children! my children! I cannot write their names / even to speak of them thus is an effort of courage. Remember me, of course, to Mr Jackson & Mrs Wilson / &c / —. May God Almighty preserve your Health & Life, for your own Happiness, & for the sake of our dear Children.—I remain faithful to you and to my own Honor in all things; and am most anxiously and affectionately

your Friend & more than Friend, S. T. Coleridge

621. *To Daniel Stuart*

Bell Inn, Friday Street / Monday Morning
August 18th, 1806

My dear Sir

I arrived here from Stangate Creek last night, a little after ten: and have found myself so unusually better ever since I leaped on land, yesterafternoon, that I am glad that neither my strength or spirits enabled me to write to you on my arrival in Quarantine, on the eleventh. Both the Captain and my fellow-passenger were seriously alarmed for my Life—and indeed such have been my unremitting Sufferings from pain, sleeplessness, costiveness, loathing of food, & spirits wholly despondent, that no motive on earth short of an awful duty would ever prevail on me to take any sea-voyage likely to be longer than three or four days. I had rather starve in [a ho]vel; and if Life thro' disease become worthless, will choose a Roman Death.—It is true, I was very low before I embarked—your kind Letter concluding with the Sums, I stand indebted to you, never for an hour ceased to prey on my mind. To have been working so hard for 18 months in a business, I detested—to have been flattered and to have flattered myself, that I should on striking the balance have payed all my debts, & maintained both myself and family during my exile, out of my savings—and earnings, including my travels thro' Germany, thro' which I had

to the very last hoped to have passed—& find myself—but
enough!—I cannot charge my conscience with a single extrava-
gance, nor even my Judgement with any other imprudences
than that of suffering one good and great man to over-persuade
me from month to month to a delay, which was gnawing away
my very vitals—and of being duped in disobedience to my first
feelings & previous Ideas by another diplomatic minister, who
is a rascal. I sent one Bill & a duplicate for 110£ to Mrs C—&
actually had entrusted another for 100£ to Mr Noble at Naples
for the same purpose, & discovered the dupery scarcely time
enough to withdraw it, which I did with an aking heart—had
I not done it, tho' at that time, it was merely for the convenience of not drawing on England, I should have been left
starving in a foreign country / for a gentleman offered to take
me without expence to Rome, which I accep[ted] with the full
intention of staying only a fortnight & then returning to Naples
to pass the winter at Noble's House, which Mr Noble offered
me partly out of compassion for the wretched state of my
finances, which were but barely sufficient for my intended
Journey in the Spring—and partly out of gratitude for my many
attentions, and one or two serious services to his Brother &
Partner at Malta, while I was the Public Secretary.—By Mr
Noble's advice I left every thing (but a good suit of cloathes, &
my shirts &c) —all my letters of credit, manuscripts, &c &c—
with him.—I had not been ten days in Rome before the French
Torrent rolled down on Naples—all return was impossible, all
transmission of Papers not only insecure, but being English &
many of them political, highly dangerous both to the Sender
and Sendee—After two months sickening anxiety I received certain tidings that Mr N. had decamped (having admirably out-
maneuvred the French) with all my papers & effects; but
whether to Malta, or Sardinia was not known. / But this is
only a fragment of a Chapter of Contents / —and I am too
much agitated to write the Detail, but will call on you as soon
as my two or three remaining [guineas] shall have put a decent
Hat upon my [head], & Shoes on my feet.—I am literally afraid
even to cowardice to ask for any person [or] of any person—Including the Quarantine, we had 55 days of Ship-board, working
up against head winds, rotting & sweating in calms, or running
under hard gales, with the dead lights secured / & from the
Captain and my fellow-passenger I received every possible Tenderness—only when I was very ill, they layed their wise heads
together, & the Latter in a Letter to his Father begged him to

inform my Family, that I had arrived & he trusted, that they
would soon see me, in better health & spirits than I had quitted
them, a Letter which must have alarmed if they saw into it, &
wounded if they did not. I was not informed of it till this morning.—God bless you, my dear Sir! I have yet chearful Hopes that
Heaven will not suffer me to die degraded by any other Debts,
than those which it ever has been & ever will be, my joy & pride
still to pay & still to owe, those of a truly grateful Heart—& to
you among the first of those to whom they are due.

S. T. Coleridge.—

642. *To George Coleridge*

2 April, 1806 [1807].—

My dear Brother

The omniscience of the supreme Being has always appeared
to me among the most tremendous thoughts, of which an imperfect rational Being is capable; and to the very best of men
one of the most awful attributes of God is, the Searcher of
Hearts. As he knows us, we are not capable of knowing ourselves
—it is not impossible, that this perfect (as far as in a creature
can be) Self-knowledge may be among the spiritual punishments
of the abandoned, as among the joys of the redeemed Spirits.
Yet there are occasions, when it would be both a comfort and
advantage to us, if with regard to a particular conduct & the
feelings & impulses connected with it, we could make known to
another and with the same degree of vividness the state of our
own Hearts, even as it exists in our own consciousness. Sure am I
at least, that I should rejoice if without the pain & struggles of
communication (pain referent not to any delicacy or self-
reproach of my own) there could be conveyed to you a fair
Abstract of all that has passed within me, concerning yourself
and Ottery, and the place of my future residence, & the nature
of my future employments (all more or less connected with
you)—but after I have been with you awhile, in proportion as
I gain your confidence & confident esteem, so I shall be able
to pour my whole Heart into you—I leave this place (a seat of
Sir G. Beaumont's) on Saturday, March [April] the 4th—& proceed to Bristol—where I am to meet Mrs Coleridge, & the two
children (for Hartley is with me) and immediately proceed to
Ottery.—If you find reason to believe, that I should be an assistance or a comfort to you by settling there in any connection with

you, I am prepared to strike root in my native place; and if you knew the depth of the friendship, I have now for ten years (without the least fluctuation amid the tenderest and yet always respectful Intimacy) felt toward, and enjoyed from, Mr W. Wordsworth, as well as the mutual Love between me and his immediate House-hold, you would not think the less of my affection and sense of duty towards you, my paternal Brother, when I confess that the resolution to settle myself at so great a distance from him has occasioned one among the two or three *very severe* struggles of my life. Previously however to my meeting you, and at the time of thus communicating to you my resolve, provided it should be satisfactory to you—it is absolutely necessary that I should put you in possession of the true state of my domestic Affairs—the agony, which I feel on the very thought of the subject and the very attempt to write concerning it, has been a principal cause not only of the infrequency & omission of my correspondence with you, but of the distraction of all settled pursuits hitherto—

In short, with many excellent qualities, of strict modesty, attention to her children, and economy, Mrs Coleridge has a temper & general tone of feeling, which after a long—& for six years at least—a patient Trial I have found wholly incompatible with even an endurable Life, & such as to preclude all chance of my ever developing the talents, which my Maker has entrusted to me—or of applying the acquirements, which I have been making one after the other, because I could not be doing nothing, & was too sick at heart to exert myself in drawing from the sources of my own mind to any perseverance in any regular plan. The few friends, who have been Witnesses of my domestic Life, have long advised separation, as the necessary condition of every thing desirable for me—nor does Mrs Coleridge herself state or pretend to any objection on the score of attachment to me;—that it will not look *respectable* for her, is the sum into which all her objections resolve themselves.—At length however, it is settled (indeed, the state of my Health joined with that of my circumstances, and the duty of providing what I can, for my three Children, would of themselves dictate the measure, tho' we were only indifferent to each other) but Mrs Coleridge wishes—& very naturally—to accompany me into Devonshire, that our separation may appear free from all shadow of suspicion of any other cause than that of unfitness & unconquerable difference of Temper. O that those, who have been Witnesses of the Truth, could but add for me that commentary on my last Words, which my very respect for Mrs Coleridge's many estimable qualities would make it little less than torture to me to attempt.—However, we part as Friends—the boys of course will be with me. What more need be said, I shall have an opportunity of saying when we are together.—If you wish to write to me, before my arrival, my address will be—Mr Wade's, Aggs' Printing-office, St Augustin's Back, Bristol.

Make my apologies to my dear Nephews; and assure them, that it will be a great Joy to me to endeavor to compensate for my epistolary neglect by my conversation with them—and that any valuable Knowledge, which it should be in my power to communicate to them, will on their account become more valuable to me.—My Love & my Duty to all, who have to claim it from me. I am, my dear Brother, with grateful & affectionate esteem

your friend & brother,
S. T. Coleridge

909. *To Thomas Roberts*

[*Circa* 19 December 1813]

. . . You have no conception of what my sufferings have been, forced to struggle and struggle in order not to desire a death for which I am not prepared.—I have scarcely known what sleep is, but like a leopard in its den have been drawn up and down the room by extreme pain, and restlessness, worse than pain itself.

O how I have prayed even to loud agony only to be able to pray! O how I have felt the impossibility of any real *good will* not born anew from the Word and the Spirit! O I have seen far, far deeper and clearer than I ever saw before the ground of pernicious errors! O I have seen, I have felt that the worst offences are those against our own souls! That our souls are infinite in depth, and therefore our sins are infinite, and redeemable only by an infinitely higher infinity; that of the Love of God in Christ Jesus. I have called my soul infinite, but O infinite in the depth of darkness, an infinite craving, an infinite capacity of pain and weakness, and excellent only as being passively capacious of the light from above. Should I recover I will—no—no may God grant me power to struggle to become *not another* but a *better man*—O that I had been a partaker with you of the discourse of Mr Robt Hall! But it pleased the Redeemer to appoint for me a sterner, fearfuller, and even more eloquent preacher, if to be impressive is to be eloquent. O God save me—save me from myself. . . .

927. *To J. J. Morgan*

14 May, Saturday [1814]
2. Queen's Square—

My dear Morgan

If it could be said with as little *appearance* of profaneness, as there is feeling or intention in my mind, I might affirm; that I had been crucified, dead, and buried, descended into *Hell*, and am now, I humbly trust, rising again, tho' slowly and gradually. I thank you from my heart for your far too kind Letter to Mr Hood—so much of it is true that such as you described I always wished to be. I know, it will be vain to attempt to persuade Mrs Morgan or Charlotte, that a man, whose moral feelings, reason, understanding, and senses are perfectly sane and vigorous, may yet have been *mad*—And yet nothing is more true. By the long long Habit of the accursed Poison my Volition (by which I mean the faculty *instrumental* to the Will, and by which alone the Will can realize itself—it's Hands, Legs, & Feet, as it were) was compleatly deranged, at times frenzied, dissevered itself from the Will, & became an independent faculty: so that I was perpetually in the state, in which you may have seen paralytic Persons, who attempting to push a step forward in one direction are violently forced round to the opposite. I was sure that no ease, much less pleasure, would ensue: nay, was certain of an accumulation of pain. But tho' there was no prospect, no gleam of Light before, an indefinite indescribable Terror as with a scourge of ever restless, ever coiling and uncoiling Serpents, drove me on from behind.—The worst was, that in *exact proportion* to the *importance* and *urgency* of any Duty was it, as of a fatal necessity, sure to be neglected: because it added to the Terror above described. In exact proportion, as I *loved* any person or persons more than others, & would have sacrificed my Life for them, were *they* sure to be the most barbarously mistreated by silence, absence, or breach of promise.—I used to think St James's Text, 'He who offendeth in one point of the Law, offendeth in all', very narsh; but my own sad experience has taught me it's aweful, dreadful Truth.—What crime is there scarcely which has not been included in or fol-

lowed from the one guilt of taking opium? Not to speak of ingratitude to my maker for the wasted Talents; of ingratitude to
so many friends who have loved me I know not why; of barbarous neglect of my family; excess of cruelty to Mary & Charlotte, when at Box, and both ill—(a vision of Hell to me when
I think of it!) I have in this one dirty business of Laudanum
an hundred times deceived, tricked, nay, actually & consciously
LIED.—And yet *all* these vices are so opposite to my nature, that
but for this *free-agency-annihilating* Poison, I verily believe
that I should have suffered myself to have been cut to pieces
rather than have committed any one of them.

At length, it became too bad. I used to take [from] 4 to 5
ounces a day of Laudanum, once ... [ou]nces, i.e. near a Pint—
besides great quantities [of liquo]r. From the Sole of my foot to
the Crown of [my h]eart there was not an Inch in which I was
not [contin]ually in torture: for more than a fortnight no
[sleep] ever visited my Eye lids—but the agonies of [remor]se
were far worse than all!—Letters past between Cottle, Hood, &
myself—& our kind Friend, Hood, sent Mr Daniel to me. At his
second Call I told him plainly (for I had sculked out the night
before & got Laudanum) that while I was in my own power,
all would be in vain—I should inevitably cheat & trick *him,* just
as I had done Dr Tuthill—that I must either be removed to a
place of confinement, or at all events have a Keeper.—Daniel
saw the truth of my observations, & my most faithful excellent
friend, Wade, procured a strong-bodied, but decent, meek,
elderly man, to superintend me, under the name of my Valet—
All in the House were forbidden to fetch any thing but by the
Doctor's order.—Daniel generally spends two or three hours
a day with me—and already from 4 & 5 ounces has brought me
down to four tea-spoonfuls in the 24 Hours—The terror & the
indefinite craving are gone—& he expects to drop it altogether
by the middle of next week—Till a day or two after that I would
rather not see you.

[Signature cut off.]

939. *To Josiah Wade*

Bristol, June 26th, 1814.
Dear Sir,

For I am unworthy to call any good man friend—much less
you, whose hospitality and love I have abused; accept, how-

ever, my intreaties for your forgiveness, and for your prayers.

Conceive a poor miserable wretch, who for many years has been attempting to beat off pain, by a constant recurrence to the vice that reproduces it. Conceive a spirit in hell, employed in tracing out for others the road to that heaven, from which his crimes exclude him! In short, conceive whatever is most wretched, helpless, and hopeless, and you will form as tolerable a notion of my state, as it is possible for a good man to have.

I used to think the text in St. James that 'he who offended in one point, offends in all,' very harsh; but I now feel the awful, the tremendous truth of it. In the one crime of OPIUM, what crime have I not made myself guilty of!—Ingratitude to my Maker! and to my benefactors—injustice! *and unnatural cruelty to my poor children!*—self-contempt for my repeated promise—breach, nay, too often, actual falsehood!

After my death, I earnestly entreat, that a full and unqualified narration of my wretchedness, and of its guilty cause, may be made public, that at least some little good may be effected by the direful example!

May God Almighty bless you, and have mercy on your still affectionate, and in his heart, grateful—

S. T. Coleridge.

964. *To Lady Beaumont*

3 April, 1815.

Dear Madam

Should your Ladyship still have among your Papers those Lines of mine to Mr Wordsworth after his Recitation of the Poem on the Growth of his own spirit, of which you honored by wishing to take a Copy, you would oblige me by inclosing them for me, addressed—Mr Coleridge, Calne, Wilts. Of the Excursion, excluding the tale of the ruined Cottage, which I have ever thought the finest Poem in our Language, comparing it with any of the same or similar Length, I can truly say, that one half the number of it's Beauties would make all the beauties of all his Contemporary Poets collectively mount to the balance; but yet—the fault may be in my own mind—I do not think, I did not feel, it equal to the Work on the Growth of his own spirit. As proofs meet me in every part of the Excursion, that the Poet's genius has not flagged, I have sometimes fancied, that having by the conjoint operation of his own ex-

periences, feelings, and reason *himself* convinced *himself* of
Truths, which the generality of persons have either taken for
granted from their Infancy, or at least adopted in early life, he
has attached all their own depth and weight to doctrines and
words, which come almost as Truisms or Common-place to
others.

From this state of mind, in which I was comparing Wordsworth with himself, I was roused by the infamous Edingburgh
Review of the Poem. If ever Guilt lay on a Writer's head, and if
malignity, slander, hypocrisy and self-contradicting Baseness
can constitute Guilt, I dare openly, and openly (please God!)
I will, impeach the Writer of that Article of it.—

These are awful Times—a dream of dreams!—To be a
prophet is & ever has been an unthankful office—at the illumi-
nation for the peace I furnish'd a design for a friend's Transparency—a vulture with the Head of Napoleon chained to a
rock, and Britannia bending down, with one hand stretching
out the wing of the Vulture, and with the other clipping it with
Shears, on the one blade of which was written Nelson, on the
other Wellington. The motto:—

> We've fought for Peace, and conquer'd it at last.
> The ravening Vulture's Leg is fetter'd fast.
> Britons, rejoice! *and yet be wary too!*
> The Chain may break, the clipt Wing sprout anew.

And since I have conversed with those who first returned from
France, I have weekly expected the Event.—Napoleon's object
at present is to embarrass the Allies, & to cool the enthusiasm of
their Subjects. The latter he unfortunately will be too successful in.—In London, my Lady! it is scarcely possible to distinguish the opinions of the people from the ravings and railings
of the mob; but in country towns we must be blind not to see
the real state of the popular mind. I do not know, whether your
Ladyship read my Letters to Judge Fletcher—I can assure you, it
is no exaggeration picture of the predominance of Jacobinism.
In this small town of Calne 500 Volunteers were raised in the
last War—I am persuaded, that 5 could not be raised now. A
considerable Land-owner, & a man of great observation, said
to me last week—'a Famine, Sir! could scarce have produced
more Evil than the Corn-bill has done under the present circumstances'—I speak nothing of the Bill itself—except that after
the closest attention, and the most sedulous Enquiry after Facts
from Land-owners, Farmers, Stewards, Millers, and Bakers, I

am convinced that both opponents & advocates were in extremes—and that an evil produced by many causes was by many
remedies to have been cured—not by the universal Elixir of
one sweeping Law.—

My Poems will be put to Press by the middle of June—A number adequate to one volume are already in the hands of my
Friends at Bristol, under conditions that *they* are to be published at all events—even tho' I should not add another volume
which I never had so little reason to doubt. Within the last ten
days I have composed three poems, containing 500 lines in the
whole.

Mr and Mrs Morgan present their respectful Compliments
to your Ladyship and Sir George—

> I remain, | my Lady, | Your Ladyship's obliged |
> humble Servant,
> S. T. Coleridge

981. *To Lord Byron*

On 18 October 1815 Byron replied to Coleridge's letter of the
15th. Since Byron's letter led Coleridge to discuss *Christabel*
and to refute Scott's charge of 'want of inclination and exertion', it may be included here:

Dear Sir,—Your letter I have just received. I will willingly
do whatever you direct about the volumes in question—the
sooner the better: it shall not be for want of endeavour on
my part, as a negotiator with the 'Trade' (to talk technically)
that you are not enabled to do yourself justice. Last spring
I saw Wr. Scott. He repeated to me a considerable portion
of an unpublished poem of yours—the wildest and finest I
ever heard in that kind of composition. The title he did not
mention, but I think the heroine's name was Geraldine. At
all events, the 'toothless mastiff bitch' and the 'witch Lady',
the description of the hall, the lamp suspended from the
image, and more particularly of the girl herself as she went
forth in the evening—all took a hold on my imagination
which I never shall wish to shake off. I mention this, not
for the sake of boring you with compliments, but as a prelude
to the hope that this poem is or is to be in the volumes you
are now about to publish. I do not know that even 'Love' or

the 'Antient Mariner' are so impressive—and to me there are few things in our tongue beyond these two productions.

Wr. Scott is a staunch and sturdy admirer of yours, and with a just appreciation of your capacity deplored to me the want of inclination and exertion which prevented you from giving full scope to your mind. I will answer your question as to the 'Beggar's Bush' tomorrow or next day. I shall see Rae and Dibdin (the acting Mrs.) tonight for that purpose.

Oh—your tragedy—I do not wish to hurry you, but I am indeed very anxious to have it under consideration. It is a field in which there are none living to contend against you and in which I should take a pride and pleasure in seeing you compared with the dead. I say this *not* disinterestedly, but as a *Committee*man. We have nothing even tolerable, except a tragedy of Sotheby's, which shall not interfere with yours when ready. You can have no idea what trash there is in the four hundred *fallow* dramas now lying on the shelves of D[rury] L[ane]. I never thought so highly of good writers as lately, since I have had an opportunity of comparing them with the bad.

Ever yours truly,
Byron

22 Octr. 1815. *Calne*

My Lord

The Christabel, which you have mentioned in so obliging a manner, was composed by me in the [year] 1797—I should say, that the plan of the whole poem was formed and the first Book and half of the second were finished—and it was not till after my return from Germany in the year 1800 that I resumed it—and finished the second and a part of the third Book.—This is all that Mr W Scott can have seen. Before I went to Malta, I heard from Lady Beaumont, I know not whether more gratified or more surprized, that Mr Scott had recited the Christabel and expressed no common admiration.—What occurred after my return from Italy, and what the disgusts were (most certainly not originating in my own opinion or decision) that indisposed me to the completion of the Poem, I will not trouble your Lordship with.—It is not yet a Whole: and as it will be 5 Books, I meant to publish it by itself: or with another Poem entitled, the Wanderings of Cain—of which, however, as far as it was written, I have unfortunately lost the only Copy—and can remember no part distinctly but the first stanza:—

Encinctur'd with a twine of Leaves,
That leafy Twine his only Dress!
A lovely Boy was plucking fruits
In a moon-light Wilderness.
The Moon was bright, the Air was free,
And Fruits and Flowers together grew
On many a Shrub and many a Tree:
And all put on a gentle Hue
Hanging in the shadowy Air
Like a Picture rich and rare.
It was a Climate where, they say,
The Night is more belov'd than Day.
But who that beauteous Boy beguil'd,
That beauteous Boy to linger here?
Alone, by night, a little child,
In place so silent and so wild—
Has he no *Friend*, no loving Mother near?

Sir G. Beaumont, I remember, thought it the most impressive of my compositions—& I shall probably compose it over again.— A Lady is now transcribing the Christabel, in the form and as far as it existed before my voyage to the Mediterranean—I hope to inclose it for your Lordship's gracious acceptance tomorrow or next day. I have not learnt with what motive Wordsworth omitted the original a[d]vertisement prefixed to his White Doe, that the peculiar metre and mode of narration he had imitated from the Christabel. For this is indeed the same metre, as far as the *Law* extends—the metre of the Christabel not being irregular, as Southey's Thalaba or Kehama, or Scott's Poems, but uniformily measured by four Beats in each Line. In other words, I count by Beats or accents instead of syllables—in the belief that a metre might be thus produced sufficiently uniform & far more malleable to the Passion & Meaning.

I was much gratified, I confess, by what your Lordship has said of this Poem, the Love, and the Ancient Mariner, but I was far more affected, and received a far deeper & more abiding pleasure from the kindness with which in the following §§ you have conveyed to me the Regrets of many concerning 'the want of Inclination and Exertion which prevented me from giving full scope to my mind.' Before God & my own Conscience I dare judge myself by no other rule, than the nihil actum si quid agendum—the limit of our faculties is the limit of our Duties. But by men I ought to be judged *comparatively*, i.e. with others possessing at least equal powers & acquirements. To think of

myself at all except *representatively* & for psychological purposes was new to me; but to think of myself comparatively was
not only new but strange. Yet the Report had done me such
exceeding Injury, such substantial Wrong—and had besides
been published in the broadest language in the Ed. Annual
Register, the Ed. Review, the Quarterly Review, and other
minors of the same family, that I felt myself bound in duty to
myself and my children to notice & prove it's falsehood. This I
have done at full in the Autobiography now in the Press: as far
as delicacy permitted.—But what I could not or at least would
not discuss in public, ought to have been taken into consideration by those who have circulated the opinion in private.—No
one of my bitterest Censors have ever charged my writings with
triviality; but on the contrary, they have been described as over
elaborate, obscure, paradoxical, over subtle &c—and I know
myself, that I have written nothing without as much effort as I
should or could have employed whatever had been the Subject—. Yet if my published Works, omitting too all that is
merely temporary, were collected, they would amount to at
least 8 considerable Octavo Volumes—if I should have any
moderate Success at Drury Lane, the ensuing year will at least
give a proof of what I have been doing for the last 10 years,
exclusive of what I have done. My Logosophia may be con-
futed or confirmed, valued or deemed useless; but I dare affirm,
that no intelligent judge will deny that the Treatises must have
been the product of intense and continued Effort both in
Thought and in systematic Reading.—

Still however the question returns—why has not some one
Work already been produced, some thing that may be referred
to?—And it is this, my Lord! which delicacy forbad me to answer
in a public work—But in private & to my friends I would ask in
return: Has there been during the whole of my Life since my
return from Germany in 1800 a single half year, nay, any three
months, in which I possessed the *means* of devoting myself
exclusively to any one of many works, that it would have been
my Delight & *hourly* pleasure to have executed? So help me
God! never one!—At all times I have been forced in bitterness
of Soul to turn off from the pursuits of my choice to earn the
week's food by the week's Labor for the Newspapers & the like.
At this very time I should have had not only the Tragedy ready
for presentation, but two other pieces, the one a musical opera
on a most interesting plot & characters, and which I had framed
and (as far as I have gone) executed con amore, and in the

belief that if there be any one quality in which I could excel, it would be in the sweetness of lyrical metres as adapted to vocal music—the other, I cannot call it a Pantomime but a Hemimime —a sort of splendid speaking Pantomime.—Now, my Lord! were it known what I have been *obliged* to do weekly, now writing Sermons, now articles for a provincial Paper—in short, almost any thing that is not dishonorable (for I write no Reviews)— it would in a kind mind rather exceed than fall short of expectation that I have done even what I have done, *towards* something less temporary.

My Lord! I will honestly tell you, that at this very time within a fortnight of this very date, instead of sending Mr Kinnaird the first act of my intended Merchant King, or the King & the Beggar, I could send the whole Play—& Mr Kinnaird's kind Communication of *his* Plan & my Confidence in his Candor, would strongly dispose me to remit it *entire* with the reasons, which long reflection has suggested to me, why I entertain *fears* concerning the success of *his* Plan—several parts of which had occurred to me, & some had been begun upon, but afterwards rejected.—But in the mean time I am almost compelled to write as much in point of paper at least, on the Duke of Wellington, Mr —— Picture Gallery, & the Lord knows what, in order to procure 15£, as the *completion* of my engagement, and it's ultimate reward!—even if I procure *as* much as fifteen pound.—Excuse my apparent Warmth, my Lord!—but I felt a desire to let you know the whole truth in proportion as your kindness inspired a wish to gain your esteem of me as a man.

If, my Lord! you were not yourself a *Committee-man,* I should have ventured to say to the Committee of D.L.—Simply *enable* me to do it—& I will pledge my Honor & my Existence, that, if I live, I will present you a Tragedy by the beginning of December, and a Romantic Comic Opera by February—and in the interim correspond with Mr Dibdin on the subject of a sort of Pantomime, on which I long ago conversed with him.—But at all events, I will rest your Lordship's opinion on the groundedness of this Self-defence on the presentation of the Tragedy by the beginning of December—. I have written to Miss Hudson; but merely as from *myself*—not exciting Hopes which perhaps may not be gratified—

I trust, your Lordship will excuse this I myself I Scrawl
from your Lordship's | obliged

S. T. Coleridge

1002. *To James Gillman*

42, Norfolk St. Strand—
Saturday Noon. [13 April 1816]

My dear Sir

The first half hour, I was with you, convinced me that I
should owe my reception into your family exclusively to motives
not less flattering to me than honorable to yourself. I trust, we
shall ever in matters of intellect be reciprocally serviceable to
each other. Men of sense generally come to the same conclusions; but they are likely to contribute to each other's enlarge-
ment of View in proportion to the distance, or even opposition
of the points from which they set out. Travel and the strange
variety of situations and employments on which Chance has
thrown me in the course of my Life might have made me a mere
man of Observation, if Pain and Sorrow and Self-miscompla-
cence had not forced my mind in on itself, and so formed habits
of *meditation*. It is now as much my nature to evolve the *fact*
from the *Law,* as that of a practical man to deduce the Law
from the Fact.

[With regard to the Terms] permit me to say, [that I offer
them as proportioned to my *present* ability; and least of all
things] to my sense of the service. But that indeed cannot be
[*payed*] for: it must be returned in kind by esteem and grateful
affection.—

And now of myself. My ever-wakeful Reason, and the keenness of my moral feelings will secure you from all unpleasant
circumstances connected with me save only one: viz.—*Evasion*,
and the cunning of a specific madness. You will never *hear* any
thing but truth from me—Prior Habits render it out of my
power to *tell* a falsehood, but unless watched carefully, I dare
not promise that I should not with regard to this detested
Poison be capable of *acting* a Lie.—No sixty hours *have yet
passed* without my having taking [taken?] Laudanum—tho'
for the last week comparatively trifling doses. I have full belief,
that your *anxiety* will not need to be extended beyond the first
week: and for the first week I shall not, I *must not be permitted*
to leave your House, unless I should walk out with you.—
Delicately or indelicately, this *must* be done: and both the
Servant and the young Man must receive absolute commands
from you on no account to fetch any thing for me. The stimulus
of Conversation suspends the terror that haunts my mind; but

when I am alone, the horrors, I have suffered from Laudanum, the degradation, the blighted Utility, almost overwhelm me—. If (as I feel for *the first time* a soothing Confidence it will prove) I should leave you restored to my moral and bodily Health, it is not myself only that will love and honor you— Every friend, I have (and thank God! spite of this wretched vice I have many & warm ones who were friends of my Youth & have never deserted me) will think of you with reverence.

I have taken no notice of your kind apologies—if I could not be comfortable in your House & with your family, I should deserve to be miserable.

I presume, there will be no Objection to Mr Morgan coming to me, as my literary Counsellor and Amanuensis at ½ past 11 every morning & staying with me till ½ past 3. I have been for so many years accustomed to dicta[te] while he writes that I now cannot compose without him—. He is an old acquaintance of Dr Adams's: and has kindly left his family for a month at Calne in order to be with me during such hours, as I should be other- wise alone.

If you could make it convenient, I should wish to be with you by Monday Evening: as it would prevent the necessity of my taking fresh Lodgings in Town.

With respectful Compliments to Mrs Gillman & her Sister I remain, dear Sir, | your much obliged

S. T. Coleridge

1071. *To Derwent Coleridge*

[July 1817]

In this volume, my dear Derwent, I have compressed all I know of the principles of a sober yet not ungenial Criticism: and most anxiously have I avoided all mere *assertion*—all *opinion* not followed or preceded by the reasons, on which it had been grounded. Of one thing I am distinctly conscious, viz. that my main motive and continued impulse was to secure, as far as in me lay, an intelligent admiration to Mr Wordsworth's Poems—and while I frankly avowed what I deemed defects, and why I deemed them so, yet to evince how *very* trifling they were not only in importance but even in the proportional space occupied by them; and lastly to satisfy at once a favorite wish as well as favorite conviction of my own, which I cannot better

express than by adopting the following stanza of old
Gascoigne's, in application to Wordsworth's Genius.

> Lo! as a Hawk that soareth tow'rd the sky
> And climbs aloft for solace of his wing,
> The greater Gate she getteth up on high,
> The truer stoupe she makes at any thing.

If in so doing I have offended where I should most wish and
did most expect to please, it is but one of many proofs that I
have been too apt to judge of the feelings of others by my
own.—   *S.T.C.*

1094. *To Derwent Coleridge*

[8] Jany. 1818

My very dear Boy

I can scarce see the paper while I am writing—my heart is so
full.—In your and Hartley's welfare for the next three or four
years all my Heart is fixed—not that I do not tenderly love
and yearn after your dear Sister; but I know not what I can
hope to effect for her in the present state of my circumstances,
more than doing my best to finish such works, as when my Death
shall have disarmed Envy and Calumny may be rendered (if
my Friends should then exert themselves for your excellent
Mother) a valuable addition to the sum assured which (should
I live to the year 1820) will, I am informed, be doubled.—But
with regard to you, I had set my very soul on having you
with me—it was my prayer every night, and my day-dream as
often as I dared take a furlow from my work: and had I not
been grossly cheated and duped by a wretch who came to me
with every holy name in his mouth, merely to suck my brains,
I should not now have been *writing* to you. Mr and Mrs Gilman
have been true friends to me—or I could not indeed have stood
up against the cruelty of—say, the World. I know not in what
respect I can lessen my expences; and my actual expences, what
I actually *cost* them, these and nothing beyond will my friends
here receive from me—a determination which they made the
moment, they became acquainted with the real state of my
means and chances. They are as anxious almost as I myself am,
that I should be enabled to lay by 200£, little by little, in the
course of the next year, for you—if I should succeed in my

Lectures and if my acquaintances should exert themselves in procuring me Subscribers for a work, to be published in weekly numbers, of which I shall soon publish a Prospectus and Specimen (I can only now tell you, that it is a biblical work, containing 1. a literal and 2. a metrical translation of all the Odes and fragments of Odes scattered throughout the Pentateuch and the Historical works of the O. Testament—as *the first* Division of the work) I shall be able to do this: and if I should, I might then safely rely on getting one hundred pound the year after—so that the money of the first year being safely lodged with your mother, there can, I trust, be no objection to your being sent to Cambridge, before your 19th year. For this year to come, my dearest Derwent! you must make yourself as happy as you can—but pray, go on with your *Mathematics* above all, and in the second place with your Greek, as earnestly as you can, but not so as to hurt your Health.—Not a word did I hear of the present plan till yesterday—but if it pleases your Mother and Mr Southey as much as it seems to please the Wordsworths, let it please you for the present—and as soon as it is settled, let me hear from you whether you are likely to have any Vacation allowed you, and if so, at what time.—I am, alas! unable to promise any thing; and till the Trial has been made of my present schemes, chiefly that of the biblical work, I dare not even disclose my Hopes. Let it satisfy you for the present, that you and Hartley are an unutterable comfort to me. Your Brother is as a blessing to me as often as I see him: and you as often as I hear concerning you—and when I reflect on God's great mercy to me in both of you and your sweet Sister, I not only feel the warmest gratitude to your Mother, but check my complaints—and thank the Almighty that I am,

my dear Derwent, | your affectionate Father,
S. T. Coleridge

1140. *To Mrs. Gillman*

Wednesday. [17 June 1818]
J. Green's, Esqre
St Lawrence near Maldon

My very dear Sister and Friend

The distance from the Post, and the extraordinary thinness of population in this district (especially of men and women of *Letters*) which affords only two days in the seven for sending to or receiving from Malden, are the sole causes of your not hearing oftener from me.—The cross roads from Margaritting St to the very House are excellent and thro' the first Gate we drove up between two large Gardens, that on the Right a Flower & Fruit Garden not without Kitchenery, and that on the left a Kitchen Garden not without Fruits and Flowers: and both in a perfect *Blaze* of Roses. Yet so capricious is our—at least my—nature, that I feel, I do not receive the fifth part of the delight from this miscellany of Flora, flowers at every step, as from the economized Glasses and Flower-pots at Highgate, so tended & worshipped by me, and each the gift of some kind Friend or courteous Neighbor. I actually make up a Flower-pot every night, in order to imitate my Highgate Pleasures.—The Country round is very beautiful—about a quarter of a mile from the garden, all the way thro' bean-fields in blossom, we come to a wood, full of Birds, & not uncharmed by the Nightingales, & which the old Workman to please his Mistress has *romanticized* with, I dare say, fifty Seats, Honeysuckle Bowers, and green Arches made by twisting the Branches of the Trees across the Paths. The view from the hilly field above the wood commanding the Arm of the Sea, ending in the open sea, reminded me very much of the Prospects from Stowey and Alfoxden in Somersetshire.—The Cottagers seem to be, and are, in possession of plenty & comfort—Poverty I have seen no marks of—nor of the least servility tho' they are courteous and respectful.—We have abundance of Cream.—The Farm must, I should think, be a valuable Estate: and the Parents are anxious to leave it as compleat as possible for Joseph, their only child—for it is Mrs J. Green's Sisters, that we have seen. G. himself has no Sister.—There is no society hereabouts—I like it the better there*fóre*—the Clergyman, a young man, is lost in a gloomy vulgar Calvinism—will read no book but the Bible—converse on nothing but the state of the soul, or rather he will not converse at all—but visits each house once in two months, when he prays and admonishes—& gives a lecture every evening at his own rooms. On being invited to dine with us, the sad and modest Youth returned for answer, that if Mr Green and I should be here when he visited the house, he should have no objection to enter into the state of our souls with us, and if in the mean time we desired any *instruction* from him, we might attend at his daily evening Lecture!—Election, Reprobation, children of the Devil, and all such Flowers of Rhetoric, and Flour of Brimstone, form his discourses both in Church and

Parlour—but my folly in not filling the Snuff Cannister is a subject of far more serious and aweful Regret with me, than the not being in the way of being thus led by the Nose by this Pseudo-evangelist. Nothing but *Scotch*: and that 5 miles off.—O Anne! it was cruel in you not to have calculated the monstrous disproportion between the huge necessities of my Nostrils or rather of my Thumb and Fore-finger, and that vile little Vial three fourths empty of Snuff! The flat of my Thumb, yea, the nail of my fore-finger is not only clean—it is white! White as the pale flag of Famine!—

Now for my health. A journey in stage or post-chaise always produces constipation with me—. Three of the Pills produced no effect, taken on Sunday Night—I took 5 on the Monday—& they answered but disagreed—& I had a sick Tuesday—But this would have—indeed has—passed off—but ludicrous as it may seem, yet it is no joke for me, that from the marshiness of these Sea Marshes, and the number of unnecessary Fish Ponds & other Stagnancies immediately around the house, the Gnats are a very plague of Egypt—and suspicious with good reason of an erisypelatous tendency I am anxious concerning the effects of the irritation produced by these canorous Visitants. While awake (and two thirds of last night I was kept awake by their Bites & Trumpetings) I can so far command myself as to check the intolerable Itching by a weak mixture of Goulard with Rose Water; but in my sleep I scratch myself, as if old Scratch had lent me his best set of Claws.—This is the only Drawback from my Comforts here—for nothing can be kinder or more cordial than my treatment—I *like* Mrs J. Green better and better; but feel that in 20 years it would never be above or beyond *liking*.— She is good-natured, lively, innocent—but wants a *soothingness,* a something I do not know what, that is tender.—

As to my return, I do not think, it will be possible without great unkindness to be with you before Tuesday Evening or Wednesday—calculating *wholly* by the progress of the Manu-script—and we have been hard at it.—Do not take it as words of course when I say and solemnly assure you, that if I followed my own *wishes,* I should leave this place on Saturday Morning: for I feel more and more that I can be well off no where away from you and Gillman.—May God bless him! For a dear Friend he is & has been to me.—

Remember me affectionately to the Milnes & Betsy—if they are at Highgate—Love to James—Kisses for the Fish of 5 waters, none of which are stagnant—& I hope that Mary, Dinah, &

Lucy are well—& that Mary is quite recovered.—Again & again & again God bless you, my most dear Friends—for I am and ever trust to remain, more than can be expressed, my dear Anne!

your affectionate, obliged & grateful
S. T. Coleridge

P.S. N.B. *Not* to put Essex, after Maldon.

1177. *To Robert Southey*

[31 January 1819]

Dear Southey

I do not remember whether or no you are acquainted with, have seen or heard of Mr Kenyon. He is a man of fortune, highly educated, a particular friend of our friend, Mr Thomas Poole, who while I was in the West shewed me *particular* kindness. He has been some years abroad with Mrs Kenyon. Last Thursday Evening just before my Lecture a Letter from him was delivered to me, earnestly requesting that I would give his friend, Mr Ticknor, an American Gentleman, an introduction to you and Mr Wordsworth. Mr Kenyon speaks highly of Mr Ticknor—both as a man and a man of liberal principles—I owe it to the memory of dear Allston to have no incredulity on this point. After the Lecture I saw him for a few seconds, and find that he leaves London tomorrow Morning for the North. I could not hesitate therefore in promising and in thus fulfilling my promise that I would give him a letter to you—and any little attentions, that your time will permit, will be put in part to my account by Mr Kenyon, and yet without lessening the sense of your kindness.

On Wednesday Night, just before 12, I was seized with a sort of ague-fit as I was sitting by a good fire—and tho' I got to bed as soon as possible, yet it kept not only me but the bed-stead in bed-and-body-quake till past 4 in the morning—It then made way for a hot fit, with pains on my limbs & across my chest and with sharp *cry-out* stitches whenever I attempted to draw my breath freely. With great Effort I contrived to get thro' the Thursday's Lecture as successfully as the subject (Lear) would allow me—but by Mr Gillman's and Mr Green's medical commands I announced a week's intermission. On Friday and Yester evening I had a relapse, but of brief continuance, ending after a short but rather alarming spasm with violent sickness. I trust, however, that by aid of Calomel, Senna+Epsom Salts =

Black Dose, Pediluvia, and as much repose as my circumstances will suffer me to give my mind, I shall be re-established in a few days.

As soon as I have sent off this letter to Mr Ticknor, I shall devote the remainder of the day to Letters to Mrs Coleridge and to Derwent, with some books for Derwent—in which Hartley, who leaves me tomorrow for Oxford, will inclose a letter.

I was as much delighted as I could be, being still more affected, by Mr Collins's exquisite Sketch-picture of Sara—and Hartley assures me, that it is not less faithful as a *portrait*.

You of course have read Antar. I have merely seen it, having read about ten pages only to Lady Errol—tho' Mr Hamilton apologized at the Lecture for not having sent me a Copy of his Brother's work. Every one, I find, has regretted the same defect—the mixture of modern phrases in pages, two thirds of the sentences of which read exactly like the Book of Kings—especially as the modernisms might be corrected currente calamo. I am anxious to read the whole—it seems to prove, as the Editor I believe has noticed, that the Arab. Nights are originally Persian—perhaps Graeco-persian.—

A Brahmin has, I hear, arisen to attempt what we have both so often wished—viz. to be the Luther of Brahmanism—and with all the effect, that could be wished—considering the times.

Mr Frere *at a heavy expence* (I was astonished to learn thro' Mr Gillman from the Scribe himself, at how heavy an expence!) has had my Lectures taken down in short-hand. It will be of service to me: tho' the Publication must of course contain much that could not be delivered to a public Audience who, respectable as they have been (scanty, I am sorry to add), expect to be kept awake.—I shall however, God granting me the continuance of the power and the strength, bring them out—first, because a History of *Philosophy*, as the gradual evolution of the instinct of Man to enquire into *the Origin* by the efforts of his own reason, is a desideratum in Literature—and secondly, because it is almost a necessary Introduction to my *magnum opus,* in which I had been making regular and considerable progress till my Lectures—and shall resume, immediately after.—I give 4 and oftener five hours twice a week, and Mr Green (Cline's Nephew and Lecturer & Demonstrating Surgeon at Guy's and Thomas's, a most amiable man, deeply studied in all the physiology and philosophy of the German Schools, and equally dissatisfied with them as myself) writes down what I say—so that we have already compassed a good handsome Volume—and hitherto we have neither of us been able to detect any unfaithfulness to the four Postulates, with which I commenced—1. That the System should be *grounded*. 2. That it should not be grounded in an *abstraction,* nor in a *Thing.* 3. That there be no chasm or saltus in the deduction or rather production. 4. That it should be bonâ fide progressive, not in circulo—productive not barren.—

Some Genius in a pamphlet entitled Hypocrisy unveiled written against Mr Wilson has pronounced poor Christabel 'the most obscene Poem in the English Lange.' It seems that Hazlitt from pure malignity had spread about the Report that Geraldine was a man in disguise—I saw an old book at Coleorton in which the Paradise Lost was described as 'an obscene Poem'—so I am in good company.—

God bless you and
S. T. Coleridge.

P.S. All remembrances &c *understood*—& all else deferred to my parcel letter—

1197. *To Charles Mathews*

Highgate.
J. Gillman's, Esqre.
6 May, 1819

Dear Sir

Strolling down Milfield Lane, my favorite Walk, I was informed by a workman who observed me gazing at Mr Tenpaint's pretty Gothic Cottage, that you had been as much pleased with it as myself: and that I owe to it the chance of having you as a Neighbor. I determined therefore to avail myself of a former introduction to you, to offer my services if in any way you can employ them, taking me either as now an old Stager at Highgate, or as the Author of Remorse, tho' at present far more disposed to the Laughable than the Tragic.—In sober earnest, however, I have long had the highest admiration of your Talents; and on whatever occasion you might wish to use either me or my Pen or the little influence with the daily & weekly or monthly Press, which I possess, *as a friend,* you will always find me AT HOME.

That Home is with my valued friend, Mr Gillman, at the Top of the Hill—your Landlord's medical attendant, & the man,

who has *the respectable* Practice of Highgate & it's vicinity, and
whose Talents and Acquirements would do honor to a larger
and more public Sphere of medical Utility. The best is—that he
has the three good qualities that most improve by keeping each
other company, i.e. He is an agreeable man, an honest man,
and a man of sound Common Sense—which last I hold to be
nine tenths of medical excellence. I hope, for your own sake
and the Public's that you may long keep your knowledge of him
confined to his merits as a good and friendly neighbor—but
should a few of the aches, you have often caused in *my* sides as
well as in those of some thousand others, be transferred to
yourself or house-hold, I dare anticipate the result of your experience,—as coincident with my own—videlicet, that no one
complains of him but his Druggist, who swears that for a man
with such a practice he sends out a *shameful small* quantity of
medicines.

But to return to a more pleasant and I trust a less remote subject—are you at all acquainted with the dramatic Pieces of Carlo
Gozzi, called (absurdly enough) the Venetian Shakspeare?
Tho' no Shakspeare, he is a delightful Fellow: and your late
bold and fortunate attempt has repeatedly reminded me of him.
The Pieces are Dramatized Popular Tales, such as our Blue-
beard, Cinderella & the like; all the comic dialogue being left
to the Actors to supply, ad libitum—the author giving the subjects, and *hints* only. It would be, I am aware, very, perhaps in-
superably, difficult to find two or three capable of playing
second or even third parts to you—even had it not been proved,
that You are yourself a sufficient Novelty for the Public. But
otherwise I am convinced that Gozzi's PLAN properly *anglicized*
and *Londonized* (*not* the works themselves) would meet with
some share of the Success which bore down every thing before
it at Venice—and fairly laughed Goldoni and the Comedie
larmoyante into mortal hysterics, and Sentimentality out of all
good society.—At all events, in the old Italian and (what perhaps may surprize you) in the *Danish* Literature there is an
inexhaustible fund of the Comic, which, as far as an hour's
conversation (now and then when you have nothing better to
do) could convey it, might supply a few serviceable Items—
which at all events would cost you nothing but the time spent
in chatting them over.—

I am not certain whether you are acquainted with Mr Arnold,
and in the Habit of seeing him. I have not forgotten his kindness during the preparation of the Remorse: and the infre-

quency of my journeys to town from my Valetudinarianism
(n.b. this is the age of *Polysyllables*) has alone prevented me
from renewing my thanks to him personally.—

Wishing you every pleasure and advantage that can be given
by the prettiest House in the best air and neighboured by the
most delightful walks that are [to] be found within ten miles
from the Strand, N. E. S. or West,

> I remain, dear Sir, | Your old and sincere | Admirer,
>   S. T. Coleridge

1215. *To Unknown Correspondent*

[November 1819?]

My dear Sir

In a Copy of Verses entitled, 'a Hymn before Sunrise in the
Vale of Chamouny', I described myself under the influence of
strong devotional feelings gazing on the Mountain till as if it
had been a Shape emanating from and sensibly representing
her own essense, my Soul had become diffused thro' 'the mighty
Vision'; and there

> As in her natural Form, swell'd vast to Heaven.

Mr. Wordsworth, I remember, censured the passage as strained
and unnatural, and condemned the Hymn in toto (which
nevertheless I ventured to publish in my 'Sibylline Leaves') as
a specimen of the Mock Sublime. It may be so for others; but
it is impossible that I should myself find it unnatural, being
conscious that it was the image and utterance of Thoughts and
Emotions in which there was no Mockery. Yet on the other
hand I could readily believe that the mood and Habit of mind
out of which the Hymn rose—that differs from Milton's and
Thomson's and from the Psalms, the source of all three, in the
Author's addressing himself to *individual* Objects actually
present to his Senses, while his great Predecessors apostrophize
classes of Things, presented by the Memory and generalized
by the understanding—I can readily believe, I say, that in this
there may be too much of what our learned Med'ciners call the
Idiosyncratic for true Poetry. For from my very childhood I
have been accustomed to *abstract* and as it were unrealize
whatever of more than common interest my eyes dwelt on; and
then by a sort of transfusion and transmission of my conscious-

ness to identify myself with the Object—and I have often thought, within the last five or six years, that if ever I should feel once again the genial warmth and stir of the poetic impulse, and refer to my own experiences, I should venture on a yet stranger & wilder Allegory than of yore—that I would *allegorize* myself, as a Rock with it's summit just raised above the surface of some Bay or Strait in the Arctic Sea,

> While yet the stern and solitary Night
> Brook'd no alternate Sway—

all around me fixed and firm, methought as my own Substance, and near me lofty Masses, that might have seemed to 'hold the Moon and Stars in fee' and often in such wild play with meteoric lights, or with the quiet Shine from above which they made rebound in sparkles or dispand in off-shoots and splinters and iridescent Needle-shafts of keenest Glitter, that it was a pride and a place of Healing to lie, as in an Apostle's Shadow, within the Eclipse and deep substance-seeming Gloom of 'these dread Ambassadors from Earth to Heaven, Great Hierarchs'! and tho' obscured yet to think myself obscured by consubstantial Forms, based in the same Foundation as my own. I grieved not to serve them—yea, lovingly and with gladsomeness I abased myself in their presence: for they are my Brothers, I said, and the Mastery is their's by right of elder birth and by right of the mightier strivings of the hidden Fire that uplifted them above me. [MS. breaks off thus.]

SPECIMENS FROM TABLE TALK, 1822-1832

Nearly everyone who ever met Coleridge came away impressed by his powers as a conversationalist or, as most of them said, as a master of the virtually uninterrupted monologue. An especially memorable account is that of his fellow opium-eater, Thomas De Quincey, who first met him on a summer's day in 1807 in the town of Bridgwater. Having introduced himself, De Quincey was presently escorted into the drawing room of the house where Coleridge was staying. With the preliminaries out of the way, the magical monologue commenced, and one may notice in particular, besides the noble periods of De Quincey's prose, the similes he feels obliged to use in order to suggest the grandeur of the listener's experience.

"Like some great river, the Orellana, or St. Lawrence, that, having been checked and fretted by rocks or thwarting islands, suddenly recovers its volume of waters and its mighty music, [Coleridge] swept at once, as if returning to his natural business, into a continuous strain of eloquent dissertation, certainly the most novel, the most finely illustrated, and traversing the most spacious fields of thought by transitions the most just and logical, that it was possible to conceive. . . . Coleridge, to many people . . . seemed to wander; and he seemed then to wander the most when, in fact, his resistance to the wandering instinct was greatest—viz., when the compass and huge circuit by which his illustrations moved travelled farthest into remote regions before they began to revolve."

We owe the specimens of *Table Talk* which follow to his nephew (and son-in-law) , Henry Nelson Coleridge. As a young man of twenty-four, he began to frequent his uncle's room in the house at Highgate, and for the next twelve years perfected a system of recording Coleridge's pronouncements on an immense range of topics, much as Boswell had done with Dr. Samuel Johnson two generations before. He well knew, as he later confessed, "how inadequately these specimens represent the peculiar splendor and individuality of Mr. Coleridge's conversation . . . his long arrow-flights of thought . . . those ejaculations of light, those tones of a prophet, which at times made me bend before him as before an inspired man." Yet he hoped, he said, "that something of the wisdom, the learning, and the eloquence, of a great man's social converse" had been at least partly captured, "and endowed with a permanent shape for general use."

For any who wish additional testimony to Coleridge's conversational powers, there is the modern compendium, *Coleridge the Talker: A Series of Contemporary Descriptions and Comments,* assembled with a critical introduction by Richard W. Armour and Raymond F. Howes, and published in 1940. This excellent volume contains selections from the remarks of seventy-six men and women who had the rare privilege of hearing Coleridge in action.

TABLE TALK

CHARACTER OF OTHELLO—SCHILLER'S ROBBERS—SHAKSPEARE— SCOTCH NOVELS—LORD BYRON—JOHN KEMBLE

OTHELLO must not be conceived as a negro, but a high and chivalrous Moorish chief. Shakspeare learned the spirit of the character from the Spanish poetry, which was prevalent in England in his time. Jealousy does not strike me as the point in his passion; I take it to be rather an agony that the creature whom he had believed angelic, with whom he had garnered up his heart, and whom he could not help still loving, should be proved impure and worthless. It was the struggle *not* to love her. It was a moral indignation and regret that virtue should so fall:—"But yet the *pity* of it, Iago!—O Iago! the pity of it, Iago!" In addition to this, his honor was concerned: Iago would not have succeeded but by hinting that his honor was compromised. There is no ferocity in Othello; his mind is majestic and composed. He deliberately determines to die; and speaks his last speech with a view of showing his attachment to the Venetian state, though it had superseded him.

Schiller has the material Sublime; to produce an effect, he sets you a whole town on fire, and throws infants with their mothers into the flames, or locks up a father in an old tower. But Shakspeare drops a handkerchief, and the same or greater effects follow.

Lear is the most tremendous effort of Shakspeare as a poet; Hamlet as a philosopher or mediater; and Othello is the union of the two. There is something gigantic and unformed in the former two; but in the latter, every thing assumes its due place and proportion, and the whole mature powers of his mind are displayed in admirable equilibrium.

I think Old Mortality and Guy Mannering the best of the Scotch novels.

It seems, to my ear, that there is a sad want of harmony in Lord Byron's verses. Is it not unnatural to be always connecting very great intellectual power with utter depravity? Does such a combination often really exist *in rerum naturâ?*

I always had a great liking—I may say, a sort of nondescript reverence—for John Kemble. What a quaint creature he was! I remember a party, in which he was discoursing in his measured manner after dinner, when the servant announced his carriage. He nodded, and went on. The announcement took place twice afterward; Kemble each time nodding his head a little more impatiently, but still going on. At last, and for the fourth time, the servant entered, and said,—"Mrs. Kemble says, sir, she has the rheuma*tise,* and can not stay." "Add *ism!*" dropped John, in a parenthesis, and proceeded quietly in his harangue.

January 3, 1823.

MATERIALISM—GHOSTS.

EITHER we have an immortal soul, or we have not. If we have not, we are beasts; the first and wisest of beasts, it may be; but still true beasts. We shall only differ in degree, and not in kind; just as the elephant differs from the slug. But by the concession of all the materialists of all the schools, or almost all, we are not of the same kind as beasts—and this also we say from our own consciousness. Therefore, methinks, it must be the possession of a soul within us, that makes the difference.

Read the first chapter of Genesis without prejudice, and you will be convinced at once. After the narrative of the creation of the earth and brute animals, Moses seems to pause, and says: —"And God said, Let us make man in *our image,* after *our likeness.*" And in the next chapter, he repeats the narrative:— "And the Lord God formed man of the dust of the ground, and breathed into his nostrils the breath of life;" and then he adds these words,—*"and man became a living soul."* Materialism will never explain these last words.

Define a vulgar ghost with reference to all that is called ghost-like. It is visibility without tangibility; which is also the definition of a shadow. Therefore a vulgar ghost and a shadow would be the same; because two different things can not properly have the same definition. A *visible substance* without susceptibility of impact, I maintain to be an absurdity. Unless there be an external substance, the bodily eye *can not* see it; therefore, in all such cases, that which is supposed to be seen is, in fact, *not* seen, but is an image of the brain. External objects naturally produce sensation; but here, in truth, sensation produces, as it were, the external object.

In certain states of the nerves, however, I do believe that the eye, although not consciously so directed may, by a slight convulsion, see a portion of the body, as if opposite to it. The part actually seen will by common association seem the whole; and the whole body will then constitute an external object, which explains many stories of persons seeing themselves lying dead. Bishop Berkeley once experienced this. He had the presence of mind to ring the bell, and feel his pulse; keeping his eye still fixed on his own figure right opposite to him. He was in a high fever, and the brain-image died away as the door opened. I observed something very like it once at Grasmere; and was so conscious of the cause, that I told a person what I was experiencing, while the image still remained.

Of course, if the vulgar ghost be really a shadow, there must be some substance of which it is the shadow. These visible and intangible shadows, without substances to cause them, are absurd.

JANUARY 4, 1823.

CHARACTER OF THE AGE FOR LOGIC—PLATO AND XENOPHON—GREEK DRAMA—KOTZEBUE.

THIS is not a logical age. A friend lately gave me some political pamphlets of the time of Charles I. and the Cromwellate. In them the premisses are frequently wrong, but the deductions are almost always legitimate; whereas, in the writings of the present day, the premisses are commonly sound, but the conclusions false. I think a great deal of commendation is due to the University of Oxford, for preserving the study of logic in the schools. It is a great mistake to suppose geometry any substitute for it.

Negatively, there may be more of the philosophy of Socrates in the Memorabilia of Xenophon than in Plato: that is, there is less of what does not belong to Socrates; but the general spirit of, and impression left by, Plato, are more Socratic.

In Æschylus religion appears terrible, malignant, and persecuting: Sophocles is the mildest of the three tragedians, but the persecuting aspect is still maintained: Euripides is like a modern Frenchman, never so happy as when giving a slap at the gods altogether.

Kotzebue represents the petty kings of the islands in the Pacific ocean exactly as so many Homeric chiefs. Riches command universal influence, and all the kings are supposed to be descended from the gods.

APRIL 30, 1823.

ZENDAVESTA—PANTHEISM AND IDOLATRY.

THE Zendavesta must, I think, have been copied in parts from the writings of Moses. In the description of the creation, the first chapter of Genesis is taken almost literally, except that the sun is created *before* the light, and then the herbs and the plants after the sun; which are precisely the two points they did not understand, and therefore altered as errors.

There are only two acts of creation, properly so called, in the Mosaic account—the material universe and man. The intermediate acts seem more as the results of secondary causes, or, at any rate, of a modification of prepared materials.

Pantheism and idolatry naturally end in each other; for all extremes meet. The Judaic religion is the exact medium, the true compromise.

MAY 1, 1823.

DIFFERENCE BETWEEN STORIES OF DREAMS AND GHOSTS.

THERE is a great difference in the credibility to be attached to stories of dreams and stories of ghosts. Dreams have nothing in them which is absurd and nonsensical; and, though most of the coincidences may be readily explained by the diseased system of the dreamer, and the great and surprising power of association, yet it is impossible to say whether an inner sense does not really exist in the mind, seldom developed, indeed, but which may have a power of presentiment. All the external senses have their correspondents in the mind; the eye can see an object before it is distinctly apprehended;—why may there not be a corresponding power in the soul? The power of prophecy might have been merely a spiritual excitation of this dormant faculty. Hence you will observe that the Hebrew seers sometimes seem to have required music. Every thing in nature has a tendency to move in cycles; and it would be a miracle if, out of such myriads of cycles moving concurrently, some coincidences did not take place. No doubt, many such take place in the daytime; but then our senses drive out the remembrance of them, and render the impression hardly felt; but when we sleep, the mind acts without interruption. Terror and the heated imagination will, even in the daytime, create all sorts of features, shapes, and colors, out of a single object, possessing none of them in reality.

But ghost stories are absurd. Whenever a real ghost appears—by which I mean some man or woman dressed up to frighten another—if the supernatural character of the apparition has been for a moment believed, the effects on the spectator have always been most terrible—convulsion, idiocy, madness, or even death on the spot. Consider the awful descriptions in the Old Testament of the effects of a spiritual presence on the prophets and seers of the Hebrews; the terror, the exceeding great dread, the utter loss of all animal power. But in our common ghost stories, you always find that the seer, after a most appalling apparition, as you are to believe, is quite well the next day. Perhaps he may have a headache; but that is the outside of the effect produced. Alston, a man of genius, and the best painter yet produced by America, when he was in England, told me an anecdote which confirms what I have been saying. It was, I think, in the University of Cambridge, near Boston, that a certain youth took it into his wise head to endeavor to convert a Tom-Painish companion of his by appearing as a ghost before him. He accordingly dressed himself up in the usual way, having previously extracted the ball from the pistol which always lay near the head of his friend's bed. Upon first awaking, and seeing the apparition, the youth who was to be frightened, A., very coolly looked his companion, the ghost, in the face, and said, "I know you. This is a good joke; but you see I am not frightened. Now you may vanish!" The ghost stood still. "Come," said A., "that is enough. I shall get angry. Away!" Still the ghost moved not. "By ——," ejaculated A., "if you do not in three minutes go away, I'll shoot you." He waited the time, deliberately levelled the pistol, fired, and, with a scream at the immobility of the figure, became convulsed, and afterward died. The very instant he believed it *to be* a ghost, his human nature fell before it.

June 15, 1827.

MAGNETISM—ELECTRICITY—GALVANISM.

PERHAPS the attribution or analogy may seem fanciful at first sight; but I am in the habit of realizing to myself Magnetism as length; Electricity as breadth or surface; and Galvanism as depth.

June 24, 1827.

SPENSER—CHARACTER OF OTHELLO—HAMLET—POLONIUS—PRINCIPLES AND MAXIMS—LOVE—MEASURE FOR MEASURE—BEN JONSON—BEAUMONT AND FLETCHER—VERSION OF THE BIBLE—SPURZHEIM—CRANIOLOGY.

SPENSER's Epithalamion is truly sublime; and pray mark the swan-like movement of his exquisite Prothalamion. His attention to metre and rhythm is sometimes so extremely minute, as to be painful even to my ear; and you know how highly I prize good versification.

I have often told you that I do not think there is any jealousy, properly so called, in the character of Othello. There is no predisposition to suspicion, which I take to be an essential term in the definition of the word. Desdemona very truly told Emilia that he was not jealous, that is, of a jealous habit, and he says so as truly of himself. Iago's suggestions, you see, are quite new to him; they do not correspond with any thing of a like nature previously in his mind. If Desdemona had, in fact, been guilty, no one would nave thought of calling Othello's conduct that of a jealous man. He could not act otherwise than he did with the lights he had; whereas jealousy can never be strictly right. See how utterly unlike Othello is to Leontes, in the Winter's Tale, or even to Leonatus, in Cymbeline! The jealousy of the first proceeds from an evident trifle, and something like hatred is mingled with it; and the conduct of Leonatus in accepting the wager, and exposing his wife to the trial, denotes a jealous temper already formed.

Hamlet's character is the prevalence of the abstracting and generalizing habit over the practical. He does not want courage, skill, will, or opportunity; but every incident sets him thinking; and it is curious, and, at the same time, strictly natural, that Hamlet, who all the play seems reason itself, should be impelled, at last, by mere accident, to effect his object. I have a smack of Hamlet myself, if I may say so.

A Maxim is a conclusion upon observation of matters of fact, and is merely retrospective: an Idea, or, if you like, a Principle, carries knowledge within itself, and is prospective. Polonius is a man of maxims. While he is descanting on matters of past experience, as in that excellent speech to Laertes before he sets out on his travels, he is admirable: but when he comes to advise or project, he is a mere dotard. You see, Hamlet, as the man of ideas, despises him.

A man of maxims only is like a Cyclops with one eye, and that eye placed in the back of his head.

In the scene with Ophelia, in the third act, Hamlet is beginning with great and unfeigned tenderness; but, perceiving her reserve and coyness, fancies there are some listeners, and then, to sustain his part, breaks out into all that coarseness.

———

Love is the admiration and cherishing of the amiable qualities of the beloved person, upon the condition of yourself being the object of their action. The qualities of the sexes correspond. The man's courage is loved by the woman, whose fortitude again is coveted by the man. His vigorous intellect is answered by her infallible tact.

———

Measure for Measure is the single exception to the delightfulness of Shakspeare's plays. It is a hateful work, although Shakspearian throughout. Our feelings of justice are grossly wounded in Angelo's escape. Isabella herself contrives to be unamiable, and Claudio is detestable.

———

I am inclined to consider The Fox as the greatest of Ben Jonson's works. But his smaller works are full of poetry.

———

Monsieur Thomas and The Little French Lawyer are great favorites of mine among Beaumont and Fletcher's plays. How those plays overflow with wit! And yet I scarcely know a more deeply tragic scene anywhere than that in Rollo, in which Edith pleads for her father's life, and then, when she can not prevail, rises up and imprecates vengeance on his murderer.

———

Our version of the Bible is to be loved and prized for this, as for a thousand other things,—that it has preserved a purity of meaning to many terms of natural objects. Without this hold-fast, our vitiated imaginations would refine away language to mere abstractions. Hence the French have lost their poetical language; and Blanco White says the same thing has happened to the Spanish. By-the-way, I must say, dear Mr. Sotheby's translation, in the Georgics, of

> "Solve mares; mitte in venerem pecuaria primus;"
> "Loose the fierce savage to the genial bed;"

and

> "Frigidus in venerem senior;"
> "Nor urge reluctant to laborious *love*"—

are the most ludicrous instances I remember of the modern slip-slop.

I have the perception of individual images very strong, but a dim one of the relation of place. I remember the man or the tree, but where I saw them I mostly forget.

Craniology is worth some consideration, although it is merely in its rudiments and guesses yet. But all the coincidences which have been observed could scarcely be by accident. The confusion and absurdity, however, will be endless, until some names or proper terms are discovered for the organs, which are not taken from their mental application or significancy. The fore-part of the head is generally given up to the higher intellectual powers; the hinder part to the sensual emotions.

Silence does not always mark wisdom. I was at dinner, some time ago, in company with a man, who listened to me and said nothing for a long time; but he nodded his head, and I thought him intelligent. At length, towards the end of the dinner, some apple dumplings were placed on the table, and my man had no sooner seen them than he burst forth with—"Them's the jockeys for me!" I wish Spurzheim could have examined the fellow's head.

Some folks apply epithets as boys do in making Latin verses. When I first looked upon the Falls of the Clyde, I was unable to find a word to express my feelings. At last, a man, a stranger to me, who arrived about the same time, said—"How majestic!" —(It was the precise term, and I turned round and was saying —"Thank you, sir! that *is* the exact word for it"—when he added, *eodem flatu*) —"Yes, how very *pretty!*"

April 17, 1830.

MOSAIC MIRACLES—PANTHEISM.

In the miracles of Moses there is a remarkable intermingling of acts which we should now-a-days call simply providential, with such as we should still call miraculous. The passing of the Jordan, in the 3d chapter of the book of Joshua, is perhaps the purest and sheerest miracle recorded in the Bible; it seems to have been wrought for the miracle's sake and so thereby to show to the Jews—the descendants of those who had come out of Egypt—that the *same* God who had appeared to their fathers, and who had by miracles, in many respects providential only, preserved them in the wilderness, was *their* God also. The manna and quails were ordinary provisions of Providence, rendered miraculous by certain laws and qualities annexed to them in the particular instance. The passage of the Red Sea, was effected by a strong wind, which, we are told, drove back the waters; and so on. But then, again, the death of the first-born was purely miraculous. Hence, then, both Jews and Egyptians might take occasion to learn, that it was *one and the same God* who interfered specially, and who governed all generally.

———

Take away the first verse of the book of Genesis, and then what immediately follows is an exact history or sketch of Pantheism. Pantheism was taught in the mysteries of Greece; of which the Cabeiric were the purest and the most ancient.

———

April 18, 1830.

POETIC PROMISE.

In the present age, it is next to impossible to predict from specimens, however favorable, that a young man will turn out a great poet, or rather a poet at all. Poetic taste, dexterity in composition, and ingenious imitation, often produce poems that are very promising in appearance. But genius, or the power of doing something new, is another thing. Tennyson's sonnets, such as I have seen, have many of the characteristic excellences of those of Wordsworth and Southey.

———

APRIL 19, 1830.

IT is a small thing that the patient knows of his own state; yet some things he *does* know better than his physician.

———

I never had, and never could feel, any horror at death, simply as death.

———

Good and bad men are each less so than they seem.

———

MAY 12, 1830.

SHAKSPEARE.

SHAKSPEARE is the Spinozistic deity—an omnipresent creativeness. Milton is the deity of prescience; he stands *ab extra,* and drives a fiery chariot and four, making the horses feel the iron curb which holds them in. Shakspeare's poetry is characterless; that is, it does not reflect the individual Shakspeare; but John Milton himself is in every line of the Paradise Lost. Shakspeare's rhymed verses are excessively condensed,—epigrams with the point everywhere; but in his blank dramatic verse he is diffused, with a linked sweetness long drawn out. No one can understand Shakspeare's superiority fully until he has ascertained, by comparison, all that which he possessed in common with several other great dramatists of his age, and has then calculated the surplus which is entirely Shakspeare's own. His rhythm is so perfect, that you may be almost sure that you do not understand the real force of a line, if it does not run well as you read it. The necessary mental pause after every hemistich or imperfect line is always equal to the time that would have been taken in reading the complete verse.

———

I have no doubt that instead of

—— the twinn'd stones
Upon the number'd beach—

in Cymbeline, it ought to be read thus:—

—— the *grimed* stones
Upon the *umber'd* beach.

So, in Henry V., instead of

His mountain (or mounting) sire on mountains standing—

it ought to be read—"his *monarch* sire,"—that is, Edward the
Third.

MAY 14, 1830.

REASON AND UNDERSTANDING—WORDS AND NAMES OF THINGS.

UNTIL you have mastered the fundamental difference, in
kind, between the reason and the understanding as faculties of
the human mind, you can not escape a thousand difficulties in
philosophy. It is pre-eminently the *Gradus ad Philosophiam*.

The general harmony between the operations of the mind
and heart, and the words which express them in almost all
languages, is wonderful; while the endless discrepances between the names of *things* is very well deserving notice. There
are nearly a hundred names in the different German dialects
for the alder-tree. I believe many more remarkable instances
are to be found in Arabic. Indeed, you may take a very pregnant and useful distinction between *words* and mere arbitrary
names of *things*.

MAY 27, 1830.

FLOGGING.

I HAD *one* just flogging. When I was about thirteen, I went
to a shoemaker, and begged him to take me as his apprentice.
He, being an honest man, immediately took me to Bowyer, who
got into a great rage, knocked me down, and even pushed
Crispin rudely out of the room. Bowyer asked me why I had
made myself such a fool? to which I answered, that I had a

great desire to be a shoemaker, and that I hated the thought of being a clergyman. "Why so?" said he.—"Because, to tell you the truth, sir," said I, "I am an infidel!" For this, without more ado, Bowyer flogged me,—wisely, as I think,—soundly, as I know. Any whining or sermonizing would have gratified my vanity, and confirmed me in my absurdity; as it was, I was laughed at, and got heartily ashamed of my folly.

MAY 28, 1830.

THE AMERICANS.

I DEEPLY regret the anti-American articles of some of the leading reviews. The Americans regard what is said of them in England a thousand times more than they do any thing said of them in any other country. The Americans are excessively pleased with any kind of favorable expressions, and never forgive or forget any slight or abuse. It would be better for them if they were a trifle thicker-skinned.

The last American war was to us only something to talk or read about; but to the Americans it was the cause of misery in their own homes.

I, for one, do not call the sod under my feet my country. But language, religion, laws, government, blood,—identity in these makes men of one country.

MAY 29, 1830.

BOOK OF JOB.

THE Book of Job is an Arab poem, antecedent to the Mosaic dispensation. It represents the mind of a good man not enlightened by an actual revelation, but seeking about for one. In no other book is the desire and necessity for a Mediator so intensely expressed. The personality of God, the I AM of the Hebrews, is most vividly impressed on the book, in opposition to Pantheism.

I now think after many doubts, that the passage, "I know that my Redeemer liveth," &c., may fairly be taken as a burst of determination, a *quasi* prophecy. "I know not *how* this can be; but in spite of all my difficulties, this I *do* know, that I shall be recompensed."

MAY 31, 1830.

ANCIENT MARINER.

MRS. BARBAULD once told me that she admired the Ancient Mariner very much, but that there were two faults in it,—it was improbable, and had no moral. As for the probability, I owned that that might admit some question; but as to the want of a moral, I told her that in my own judgment the poem had too much; and that the only or chief fault, if I might say so, was the obtrusion of the moral sentiment so openly on the reader as a principle or cause of action in a work of such pure imagination. It ought to have had no more moral than the Arabian Nights' tale of the merchant's sitting down to eat dates by the side of a well, and throwing the shells aside, and lo! a geni starts up, and says he *must* kill the aforesaid merchant, *because* one of the date-shells had, it seems, put out the eye of the geni's son.

JUNE 14, 1830.

STUDY OF THE BIBLE.

INTENSE study of the Bible will keep any writer from being *vulgar*, in point of style.

JUNE 15, 1830.

RABELAIS—SWIFT—BENTLEY—BURNET.

RABELAIS is a most wonderful writer. Pantagruel is the Reason; Panurge the Understanding,—the pollarded man, the man with every faculty except the reason. I scarcely know an example more illustrative of the distinction between the two. Rabelais had no mode of speaking the truth in those days but in such a form as this; as it was, he was indebted to the King's protection for his life. Some of the commentators talk about his book being all political; there are contemporary politics in it, of course, but the real scope is much higher and more philosophical. It is in vain to look about for a hidden meaning in all that he has written; you will observe, that after any particularly deep thrust, as the Papimania, for example, Rabelais, as if to break the blow, and to appear unconscious of what ne has done, writes a chapter or two of pure buffoonery. He every now and then flashes you a glimpse of a real face from his magic lantern, and then buries the whole scene in mist. The morality of the work is of the most refined and exalted kind; as for the manners, to be sure, I can not say much.

Swift was *anima Rabelaisii habitans in sicco,*—the soul ot Rabelais dwelling in a dry place.

Yet Swift was rare. Can any thing beat his remark on King William's motto,—*Recepit, non rapuit,*—"that the Receiver was as bad as the Thief?"

The effect of the Tory wits attacking Bentley with such acrimony has been to make them appear a set of shallow and incompetent scholars. Neither Bentley nor Burnet suffered from the hostility of the wits. Burnet's "History of his own Times" is a truly valuable book. His credulity is great, but his simplicity is equally great; and he never deceives you for a moment.

JUNE 25, 1830.

GIOTTO—PAINTING.

THE fresco paintings by Giotto and others, in the cemetery at Pisa, are most noble. Giotto was a contemporary of Dante; and it is a curious question, whether the painters borrowed

from the poet, or *vice versâ*. Certainly M. Angelo and Raffael
fed their imaginations highly with these grand drawings, especially M. Angelo, who took from them his bold yet graceful
lines.

———

People may say what they please about the gradual improvement of the Arts. It is not true of the substance. The Arts and
the Muses both spring forth in the youth of nations, like
Minerva from the front of Jupiter, all armed: manual dexterity
may, indeed, be improved by practice.

Painting went on in power till, in Raffael, it attained the
zenith, and in him too it showed signs of a tendency down-
wards by another path. The painter began to think of overcoming difficulties. After this the descent was rapid, till sculp-
tors began to work inveterate likenesses of periwigs in marble,
—as see Algarotti's tomb in the cemetery at Pisa,—and painters
did nothing but copy, as well as they could, the external face of
nature. Now, in this age, we have a sort of reviviscence,—not,
I fear, of the power, but of a taste for the power, of the early
times.

———

JUNE 26, 1830.

SENECA.

You may get a motto for every sect in religion, or line of
thought in morals or philosophy, from Seneca; but nothing is
ever thought *out* by him.

———

JULY 2, 1830.

PLATO—ARISTOTLE.

EVERY man is born an Aristotelian or a Platonist. I do not
think it possible that any one born an Aristotelian can become a Platonist; and I am sure no born Platonist can ever
change into an Aristotelian. They are the two classes of men,
beside which it is next to impossible to conceive a third. The
one considers reason a quality, or attribute; the other considers
it a power. I believe that Aristotle never could get to under-

stand what Plato meant by an idea. There is a passage, indeed, in the Eudemian Ethics which looks like an exception; but I doubt not of its being spurious, as that whole work is supposed by some to be. With Plato ideas are constitutive in themselves.

Aristotle was, and still is, the sovereign lord of the understanding;—the faculty judging by the senses. He was a conceptualist, and never could raise himself into that higher state which was natural to Plato, and has been so to others, in which the understanding is distinctly contemplated, and, as it were, looked down upon from the throne of actual ideas, or living, inborn, essential truths.

Yet what a mind was Aristotle's—only not the greatest that ever animated the human form!—the parent of science, properly so called, the master of criticism, and the founder or editor of logic! But he confounded science with philosophy, which is an error. Philosophy is the middle state between science, or knowledge, and sophia, or wisdom.

SEPTEMBER 26, 1830.

SCOTCH AND ENGLISH LAKES.

THE five finest things in Scotland are—1. Edinburgh; 2. The antechamber of the Fall of Foyers; 3. The view of Loch Lomond from Inch Tavannach, the highest of the islands; 4. The Trosachs; 5. The view of the Hebrides from a point, the name of which I forget. But the intervals between the fine things in Scotland are very dreary;—whereas, in Cumberland and Westmoreland there is a cabinet of beauties,—each thing being beautiful in itself, and the very passage from one lake, mountain, or valley, to another, is itself a beautiful thing again. The Scotch lakes are so like one another, from their great size, that in a picture you are obliged to read their names; but the English lakes, especially Derwent Water, or rather the whole vale of Keswick, is so rememberable, that after having been once seen, no one ever requires to be told what it is when drawn. This vale is about as large a basin as Loch Lomond; the latter is covered with water; but in the former instance, we have two lakes with a charming river to connect them, and lovely villages at the foot of the mountain, and other habitations, which give an air of life and cheerfulness to the whole place.

_____

The land imagery of the north of Devon is most delightful.

_____

SEPTEMBER 27, 1830.

LOVE AND FRIENDSHIP OPPOSED—MARRIAGE—CHARACTERLESSNESS OF WOMEN.

—— ONCE said, that he could make nothing of love, except that it was friendship accidentally combined with desire. Whence I conclude that he was never in love. For what shall we say of the feeling which a man of sensibility has toward his wife with her baby at her breast! How pure from sensual desire! yet how different from friendship!

_____

Sympathy constitutes friendship; but in love there is a sort of antipathy, or opposing passion. Each strives to be the other, and both together make up one whole.

_____

Luther has sketched the most beautiful picture of the nature, and ends, and duties of the wedded life I ever read. St. Paul says it is a great symbol, not mystery, as we translate it.

_____

"Most women have no character at all," said Pope, and meant it for satire. Shakspeare, who knew man and woman much better, saw that it, in fact, was the perfection of woman to be characterless. Every one wishes a Desdemona or Ophelia for a wife,—creatures who, though they may not always understand you, do always feel you, and feel with you.

_____

SEPTEMBER 28, 1830.

MENTAL ANARCHY.

WHY need we talk of a fiery hell? If the will, which is the law of our nature, were withdrawn from our memory, fancy, understanding, and reason, no other hell could equal, for a spiritual being, what we should then feel, from the anarchy of our powers. It would be conscious madness—a horrid thought!

SEPTEMBER 12, 1831.

MR. COLERIDGE'S SYSTEM OF PHILOSOPHY.

MY system, if I may venture to give it so fine a name, is the only attempt I know ever made to reduce all knowledges into harmony. It opposes no other system, but shows what was true in each; and how that which was true in the particular, in each of them became error, *because* it was only half the truth. I have endeavored to unite the insulated fragments of truth, and therewith to frame a perfect mirror. I show to each system that I fully understand and rightly appreciate what that system means; but then I lift up that system to a higher point of view, from which I enable it to see its former position, where it was, indeed, but under another light and with different relations;— so that the fragment of truth is not only acknowledged, but explained. Thus the old astronomers discovered and maintained much that was true; but, because they were placed on a false ground, and looked from a wrong point of view, they never did, they never could, discover the truth—that is, the whole truth. As soon as they left the earth, their false centre, and took their stand in the sun, immediately they saw the whole system in its true light, and their former station remaining, but remaining as a part of the prospect. I wish, in short, to connect by a moral *copula* natural history with political history; or, in other words, to make history scientific, and science historical—to take from history its accidentality, and from science its fatalism.

I never from a boy could under any circumstances feel the slightest dread of death as such. In all my illness I have ever had the most intense desire to be released from this life, unchecked by any but one wish, namely to be able to finish my work on Philosophy. Not that I have any author's vanity on the subject: God knows that I should be absolutely glad, if I could hear that the thing had already been done before me.

———

Illness never in the smallest degree affects my intellectual powers. I can *think* with all my ordinary vigor in the midst of pain; but I am beset with the most wretched and unmanning reluctance and shrinking from action. I could not upon such occasions take the pen in hand to write down my thoughts for all the wide world.

———

OCTOBER 26, 1831.

KEENNESS AND SUBTLETY.

FEW men of genius are keen; but almost every man of genius is subtle. If you ask me the difference between keenness and subtlety, I answer that it is the difference between a point and an edge. To split a hair is no proof of subtlety; for subtlety acts in distinguishing differences—in showing that two things apparently one are in fact two; whereas to split a hair is to cause division, and not to ascertain difference.

———

JUNE 10, 1832.

CHARM FOR CRAMP.

WHEN I was a little boy at the Blue-coat School, there was a charm for one's foot when asleep; and I believe it had been in the school since its foundation, in the time of Edward the Sixth. The march of intellect has probably now exploded it. It ran thus:—

> Foot! foot! foot! is fast asleep!
> Thumb! thumb! thumb! in spittle we steep;
> Crosses three we make to ease us,
> Two for the thieves, and one for Christ Jesus!

And the same charm served for a cramp in the leg, with the following substitution:—

The devil is tying a knot in my leg;
Mark, Luke, and John, unloose it, I beg!—
Crosses three, &c.

And really, upon getting out of bed, where the cramp most
frequently occurred, pressing the sole of the foot on the cold
floor, and then repeating this charm with the acts configurative
thereupon prescribed, ı can safely affirm, that ı do not remember an instance in which the cramp did not go away in a few
seconds.

JULY 21, 1832.

WORDSWORTH.

I HAVE often wished that the first two books of the Excursion
had been published separately, under the name of "The
Deserted Cottage." They would have formed, what indeed they
are, one of the most beautiful poems in the language.

Can dialogues in verse be defended? I can not but think
that a great philosophical poet ought always to teach the reader
himself as from himself. A poem does not admit argumenta-
tion, though it does admit development of thought. In prose
there may be a difference; though I must confess that, even in
Plato and Cicero, I am always vexed that the authors do not say
what they have to say at once in their own persons. The introductions and little urbanities are, to be sure, very delightful in
their way; I would not lose them; but I have no admiration
for the practice of ventriloquizing through another man's
mouth.

I can not help regretting that Wordsworth did not first publish his thirteen books on the growth of an individual mind—
superior, as I used to think, upon the whole, to the Excursion.
You may judge how I felt about them by my own poem upon
the occasion. Then the plan laid out, and, I believe, partly suggested by me, was, that Wordsworth should assume the station

of a man in mental repose, one whose principles were made up, and so prepared to deliver upon authority a system of philosophy. He was to treat man as man,—a subject of eye, ear, touch, and taste, in contact with external nature, and informing the senses from the mind, and not compounding a mind out of the senses; then he was to describe the pastoral and other states of society, assuming something of the Juvenalian spirit as he approached the high civilization of cities and towns, and opening a melancholy picture of the present state of degeneracy and vice; thence he was to infer and reveal the proof of, and necessity for, the whole state of man and society being subject to, and illustrative of, a redemptive process in operation, showing how this idea reconciled all the anomalies, and promised future glory and restoration. Something of this sort was, I think, agreed on. It is, in substance, what I have been all my life doing in my system of philosophy.

———

I think Wordsworth possessed more of the genius of a great philosophic poet than any man I ever knew, or, as I believe, has existed in England since Milton; but it seems to me that he ought never to have abandoned the contemplative position, which is peculiarly, perhaps I might say exclusively, fitted for him. His proper title is, *Spectator ab extra.*

————

AUGUST 12, 1832.

MALTHUSIANISM.

Is it not lamentable—is it not even marvellous—that the monstrous practical sophism of Malthus should now have gotten complete possession of the leading men of the kingdom! Such an essential lie in morals—such a practical lie in fact, as it is too! I solemnly declare that I do not believe that all the heresies, and sects, and factions which the ignorance, and the weakness, and the wickedness of man have ever given birth to, were altogether so disgraceful to man as a Christian, a philosopher, a statesman, or citizen, as this abominable tenet. It should be exposed by reasoning in the form of ridicule. Asgill or Swift would have done much; but, like the Popish doctrines, it is so vicious a tenet, so flattering to the cruelty, the avarice, and sordid selfishness of most men, that I hardly know what to think of the result.

AUGUST 14, 1832.

STEINMETZ—KEATS.

POOR dear Steinmetz is gone—his state of sure blessedness accelerated; or, it may be, he is buried in Christ, and there in that mysterious depth grows on to the spirit of a just man made perfect! Could I for a moment doubt this, the grass would become black beneath my feet, and this earthly frame a charnel-house. I never knew any man so illustrate the difference between the feminine and the effeminate.

A loose, slack, not well-dressed youth met Mr. Wordsworth and myself in a lane near Highgate. Wordsworth knew him, and spoke. It was Keats. He was introduced to me, and stayed a minute or so. After he had left us a little way he came back, and said: "Let me carry away the memory, Coleridge, of having pressed your hand!"—"There is death in that hand," I said to Wordsworth when Keats was gone; yet this was, I believe, before the consumption showed itself distinctly.

AUGUST 16, 1832.

CHRIST'S HOSPITAL—BOWYER.

THE discipline at Christ's Hospital in my time was ultra-Spartan;—all domestic ties were to be put aside. "Boy!" I remember Bowyer saying to me once when I was crying, the first day of my return after the holydays, "Boy! the school is your father! Boy! the school is your mother! Boy! the school is your brother! the school is your sister! the school is your first cousin, and your second cousin, and all the rest of your relations! Let's have no more crying!"

No tongue can express good Mrs. Bowyer. Val. Le Grice and I were once going to be flogged for some domestic misdeed, and Bowyer was thundering away at us by way of prologue, when Mrs. B. looked in, and said, "Flog them soundly, sir, I beg!" This saved us. Bowyer was so nettled at the interruption, that he growled out, "Away, woman! away!" and we were let off.

NOTES TO THE POEMS

Coleridge is here referred to throughout by his initials STC.

MYSTERY POEMS.

The Ancient Mariner. This was STC's major contribution to *Lyrical Ballads* (1798). Reprinted in successive editions (1800, 1802, 1805), it did not carry his name until *Sibylline Leaves* (1817). The glosses in the margins, designed to suggest a poem of some antiquity, first appeared in the latter edition.

The epigraph from T. Burnet has been translated as follows by Ernest Bernbaum: "I readily believe that there are more invisible things in the universe than visible. But who shall explain to us the nature, the rank and kinship, the distinguishing marks and graces of each? What do they do? Where do they dwell? The human mind has circled round this knowledge, but never attained to it. Yet there is profit, I do not doubt, in sometimes contemplating in the mind, as in a picture, the image of a greater and better world: lest the intellect, habituated to the petty details of daily life, should be contracted within too narrow limits and settle down wholly on trifles. But, meanwhile, a watchful eye must be kept on truth, and proportion observed, that we may distinguish the certain from the uncertain, day from night."

For a useful summary of earlier interpretations of the poem, see the introductory essay by Robert Penn Warren cited in the bibliography below. The famous study of the sources of the poem is by John Livingston Lowes, *The Road to Xanadu.*

Christabel. The two parts of the fragment were composed respectively in 1797 and 1800. Late in life (*Table Talk*, July 6, 1833) STC said: "The reason of my not finishing *Christabel* is not, that I don't know how to do it—for I have, as I always had, the whole plan entire from beginning to end in my mind; but I fear I could not carry on with equal success the execution of the idea, an extremely subtle and difficult one . . ."

According to his benefactor, Dr. James Gillman (*Life of Coleridge,* London, 1838, vol. 1, pp. 301–302), STC had the following plan in mind for completing *Christabel.* Bracy the Bard, with a youthful harp-bearer, rides across the mountains to Tryermaine only to find that Sir Roland's castle has been washed away. Aware of what is happening, Geraldine temporarily vanishes, but reappears to await the Bard's return, meantime working on the Baron to excite his anger and jealousy. When Bard Bracy and his youthful companion arrive, Geraldine transforms herself into a semblance of Christabel's absent lover. During the courtship which ensues, Christabel feels a deep disgust towards "her once favoured knight" for reasons which she cannot understand. But at her father's urging she at last agrees to marry "this hated suitor." At the crucial moment the real lover returns, and produces a betrothal ring to identify himself. The defeated Geraldine disappears finally, "the castle bell tolls, the mother's voice is heard, and . . . the rightful marriage takes place, after which follows a reconciliation and explanation between the father and daughter." This may be roughly the plan of which STC spoke in the passage from *Table Talk* quoted above.

An able study of the sources of the poem is A. H. Nethercot's *The Road to Tryermaine.* (See bibliography below.)

Kubla Khan. The classic source study for this poem is Lowes', *The Road to Xanadu.* (See bibliography below.) A thorough and up-to-date study of such vexed questions as the dating, the alleged influence of opium upon the act of composition, and the matter of interpretation, is Elisabeth Schneider's *Coleridge, Opium, and Kubla Khan,* listed in the bibliography below.

CONVERSATION POEMS.

The Eolian Harp (like the next poem, *Reflections on Having Left a Place of Retirement*) is a product of the first rapture of STC's marriage in the fall of 1795, when he spent three months with his bride in a vine-covered cottage near Clevedon, County Somerset, within view of the Bristol Channel. "The prospect around us," he wrote on 7 October, "is perhaps more *various* than any in the kingdom—Mine Eye gluttonizes.—I shall assuredly write Rhymes—let tne nine Muses prevent it, if they can . . ."

This Lime-Tree Bower My Prison. The accident which kept STC "imprisoned" in his lime-tree bower at Nether Stowey was occasioned by his wife's accidentally spilling a skillet of boiling milk on his foot. While Wordsworth and his sister Dorothy were out walking with Charles Lamb one evening in July, 1797, the incapacitated STC settled down in tne arbor in Tom Poole's garden next door and wrote the poem. Contrary to STC's belief, Charles Lamb did not "hunger after nature." He loved nothing so much as teeming London. The "evil and pain and strange calamity" which STC mentions had to do with the insanity of Lamb's sister Mary. STC was not always so sentimental about Lamb and his spinster sister. On 14 March, 1804, he wittily but vulgarly wrote John Rickman that he would come to see him, accompanied by "the Virgin Mary and the uncrucified Lamb."

Frost at Midnight. This fine poem in which STC reviews his past life and confidently predicts his son Hartley's future life has struck many readers as peculiarly Wordsworthian. Formally speaking, as M. H. Abrams has remarked, the poem closely resembles Wordsworth's *Tintern Abbey.* "The stranger" which the ruminator sees fluttering in the fire is a kind of film which appears on the outside of burning peat. A country superstition held that when one saw "the stranger" it foretold an unexpected visit from a friend.

Fears in Solitude. STC's fears were occasioned by the rumored invasion of England by the Napoleonic armies. The language in which he speaks of his beloved England is oddly reminiscent of the domains of Kubla Khan.

The Nightingale. The quotation in line 13 is from Milton's *Il Penseroso,* and STC is anxious to contradict Milton's opinion. The allusion to Philomela in line 39 echoes the classical name for the nightingale in Ovid and others. The "dear babe" of line 91 is STC's son Hartley, the same who slept near him in *Frost at Midnight.* STC is still anxious here to make him "Nature's playmate." "My Friend, and thou, our sister" are William and Dorothy Wordsworth, who shared STC's views on the therapeutic values of contact with natural scenes.

To William Wordsworth. Early in 1807, STC spent some time with the Wordsworths, who were wintering at Coleorton, not far from Leicester. While Wordsworth was writing *The Prelude,* his long autobiographical poem (finally published in 1850), he often called it "Coleridge's poem." By the time STC had come back from his years in Malta and Italy, the poem was finished in first draft, and Wordsworth read it aloud to the family circle. STC's poetic tribute to his friend, composed "on the night after his recitation" of *The Prelude,* is all the more touching when we remember that STC felt himself inferior to Wordsworth both as poet and person, and that, as he listened to the poem, he was fully aware of his failure to throw off the opium habit, the failure of his marriage, and the decline of his own powers of poetic expression.

Poems before Wordsworth, 1790–1794.

Sonnet (To the Autumnal Moon). Included as an example of STC's earliest work, composed while he was still a schoolboy at Christ's Hospital, and of course very eighteenth-century in manner.

Monody on the Death of Chatterton. Thomas Chatterton (1752–1770) was a favorite among the English romantic poets partly because he committed suicide by taking arsenic at the tender age of seventeen. He was the progenitor of a famous hoax in which he wrote poems which he passed off as the work of a fifteenth-century monk of Bristol. The fraud was exposed after Chatterton's death by one Mr. Tyrwhitt. The headnote is intentionally made over from the thirteenth stanza of Gray's *Elegy: Written in a Country Churchyard.*

Music. STC had in mind the Church-Music of Ottery and Tiverton in his native Devonshire.

Imitated from Ossian. Like Chatterton's Rowley poems, the Ossianic epics were a fabrication, this time by a learned Scot named James Macpherson (1736–1796) who published in 1760–1763 several long poems which he said were gathered in the Scottish highlands and translated out of Gaelic. The most famous of these was *Fingal,* an epic in six books, purportedly the work of a Gaelic poet named Ossian. This and its sequel, *Temora,* another epic in eight books, were immensely popular at the end of the eighteenth century, but their authenticity was soon questioned, among others by Dr. Samuel Johnson, and the hoax was exposed after Macpherson's death. STC's poem was composed three years before Macpherson died and published in the year of his death.

Sonnet (To the River Otter). This sentimental tribute to the river he knew at home in Devonshire marks STC's habitual nostalgia.

Pantisocracy and *On the Prospect of Establishing a Pantisocracy in America* are the poetical record of STC's abortive scheme to found a settlement on the banks of the Susquehanna River with his brother-in-law-to-be, Robert Southey, and some others.

To a Young Ass. STC says he sometimes dreamed of taking this animal along with him on the voyage to America, there to disport itself in the green meadows of the new world. When Byron brought out *English Bards and Scotch Reviewers* in 1809, he used this poem as a satirical club against STC:

> Yet none in lofty numbers can surpass
> The bard who soars to elegise an ass.
> So well the subject suits his noble mind,
> He brays the laureat of the long-ear'd kind.

ODES, HYMNS, AND SONGS.

France: An Ode. STC's argument, prefixed to his poem, pretty well sums up his changing views of France between the time of his highest hopes for French liberty at the outbreak of the French Revolution to his disillusionment in 1798 when French forces invaded Switzerland. This change of heart was not uncommon among men of liberal principles at the end of the eighteenth century.

Lewti. This imitation of an Eastern love-song was to have been included in the first edition of *Lyrical Ballads* (1798) but was cancelled at the last minute. Despite its representative quality in an age when the Oriental-exotic attracted many minds, *Lyrical Ballads* was not much poorer for its exclusion.

Dejection: An Ode. The two versions of this famous ode make a useful comparative study. The original version, from which the later was extracted, is in the form of a verse-letter to Sara Hutchinson, with whom STC had fallen in love. The revised version is almost exactly 200 lines shorter, and carefully disguises the identity of the "Lady" whom STC is addressing. The original version was not published until 1937, when the late Ernest De Selincourt brought it out with a valuable essay explaining the circumstances. The second version is in many ways STC's best poem after 1800. With this ode may be compared Wordsworth's better-known *Ode: Intimations of Immortality.*

The Picture. Though it is cast in the form of a dramatic monologue, this poem's tone and manner suggest that of STC as a writer of odes. It is a curious specimen, included here mainly to show how much less of a poet he was in 1802 than he had been five, four, or even three years earlier. Alcaeus (line 171) was a lyric poet of Lesbos who addressed an ode to Sappho, "the Lesbian woman" of line 172.

Hymn Before Sun-rise, in the Vale of Chamouni. The valley of Chamouni is in the Haute Savoie not far from Mont Blanc, and still offers breathtaking vistas like those described in the poem. STC had not in fact visited the region, but based his account on another *Ode to Chamouny* by Friederika Brun, which he freely adapted to his own purposes, one of the many instances of near-plagiarism in this great man's career. When STC's poem first appeared in the *Morning Post* for September 11, 1802, the prose note to the *Hymn* asked, "Who *could* be an Atheist in this valley of wonders?" This is in brief the point of the poem.

The Pains of Sleep. Although again not quite a hymn or quite an ode, this confessional piece belongs close to such legitimate odes as *Dejection*, signifying STC's remorse at having contracted the opium habit, his burrowing sense of what he calls "the unfathomable hell within."

Song and *Hunting Song* are lyrical interludes from STC's play *Zapolya* which he composed, he asserted, "in humble imitation of the *Winter's Tale of Shakespeare.*" The first is sung by Glycine, orphan daughter of Chef Ragozzi, and the second by a chorus of huntsmen. STC composed his play in 1815, hoping for a repetition of the mild success which had greeted his tragedy *Remorse,* produced at the Drury Lane Theatre two years earlier. His luck did not hold.

Limbo. In one manuscript version STC called this "A Dream of Purgatory." The poem itself is, however, a kind of awful hymn to Nothing-at-all, one of the ultimate horrors.

Song ("Though veiled in spires") shows that though STC wrote little verse after he was past fifty he was still capable of turning some ironic couplets.

EPIGRAMS AND EPITAPHS.

[Hippona] is adapted from a little poem of Lessing's.

On a Volunteer Singer. The singer has not been identified, but his (or her) name is legion.

On the Above [Major Dieman]. In his first epigram on the late soldier, STC had remarked that though he had died a major, he had now become "merely Corporal."

[What Is an Epigram?] STC here merely versifies the original statement in *Hamlet,* Act II.

For a House-Dog's Collar. When he published this in *The Friend* in 1809, STC changed the title to read: *For a French House-Dog's Collar.*

Epitaph on a Mercenary Miser. One of STC's contributions to the *Morning Post.*

Epitaph on Himself. STC's own note to this poem reads: "Composed in my sleep for myself while dreaming that I was dying." The inn was the Black Bull, Edinburgh. The date was Sept. 13, 1803.

Psyche. According to STC's own note, Psyche in Greek is the common name for both the soul and the butterfly.

[*Epitaph*] ("An excellent adage commands"). Such cruel pronouncements as this were not uncommon in STC's time. Lord Byron outdid him in this respect.

[*Wine*]. The date of these couplets is uncertain, but they may stem from STC's trip to the Rhine with Wordsworth in 1828.

On Donne's Poetry. STC actually admired Donne's poetry, though he is somewhat wry, like Dr. Samuel Johnson, on "metaphysical verse."

Reason. STC first published these lines as the conclusion to his book *On the Constitution of Church and State*.

Epitaph ("Stop, Christian passer-by"). STC's "auto-epitaphium" shows him still playing with the *death-in-life: life-in-death* concept he had used in *The Ancient Mariner* thirty-five years earlier.

SELECTED BIBLIOGRAPHY

EDITIONS

W. G. T. SHEDD, ed., *Complete Works of Samuel Taylor Coleridge*, 7 vols. New York, 1853; reissued 1884. Still the most nearly complete edition.

E. H. COLERIDGE, ed., *The Complete Poetical Works of Samuel Taylor Coleridge*, 2 vols. Oxford, Clarendon, 1912; reprinted 1957. Vol. I contains the poems; Vol. II, the dramatic works and appendices.

E. L. GRIGGS, ed., *Letters of Samuel Taylor Coleridge, 1785–1806*, 2 vols. Oxford, Clarendon, 1956.

——, ed., *Letters of Samuel Taylor Coleridge, 1807–1819*, 2 vols. Oxford, Clarendon, 1959. These four volumes, with two more to come, will be the authoritative edition of the letters.

KATHLEEN COBURN, ed., *The Philosophical Lectures of Samuel Taylor Coleridge*. London, Pilot Press, 1949.

——, ed., *Inquiring Spirit*. New York, Pantheon, 1951.

——, ed., *The Notebooks of Samuel Taylor Coleridge, 1794–1804*. Vol. I in two volumes, New York, Pantheon, 1957. Vol. II, same, 1961. Further vols. forthcoming.

E. H. COLERIDGE, ed., *Anima Poetae*. Boston, Houghton Mifflin, 1895.

JOHN SHAWCROSS, ed., *Biographia Literaria*, 2 vols. London, Oxford University Press, 1907. Reprinted with corrections, 1954.

THOMAS M. RAYSOR, ed., *Coleridge's Shakespearean Criticism*, 2 vols. Cambridge, Harvard U. Press, 1930.

——, ed., *Coleridge's Miscellaneous Criticism*. London, Constable, 1936.

ALICE D. SNYDER, ed., *Coleridge on Logic and Learning*. New Haven, Yale U. Press, 1929.

——, ed., *Coleridge's Treatise on Method*. London, Constable, 1934.

Biography and Criticism

R. W. Armour and R. F. Howes, *Coleridge the Talker*. Ithaca, Cornell U. Press, 1940. Reveals the personality in conversation.

James V. Baker, *The Sacred River: Coleridge's Theory of the Imagination*. Baton Rouge, Louisiana State U. Press, 1957. An able study of a vexed subject.

E. K. Chambers, *Samuel Taylor Coleridge*. Oxford, Clarendon, 1938. Good factual biography.

Humphry House, *Coleridge*. London, Rupert Hart-Davis, 1953. Good on the poetry.

J. L. Lowes, *The Road to Xanadu*. Boston, Houghton Mifflin, 1927; revised and enlarged, 1930. Imagery in *The Ancient Mariner* and *Kubla Khan*.

J. H. Muirhead, *Coleridge as Philosopher*. New York, Macmillan, 1930.

A. H. Nethercot, *The Road to Tryermaine*. Chicago, U. of Chicago Press, 1939. Imagery in *Christabel*.

I. A. Richards, *Coleridge on Imagination*. New York, Harcourt, 1935.

Elisabeth Schneider, *Coleridge, Opium, and Kubla Khan*. Chicago, U. of Chicago Press, 1953.

Robert Penn Warren, ed., *The Rime of the Ancient Mariner*. New York, Reynal and Hitchcock, 1946. Contains a useful interpretive introduction.

Note: The chapters on Coleridge in *The English Romantic Poets: A Review of Research*, New York, The Modern Language Association of America, 1950, edited by T. M. Raysor, contain a useful systematic summary of books and articles on Coleridge through 1949. A good source for subsequent scholarship are the annual bibliographies in *Publications of the Modern Language Association*, New York.

BANTAM CLASSICS